D1050664

STRANGE CREATIONS

STRANGE CREATIONS

Aberrant Ideas
of
Human Origins
from
Ancient Astronauts
to
Aquatic Apes

Donna Kossy

FERAL HOUSE

ACKNOWLEDGMENTS

Many thanks to all those who lent source materials, commented on the manuscript and discussed aberrant anthropology with me. I'd especially like to thank Walter Minkel who devoted many hours helping me improve the manuscript. Also thanks to Lyell Henry and Chris Roth whose expert advice was indispensable, to Phil Lipson at the As You Like It Library in Seattle, for calling my attention to *The Beginning Was the End*, the original inspiration for the article that grew into this book, and to Steve Connell and Katherine Spielmann for publishing and commenting on that article. Thanks also to Greg Bishop, Trevor Blake, David Hauptschein, Dan Kelly, and Adam Parfrey for sources and comments, and to Gerald Casale, Robert Girard and Elaine Morgan for answering my questions. And finally, thanks to Ken DeVries for sparking my interest in the broader impact of aberrant anthropology books when he casually commented, "That's the book that inspired DEVO," and for bearing with me while I labored over this project.

The De-evolution chapter grew out of an article, "The Truth about De-evolution," which originally appeared in *Puncture* magazine #34.

FERAL HOUSE
P.O. BOX 13067
LOS ANGELES, CA 90013

DESIGN BY LINDA HAYASHI

10 9 8 7 6 5 4 3 2 1

Contents

CHILDREN OF ANIMALS, OR SLAVES OF THE GODS?

*W*here did we human beings come from? There's never been a shortage of answers to this question—in world mythology, religious texts and scientific theories. While we think of the "evolution versus creation" debate as belonging to the past hundred years or so, a similar debate might have been staged, say, five or 1,500 years ago, between tribal cultures. Some mythologies leaned towards a more "evolutionary" tale of human origins, while others described instantaneous creation; some people thought of themselves as the children of gods, others, as the children of animals.

For example, tribal pre-"evolutionists" such as the Zunis of New Mexico, thought of humans as, literally, the children of animals. They say that long ago, pre-human animals roamed the underworld on all fours. When these creatures made their way to the earth's surface they continued to crawl like toads, and only became human after the twin war gods cut off their tails and horns, slit their webbed feet and gave them fingers. Far to the northeast of Zuni territory, another North American tribe, the Algonquins of the Ottawa River valley, told a different story about the creation of humanity: the god Nokomis fell from the moon and bore a daughter, who became the mother of Hiawatha and, through him, the Algonquin people—human beings, to the Algonquins, were not born of *animals*, but of *gods*.

On the other side of the world, in what is now Iraq, ancient Babylonians told a story that may go back as far as 1900 B.C. Their *Poem of Creation* (also known as the *Epic of Creation*) tells how the gods fashioned human beings from the blood of a sacrificial god to be their *slaves*. The ancient Hebrews' creation myth, recorded in the biblical book of Genesis, was similar; their variation on this "creationist" theme was that the first man, Adam, was created from dust by one all-powerful creator-god, Jehovah.

Each alternative—descent from animals, descent from gods, creation by gods, or creation by one god—tells us the place of humanity in the universe. Descent from animals emphasizes our kinship to and dependence upon the natural world and to the creatures living in it. Sir James Frazer, author of *The Golden Bough*, a 1922 study of comparative mythology, concurred. "The reason why a clan revere a particular species of animals and call themselves after it," he wrote, "would seem to be a belief that the life of each individual of the clan is bound up with some one animal."[1] Descent or assistance from sky gods suggests a kinship with the sky and heavens. The sky, according to historian of religion Mircea Eliade, "directly reveals a transcendence, a power and a holiness," while the beings who dwell there "are [universally] endowed with foreknowledge and wisdom."[2] When such beings come to Earth, says Eliade, they impart culture and metaphysical truths. Similarly, the idea that human beings are the *children* of sky gods means that we each have sky god qualities *in our blood*, intimating a supernatural, higher nature combining with our earthly existence.

Instantaneous creation by one powerful creator deity, on the other hand, implies both the existence of an unseen world and our *subservience* to it. Jehovah, for example, the creator-god of the Bible, insists that his people obey his laws or be severely punished . When Adam and Eve disobeyed Jehovah by eating the fruit of "the tree of the knowledge of good and evil," Jehovah promised Eve that "in sorrow thou shalt bring forth children," and Adam, "in the sweat of thy face shalt thou eat bread." Adam and Eve were only the first of many in the Bible to pay a heavy price for disobedience to the creator-god. At the same time, the biblical story makes clear that humanity, created in God's image, rules the beasts, just as God rules us.

EVOLUTION OR CREATION: IS THAT ALL THERE IS?

Ever since they converted to Christianity early in the first millennium A.D., most Europeans became "creationists" by accepting the creation story of the Bible. Even when later geologic discoveries implied the earth was much older than the age deduced from Scripture, many scientists continued in their religious faith. Jean André Deluc, for example, a Swiss chemist, geologist and physicist of the late eighteenth century, attempted to reconcile his scientific theory of an ancient Earth with Scripture. He did so by dividing history into two distinct eras: one before the birth of the continents, and one after. Earth is very old, he concluded, but it was only during the second era that the biblical book of Genesis applied. Therefore, he could continue to believe events such as Noah's Flood had occurred as recorded in the Bible. His dating methods, which he called "natural chronometers," pinned the date of that catastrophe at 2200 B.C.[3] Many of Deluc's contemporaries dedicated themselves, as well, to conducting science in the service of traditional faith.

After Charles Darwin's *Origin of Species* appeared in 1859, however, it became increasingly difficult for intellectuals to accept both natural science and the creation story in Genesis. Darwin himself couldn't reconcile the two. "I cannot persuade myself," he wrote, "that a beneficent and omnipotent God would have designedly created the Ichneumonidae with the express intention of their feeding within the living bodies of caterpillars, or that a cat would play with mice."[4] In his autobiography he wrote, "There seems to be no more design in the variability of organic beings and in the action of natural selection, than in the course which the wind blows. Everything in nature is the result of fixed laws."[5] Meanwhile, many of the clergy and their pious flocks retained their faith in Scripture. The question put to moderns ever since has been: creation or evolution?

But are these the only two choices? What about a third option? What if we accepted some combination of evolution and creation at the same time? Several theories which claim to do just that—combine creation and evolution—have become increasingly visible. The "alien intervention" theories, for example, suggest most living things on Earth may have evolved over millions of years, but humanity is the result of intervention by gods. In this scenario, the human species is often a hybrid between an evolved ape-creature and sky gods, explaining the dual nature—animal and spirit—of humanity. The race-based theories, on the other hand, propose that God or gods created "superior" races, but that "inferior" peoples evolved from animals. Meanwhile, "de-evolutionary" theories rest on an approximate reversal of evolution that has its roots in ancient myth and esotericism.

These "third" options between evolution and creation map out alternative ways of looking at human origins and therefore mankind's place in the universe. In addition to these attempts to combine science with spirit or evolution with creation, there are other unorthodox theories. The Aquatic Ape theory suggests there was an aquatic phase in human evolution, and it is attractive to feminists who see our ancestors not as hunters but, rather, as mothers wading neck-deep in water with their infants. Another view of mankind—as a species that can be perfected by better breeding—was embraced by the eugenics movement of the late nineteenth and early twentieth centuries. I call these ideas "aberrant anthropologies"—theories of human origins or human nature that diverge, sometimes wildly, from the mainstream.

Aberrant anthropologies naturally group themselves into several categories: alien intervention theories of human origins, de-evolution, race theories, eugenics and the Aquatic Ape theory. And although creationism is a traditional way of looking at mankind, I treat it as an aberrant anthropology for the purposes of this book; it is currently on the defensive, trying to fight its way back into polite society and public education. As in my previous book, *Kooks*, I seek not to debunk strange ideas, but to present them as a necessary segment of the full spectrum of human thought.

⇒·◆·⇐

1. Frazer, *Golden Bough*, p. 689.
2. Mircea Eliade, *Myths, Rites, Symbols*, 2:352.
3. Gillispie, *Genesis and Geology*, pp. 56–66.
4. Greene, *Death of Adam*, p. 303. In a letter from Darwin to Asa Gray.
5. Greene, *Death of Adam*, p. 303.

CHAPTER ONE

EXTRATERRESTRIAL ORIGINS

*The chief difference between the man of the archaic and
traditional societies and the man of the modern
societies lies in the fact that the former
feels himself indissolubly connected with
the Cosmos and the cosmic rhythms, whereas
the latter insists that he is connected only with History.*
MIRCEA ELIADE, *The Myth of the Eternal Return*

One of the best-known aberrant anthropologies—often touted as the middle ground between creationism and evolution—is the "alien intervention" theory of human origins. This theory—or family of theories—is well summarized by authors Max Flindt and Otto Binder in their 1974 book *Mankind: Child of the Stars.* "Starmen visited Earth," they wrote, "and mated with early females (perhaps hominids) to sire the modern human race of *Homo sapiens.*"[1] Upon discovery of this theory during a surge of UFO popularity in the 1970s, it struck me as instantly appealing and exciting. Not only might we humans come in contact with extraterrestrial beings, but ETs might actually be our ancestors, or maybe even our brothers: we ourselves could be "star people."

MADAME BLAVATSKY

This entertaining theory, which seems tailor-made for the space age, is not as new as it might seem. On the one hand, it updates the old creation myths that depict human beings as the children or creation of sky gods— only the "sky gods" are advanced extraterrestrial beings who colonized Earth and created mankind via experiments in genetic engineering or by inter- breeding (themselves) with terrestrial ape creatures. On the other hand, the ET theory's true roots lie in Western esoteri- cism and nineteenth century Theosophy.

NEW LIFE TO AN OLD MYTH

The belief that men and women descended from (or were created by) space gods stems from neither science nor organized religion, but a third, esoteric tradition. This tradition and

its practices go by various names: esotericism, occultism, gnosticism, spiritualism, Theosophy, and, most often, the New Age. Like organized religion, esotericism acknowledges an unseen world, but unlike organized religion, it invites direct participation in it. Rather than place themselves, permanently, far below the level of the all-powerful creator-spirit, esotericists seek to ascend to the level of the gods, to experience spirituality first-hand, to contact invisible entities, even to influence the cosmos.

Fundamentalist clergy and born-again former participants in the "New Age" movement denounce esoteric traditions for promoting witchcraft, Satanism or demon-worship. *The Hidden Dangers of the Rainbow: The New Age Movement and Our Coming Age of Barbarism*, and *A Planned Deception: The Staging of a New Age 'Messiah,'* by Constance Cumbey as well as *Inside the New Age NIGHTMARE* by Randall Baer are some of the better known anti-New Age volumes. Baer—who, before he found Christ, had authored books on self-transformation through crystals—described the realization that he'd been 'seduced' by the New Age. "What I thought was 'up' was actually 'down,'" he explained. "What I thought was 'heaven' was actually 'hell' wrapped in Satan's finest counterfeit garments. What I thought were Ascended Masters, extraterrestrials and angels were actually demons in cunning, glowing disguises."[2] For conservative Christians like Baer, contacting entities other than Jesus Christ is tantamount to Devil-worship; human beings must remember that their place remains far below God the creator, at least until the Second Coming of Christ.

Even though the esotericists are seriously interested in spiritual matters, they are often alienated from traditional, organized religion. At the same time, they distrust scientific theories because those theories are devoid of spiritual meaning. Modern participants in the "unseen world" believe that the role of the human being in the cosmos is more than just as a complex, accidental animal or a lowly servant of a jealous creator. To them, men and women are vital players in a grand, cosmic drama. So, naturally, they are attracted to myths that depict humanity as the children or creation of space gods.

Esoteric Background of Alien Intervention Theories

In 1851, Charlotte Bronte, author of *Jane Eyre*, attended the Great Exhibition of London. Its marvels left the great novelist, like thousands of others, awestruck. But it was the Crystal Palace, containing more than 800,000 square feet of floor space and over eight miles of display tables that especially enchanted her. Afterward she was moved to write:

> Yesterday I went for the second time to the Crystal Palace. Its grandeur does not consist of one thing, but in the unique assemblage of all things. Whatever human industry has created you find there. It seems as if only magic could have gathered this mass of wealth from all the ends of the earth—as if none but supernatural hands could have arranged it thus, with such a blaze and contrast of colours and marvellous power of effect. The multitude filling the great aisles seems ruled and subdued by some invisible influence. Amongst the thirty thousand souls that peopled it the day I was there not one loud noise was to be heard, not one irregular movement seen; the living tide rolls on quietly, with a deep hum like the sea heard from the distance.[3]

The hush amidst material splendor Ms. Bronte observed suggests the first stirrings of a new faith—a faith in human progress. As historian J.B. Bury put it, the Great Exhibition of London was "a public recognition of the material progress of the age and the growing power of man over the physical world." The *Edinburgh Review* said it had seized "the living scroll of human progress, inscribed with every successive conquest of man's intellect." Those who wrote about it saw the exhibition as a symbol, not only of material progress, but also the unity of mankind and of universal peace.[4]

Just two decades later, wrote Bury, "The idea of Progress was becoming a general article of faith."[5] At the same time, belief in evolution was on the rise and industrial growth was booming. Intellectuals and captains of industry embraced the new faith, but worship of material progress was an affront to occultists and spiritualists. Rather than material growth, they wanted spiritual growth. While engineers looked forward to a utopia filled with flying machines and instant communications, esotericists looked backward to a Golden Age inhabited by winged beings who communicated by telepathy. While scientists looked outward for answers, spiritualists looked inward for theirs.

It was in this anti-materialist spirit that H.P. Blavatsky and Col. H.S. Olcott founded the Theosophical Society in 1875. Theosophy would provide starry-eyed misfits—from spiritualists to flying saucer contactees to contemporary New Agers—with "ancient wisdom" for years to come. The purported sources for this ancient wisdom were "Ascended Masters" from Tibet and ancient sacred texts known only to Madame Blavatsky. For example, Blavatsky's dense two-volume tome, *The Secret Doctrine* (first published in 1888), is, according to its author, based on an ancient book of wisdom called the "Book of Dzyan," written in a language called "Senzar."

The single most influential esotericist of our time, Madame Blavatsky (1831–1891), known as HPB to her followers, lived a life of defiance in almost every sphere: personal, societal, scientific and religious. After rebelling against her aristocratic family and running away from her husband, the spirited young woman fashioned a philosophy—dubbed "Theosophy"—that rejected traditional Western religion on the one hand, and "materialist science" on the other. Most fervently of all, and to the very end of her life, Blavatsky rejected Darwin. In her last work, the ponderous *Secret Doctrine*, the controversial medium spilled much ink attacking science in general, and Darwin in particular.

Born Helena Petrovna von Hahn in southern Russia, Blavatsky showed a rebellious and exceptional spirit early on. According to her sister, she practiced her mystical storytelling abilities on her younger siblings, whom she held in rapt attention:

> Helena used to dream aloud, and tell us of her visions, evidently clear, vivid, and as palpable as life to her. . . . It was her delight to gather around herself a party of us younger children, at twilight, and after taking us into the large dark museum, to hold us there, spellbound, with her weird stories. Then she narrated to us the most inconceivable tales about herself; the most unheard of adventures of which she was the heroine, every night, as she explained. Each of the stuffed animals had taken her in turn into its confidence, had divulged to her the history of its life in previous incarnations or existences.[6]

Though married at just 18—to Nikifor V. Blavatsky, middle-aged friend of the family and Vice-Governor of the Province of Erivan—Helena was not cut out for marriage. The bold young woman ran away after only a few months, before the marriage was consummated. Instead, she consummated a career—brazen at the time—as an itinerant mystic, initiate, oriental scholar and medium. Her influence is still felt today: in Theosophy, countless versions of the New Age, in pseudoscientific speculations on the lost continents of Atlantis and Lemuria, and in racist theories of human development. Even the Nazis were influenced by Madame Blavatsky.[7]

Madame Blavatsky was a large woman. Peter Washington, in his 1993 biography *Madame Blavatsky's Baboon*, relates that many who encountered Blavatsky found her physical presence difficult to forget:

> Though not approaching the seventeen and a half stone she later achieved by eating fatty foods, including her favorite fried eggs floating in butter, she was already stout. She had light brown hair "crinkled like a negro or a cotswold ewe," and magnetic eyes, variously described as blue, grey-blue and azure. High cheekbones and a broad, massive face with a flattened nose completed the exotic appearance suggested by shabby, fantastic clothes. At the first meeting with

Olcott she was wearing a Garibaldi red shirt. In later life she developed a taste for loose, badly fitting robes, preferring a sort of red flannel dressing-gown. Smoking incessantly, she carried the materials for her cigarettes in a furry pouch made out of an animal head worn round her neck. Her hands were usually covered with rings, some with genuine stones, and she looked overall like a badly wrapped and glittering parcel. She talked incessantly in a guttural voice, sometimes wittily and sometimes crudely. She was indifferent to sex yet frank and open about it; fonder of animals than of people; unsnobbish, unpretentious, scandalous, capricious and rather noisy. She was also humorous, vulgar, impulsive and warm-hearted, and she didn't give a hoot for anyone or anything.[8]

Madame Blavatsky lived in a grand style, well-suited to her persona as "Oriental Mystic." As detailed in Washington's account, she furnished her rooms in New York in the Victorian manner, filling them with foreign tchotchkes of every description. She amazed her guests with an impressive collection of stuffed animals, which included a lioness' head over the door, monkeys "peeping out of nooks," birds, lizards, a grey owl and a snake. As her own little joke on her nemesis Darwin, she displayed—as the centerpiece of her collection—a "large bespectacled baboon, standing upright, dressed in wing-collar, morning-coat and tie, and carrying under its arm the manuscript of a lecture on *The Origin of Species*." She named it "Professor Fiske" after John Fiske, a prominent Darwinian of the time.

Aside from her notoriety in the States and in London, the specifics of Blavatsky's life and travels, not to mention the veracity of her many outlandish claims are still a matter of some dispute. Here is the official Theosophical Society account: After she ran away from her husband, Blavatsky traveled for a couple of years in Egypt, Greece and Eastern Europe. Then, on her 20th birthday, in London, she met the Tibetan "Master Morya" of the Great White Brotherhood. The next year she attempted to enter Tibet but only made it as far as Nepal. Then, instructed by the Masters, she sailed to the United States. After two years in America, she returned to Asia and successfully entered Tibet, where she studied with her master for three years. Afterward she wandered in Egypt, Syria and Constantinople. She returned to New York in 1873, where she met Col. H.S. Olcott. Two years later, Blavatsky and Olcott founded the Theosophical Society. She published her first major book, *Isis Unveiled*, in 1877, and, according to the Society, it was an immediate success. In 1878 she returned to India with Olcott, and shortly thereafter they established Theosophical Headquarters at Adyar, near Madras. Back in London and Europe in 1884, Blavatsky was well-received for her brilliant conversation, for her knowledge, and for her psychic powers. In 1888 she published her final work, *The Secret Doctrine*, which she wrote in London. She died there in 1891.

Disinterested biographers are skeptical of many particulars of this account. Though many of Blavatsky's travel claims are possible, fewer are plausible, and none of them are verifiable. Her claims of occult initiation are even less so. Her most significant boast was that she'd traveled alone to Tibet and had reached the highest level of initiation into the occult hierarchy there, having received instruction from the "Himalayan Masters." Tibet was "closed" in the nineteenth century and all but the most devious and skilled were turned away by guards. Peter Washington points out that due to the eccentric lady's notoriously wide girth, "The thought of the breathless, tactless and massively stout Blavatsky managing to climb steep mountains in brutal weather while concealing herself from trained observers is just too difficult to imagine." Nor is there any evidence of the existence of Master Morya or any of the other Masters of the Divine Hierarchy, Blavatsky's alleged sources of esoteric knowledge.

It is more likely that Blavatsky utilized a variety of published documents on Eastern religion and Western esotericism for source material. During the late eighteenth century, when Asian religion was first pried open by Western scholars, Hindu scriptures, for example, were being translated into French and English for the first time. Peter Washington suggests that HPB's single most important source for Western esotericism was the work of popular novelist Edward Bulwer-Lytton (1803–73), an expert in alchemy and neo-Platonism. Bulwer-Lytton, in turn, was largely influenced by the writings of seminary-trained Frenchman Eliphas Levi (1810–75). Levi drew heavily on Eastern sources and Hindu scriptures; he taught the existence of a "secret doctrine" uniting all magical and religious systems, transmitted by long-lived adepts with magical powers. According to Peter Washington, there is a direct connection between Eliphas Levi's "secret doctrine" and Madame Blavatsky's *Secret Doctrine*.

Madame Blavatsky's claims of mediumship, as well, were challenged during her lifetime. Two of her employees at Theosophical Society headquarters in Adyar, India accused her of fraud in connection with her career as a medium by exposing two letters. In the letters, Blavatsky had instructed her servants to arrange phony mediumistic effects for an upcoming séance. Blavatsky "flatly repudiated" the letters and wrote the incident off as a case of revenge by employees she'd dismissed for their incompetence. After this incident, however, she never returned to India.

Scholars have leveled even more serious accusations: not only did Blavatsky arrange phony séances and lie about her sources, but much of her work was actually *plagiarized*. Nicholas Goodrick-Clarke wrote: "[Nineteenth century scholar] W.E. Coleman has shown that [Blavatsky's] work comprises a sustained and frequent plagiarism of about 100 contemporary texts, chiefly relating to ancient and exotic religions, demonology, freemasonry and the case for spiritualism." Moreover, her first major work, *Isis Unveiled*, "was less an outline of her new religion than a rambling tirade against the rationalist and materialistic culture of modern Western civilization."[9] Thus, Theosophy was (and continues to be) essentially a reactionary philosophy. It claims to revive traditional wisdom and ancient doctrines that are, in fact, the products of contemporary minds, bred of a nostalgia for a world which never existed.

Believers, however, aren't much bothered by skeptics and exposés. Their mythic world's objective reality, or lack thereof, is simply irrelevant. For those who don't feel quite at home in the material world, it's an easy choice: between a purely physical Earth, guided by greed and heartless intellectualism, condemned by science to meaningless oblivion in the end—and a spirit-infused Earth, guided by wise masters who will lead humanity to a noble, cosmic destiny.

THE SECRET DOCTRINE AND THE COSMIC SPARK

The first volume of *The Secret Doctrine*, "Cosmogenesis," is concerned with the creation of the universe, and the second, "Anthropogenesis," with human origins. It is in the second volume that Madame Blavatsky provides a third alternative to the creation/evolution dichotomy, one well-suited to New Age sensibilities. According to Blavatsky's spiritual guides, humanity developed not by natural forces, nor by one creator-god, but with the help of many other-worldly beings. Those seekers willing to tackle the mystical lady's difficult prose learn that the process of humanity's evolution was anything but simple. The basic idea, however, is that human beings evolved from spirit to matter and back again through seven "Root-Races," each Root-Race evolving through seven "Sub-Races."

"The first Root-Race," wrote Blavatsky, "was as ethereal as ours is material." It was "a pale copy of its Progenitors; too material, even in its ethereality, to be a hierarchy of Gods," while "too spiritual and pure to be MEN, endowed as it is with every negative perfection."[10] These first human races were asexual. It wasn't until the third race that "separation of the sexes" occurred:

> From being previously a-sexual, Humanity became distinctly hermaphrodite or bi-sexual; and finally the man-bearing eggs began to give birth, gradually and almost imperceptibly in their evolutionary development, first, to beings in which one sex predominated over the other, and, finally, to distinct men and women.[11]

About 18 million years ago lived the fourth Sub-Race of the third Root-Race, the Lemurians. They stood 16 feet tall, lacked souls and consciousness and possessed no capacity for sexual reproduction. Then, extraterrestrial, spiritual "princes" called *Kumaras* inhabited the bodies of the Lemurians, implanting them with both consciousness and sexual reproduction. Humanity's asexual, material development had taken place on Earth, but spirit, consciousness and sex came from elsewhere. Some of the Lemurians, the "narrow-headed," wrote Blavatsky, weren't ready to receive their cosmic spark, because of an unfortunate cosmic error:

And those which had no spark (the "narrow-headed") took huge she-animals unto them. They begat upon them dumb races. Dumb they were (the "narrow-headed") themselves. But their tongues untied. The tongues of their progeny remained still. Monsters they bred. A race of crooked, red-hair-covered monsters, going on all fours. A dumb race, to keep the shame untold.[12]

The soulless monsters attacked and ate the other Lemurians, introducing sin and murder to the world. Eventually, help arrived by way of the "wise Serpents and Dragons of Light" from Venus. They taught sentient humanity agriculture and weaving. The most virtuous Lemurians received secret teachings and became the first Masters, living invisibly alongside the others while guiding their development.

Blavatsky's message is that without intervention from otherworldly beings, humanity would have been doomed to monstrous carnality. At the same time, she taught that some men and women are capable of elevating themselves even higher by receiving secret teachings from Ascended Masters. Blavatsky's revival of an old idea—that sky gods intervened in the birth of humanity—was the germ from which "alien hybrid" and "alien intervention" theories of human origin later emerged.

OAHSPE AND THE JEHOVIH'S ANGELS

Many of Blavatsky's readers were "spiritualists," who believed in the survival of the human soul after death. The spiritualist movement was born in 1848, when Margaret and Kate Fox, aged 6 and 8, of Hydesville, New York, became famous for communicating with disembodied spirits that made "rapping" noises in their house at night. On October 21, 1888, Margaret Fox's written confession of fraud—and denunciation of spiritualism—appeared in the *New York World*. She admitted that she and her sister Kate—not spirits of the dead—were responsible for the mysterious rappings at their farmhouse. But spiritualism continued to grow in popularity, despite Fox's and others' exposés. The phenomena associated with spiritualism and seances, meanwhile, grew from rappings to table tilting, spirit writing, bell ringing, levitation and the playing of musical instruments by invisible hands.

JOHN NEWBROUGH,
mediumistic channel
for *Oahspe*

While mediums were usually the ones making the call to "the other side," sometimes disembodied entities with a story to tell initiated contact. In 1880, eight years before Fox's confession, a disembodied spirit contacted a spiritualist named John Newbrough and told Newbrough it wished to tell him the history of the universe. Since the crude communication method of knocks and rappings wouldn't do for such an epic tale, the spirit instructed Newbrough to buy a typewriter. Every day for the next year, the spirit awakened Newbrough before dawn to sit at the typewriter while the spirit controlled his fingers. What emerged from these sessions was an enormous book: *Oahspe: A New Bible in the Words of Jehovih and his Angel Embassadors; A Sacred History of the Dominion of the Higher and Lower Heavens on the Earth for the Past Twenty-four Thousand Years*. It was published in 1882 and has since become a spiritualist classic. (*Oahspe* was later reprinted by flying saucer publisher Ray Palmer and sold through *FATE* magazine.) In a dense, imitation biblical style, *Oahspe* recounts the deeds of the creator Jehovih and his angels, and the creation of Man, an immortal being:

> At the time of the creation of man, the earth was travelling in the arc of Wan, where dwell thousands of Orian chiefs, with thousands of millions of high-raised angels.
>
> The Holy Council of Orian Chiefs, through the Wisdom and Voice of Jehovih, appointed one of their number, Sethantes, to take charge of the earth, and to people it with immortal beings, during its travel in Wan.
>
> The rank and title of Sethantes, thus raised up by Jehovih, Creator of worlds, was first god of the earth and her heavens.[13]

Sethantes "raised up from the earth fifteen hundred million Brides and Bridegrooms to Jehovih." Each subsequent cycle brought more "harvests" until the earth was full of people. Subsequently, the people divided into spiritually inclined, small, white and yellow "I'hins," and large, black and brown "ground people, with long arms" who lived to be 200 to 400 years old.

I'hins, I'huans and Yaks, pre-human creatures from *Oahspe*

Oahspe, like Theosophy, provided readers familiar with the Bible with an alternative view of creation and immortality, as well as skewed versions of all the major Bible stories. Despite its lack of clarity—or perhaps because of it—*Oahspe* sat proudly near *The Secret Doctrine* on many a metaphysical bookshelf, adding its weight to the alternative mythos of divine humanity.

Ancient Astronauts & the Creation of Humanity

GOD DRIVES A FLYING SAUCER

Before the first "flying saucer" appeared in 1947, sky people and angels dwelt in the spirit world, their "bodies" made of an entirely different, "lighter" substance than physical bodies in the material world. By the late 1940s, however, a new generation began to identify sky people and even God Himself as simply "men of other planets." The veil of mystery was being removed in everything from electricity to deadly disease, so why not remove the mystery from spirits and gods as well? It would be safe to believe in the gods again—even in the nuts-and-bolts worshipping twentieth century—if they were simply extraterrestrials who were not too different from human beings. "Flying saucer contactees" began receiving visits from "saucer men" much like mystics receive visits from spirits or angels. Cosmic tutors in the guise of kindly extraterrestrials or "space brothers" began meeting with selected members of our human tribe, providing sorely needed philosophical tutelage on such urgent topics as nuclear war and the fate of the human race. Nobody seemed to notice, however, that they had traveled all that way to impart information gleaned just as easily from the Bible or the *Secret Doctrine*.

In 1953, *Flying Saucers Have Landed* by British novelist and musician Desmond Leslie (born 1921) and American contactee George Adamski (1891–1965) became an overnight best-seller. Adamski, who had taught what he called the "Universal Laws" since the 1930s, claimed to have seen flying saucers with his own eyes. Leslie, however—as he told a Detroit flying saucer club in 1954—hadn't given flying saucers much thought until his publisher asked him to write a science fiction story about them. While researching the story, the young author concluded that flying saucers were, in fact, real.[14] The resulting nonfiction book, *Flying Saucers Have Landed*, was a landmark, eventually translated into 16 languages. Adamski detailed his encounter with Venusians in the Mojave Desert, while Leslie broke new ground with his discussion of ancient astronauts.

Not only were spacemen visiting Earth now, suggested Leslie, but they have been landing on our planet for millennia. The first saucer landing (from Venus) took place around 19 million B.C. Extraterrestrials have left thousands of artifacts since ancient times, including Stonehenge and the Egyptian pyramids; they have also inspired myths and legends, including the story of Ezekiel's Wheel from the

DESMOND LESLIE, 1955
(from *Flying Saucer
Pilgrimmage*)

Bible. These claims were soon repeated by other authors. Leslie seems to have been the first, however, to ask how ancient peoples could have achieved such difficult feats as moving the blocks of Stonehenge without help from space people. Best-selling authors *still* haven't stopped repeating that question.

Leslie also addressed the question of human origins, updating and simplifying Blavatsky's story in *The Secret Doctrine* for the postwar audience. The Hindu *Puranas*, wrote Leslie, "contain records, in allegorical form, of Universal Man's ceaseless pilgrimage through space." According to these ancient documents, human seeds arrive on each new planet, and then grow up through the mineral, vegetable, animal and human kingdoms, and ultimately the kingdom of

God. At the end of each planetary cycle, the hidden God within humanity emerges and "the seeds are gathered up and taken through space in immense shining ships to the next planet for development." Leslie called such ships "Interplanetary Noah's Arks."

Our own seeding occurred in the year 18,617,841 B.C. when a ship arrived from Venus, the "Home of the Gods." While Venus is an ideal, advanced world, Earth is "the tough school—a kind of solar commando course whose successful graduates may surpass all other solar humans in strength and powers of resistance." The seeding, said Leslie (citing the "Book of Dzyan"[15]), could only take place after "something resembling a man had evolved." This creature was mindless, and "may have been," wrote Leslie, "the 'Missing Link' between the human and animal kingdoms that still eludes anthropologists."

GEORGE ADAMSKI
(from *Flying Saucer Pilgrimmage*)

> In other words, evolution had gone so far but could go no farther [sic] until it received some tremendous stimulus outside the ordinary powers of the earth. And so from our nearest neighbour came the greatest of Venus, "The Sanat Kumara", "The Lord of the Flame", the Spirit of the Venusian Logos Itself, whose memory is revered and held sacred in every ancient religion. From Venus, say the old teachings, came the elder brothers, the "Lords of the Flame", the highly perfected humans from an older branch of the planetary family. Of their free will they came; out of love and compassion for the groping, mindless things in the steaming primal jungles.[16]

Only after the Lord of the Flame "projected the Spark" were the groping mindless things called men stimulated to rationality and productivity. The Lord of the Flame then continued to live among "the huge black creatures [who] worshipped Him as the 'Holy of Heaven.'"

Though this kind of information might have been new to teenaged UFO buffs, it was old hat to students of Theosophy, since Leslie's message drew overtly from *The Secret Doctrine*. Meanwhile, Adamski's Venusians spoke of the same "Universal Laws" he had been pushing since the '30s. In his first book, *Wisdom of the Masters of the Far East* (1936), "Professor G. Adamski" revealed secret teachings of the "Royal Order of Tibet." Later, after he'd encountered flying saucers, the contactee penciled in "Space Brothers" wherever he'd written "Royal Order of Tibet."[17] The Venusian space brothers were also religious and wary of materialism, just like their Earth friend. "[The Venusians] made me understand," wrote

Adamski, "that we on Earth really know very little about this Creator [God]. In other words, our understanding is shallow. Theirs is much broader, and they adhere to the Laws of the Creator instead of the laws of materialism as Earth men do."[18] The space brothers—just like the "Ascended Masters" before them—told them nothing truly new or revolutionary, but confirmed the anti-materialist sentiments of their listeners.

NAZIS FROM SPACE?

Over the next 10 years, many of the messages received from "extraterrestrials" would also resemble the pre-World War II doctrines of American racists, Nazis and fascists. Only now they would carry the authority of higher intelligences, their reactionary messages cloaked in space jargon.

According to Jacques Vallee in *Messengers of Deception*, this resemblance was no accident. Adamski had pre-war connections with William Dudley Pelley (1890–1965), who was once called "the most dangerous man in America."[19] Pelley founded the Nazi-inspired Silver Shirts—also known as the Christian American Patriots—on January 31, 1933, the day after Hitler took power. At their height, as many as two million of Pelley's would-be storm troopers could be seen in uniforms of silver shirts, blue corduroy pants and gold socks. Pelley ran for President in 1936 as a candidate of the Christian Party, which, according to John Carlson in *Under Cover*, was "backed mainly by Nazi funds." Pelley's voice rang out with the slogans "Christ or Chaos!" and "For Christ and Constitution."[20] He declared in his party's platform:

> I propose to defranchise the Jew by Constitutional Amendment, to make it impossible for a Jew to own property in the United States excepting under the same licensing system successfully employed against Occidentals in Japan, and to limit Jews in the professions, trades and sciences by license according to their quotas of representation in the population.[21]

In a campaign speech before the German-American Folk Union in Seattle, Pelley cried:

> The time has come for an American Hitler and a pogrom. When I'm President I'll incorporate the Silver Shirts into a combination of Federal army and police force. I'm going to do away with the Department of Justice entirely.[22]

In 1942 the federal government arrested Pelley for sedition; he was convicted and received a sentence of 15 years in federal prison. But by 1950 he won parole after serving only half of his term. Once released, Pelley resumed his activities, founding the occult group "Soulcraft" and publishing the racist magazine *Valor*.[23]

Pelley's influence could be seen in Adamski's ideas, but even more so in those of another well-known contactee, George Hunt Williamson.[24] Williamson, who had begun working at the offices of Pelley's Soulcraft Publications in Noblesville, Indiana in 1950, was with Adamski when he met the Venusians. He later claimed that his expertise in linguistics helped him to interpret the symbolic message the Venusians left via their footprints.[25] From three horizontal lines found in one left footprint he derived the message, "The

GEORGE HUNT
WILLIAMSON

spacemen have found three different types of people on Earth. Unless a man puts away the materialism that is in him, he cannot rise to the emancipated heavens of the Creator. The Creator has sent people from outer space to guide Earthmen as they free themselves from darkness and bondage."

Although he never achieved the fame of his friend George Adamski, Williamson's book *Other Tongues—Other Flesh*, published in 1953 by Ray Palmer's Amherst Press, influenced later speculative books. In it Williamson aimed to tell the world the *purpose* of the saucers, as well as the epic story behind their landings which, he says, began millions of years ago.

Williamson's version of the origin of humanity draws from Pelley's *Star Guests*,[26] which itself draws from "I AM" (Guy and Edna Ballard's "Ascended Master" cult which flourished in the '30s), Theosophy, the Bible and possibly other sources. "In the beginning," writes Williamson, "the earth was a comet." Humanity came to Earth when "spiritual life migrated through interstellar space," from Sirius "and began to struggle independently with the problems of Earth planet environment." These spirits, known as angels, souls and Sons of God, came here to "gain experience on the physical plane," to be "prisoners of pain for education."

After their arrival, the Sons of God "incarnated in certain animal forms" that had evolved on Earth. They considered using the cat form, but discarded it in favor of the ape, which had useful, opposable thumbs. The "'Sons of God' made wives of the ape creatures," writes Williamson, "and the progeny was antediluvian man, or prehistoric-primitive man," whose "physical attributes belonged to the anthropoid apes and spiritual attributes belonged to the migration which came from the planets of the star-sun Sirius." Humanity, then, is a hybrid, combining the physical nature of the ape with the spiritual nature of space

Other Tongues-
Other Flesh

George Hunt Williamson

people. This idea is so attractive that it has been repeated time and again in "ancient astronaut" literature.

Williamson most clearly reveals Pelley's influence when he discusses "purity." He relates how the Sons of God tried living forms other than the ape during the "abomination period." Mankind took the form of half-angels, half-beasts such as the Griffin (half eagle, half lion), Medusas, Gorgons, Furies, Centaurs and the Sphinx. But during the Great Flood, says Williamson, the earth was "cleansed" of these "abominations," and all that were saved were the "pure" species. Williamson also quotes extensively from Pelley's *Star Guests*, channeled from a "higher intelligence" during the '30s. Its message closely resembles that of the proto-Nazi Ariosophists of Austria:[27]

> Man was pure ape or pure spirit. He had escaped the Great Catastrophy [sic] in areas where his species was clean. He was beast-ly but cleanly beastly. . . . Man was to suffer and die as beast, return-ing to the planets of the star-sun Sirius on physical death of beastly body. But came I [Son of Thought Incarnate] to the Father with bet-ter plan. The world of men could be cleansed of the beast by my instruction. Over countless generations could man be lifted back slowly to his lost angelic status. Thus was reincarnation born. So man came to remain in possession of ape-body.[28]

Though this message came during the '30s, Williamson notes that it "ties in perfectly with knowledge now being received from space intelligences." The Venusians agree with Pelley that our heritage comes from "races of angels mixed with beasts," and that humanity is now "engaged in separating the brute from the angel."

Several non-human intelligent life forms dwell on this planet, writes Williamson, among them "The Migrants," "The Harvesters," and "The Intruders." The earth, it seems, is a grand convention site for wandering aliens. The Migrants, or "Christ People," help humans win back their angelic status. The Harvesters occupy flying saucers; they are now preparing us for the New Age by exterminating all the "evil children" on Earth. The evil Intruders from the constellation Orion are infiltrators here on Earth. They were "discharged" and "secreted" onto the planets in Orion because they are literally the "slop" and the "waste" of the universe. Always looking for trouble, these beings are out to dis-turb all the other planets. Space intelligences have warned us:

> People of Orion are not our kind of people, they do not belong to our Confederation. They interrupt and are unruly. At present time there is a small group of people on Earth working for Orion. These people are sometimes small in stature with strange, oriental type

eyes. Their faces are thin and they possess weak bodies. They prey on the unsuspecting; they are talkative; they astound intellects with their words of magnificence. While their wisdom may have merit, it is materialistic, and not of pure aspiration toward the Father. They are the Universal parasites! Disturbers, negative elements; soon they will be eradicated.[29]

Many of the space brothers' messages, as received by contactees such as Williamson and Adamski, are transparent right-wing political statements whose authority is legitimized because they come from a "higher intelligence." When we are told that the spiritual side of human beings came here from another planet, we are often told that some of us are more "spiritual" than others and that the least spiritual of all, the interstellar enemies of humanity, will be exterminated.

THE SAGE OF GIANT ROCK

Williamson and Adamski often cited another contactee, George Van Tassel (1910–1978) who, during the '50s and '60s, preached humanity's star heritage. Born in Ohio, Van Tassel had worked as an aircraft mechanic for Douglas, Hughes and Lockheed. He moved to California in 1930 to an abandoned airport near Yucca Valley called "Giant Rock," which he leased from the U.S. government; he and his wife later bought the adjoining 40-acre ranch. After settling in at the ranch, they founded "The Ministry of Universal Wisdom" (a "science philosophy" organization), and "The College of Universal Wisdom" to facilitate "electro-magnetic" research.

Van Tassel's admirers soon began calling him the "Sage of Giant Rock," while his many friends knew him simply as "Van." The warm, hospitable Van Tassel family encouraged fellow flying saucer fans to visit and camp out at Giant Rock, where they would exchange contactee gossip, saucer sightings and philosophy.[30] When fans Bryant and Helen Reeve visited the site in 1955, they were struck by the constant activity there:

> People were coming and going all the time. . . . They all wanted to see and talk to Van. We marvelled at the stature and qualities of this man they came to see, his incredible patience with the most flippant and annoying questions, his unfailing courtesy, his amazing self-restraint and unselfish helpfulness toward all who came.[31]

Hundreds also showed up each year for the Van Tassels' UFO conventions (held 1954–1977), which became notorious for the strange characters they attracted.

Besides the sage himself, the other main attraction at Giant Rock was a unique, dome-shaped structure called the "Integratron." Van Tassel built the four-story machine (according to specifications of space brothers) to "recharge

GEORGE VAN TASSEL,
standing in front of
the Giant Rock (from *Flying
Saucer Pilgrimmage*)

energy into living cell structure, to bring about longer life with youthful energy." The beneficent brothers designed it "to handle up to 10,000 people a day," and its principle of operation, Van Tassel claimed, was "ten times simpler than color television."

In 1958, Van Tassel combined spiritualist philosophy and UFO belief in a book entitled *The Council of the Seven Lights*. (He reprinted it in 1968 as *Religion and Science Merged*.) The book's account of "the 12 densities, cycles, and arcs" reveals the influence of *Oahspe* from which Van Tassel borrows terminology as well as general spiritualist philosophy. He updates the spiritualist view, however, by arguing that "religion and science are the same thing." The only difference between them is that "they are two opposite viewpoints," like opposite sides of a wall. While science encroaches on previously religious territory, mystics like Van Tassel seek to rope in science by redefining it in their own terms; terms which are, at bottom, spiritual. The desire to combine science and religion underlies much of the contactee and later New Age literature; the sentiment is typified by creation stories that pay lip service to evolution but owe their substance to the Bible. Van Tassel's view of human origins, for example, has far more in common with the biblical account than with Darwin's.

Van Tassel reveals the true meaning of evolution and the book of Genesis in a chapter of *Religion and Science Merged* entitled "The Missing Link." God created Man, Van Tassel tells us—on many planets in many solar systems—before He created Earth. We didn't evolve from "lower animals," but were created "to serve as the instrument of God's doing." Adam wasn't the first man, he was an entire race of men brought here by the Adamic Federation in a spaceship. But the colonizers forgot to bring women along—a rather large oversight for a supposedly perfect race. If they wanted to people the earth, the Adamic race would have to mate with female Earth creatures. Fortunately, they were able to breed with one of the animal races here on Earth, the race of Eve, which Van Tassel describes as "upright walking animals . . . the highest form of lower animal life" on Earth, but they were not apes.

The Bible story of Adam and Eve and the serpent, writes Van Tassel, is really an account of God's displeasure with this coupling between man and beast; eating *the wrong apple* is a metaphor for mating with *the wrong species*. "This," says Van Tassel, "is where Man became *hu-man*." "Hu" represents the animal, killer nature of the tribe of Eve, while "man" is the higher nature, created by God. People on Earth today are crossbred descendants of the Adamic sons of God and the animal race of Eve, with an earthly dense animal body and an inner godly body. "The human race is a degenerate species of Man," writes Van Tassel, "as a result of following the bestial tendencies."

Van Tassel's fractured account of Genesis accomplishes several things: it explains the good and evil aspects of human nature and it suggests humanity can "choose" higher levels of spirituality, like its godly ancestors, or degenerate back into beasts. The theme of humanity as a hybrid between god and beast pervades not only the writings of flying saucer contactees, but also the metaphysical writings on the "degeneracy" of some or all members of the human race, as we'll see in the following chapters.

THE SKY PEOPLE

BRINSLEY LE POER TRENCH, THE EIGHTH EARL OF CLANCARTY (from *Eccentric Lives and Peculiar Notions*)

Van Tassel wasn't the only one to read the Bible as a space opera, nor was he the only contactee to claim that humanity is a cross between extraterrestrials and beasts. Brinsley Le Poer Trench discussed the same concept in his 1960 book *The Sky People*. Van Tassel had written that humanity was a cross between the beastly Eve race and the ET Adam race; Trench agreed, but used slightly different terminology. Trench suggested that humanity had been born of "Chemical-Man" and "Galactic-Man" to create the hybrid, "Cross-Man."

Trench, born in 1911, is a bona-fide English lord, the eighth Earl of Clancarty; he took "Brinsley Le Poer Trench" as his "civilian" name. UFOs intrigued Trench after World War II when he began clipping the plentiful news stories on the subject. He met Desmond Leslie, co-author of *Flying Saucers Have Landed*, who encouraged him to attend a lecture about flying saucers in London. Trench then became a vocal and powerful force in the British UFO world.

In 1955, with Derek Dempster (aviation correspondent for the *Daily Express*) and others, Trench founded the Flying Saucer Service, Ltd. and the *Flying Saucer Review*, which he edited from 1956 to 1959. In 1967 Trench founded Contact International, a UFO organization with members in 37 countries.

In the grand tradition of wealthy British eccentricity, the Earl used his position in the House of Lords to advance his pet cause: UFOs. In 1979, Trench introduced the first debate on UFOs into British Parliament, which led to the formation of the House of Lords All-Party UFO Study Group.

The Sky People (1960) was Trench's first book, followed by Forgotten Heritage (1964), *The Flying Saucer Story* (1966), *Operation Earth* (1969), *The Eternal Subject* (1973) and *Secret of the Ages: UFOs from Inside the Earth* (1974).

In *The Sky People*, Trench drew explicitly from the '50s flying saucer mythology, as well as from earlier Theosophical and occultist belief systems. "Sky People," wrote Trench, "have been coming to Earth for millions and millions of years." He interpreted ancient myths as veiled accounts of history, in anticipation of writers like Zecharia Sitchin.[32] Myths of the Golden Age when gods mingled with mortals, he wrote, are "but the fairy story coverings these true happenings of a bygone age were wrapt up in to preserve them for posterity." Whenever mythological gods such as Zeus, Hermes and Aphrodite, were said to come down from the clouds, this really meant that real Sky People—extraterrestrials—had emerged from spacecraft.

HU MAN
a homegrown metaphysical novel about mankind's extraterrestrial origins published in Springfield, Missouri in 1982.

The Bible, as well, tells us the truth about the Sky Gods. In the first chapter of Genesis, after He has created light, earth, water, plants, fish, animals and everything else, God (Elohim) creates man and woman in his own image and tells them to "be fruitful and multiply" (Gen. 1:26–28). This, writes Trench, "refers to the establishment of the Golden Age and to the creation of Galactic Man," by a race of Sky People called Elohim. In the second chapter of Genesis, Lord God (Jehovah) forms man from dust, places him in the Garden of Eden, and then forms woman from the rib of the man (Gen. 2:7–25). This story refers to a much later creation, writes Trench, by another group of Sky People called Jehovah. They made "Adam II humanity"— or "Chemical Man"—from dust of the ground to be their servants in the Garden of Eden.

The Garden of Eden, we learn, was "an enormous agricultural project" located in a former desert on Mars, developed with the aid of irrigation. "In this garden," writes Trench, the Jehovahs "placed the new animal hu-man type, specifically to till the ground, care for the vegetation and to guard the area."[33] The diet of the Adam-II servants was restricted to make them sterile; they were created for strictly commercial use. They could eat anything in the garden except two prohibited varieties, the proverbial "forbidden fruit." The story of Adam and Eve and the forbidden fruit is, according to Trench, an account of an agricultural experiment gone wrong. The Adam-II women, in disobedience to their masters, interbred with the Galactic Race, serving forbidden fruit to the men and wearing clothes, causing the Jehovahs to shut down the operation.

Just after the failure of the agricultural experiment, the polar cap of the red planet melted. The Jehovahs fled to nearby Earth in a spaceship, taking some of the Adam-II people with them. This spaceship later became known as Noah's

Ark. Because they had interbred with the Galactic Race, the Adam-II people who arrived on Earth were what Trench calls "Cross-Men," a cross between the two races. Much like in Van Tassel's account, in Trench's human ancestry includes both Chemical and Galactic elements, explaining the humanity's dual nature, one portion oriented towards the stars, the other toward the earth. As Cross-men, however, we humans are destined to some day join with our "higher kin," the Galactic Men, and the "Age of Darkness will come to an end."

Trench parallels Van Tassel when he asserts in *The Sky People* that humanity is a cross between Galactic-Man and Chemical-Man. His message is basically religious, an esoteric interpretation of the Christian Bible: dual-natured, cross-bred humanity will one day "reach Galactic manhood," closing the Age of Darkness and ushering in the Age of Light and Christ. Trench was providing the flying saucer fans with new interpretations of old myths. The updated mythology, along with messages from the space brothers about "Universal Law" and the like, would form the backbone of a new space-age religion. Hence, flying saucer contactees believed humans were planted on Earth by spacemen for, essentially, religious reasons.

MANKIND — CHILD OF THE STARS

A couple of years after *The Sky People* first appeared, Max H. Flindt (1915–?) — son of science fiction pioneer Homer Eon Flint (1892–1924) — attempted to give the "Space Gods" theory of human origins a more scientific veneer.

Judging from his father's stories, Max Flindt grew up in an environment friendly to speculative ideas from science to spiritualism. His father had authored such pulp space operas as "The Lord of Death," "The Queen of Life," "The Devolutionist" and "The Emancipatrix," which appeared in *Argosy All Story Weekly* in the late teens and early twenties.[34] These stories depict not-too-alien worlds inhabited by

The Devolutionist and The Emancipatrix by HOMER EON FLINT, father of MAX H. FLINDT

advanced people who have mastered, for example, space travel via telepathy. In "The Devolutionist" and its sequel, "The Emancipatrix," a small group of friends (on Earth) learn a technique of telepathic space travel — which strongly resembles a séance — from advanced, enlightened Venusians. Using this technique, they visit a world very much like Earth — only it revolves around its sun every 25 hours — inhabited by people very similar to themselves — only they wear their wedding rings on the *third* finger of the *right* hand. It would be easy to imagine the sort of "aliens" portrayed by Homer Eon Flint as our "cousins," since they were essentially no different from Earth people. Homer Flint's son Max introduced his own speculations concerning the human past in 1962, in a self-published booklet entitled *On Tiptoe Beyond Darwin*. The booklet was expanded and re-published in 1974 as *Mankind—Child of the Stars* to cash in on the popularity of Erich von Däniken's *Chariots of the Gods?*

According to the paperback's biographical blurb, Max Flindt was born in 1915 and worked as a "Senior Laboratory Technician under Nobel winners Dr. Edward Teller, Dr. Glenn Seaborg, and Dr. Melvin Calvin at Lawrence Radiation Laboratory, . . . and [did] research on human blood anomalies under the late Professor Emeritus Percival Baumberger of Stanford University."

Flindt's co-author, Otto Binder (1911–1974), was a well-known science fiction writer during the '50s, '60s and early '70s, who often used the pseudonym Eando Binder. He also churned out nonfiction flying saucer paperbacks such as *Flying Saucers Are Watching Us* and articles for pulps such as *Argosy, Mechanix Illustrated* and *Saga*, with titles like "How Flying Saucers Can Injure You" and "Sex and the Saucerman."

In their effort to argue "scientifically" that humanity is a hybrid between apeman and spaceman, the co-authors of *Mankind—Child of the Stars* didn't hesitate to quote extensively from Binder's own flying saucer titles. They also, however, attempted to transcend the flying saucer genre with research into human evolution. Familiarizing themselves with the scientific problems of the field (such as the "missing link" problem), they generated a long list of what they took to be the riddles, enigmas and anomalies of human evolution. All these enigmas, Flindt and Binder claimed, were solved if we realized that our species is a hybrid between "Apeman" and "Spaceman."

Although they try very hard to look scientific, Flindt and Binder find their clearest evidence for the improbable coupling of apeman and spaceman in the Bible. From Genesis 6:2, in which the sons of God marry the daughters of men—"And it came to pass, when men began to multiply on the face of the earth, and daughters were born unto them, that the sons of God saw the daughters of men that they were fair, and they took them wives of all which they chose"—they conclude that "starmen visited Earth and mated with early females (perhaps hominids) to sire the modern human race of *Homo sapiens*."

Flindt and Binder conclude that not only humans—but just about every species on Earth—were originally brought here by aliens. The space people first arrived here long before hominids appeared, making countless trips to Earth, each for a different "hybridization project." They brought with them such creatures as the coelacanth and the duck-billed platypus. (The existence of these "living fossils," say Flindt and Binder, disproves evolution because—according to their story-book understanding of the theory—those creatures should have died out eons ago.) The aliens also imported the first apes and then returned about 12 million years ago, in time to breed with *Ramapithecus*, an early hominid. Not quite 12 million years later, the offspring of this strange coupling had developed into *Australopithecus*, an early ancestor of *Homo sapiens*. The idea of humanity as a hybrid between apeman and spaceman, already circulating among flying saucer fans, is a good metaphor for the coupling of science/nature and religion/spirit, with the apeman (or, more often apewoman) representing science/nature and the spaceman representing religion/spirit. This coupling of nature and spirit is also the underlying motive for trying to reconcile evolution and the Bible.

The contactees in the 1950s, and then Flindt, in 1962, were among the first to discover the ancient astronauts as symbolic of the fusion between science and spirit. But it wasn't until the late '60s and early '70s that "ancient astronauts" would become a household phrase.

ANCIENT ASTRONAUTS CONQUER THE WORLD!

In 1969, Erich von Däniken's mass market paperback, *Chariots of the Gods?*, published in Germany the previous year, blanketed the United States. In the traditions of Desmond Leslie and Brinsley LePoer Trench, von Däniken saw "ancient astronauts" as responsible for every earthly mystery from Ezekiel's Wheel to the Mayan and Egyptian Pyramids to the enigma of our own existence. Sales of this blockbuster approached 50 million copies. I personally remember the book provoking many heated debates in my high school cafeteria. Von Däniken was obviously touching a nerve that went far beyond the saucer clubs and space brother contactees.

Erich von Däniken was born in Zofingen, Switzerland in 1935 and was raised in a strict, Catholic household. He often butted heads with his pious father and with his teachers at the Jesuit College of Saint-Michel (a secondary school) in Fribourg, Switzerland. His father removed him from the school after he had completed only three years there. Von Däniken then began a career as hotelier, working his way up from cook and waiter to manager. But his real passion lay elsewhere. After hours, von Däniken would devote himself to archeology, astronomy and metaphysics.

Von Däniken's search for "the gods" began when he first experienced the paranormal in 1954, at age 19. He later told *Der Spiegel* magazine that ESP was "a source which led me to the firm belief that the earth had been visited by extraterrestrial astronauts." In the ESP experiences, "one makes a sort of 'journey through time.' I step out of time, so I stand outside time and see everything simultaneously—past, present, and future." [35]

In 1966 the starry-eyed hotel manager finished his first book, *Memories of the Future*, the result of late-night sessions until three and four in the morning. The following year, von Däniken's book—out of all the thousands of amateurs in search of a publisher—was accepted by Econ-Verlag. In March of 1968, after extensive rewriting by Wilhelm Roggersdorf, a film producer and screenwriter, the first 6,000 copies of *Memories of the Future* were printed. The book was an unqualified hit. The next year it was published and renamed *Chariots of the Gods?* in West Germany and became that country's number one best-seller.

While von Däniken was still toiling away as a hotel manager, he began spending his vacations in Egypt, Lebanon and America to see the ancient astronaut evidence himself. In order to finance his journeys, however, he had to embezzle over 400,000 Swiss francs. In 1968, as his book was climbing the best-seller lists, he was arrested for fraud. In court, he pleaded that this behavior was justified by the scholar's impassioned quest for knowledge. But the judges were not convinced, and in 1970 von Däniken was convicted of embezzlement, fraud and forgery. His sentence was three and a half years in prison and a fine of 3,000 francs. This sum was easily paid off by his ever-growing royalty checks, and he was let out of prison early. Free of legal entanglements, now the budding author could fulfill his dream of devoting himself to ancient astronauts full time. Von Däniken is still churning out sequels, 30 years later.

In *Chariots of the Gods?* von Däniken attributed artifacts and monuments such as the Great Pyramid of Cheops and the markings on the Plain of Nazca in Peru— and humanity itself—to ancient astronauts. In the chapter entitled "Was God an Astronaut?" he asks another question: "Does not [evidence from the Bible] seriously pose the question whether the human race is not an act of deliberate 'breeding' by unknown beings from outer space?" He later suggested a scenario that was old hat to the flying saucer buffs but seemed daring to the uninitiated:

> Dim, as yet undefinable ages ago an unknown spaceship discovered our planet. Obviously the "man" of those times was no *Homo sapiens* but something rather different. The spacemen artificially fertilized some female members of this species, put them into a deep sleep, so ancient legends say, and departed. Thousands of years later the space travelers returned and found scattered specimens of the genus *Homo sapiens*. . . .[36]

Von Däniken's version of humanity as an alien breeding experiment, like those that came before, loosely follows the Bible. Like Blavatsky's narrow-headed Lemurians[37] and Van Tassel's alien-beast hybrids, some of Adam's genetically altered progeny were unable to control themselves, and continued to mate with animals. This "backsliding" represented the Fall of Man because it "impeded evolution," and retained the bestial in man. A few thousand years later, however, presumably at the time of Noah's flood, the cosmonauts corrected this situation. "They destroyed the hybrid animal-men, separated a well-preserved group of new men, and implanted new genetic material in them by a second artificial mutation."

Though derivative of earlier authors, von Däniken was able to reach those who had never touched a flying saucer book in their lives. After the appearance of *Chariots of the Gods?* the idea that spacemen created humanity as a genetic experiment was circulating in perhaps 50 million minds. "Impossible?"

The religious angle of the ancient astronaut story is perhaps its biggest selling point. Many people are relieved to find out that God isn't dead after all, He's just a misunderstood colony of spacemen. After von Däniken and others cleared the field for speculation in this vein, the market was flooded with reinterpretations of the Bible as an extraterrestrial epic.

THOSE WHO CAME FROM THE SKY

Von Däniken wasn't the only European to popularize ancient astronauts during the late '6os. In 1968, French author Jean Sendy, who had previously written on biblical and occult subjects, came out with a new title, *La Lune, Cle de la Bible*. It was translated as *The Moon: Outpost of the Gods* for U.S. distribution in 1975. In this book Sendy, like Brinsley LePoer Trench before him, suggested that the biblical book of Genesis is a literal account of the coming of extraterrestrial colonists to Earth, known biblically as Elohim.

Space Aliens Took Me To Their Planet
(RAËL circa 1975)

Five years later, on December 13, 1973, Sendy's disclosure of the true identity of the Elohim was dramatically confirmed by auto racing journalist Claude Vorilhon; he spoke to an extraterrestrial who emerged from a hovering spaceship in a dormant volcano in the French countryside. A small humanoid in a green suit told Vorilhon that he had come from "a far distant planet" similar to Earth "to observe the evolution of human beings and to watch over them." He had chosen Vorilhon specifically to be his messenger, and his new name would be Raël. Vorilhon/Raël was to return the next day, at the same time, with a Bible and note pad.

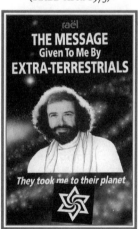

During their second meeting, the extraterrestrial instructed his French pupil in the true meaning of the Bible, confirming the speculations of authors such as von Däniken, Sendy and Flindt. Raël learned that sci-

The Message Given to me by Extraterrestrials
(RAËL circa 1986)

entists from the ET's planet had come to Earth long ago to conduct experiments in creating life, and that the word "Elohim" from the Bible, when properly translated, means "those who came from the sky." The humanoid explained that the line, "And the spirit of Elohim moved across the waters" in Genesis 1:2, really means, "[The extraterrestrials] made reconnaissance flights, and what you might call artificial satellites were placed around the earth to study its constitution and atmosphere." Likewise, the true story behind the line "Elohim saw that the light was good" in Genesis 1:4, is, "To create life on Earth it was important to know whether the sun was sending harmful rays to the earth's surface." [38]

The Elohim, of course, also created mankind, but it wasn't until August 6, 1945, the day the United States dropped the atomic bomb on Hiroshima, that humanity had finally "reached the stage in its scientific evolution where it was now ready to understand the truth about its origins." And now that we know the truth, the Elohim are imploring us, through Raël, to welcome them back to Earth by building an embassy for them in Jerusalem. It is up to the International Raëlian Movement to spread the Elohim's messages, to build the embassy and to prepare humanity for their imminent arrival.

The Raëlian movement claims over 30,000 members in 67 countries; the messages of the Elohim have been translated into 19 languages. This classic New Age religion embraces sensual practices and meditations inspired by Eastern religion, as well as a religious philosophy which updates the standard Judeo-Christian mythology with space-age technology. The Raëlians are overtly opposed, however, to the scientific establishment and regard evolution by "chance" as a "myth." They embrace technological progress while rejecting the scarier atheist underpinnings of science.

SLAVES OF THE ALIENS

During the ancient astronaut boom in the '70s, Zecharia Sitchin's 1976 offering, *The 12th Planet*, almost got lost in the shuffle. Twenty years later, however, Sitchin became heir to von Däniken's blockbuster kingdom. During the '90s, Sitchin's series of best-selling pseudo-scholarly books have fostered a huge and fanatical following. While his fans believe the author's claim to scholarly credentials, his actual scientific understanding is limited, at best. Sitchin may be, as he insists, an expert in ancient languages, but his greatest expertise is his ability to twist the logic of modern languages. Yet people who would laugh at von Däniken or Van Tassel are beguiled by the scholarly bait-and-switch of Zecharia Sitchin.

Sitchin was born in 1920 in Baku in the former USSR,[39] later emigrating to England and then Israel. Before delving into the arcane field of extraterrestrial inter-

vention, Sitchin served in the British and Israeli Armies and then distinguished himself in journalism, foreign trade and public service. He served as Assistant Town Clerk of Tel Aviv, Executive Director of the American-Israel Chamber of Commerce and Industry and president of the American-Israel Pavilion at the 1965 New York World's Fair, for which he received the New York World's Fair Award.

Sitchin claims, as well, to be an "expert" in ancient languages, trained at Hebrew University in Jerusalem. However, the biographical source I checked lists his only degree as Bachelor of Commerce (B.Com.) from the

University of London. Aside from his membership in various museum and Oriental societies, there is no mention of any scholarly credentials; his most obvious talents are promotion and marketing.

Sitchin adds the pretense of expertise to standard ancient astronaut lore. His chains of argument, however, are as flawed as von Däniken's. He frequently points to ancient illustrations, claiming they depict rockets, batteries, helmets and electronic devices used by people who lived thousands of years ago. Yet he never wonders why archeologists haven't yet found any hi-tech equipment buried in the rubble of the ancient cities.

Sitchin's fans perceive him as an original thinker. But his hallmark, interpreting battles between gods in Sumerian texts as collisions between planets, is nothing

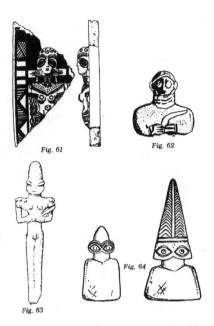

Fig. 61

Fig. 62

Fig. 63

Fig. 64

Ancient depictions of our ET creators says SITCHIN (from *The 12th Planet*)

new. In the early '50s, George Hunt Williamson used arguments based on made-up word associations that Sitchin would perfect later; he identified the Babylonian god Marduk with an extra planet called "Maldek"—an idea that was a direct precursor to Sitchin's *12th Planet*.

In the *12th Planet*, Sitchin claims to read the Sumerian *Epic of Creation* (a work we can assume is unfamiliar to much of his audience) at "face value." At face value, the tale is one of the creation of the waters, heavens and earth by gods. Sitchin, however, reads it as a tale about the peregrinations of planetary bodies. Sitchin provides bits and pieces of the epic, but he never summarizes the original story in full. If he did, his argument would fall apart. One must turn to Near Eastern scholars, such as Dr. Georges Roux, for a straightforward interpretation of the poem:

> When nothing yet had a name, that is to say when nothing had yet been created, Apsu (the sweet waters), Tiamat (the salt waters) and Mummu (the clouds) formed together one single confused body.
>
> [L]arger patches of land emerge from the mist as the sun rises, and soon a clear-cut line separates the sky from the waters and the waters from the earth. So in the myth the first gods to emerge from the chaos were Lahmuand Lahamu, representing the silt; then came Anshar and Kishar, the twin horizons of sky and earth. Asharand Kishar begot Anu, and Anu in turn begot Ea (Enki).[40]

In Sitchin's mind, each Sumerian god represents a planetary body in our solar system: Apsu is the sun, Mummu is Mercury and Tiamat is "the missing planet." Tiamat and Apsu "commingled" to beget not gods, but two more planets, Lahmu (Mars) and Lahamu (Venus). Then, another two planets—Anshar (Saturn) and Kishar (Jupiter)—were formed and grew larger than Mars and Venus. Finally, a third pair of planets, Anu, "Anshar's first-born" (Uranus) and Ea (Neptune) were formed. To complete the picture, Gaga (Pluto) materialized, as a satellite to Saturn. The completed solar system consisted of ten bodies: the sun, Mercury, Venus, Mars, Tiamat, Jupiter, Saturn, Pluto, Uranus and Neptune.

In the next part of the poem—as presented by Roux—the great god Marduk, son of Ea and Damkina, is born: "Perfect were his members beyond comprehension. Four were his eyes, four were his ears; when he moved his lips, fire blazed forth. His members were enormous, he was exceedingly tall." [41] After Marduk appears, the goddess Tiamat and Marduk engage in a great battle; the battle ends when Marduk splits Tiamat's body open "like a shellfish." Half of the goddess becomes the sky, and the other half, the underworld. According to Sitchin, however, the battle represents a series of collisions between the "missing planet" Tiamat and the "12th planet" Marduk, "a large, comet-like planet from outer space." These collisions, says Sitchin, created the earth, moon and all the other bodies of the solar system. Marduk still exists, and enters our solar system every 3,600 years.

Marduk, according to Sitchin, is the home planet of our creators, an intelligent, humanoid race he calls the "Nefilim." They first landed on Earth about 450,000 years ago, during the second ice age.

The word "Nefilim" comes not from Sumerian, but from Genesis 6:4, "The Nefilim were upon the earth, in those days and thereafter too, when the sons of the gods cohabited with the daughters of the Adam, and they bore children unto them. They were the mighty ones of Eternity—The People of the *Shem*." [42] *Shem*, usually translated as "name" or "reputation," Sitchin identifies as "fiery rocket." In defense of this strange translation, Sitchin employs von Däniken-style arguments based on how much all those ancient artifacts seem to depict rockets and space helmets and airports. Hence, the Nefilim are the "people of the fiery rockets."

Similar arguments reveal to Sitchin that the Nefilim were advanced petroleum-hungry beings who chose to settle in Mesopotamia (now Iraq), the biblical "Eden," because of its abundance of oil. They also chose this site for its proximity to two seas, in which their hermetically sealed space capsules could "splash down," as NASA does.

The reason the Nefilim came to Earth, says Sitchin, was the mundane quest for *gold*. After settling in Mesopotamia, they established colonies in southeast Africa to mine gold and other precious metals, which were needed for their electronic equipment. The Annunaki—the rank and file Nefilim—would be shipped to Earth to work the mines and raw materials would be shipped back to the home planet. Thus, the deity, Enki (or Ea), which Mesopotamian scholars identify as the god of *wisdom*, was really the god of *mining*. After all, Sitchin points out, the artists who depicted Ea showed him "holding a miner's rock saw."

Sitchin returns to the *Epic of Creation* for the story of the creation of mankind. Only now the "gods," whom he'd previously interpreted as "planets," transform magically into extraterrestrials from Marduk; Sitchin seems too busy spinning his sensational story to worry about details. Mankind, asserts Sitchin, was created 300,000 years ago, as a result of a mutiny by the Annunaki. When they set fire to their tools and aired their grievances, their bosses decided to create a "primitive worker" to relieve them. The Nefilim and "their chief scientist, Ea," created *Homo sapiens* to be that primitive worker by genetically manipulating the most advanced human at the time, *Homo erectus*. This was accomplished by inserting the sperm of a Nefilim male into the ovum of a female *Homo erectus*, and then implanting the fertilized egg into the womb of Ea's spouse. The child of this antiseptic union was the first modern man, Adam. Adam, however, was only a "model" or "mold" from which duplicates (clones, presumably) were obtained and then implanted in the wombs of female Nefilim, or "birth goddesses."

Since the first specimens of *Homo sapiens* were created as hybrids—like mules—they were infertile. It was only through genetic engineering that our ancestors were given two sets of sex cells so that they could reproduce. This is what the story of Adam and Eve is about. In the story, eating the fruit of the tree of knowledge is a symbol for the primeval pair's newfound ability to reproduce.

Sitchin, true to the ancient astronaut credo, tells us that humanity is a hybrid between evolved hominids and advanced extraterrestrials, while providing a vague critique of Darwin. He wonders, "Are we really nothing more than 'naked apes'?" "No!" he answers. Darwinian evolution is correct, but only up to a point. When it identifies humanity as an accident that befell a band of apes, he's forced to bail out. Like almost every author discussed in this chapter, he asserts that "evolution can explain the general course of events that caused life on Earth, but evolution cannot account for the appearance of *Homo sapiens*." Instead, he finds it more likely that humankind was genetically engineered as a slave for extraterrestrial gold miners.

Obviously, Sitchin's popularity comes not from the strength of his arguments. He's more concerned with "proving" his alternative history by bending the available evidence than with altering his theory to fit the facts. Like von Däniken, he has tapped into the imagination of the popular mind which is disillusioned and distrustful of hard science, even while embracing many of its accomplishments.

Ironically, Sitchin's interpretations of myth are embedded in a stubborn materialism usually identified with science. To Sitchin, myths don't depict anything spiritual or intangible at all; they depict only hard, historic events. Ea wasn't the god of wisdom; he was the god of mining. Though Sitchin's conclusions seem imaginative, they stem from a *lack* of imagination shared with some fundamentalists, an inability to connect with the cosmos and its mysteries in any but the most literal way.

Many of Sitchin's followers come from the New Age tradition, which sees humanity as something more than just a particularly successful genotype. Blavatsky, the spiritualists, the flying saucer contactees and current esoteric believers all maintain that our culture's sacred texts, including the Bible, are *not* incorrect, just incorrectly interpreted. The human race was created by powerful beings, after all—extraterrestrials to whom we are inextricably and genetically linked.

Sitchin and his followers—like the creationists we will meet later—seek hard, "scientific proof" of spiritual conclusions. Faith, these days, is not enough. If they find this evidence, they tell themselves, the atheists and materialists will finally have to admit defeat.

THE ANNUNAQI AND THE THORIANS

Though Sitchin would deny that his books are "religious," they have touched a religious nerve with many. Take the Holy Tabernacle Ministries, for example. Dr. Malachi Z. York, who claims to hail from the planet Rizq in the 19th galaxy called Illyuwn, founded this black Muslim group. The Holy Tabernacle Ministries is, in fact, just one of a string of black Muslim sects he's started since the 1970s. During the '70s and '80s, while leading the most well-known of his sects, the Nubian Islamic Hebrew Mission (the "Nubians"), York called himself As Sayyid Isa Al Haady Al Mahdi and claimed descent from a royal family in the Sudan, in Africa. In fact, however, this extraordinary charlatan was born with the name Dwight York and really comes from New Jersey. York had penned all of the Nubians' lengthy texts, much of them plagiarized or derived from other fringe sources. Two of these books, *Leviathan 666* and *The Paleman*, contain diatribes against the race of white devils who mate with dogs and run the world.[43] But now that he has been exposed to Zecharia Sitchin, York embraces an entirely new theology and, of course, a new name. His "galactical name" is Yaanuwn, though in ancient times he was known as Murdoq, Michael or Melchisedek.

Many of the ideas in York's texts (which I obtained from Holy Tabernacle Ministries websites) are lifted almost word for word from Sitchin—with a Nubian twist. York reveals that he traveled here by a small passenger craft called a "Sham." Sitchin had written that the Nefilim spaceships were called "Shem." York says it takes the Annunaqi 3,600 years to travel to Earth, and that the orbit is called a "Shar." Sitchin had argued that it took the Nefilim 3,600 years to travel to Earth, the orbit of the planet Marduk, which the Sumerians called a "Shar."

In York's version, however, the gods, or Annunaqi, came not from Marduk, but from "the eighth planet Rizq in the 19th Galaxy Illyuwn." An elite, woolly-haired race of beings, the Annunaqi created *Homo sapiens* and now "travel through this galaxy by way of a planet ship named Nibiru: the Mother ship." The Annunaqi originally came to Earth to mine gold, and then created a primitive worker by crossbreeding with apemen, or "Shaggies," to ease the toil. The Shaggies, or "Enkiduites," are "beings covered in fur from other galaxies," also known as "your Big Foot." York himself is one of the Annunaqi and incarnated on Earth "for the sole purpose of saving the children of the Eloheem (Anunnaqi), The Banaat, the chosen 144,000."

It is not surprising to find alien intervention theories of human origins popping up in messianic religions, for these theories directly address religious needs, no matter how much lip service they pay to "science." What is a bit surprising is the number of variations suggested over the years, with many new titles still coming out. The authors range from hack writers to professional UFO investigators to rank amateurs who must self-publish. Most such theories merely reiterate previous theories, which show little originality.

The Thorians, by amateur astronomer Finnvald Hedin, is more original than most offerings. It was published in 1980 by Vantage, a leading vanity press; I may be the only person not related to Finnvald Hedin to own a copy of the book. It's a good example of homespun alien intervention theory, inspired by a panoply of cultural influences: ancient astronaut and saucer books; Norse mythology; Scandinavian pride; mathematics; astronomy; physics; numerology; and a mild dose of inner vision.

Hedin, a retired Boeing engineer and co-designer of the 747, was born in Norway in 1929, and later settled in the Seattle area. Finnvald Hedin, however, is no ordinary engineer, as he also dabbles in astronomy, physics and a kind of antiquated numerological mysticism inspired by astronomer Johannes Kepler (1571–1630).

Because of Hedin's training he is well aware of the speculative nature of his theories; nor is he under any delusions concerning his own importance. He does, however, plea for the value of mysticism, "quasi-science" and the contribution of amateurs like himself.

Though *The Thorians* is standard ancient astronaut fare, Hedin takes a novel approach to documenting his ideas. His theories hinge on Bode's Law in astronomy and the concept of "perfect" numbers from mathematical number theory.[44] Bode's Law, based on empirical data, states a predictable, numerical relationship between the distances from the sun of the planets in our solar system. All the planets—including the asteroid belt, which scientists once thought contained the remains of a planet—conform to Bode's Law, except for Neptune and Pluto. Hedin speculates that there were originally two bodies—roughly the size of the earth and our moon—that broke apart to become the asteroid belt. George Hunt Williamson called this "fifth planet" Maldek and Zecharia Sitchin called it Tiamat. The numerical sequence given by Bode's Law gives six for the earth and 28 for the asteroid belt.

It is more than coincidence, says Hedin, that these are both perfect numbers. He speculates that any planet associated with a perfect number in the Bode's Law sequence harbors life. Thus, Earth, associated with the perfect number six, contains life, and the fifth planet (which Hedin calls "Thor"), associated with perfect number 28, also once contained life—intelligent life, in the form of "Thorians."

Thorians, writes Hedin, were eight feet tall and lived 400 years. 20,000 years ago, however, Thor and its moon were destroyed in a nuclear explosion, creating the asteroid belt. Some of the Thorians escaped and fled to Earth. One of the Thorian invaders was, in fact, Noah, his spaceship the "Ark"; Noah's "flood" was really a nuclear explosion on Thor, caused by Godless pride. To avoid the same kind of disaster on Earth, Noah and the other Thorians imported the concept of God.

The original Thorian colonies were located in Scandinavia, where otherworldly Vikings bred with humans to create hybrids. This accounts for the large stature and light pigmentation of the Scandinavian people. As they moved south, the giant blond extraterrestrials brought aggression and civilization to humanity. The remains of these colonies lie mostly under water now, in the northern Atlantic.

The Thorians, along with Dr. Malachi Z. York's Sitchin-like theology, are testaments to the pervasiveness and malleability of the ancient astronaut myth. It can be molded to anybody's ethnic bias, pet theory or religion, enhancing their status by transforming them from colorless mortals to children the of gods.

Malevolent Aliens and Hidden Histories

DERO, SERPENT PEOPLE AND REPTOIDS

In ancient astronaut and other "hidden history" myths, the god-like extraterrestrials who colonized Earth often battle an evil enemy. The fallen angels and evil spirits of old are personified in these myths by Serpent People, Reptoids (or Reptilians), Dinoids, the Greys and the Dero[45]—just as the gods and angels are often seen as beautiful, blond-haired Space Brothers. The myths in which these sinister beings appear usually involve the same, or similar elements: a Golden Age when the earth's axis was upright;[46] malevolent Serpent or Snake People; genetically engineered robot slaves (the Dero) or extraterrestrials (the Greys); former civilizations on Atlantis and Lemuria; and a cataclysm that destroys the ancient civilizations, tilts the earth on its axis and cleanses the world of its evil inhabitants who flee to the hollow earth and outer space, making room for godly humanity.

Richard Shaver's 1945 memoir "I Remember Lemuria" gave birth to the "Shaver Mystery" craze (which lasted about three years) and strongly influenced subsequent "hidden histories" of the human race. In this work of alleged nonfiction, first published in Ray Palmer's science fiction magazine *Amazing Stories*, the evil race is personified by the Dero, a degenerate race of genetically engineered robot slaves abandoned in the hollow earth by the extraterrestrial super-race who once colonized Atlantis before emigrating to another world.

Meanwhile, the fallen angels of Christianity had been transformed by Theosophists into "Lucifer spirits" and "Serpent People," eventually finding their way into the hidden history and ancient astronaut myths as rivals of the benevolent angels who assisted in the creation of humanity. These Serpent People often originated from the constellation Orion—as George Hunt Williamson's "Intruders" had. Dr. Maurice Doreal (1898–1963), the "Supreme Voice" of the Brotherhood of the White Temple,[47] wrote that the home of the Serpent People—eternal enemies of the Arctic Sons of God—was Antarctica; they were wiped out by a superweapon which also tilted the earth on its axis. The Snake People, the evil race found in the telepathically received "Hefferlin Manuscript" (1947), came simply from outer space. They chased humans from planet to planet for a thousand years until the last remnants of the human empire fled the dying planet Mars and colonized Earth. The Snake People continued to plague the human race, however, their surprise attack causing a catastrophe that tilted the earth.

Aliens, The Final Answer? suggests humanity was created by super-intelligent Dinosaurs

In 1951 a "Messenger of Buddha" named Robert Ernst Dickhoff a.k.a. Sungma Red Lama published a book entitled *Agharta: The Subterranean World*, in which the Serpent People came from Venus. In this scenario, Earth humans were created as slaves by Martian "super-scientists" who colonized the planet 2.5 million years ago. The Serpent People, however—who resembled crocodiles, walked erect, stood 14 feet tall, and possessed humanoid hands and feet with six fingers and toes plus a thumb—wanted Earth for themselves. They invaded the planet, causing some of the Martians and humans to flee to the inner earth. The battle developed into nuclear warfare, destroying Atlantis and Lemuria and tilting the earth on its axis. The conflict continues to this day, inside the hollow earth, while the Serpent People try to exterminate the humans by triggering World War III.

Hidden histories continue to be received from Ascended Masters and Tibetan lamas or—more often—channeled from the extraterrestrials themselves. The messages of "Cosmic Awareness," a voice currently being channeled by Paul Shockley in Olympia, Washington,[48] contain a mishmash of seemingly every hidden history, extraterrestrial intervention and hollow Earth book in existence. Cosmic Awareness frequently reports that works of science fiction, including blockbuster movies like *Close Encounters of the Third Kind*, are factual. The entity also has much to say about the Serpent People, whom it calls Reptoids, malevolent creatures who are trying to alter human genetics and seize our planet.

A 1992 issue (#396) of the Cosmic Awareness Communications newsletter, *Revelations of Awareness*, is devoted almost exclusively to the Reptoids (who originate from the constellation Orion). With an unemotional tone of authority, Cosmic Awareness describes the Reptoids as scaly humanoids who see "with infrared capacity," detecting "heat rather than visual qualities." The average Reptoid is seven feet tall and four times as strong as a man. The creatures reproduce by laying eggs, as earthly reptiles do, though they place their eggs in an incubator rather than a nest. Some, but not all, have tails. The longer tails are, to them, signs of virility.

The Greys (aliens from Zeta Reticuli) are servants of the powerful Reptoids. The Greys, warns Cosmic Awareness, were once similar to humans. After the Reptoids saved them from their dying planet, however, the Reptoids modified the Greys "through genetic engineering to incorporate insect and reptilian genes to become what they presently are, being born in a sack of hundreds, perhaps, of genetically engineered fetuses of Zeta Reticuli so that an entire hive or group might be born at one time." The sinister creatures have similar designs on Earth people, sometimes mating with them to create test-tube half-breeds for military purposes.

The Reptoids are currently engaged in attempting to conquer Earth. Zecharia Sitchin's hypothesized 12th Planet, which Cosmic Awareness calls Nemesis, now travels toward our solar system at 6,000 miles per hour. It contains 30 to 40 million frozen warriors which the Reptoids plan to thaw and use as an army for the takeover of Earth.

Though sophisticated in warfare, Cosmic Awareness reports that the Greys and Reptoids are boorish when it comes to culture. When asked what his favorite musical group was, one Grey answered, "New Kids on the Block." When the Greys attempt to dance, they move stiffly and awkwardly, like robots. The Reptoids, on the other hand, have a bit more soul than the Greys; they enjoy rhythm and vibrations, though they have little appreciation for lyrics. "They are not impressed," reports Cosmic Awareness, "by singers who shout and groan and growl to hard rock type music." While the Reptoids attempt to understand our culture, our leaders and media prepare us to accept theirs. Television shows such as *Barney the Purple Dinosaur* and *Teenage Mutant Ninja Turtles* are "conditioning tools for children," designed so we won't be afraid of the Reptoids when they finally take over. The Reptoid presence, like that of traditional evil demons, is eternally looming somewhere nearby, attempting to undermine humanity's godly, galactic destiny.

HOMO-SAURUS

According to David Barclay, author of the 1995 book *Aliens: The Final Answer*, the Reptoids—a race of super-intelligent dinosaurs once in charge of Earth—are now trying to get their planet back. UFOs are not piloted by aliens from space, but by super-intelligent dinosaurs from Earth. While most people think of dinosaurs as dumb giants that became extinct 65 million years ago, many of them were smarter than we are—and survive to this day. The Reptoids, in fact, created the human species. They domesticated us through selective breeding from a race of bright but less intelligent dinosaurs, just as we domesticated dogs. Barclay maintains that once the human race accepts its true identity—as a dinosaur pet—all kinds of unsolved problems in the UFO field and history will be made clear. We must face the fact, he writes, that "in more ways than one, the individual who stares back at you from your bathroom mirror every morning is probably just as alien as the life form you have been led to believe drives around in flying saucers. Gaze deeply into its eyes and try to realize that you are not the biggest mistake that nature ever made, but more probably the descendant of a dog-like domesticated dinosaur."

Barclay—again, true to the ancient astronaut creed—condemns science and evolution while offering to reconcile science and the Bible. Like Sitchin and the others, he likes evolution, but only up to a point, and that point is *humanity*. This is not surprising, since Barclay seems to get all his information about science from UFO books: almost all his citations are from paranormal paperbacks, flying saucer books and his own writings; he especially holds Flindt and Binder's *Mankind: Child of the Stars* in high esteem. Barclay quotes them as classic scholars might quote Plato or Pliny the Elder.

Homo-saurus or "Reptile Man" may have been the "Missing Link" according to R.A. BOULAY in his 1997 book, *Flying Serpents and Dragons: The Story of Mankind's Reptilian Past*

The continuing saga of our saurian masters' attempts to regain control of the earth can also be found in both the Old and New Testaments, which are "nothing more than pre-scientific contactee narratives." The ancient astronauts—pillars of fire, Ezekiel's wheel, the burning bush—were in fact dinosaurs masquerading as gods.

Humanity's creators are dinosaurs from Earth who, in essence, serve the same purpose as the space gods. Barclay's theory—unbelievable as it is—updates the Bible, confirms the reality of the paranormal and provides a "middle ground" between evolution and creation.

A similar offering, *Flying Serpents and Dragons: The Story of Mankind's Reptilian Past* (1990, 1997) by R.A. Boulay, contains "evidence" that we are the children of extraterrestrial serpent-gods. It's a Reptoid variation on the ancient astronaut theme, based directly on the books of Zecharia Sitchin. The only difference is that where Sitchin saw humanoid extraterrestrials, Boulay sees winged, *serpent* extraterrestrials.

"All myth," writes Boulay, "is derived from historical fact or event." [49] This assumption, cast as a sensible alternative to hard evidence, is the guiding logical principle behind the works of almost all the ancient astronaut authors discussed so far. Those who use the principle seem oblivious to its implications: once you accept the historical basis of myth, then you can prove almost anything you like about the human past, as long as you interpret the myths in a certain way.

If you believe certain myths as history, and if you interpret them the way he does, you will agree with R.A. Boulay that dragons and flying serpents of mythology were real, they were extraterrestrials, and they were our creators:

> The dragon symbolism [in mythology] may be the result of trau-matic events so deeply rooted in man's subconscious that the knowledge of their true nature has been suppressed. These dragons or flying serpents apparently co-existed with ancient man who por-trayed them as gods who could effortlessly move about the skies in their 'fiery chariots' or 'boats of heaven.' They lived in the sky in a 'heavenly abode' from where they often descended to interfere in the affairs of men.[50]

Using Sitchin's blueprint for interpreting Sumerian and Hebrew mythology, Boulay concludes that the gods of Mesopotamia, the Annunaki, were extrater-restrial serpent people who created a "Homo-saurus" as an experiment:

> The Annuna were an alien race of sapient reptiles. They required a labor force to do the necessary menial work, and for this reason a primitive man was created. They accomplished this by combining the characteristics of the native ape-man with their own saurian nature. In this way they produced the "Adam" of the Old Testament. This Adam was half human and half reptile, what can be called a Homo-saurus. It was a failed experiment for the main reason it was a "mule" and could not reproduce itself.[51]

The "Fall of Man" occurred when the "Adam" gained the ability to reproduce, losing his "saurian" nature, "his shiny, luminous skin and scaly hide," and acquir-ing mammalian characteristics. "He no longer ran around naked. He now had to wear clothing for comfort and protection. For all purposes he was a *Homo sapi-ens*." But the gods "never forgave mankind for straying so far from the reptilian pattern."[52]

Boulay's vision of mankind, as genetically engineered hybrid between ape-man and space-reptile, serves as yet another "middle ground" solution to the problem of creation vs. evolution. His interpretation of the gods of sacred texts as extraterrestrial Reptoids—fabulous though it is—at least transforms the gods of old into physical creatures accessible and understandable to modern minds.

YOU ARE BECOMING A GALACTIC HUMAN

"My name is Sheldon Nidle and I have been appointed as a representative of the Galactic Federation. This position was given to me by a Sirian counselor and galactic presence named Washta. . . ."

So writes the co-author of *You Are Becoming A Galactic Human* (1994), a hidden history with a sweeter, New Age flavor. It's typical of many channeled New Age offerings in its synthesis and elaboration of a host of modern myths. In addition to the news of the "Photon Belt" and the "Interdimensional Rescue Bubble," Washta told Virginia Essene and Sheldon Nidle of the mysterious origins of dolphins and alien dinosaurs, and of our own heritage as extraterrestrial aquatic apes.[53]

In 1988 the "Galactic Federation," via Sirian council members Washta, Teletron and Mikah, began instructing Nidle in the forgotten history of mankind, so he could tell the rest of us.

Approximately 35 million years ago, they said, the "Time Lords" and the "Spiritual Hierarchy" of our solar system placed an etheric life form on Earth to be the guardians of the solar system, in accordance with the divine plan of the Creator. Their "etheric civilization" lasted until 26 million years ago. Then the Reptoids from Sagittarius and the Dinoids from Orion invaded the planet. (Both are creatures the authors may have read about in "Cosmic Awareness" or similar literature.)

Meanwhile, the first intelligent Earth mammals had developed. They were the ancestors of dolphins and whales, the "Pre-cetaceans." They had ten fingers and toes and were covered with thick fur. Their faces consisted of "a large, horse-like snout" and their teeth were rounded. Their eyes were human-like and they had "a small stump of a tail." These proto-porpoises developed a "primitive agrarian society." The Spiritual Hierarchy helped them out by giving them "advanced technology" to improve food production.

The three races on Earth at that time, the Pre-cetaceans, as well as Dinoids and Reptoids, were at peace. The Dinoids and Reptoids on other planets, because they considered themselves superior to all other species, set out immediately to destroy Earth's Pre-cetaceans. The Pre-cetaceans, however, were ready for them and planned a counterattack—the strategy was to "utilize their vast series of fusion generators to create a worldwide catastrophe that would destroy the other two civilizations." They split into two societies: one half evacuated to outer space, and the other half to the oceans. They "imploded" the fusion generators, destroying most of the Dinoids and Reptoids, whose survivors escaped to the large planet then orbiting between Mars and Jupiter called Maldek (the same planet George Hunt Williamson had written about).

Because the Pre-cetaceans had escaped to the oceans and outer space, Earth needed a land-based caretaker to replace them. The Spiritual Hierarchy searched the galaxy and discovered a promising aquatic primate species[54] in the Vega star system, which they genetically altered to speed up its evolution. These were the first galactic humans. They spread out across the galaxy, banded together to form a human Galactic Federation and colonized our solar system. Their first colony on Earth was called Hybornea.

The humans controlled most of the solar system; only Maldek and a few outposts on the fringes of the solar system were left to the Dinoids and Reptoids. The Dinoids and Reptoids, however, wanted their planets back. They destroyed the human colonies on Mars, Venus and the Hybornean colony on Earth. They were then able to take control of the solar system.

Around 900,000 years ago, the galactic humans pushed the enemy back and planned their return. They brought a "large battle planet" into the region and succeeded in destroying Maldek, whose remains can be found in the asteroid belt.

Not even the humans, however, were able to live in peace. When they returned to Earth, they colonized the continent of Lemuria and then spread out across the planet. The "daughter empire" of Atlantis was envious of Lemuria and set out to destroy it. The Atlanteans allied themselves with renegade colonies in other solar systems; 25,000 years ago they were joined by Pleiadean and Centaurian rebels to destroy Lemuria.

At that time, two different moons circled Earth:

> What the renegades proposed to do was to move one of these two moons into a downward spiraling orbit using force fields. Before this moon reached a critical mass position (the Lagrange Point) with the earth, it would be exploded so that it would fall down as an incredible shower of meteors upon the Lemurian continent.[55]

This explosion created "a volcanic catastrophe that caused the great gas chambers underneath Lemuria to implode, sink the continent, and destroy Lemurian dominance."

Atlantis too, fell around 10,000 B.C. "Its final demise," says Washta, "would leave Earth humans in a genetically reduced mutant condition from which you are still suffering."

Even after the fall of Atlantis, Earth retained its "crystal temples" that "housed the network of crystals that kept the Firmament in place above the surface of the earth." The Firmament was "a huge crystalline shield of water situated at two positions, one roughly 15,000–18,000 feet from the earth's surface and a second higher layer roughly 35,000–38,000 feet from the earth's surface." The layers provided the earth with a protective, life-giving atmosphere. At that time, there was no "weather" to plague us: no rain, little wind and no seasons.

But 6,000 years ago, three warring empires attacked the crystal temples. Millions of gallons of water fell from the sky, causing the great flood. During the flood all written records of human history were washed away; all that remained

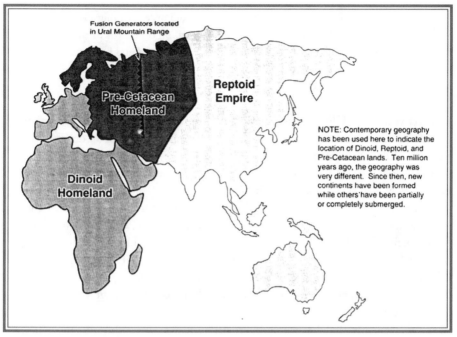

Map of Pre-Cetacean Homeland and Sites of Fusion Generators
(from *You Are Becoming a Galactic Human*)

were oral histories and legends of the Golden Age. Even worse, those who survived the flood were "partially conscious mutants." Our life spans shrank from a millennium to decades, while our statures shriveled from eight to ten feet to just five or six feet.

Despite our great fall, there is hope. Now is the time we may reclaim our "full molecular capability." With help from the Spiritual Hierarchy we will be able to rise out of quarantine and mutancy, to claim our "cellular credentials of galactic birthright" via such practices as meditation, deep breathing, bodywork and the study of metaphysics.

HOMO FUTURUS

George Hunt Williamson wrote, in 1953:

> What people on Earth will survive to inherit the New Age? The world population will be reduced greatly. Where there are now thousands there will be tens. But it is not tragic if one loses his physical equipment on Earth. Certain souls have evolved to the place where the old earth can no longer teach them anything, therefore either they or the earth must graduate to a higher level. Shortly, the entire earth will be made new in the new vibratory rate and the advanced souls, or The Remnant, will inherit the kingdom of God on Earth.

> The other souls, who refused to give up the old order of things, will
> be taken out of flesh life and will be re-settled on other worlds that
> can give them the lessons they need. So only the good and beautiful
> is to come to all men; there is no retrogression, for all are advancing
> toward the Father.[56]

Forty years later, UFO bookseller Robert Girard would expand and update the idea that aliens—our masters and, perhaps, our creators—will soon de-populate the earth. Like Williamson, Girard supports genocide, as long as the aliens carry it out. But unlike Williamson, he doesn't try to hide his racist assumptions behind New Age sweetness and light.

Girard has been involved in the UFO community for a long time and currently is the owner of Arcturus Books, a mail order book distributor in Point Saint Lucie, Florida that specializes in UFO literature. The Arcturus catalog contains frank, skeptical and sometimes very funny reviews of each item for sale. Girard honestly describes much of the literature in his catalog as unadulterated crap. He saves his uncritical enthusiasm for authors such as Zecharia Sitchin and David Icke.[57]

Girard told me that he was born in 1942 and "came up through the flying saucer ranks" starting around 1950 when he "saw something in the sky." Originally, he thought UFOs were extraterrestrial in origin, but around the mid-'70s began reading the books of John Keel and Jacques Vallee, who suggested otherwise. He began to agree with them that "the origin was a lot closer to us than it was to, say, Alpha Centauri or some other solar system." He rejected the ET hypothesis[58] and replaced it with "a hypothesis which supposed the existence of beings right here on the earth, in the same way that we can look down the scale of life, down through the animals, down through the plants, down through the fungi and right down to the microscopic stuff."

In his self-published book *Futureman: A Synthesis of Missing Links, the Human Infestation of Earth, and the Alien Abduction Epidemic* (1993), Girard suggests that the "aliens" are as earthly as we are, only on a higher level or "Octave," as he puts it. The higher the Octave, the higher the "conscious awareness," so that Octaves 1–5 represent earth, fungi, plants, animals, and humans respectively. The beings we know as "aliens" inhabit the Sixth Octave. Humans are the "lowest of the self-aware earthly species," and "each Octave of life is exponentially more complex in terms of awareness than the Octave immediately beneath it." Therefore, it's difficult for us to understand those beings who inhabit any of the Octaves above us, just as it's difficult for animals to understand us. To a certain extent we can control animals, and to a certain extent the aliens can control us; they are our masters.

In discussing the origins of the human race, Girard focuses not on our physical attributes but on our "Self-Awareness." And, though using a more sophisticated argument, Girard concurs with the ancient astronaut authors that evolution accounts for life on Earth—save humanity. He wonders whether evolution is "all a strictly natural process, or is there some conscious intelligence present wherever life is found which nudges things along whenever conditions are favorable for change?" At the level of humanity, evolution is no longer sufficient to accomplish a jump to the next Octave; there must have been some kind of intervention for the human race to acquire self-awareness.

The "missing link" that interests him is that between non-self-aware humans and self-aware humans. He argues that this missing link won't be found "as long as 'expert' eyes are squinting at the dirt, death and bones beneath the surface." Instead, it will only be found "by looking *upward*, not downward," not as "a stony fossil, but as a *living example*." Girard is suggesting, in other words, that the higher-dimensional aliens—who have been abducting us of late—might be our creators. How was humanity created? He submits the following scenario:

> [The aliens] raised us from an animal-instinctive level until, after long and patient work, they had matched an efficient, though failure-prone physical body with a rudimentary self-aware consciousness. Cro-Magnon man is the most recent in an apparently ongoing series of creations perfecting a self-aware physical hominid. This type of man has, since his inception some 40,000 years ago, been developing his awareness and his abilities while co-existing among the descendants of the earlier, less-capable human creations. In the course of time, Cro-Magnon man and his descendants have achieved dominance over the other human types, a dominance which some have called "imperialist." Self-Aware man has created great conflict within the entire human species because of his insatiable and unquenchable need to create change and make progress, while other kinds of man are content to exist passively, at an animal level of consciousness and a herd-level mentality.[59]

The vestiges of these multiple creations can be found in the variety of human spiritual states—and in our racial make-up. Girard identifies two main groups of humanity: first, the vast herd-like majority who live basically on the "animal" level, and second, those rare self-aware individuals capable of independent thought. The first group, he speculates, are descended from three earlier human creations—the black, red, and yellow races—while the second group are the fourth, white race, descended from Cro-Magnon man, the first fully modern humans.[60] Girard tries to temper this transparently racist theory by pointing out that the "progressive, aggressive" white race is responsible for the terrible mess we're in now. But it's clear that he considers whites to be far in advance of the brown "herd."

Girard, much like some of the racist thinkers we will soon meet, equates spiritual states with biological ones. He disregards the fact that creative, progressive "self-aware" individuals (by his definition) appear in all human groups, and that there are plenty of "herd-like" whites living on what he would identify as the "animal level" of existence. Nor does he seem to be aware that so much mixing has occurred in the 30-some millennia since the appearance of Cro-Magnon, that one can hardly identify their descendants as belonging to one race. He uses the concepts of "race" and of "species" interchangeably, identifying the darker races of man as constituting earlier human species. This is a conception he shares with eighteenth and nineteenth century anthropologists and twentieth century white and black supremacists, as detailed in the "race" chapter.

Girard calls the human presence on Earth an "infestation." This infestation is the result of (white) technology; when this technology was exported to the (non-white) passive, cooperative herd, it caused them to breed uncontrollably. The aliens, however, are now preparing to fumigate the lot of us, just as we might fumigate an infestation of cockroaches or ants. Or, just as the Nazis tried to fumigate non-Aryans. They're abducting us to retain some of our genetic material, so that a new species can emerge after the infestation is eliminated. The testimony of abductees, says Girard, reveals that the aliens are "working at a feverish pace to complete experiments involving the hybridization of humans and another species." The hybrid will be a "transitional species," a kind of missing link between ourselves and the fifth human species, *Homo futurus*, or "Futureman." Futureman, incidentally, will completely replace *Homo sapiens*. "The best of our qualities and spirit," Girard writes, "will be introduced into a part-human, part-alien hybrid humanoid." Rather than evolve naturally, we will evolve—with the help of our higher-dimensional big brothers—at "warp speed." The hybrids won't live on Earth, but in incubation, until the earth is rid of the rest of us and restored to health. "Within these incubatory mediums," Girard speculates, "are fully operational 'production lines' in which hundreds or even thousands of human-alien hybrids are being gestated and 'born.'" As soon as enough fully functional hybrids are formed, the aliens will exterminate the rest of us. Though it will be impossible for the current humans to co-exist with the new humans, Girard is optimistic that "certain human spirits now living" will achieve a "super-aware level of existence" and thus have the opportunity to reincarnate into the next human form. He's also confident that there will be a "harvest of souls" to determine who will reincarnate and who must die; he speculates that the number of such souls might even be close to the 144,000 mentioned in the Bible. While the new species is being perfected, the earth will be free of humanity for 25,000-50,000 years. When the new species is finally ready, it will look like a cross between present humans and the large-headed aliens. But most importantly, they will be spiritually, mentally and morally superior to us, with awareness of their true place in the world. "Futureman," Girard writes, "is, above all else, aware of his obligations to all other earthly life and to the earth itself."

ALIENS: THE "MISSING LINK" BETWEEN HUMANITY AND THE COSMOS

Though they disagree on details, the ancient astronaut authors agree that neither organized religion nor science adequately answer the big questions. They are anxious to bridge the gap between science and religion, and claim to do so by reading the Bible as a historic document about extraterrestrials. Though they embrace technology, they are disturbed by scientific materialism and atheism, which leaves humanity without a spiritual link to the cosmos. As these authors see it, scientific progress, through the years, has placed humanity further and further out on the periphery of reality. The human has become an accidental sequence of DNA, an insignificant beast that might not have been. By suggesting that we were created by space aliens or angelic beings, the alternative anthropologies say that humanity isn't an accident like a virus or a sea sponge, that we are as essential to the universe as God. As the creation of aliens, we have a distinct *purpose* and place in the universe. Evolution, though it might explain the existence of animals, does not apply to humans. The bestial part of our nature, they believe, can be eradicated. During an interview with *Connecting Link* online magazine, Zecharia Sitchin remarked that "physically, outwardly and inwardly," we are much like the aliens who created us. "So much of what they are, we are." And he emphasizes that they don't look like us, "we look like them," and adds, "that is what the Bible says." They share their destiny with us. Sitchin predicts that "just as they came to Earth and created us through genetic engineering, and mixed their genes with those of Ape-woman, one day we will go out in space and land on another planet somewhere and do the same thing. In this sense," Sitchin says, "things are ordained in a grand pattern."

---

1. Binder and Flindt, *Mankind*, p. 26

2. Baer, *New Age Nightmare*, p. 54.

3. Charlotte Bronte, "Inside the Crystal Palace," pp. 324–25.

4. Bury, *Idea of Progress*, pp. 329–31.

5. Ibid., p. 346.

6. Washington, *Blavatsky's Baboon*, p. 30. Quote previously published in *The Truth about Madame Blavatsky*, by V. Jelihovsky (n.p., n.d.).

7. Goodrick-Clarke, *Occult Roots of Nazism*. For more on Blavatsky and racist theories, see chap. 3.

8. Washington, *Blavatsky's Baboon*, p. 41.

9. Goodrick-Clarke, *Occult Roots of Nazism*, p. 18

10. Blavatsky, *Secret Doctrine*, p. 171.

11. Ibid., p. 180.

12. Ibid., pp. 195–96.
13. Newbrough, *Oahspe*, p. 62.
14. B. and H. Reeve, *Flying Saucer Pilgrimage*, pp. 29–30.
15. Blavatsky, *Secret Doctrine*. This book cites the "Book of Dzyan" as a source; as far as I know, it exists only within the world of Theosophy.
16. Adamski and Leslie, *Flying Saucers*, p. 166.
17. Zinsstag and Good, *George Adamski*.
18. Ibid., p. 201.
19. Carlson, *Under Cover*, p. 150.
20. Ibid., p. 151.
21. Pelley's Christian Party platform statement quoted in Roy, *Apostles of Discord* (n.p., n.d.), p. 61.
22. Carlson, *Under Cover*, p.151.
23. Vallee, *Messengers of Deception*, pp. 210–11.
24. George Hunt Williamson is the pen name of Michel d'Obrenovic.
25. Though he enrolled in college-level courses in anthropology, sociology, philosophy, biology and geology, Williamson never earned a college degree.
26. Williamson, *Other Tongues*. Pelley's book is listed in Williamson's bibliography as follows: Pelly, W. D., *Star Guests*, Noblesville, Indiana, 1950.
27. See chap. 3, "Race."
28. Pelley quoted in Williamson, *Other Tongues*, p. 203.
29. Ibid., p. 387.
30. B. and H. Reeve, *Flying Saucer Pilgrimage*, pp. 90–91.
31. Ibid., pp. 92–93.
32. See "Slaves of the Aliens" section in this chapter, for more on Sitchin.
33. Trench, *Sky People*, p. 30.
34. These stories were later re-published by Ace as two paperbacks in their Science Fiction Classic series: *The Lord of Death and the Queen of Life* (F-345) and *The Devolutionist and the Emancipatrix* (F-355), both circa 1960s.
35. Story, *Guardians of the Universe?* p. 16.
36. von Däniken, *Chariots of the Gods?* pp. 51–52.
37. Indeed, Blavatsky's *Secret Doctrine* is included in the bibliography.
38. Vorilhon/Raël, *Message Given*, pp. 15–16.
39. Baku now belongs to Azerbaijan.
40. Georges Roux, *Ancient Iraq*, p. 98.
41. Ibid., p. 99.
42. Sitchin, *12th Planet*, p. 171.
43. Kossy, "Black Messiahs" section, *Kooks*.
44. A perfect number is a number which equals the sum of all its factors, a fairly rare occurrence, e.g. 6=1+2+3; 28=1+2+4+7+14.
45. Kafton-Minkel, *Subterranean Worlds*. This is the source used for information on Shaver, the Hefferlin Manuscript and Dickhoff.

46. See chap. 2 for details on de-evolution.
47. See Kossy, *Kooks*, pp. 125–31 and Kafton-Minkel, *Subterranean Worlds*, pp. 154–60, for background on Doreal and the Brotherhood of the White Temple.
48. Cosmic Awareness was first channeled by ex-army officer William Ralph Duby, in 1962. *The Revelations of Awareness* newsletter contains records of all channeling sessions; it is circulated widely, in print and on the internet.
49. Boulay, *Serpents and Dragons*, p. 6.
50. Ibid., p. 3.
51. Ibid.
52. Boulay, *Serpents and Dragons*, pp. 3–4.
53. See chap. 6, "The Aquatic Ape Theory," for further details.
54. See chap. 6 for the origin of this "aquatic primate" concept.
55. Essene and Nidle, *Galactic Human*, p. 91.
56. Williamson, *Other Tongues*, pp. 428–29.
57. David Icke is a popular British New Age conspiracy author with alleged right-wing, anti-Semitic ties.
58. The ET Hypothesis states that UFOs are of extraterrestrial origin.
59. Girard, *Futureman*, p. 48.
60. Ibid., pp. 24–30.

Chapter two

De-evolution

[Man] became physically and mentally sick.
He is swimming in a raging ocean of uncertainty the billows of
which he himself has caused to rage. The lifeboats which he is forever
constructing in the name of progress are puny straws to which he
tightly clings, but they are not able to carry him. And one day not
even a straw will be left, there will be no lifeboat for him.
Oscar Kiss Maerth, *The Beginning Was the End*

DEVO: Humanity in Decline

It was the spring of 1979, and I was about to graduate from college. I shared a house in western Massachusetts with five other students. Several of my housemates had a taste for punk rock, which I didn't altogether appreciate. That all changed in one terrifying moment. Someone turned on the TV and we all sat silently as we learned about the near meltdown of the Three Mile Island nuclear plant just 300 miles away. The silence was broken when someone began to blast the new DEVO album.

Oscar Kiss Maerth, circa 1973 (from jacket of *The Beginning Was the End*, photo by Klaus Schleusener)

The voices mechanically chanted, "Mongoloid/He was a mongoloid/happier than you and me . . ." and "They tell us that we lost our tails/evolving up from little snails/I say it's all just

wind in sails . . . We are DEVO—D-E-V-O."[1] It was like the soundtrack to our worst nightmares of hideous mutant armies that would overrun the earth after some future nuclear accident. I was instantly transformed from a scoffer—I had previously complained the band was soulless and boring—to an ardent fan. DEVO had become strangely relevant. After that day, I couldn't get enough; DEVO crystallized my rage—and bemusement—with the dangers and enigmas of modern life and its idealistic handmaiden, progress.

But what did the former art students who made up the band DEVO (Gerald "Jerry" Casale, Mark Mothersbaugh, Bob Mothersbaugh and Jim Mothersbaugh from 1974–early 1976; Jerry Casale, Mark

Mothersbaugh, Bob Mothersbaugh, Bob Casale and Alan Myers from late 1976–1985) mean by "de-evolution"? The images in their movies and collages featured apes, degenerate humans, and a kind of mentally deficient mascot, Booji Boy.[2] De-evolution obviously meant some kind of reverse evolution, in which humanity degenerates through the years, rather than improves. It seemed like heresy at the time, but little did I know that this loose idea of human degeneration had a long history that could be traced through the eugenics movement of the late 1800s and early 1900s,[3] early scientific theories of race,[4] Theosophy, and back to ancient times. I'm not sure that DEVO themselves knew of de-evolution's universality or its antiquity.

Broadly speaking, de-evolution—the idea that humanity is in a decline, be it spiritual or physical—is a universal concept, common throughout history and among diverse cultures. According to historian J.B. Bury, the modern notion of "progress," from which sprouted the theory of evolution, is a historical anomaly. Diverse peoples through the ages more often viewed life and history cyclically, with humanity sliding down the declining arc of the cycle. Bury wrote in the opening pages to his classic study, *The Idea of Progress*, "the profound veneration of antiquity . . . seems natural to mankind." Time is usually regarded as the enemy of humanity. The ancient Latin poet Horace wrote that "time depreciates the value of the world," a pessimism Bury notes is shared by "most systems of ancient thought."

With the veneration of antiquity goes the denigration of the present. Since ancient times, people who had both the sensitivity and the leisure to look around and take note of the human condition all concurred that the world is an unrelenting horror show of pain, injustice and human meanness. They consoled themselves with the notion that things must have been better back in the "good old days." Today we're no different; we're nostalgic for simpler times. Those wishing for a return of the 1950s, however, might remember the smooth sounds of Doo-Wop or the excitement of rock 'n' roll but forget the terrors of living in fear of the H-Bomb.

Otto Bettmann, founder of the Bettmann Archive of historic photos and prints, devoted his book *The Good Old Days—They Were Terrible!* to exploding the myth that the period between the Civil War and 1900 were the "good old days" in America. Those who have never experienced it especially romanticize rural life in those days. "We are always tempted to invest [rural life]," writes Bettmann, "with virtues that appear to have been corrupted in urban culture. Country living presents visions of nostalgia to soothe city nerves." The reality, however, was far from bucolic:

> Country life in the post-Civil War era was an unremitting hardship.
> The farmer and his family toiled fourteen hours a day merely to sustain themselves, primarily on a landscape that lacked the picturesque inspiration of Currier & Ives' prints.

> Nor did their endless drudgery reward the farmers with prosperity; during the economic distress of 1870–1900 few small and middle-sized farms produced anything beyond bare subsistence, and many were foreclosed.
>
> In place of a neat rose garden, an expanse of muck and manure surrounded the farmhouse, sucking at boots and exuding a pestilential stench that attracted swarms of flies, ticks and worms to amplify the miseries of man and beast. The elementary task of survival precluded any concern for hygiene or sanitary installations. And the punitive winter brought with it isolation and terrible loneliness.[5]

In the foggy view of a fading memory everything looks better. Bettmann felt it necessary to write his book, not because the late nineteenth century was worse than any other, or because that era was all bad, but because foggy nostalgia for a "Gilded Age" filled with carefree gaiety had overshadowed the miseries of the common people.

Nostalgia for the "Gilded Age" is much like the nostalgia for the "Golden Age" of myth, a perennially popular, kind of super-good-old-days, thought to be deep in the human past. The Golden Age has long appealed to those disgusted by the time in which they lived, whether that time was 500 B.C. or 2000 A.D. In the Golden Age, people were more intelligent, kinder to one another, and, in general, better than they are now. It follows that humanity is now *in decline*.

De-evolution explains "the awful mess we're in now." DEVO, certain "hidden histories" of mankind, racial theories of human decline and de-evolutionary theories of anthropology are all based on the ancient myth of the Golden Age—but repackaged for modern tastes. In this chapter we will explore these new expressions of the myth of the Golden Age: their origins in antiquity, their universality, and their popular appeal. We will find that, at bottom, myths and theories of the Golden Age, human decline and de-evolution—like the alien intervention myths discussed in the previous chapter—stem from spiritual discontent. Their adherents believe material progress can only spell spiritual decline for the human race.

THE GOLDEN AGE

The ancients, as appalled by their current state of affairs as we are by ours, imagined a Golden Age of perfection in the distant past. Egyptians believed that earlier citizens were ruled not by mortals, but by god-kings. The Babylonians wrote of three ages, the first being the Golden Age which ended in the universal flood. The Persian Zoroastrian scriptures speak of the thousand-year-old Golden Reign of Yima, when cold, heat, sickness, old age and death were unknown. We are all familiar with the Judeo-Christian version, the idyllic Garden of Eden, scene of the Fall of Man.

The ancient Hindus developed an intricate, cyclic version of original perfection and gradual decline, the doctrine of the Four Ages, or Yugas. According to this scheme, the universe is reborn every 12,000 years. In the beginning of the 12,000 year cycle, the Krita or Satya Yuga, all needs are fulfilled and every being is in a state of moral perfection:

> In the first krita yuga, after the creation of the earth, Brahman created a thousand pairs of twins from his mouth, breast, thighs, and feet respectively. They lived without houses; all desires which they conceived were directly fulfilled; and the earth produced of itself delicious food for them, since animals and plants were not yet in existence. Each pair of twins brought forth at the end of their life a pair exactly like them. As everybody did his duty and nothing else there was no distinction between good and bad acts.[6]

In subsequent ages, everything gets progressively worse: life is shorter, intelligence wanes, and greed and immorality increase. Finally, during the Kali Yuga or Age of Darkness (you guessed it: the current age), disease, drought, famine, revolution and war prevail until the end of the cycle, when the world is set on fire, deluged with water, and then reborn.

In *The Myth of the Eternal Return*, historian of religion Mircea Eliade observes that by providing an explanation "of historical catastrophes, of the progressive decadence of humanity, biologically, sociologically, ethically and spiritually," the doctrine of the Four Yugas guards against the "terrors of history."[7] Because we are now living in the worst of times, we can console ourselves that we suffer in harmony with the cycles of the universe. We degenerate only because the universe is getting ready to be reborn.

Ancient Westerners too, believed history and time were cyclic. Originally, during the Golden Age, everything was perfect, and after the degeneration of mankind and the world the process would begin again. This non-linear de-evolution was part of the natural order of the cosmos; humanity and the world degenerate as we watch, and nothing is permanent. J.B. Bury describes Plato's version of this myth:

> The world was created and set going by the Deity, and, as his work, it was perfect; but it was not immortal and had in it the seeds of decay. The period of its duration is 72,000 solar years. During the first half of this period the original uniformity and order, which were impressed upon it by the Creator, are maintained under his guidance; but then it reaches a point from which it begins, as it were, to roll back; the Deity has loosened his grip of the machine, the order is disturbed, and the second 36,000 years are a period of gradual decay and degeneration.

At the end of this time, the world left to itself would dissolve into chaos, but the Deity again seizes the helm and restores the original conditions, and the whole process begins anew.[8]

Around 700 B.C., Hesiod, the Greek farmer-poet, distilled the folk legends of the Golden Age in his poem, *The Works and Days*. The most oft-cited source for such legends, the poem contains the first mention in Greek literature of the origin of mortals. B.C. Dietrich, in his study of Greek myth and legend, *Death, Fate and the Gods*, points out that Hesiod's account of the Five Ages of Man, though derived from popular traditions of hero and ancestor worship, also probably contained a fair dose of Hesiod's personal beliefs.[9]

During the Golden Age in the time of Kronos, Hesiod wrote, the mortals lived as gods, without sorrow, work, pain or old age. The food was free and the pleasures were many. "When they died, it was as if they fell asleep."

Next came the Silver Age, "far worse than the other." Children stayed children at home, looked after by their mothers for a hundred years as "a complete booby." When they finally grew up, the people lived only for a short time. They were foolish, irreligious, and unable to stay away from reckless crime. Finally Zeus, in his anger, destroyed them because they refused to pay tribute to the gods.

Then Zeus created a new generation, "from ash spears," which would live in the Bronze Age. This warlike race was "terrible and strong." Hesiod wrote, "They ate no bread, but maintained an adamantine spirit." They were huge and strong "and from their shoulders the arms grew irresistible on their ponderous bodies." Not only their weapons, but their houses as well were made of bronze. They worked as bronze smiths. "Yet even these," wrote Hesiod, "destroyed beneath the hands of each other, went down into the moldering domain of cold Hades; nameless; for all they were formidable black death seized them, and they had to forsake the shining sunlight."

Things improved during the Heroic Age, in which the Trojan War was fought. Zeus created a "better and nobler wonderful generation of hero-men also called half-gods, the generation before our own on this vast earth." Carnage and war, however, were not unknown. During this age men "fought together over the flocks of Oedipus."

Fifth, comes our own ghastly Iron Age, which is the worst of all. Hesiod's description applies as well to the 1990s—or any other time—as it did to 700 B.C. The poet lamented, "And I wish that I were not any part of the fifth generation of men, but had died before it came, or been born afterward." For it is during the present age that there is no end to hard work, pain or weariness. And in the night "the gods send anxieties to trouble us." There are good things as well, "mixed with the evils." But in the end, when "the father no longer agrees with the children, nor children with their father, when guest is no longer at one with host, nor companion to companion, when your brother is no longer your friend," when "men will deprive their parents of all rights," and "there will be no favor for the man who keeps his oath," when "men shall give their praise to violence and the doer of evil," and might is right and nobody knows any shame, when "the spirit of envy, with grim face and screaming voice, who delights in evil, will be the constant companion of wretched humanity," then Zeus will destroy us all.

The Greeks, who assumed humanity was inevitably sliding downward—like the Hindus—were comforted in their belief that this situation "was prescribed by the nature of the universe." [10] (Plato, for his part, added a novel, historical dimension to this non-explanation. He thought the degeneration of humanity was also due to "laxity and errors in the State regulation of marriages, and the consequent birth of biologically inferior individuals." [11] This belief would be echoed much later by the modern eugenics movement, as we'll see in the fourth chapter.)

The cyclic view of history—perfection-decline-destruction-rebirth—was superseded by Judeo-Christian doctrine in the Middle Ages. Now, thinkers saw events in history as linear and unique, not just another part of a cycle. They still believed in human degeneration—the fall of mankind in the Garden of Eden—but this fall occurred only once. All men and women were, from the beginning, fallen, sinful creatures whose only chance for redemption came from God. The destruction and rebirth of the world—the Battle of Armageddon and the return of Christ—would also happen only once; after that justice and happiness would prevail for eternity.

In Judeo-Christian Europe, the decline of humanity was as much a foregone conclusion as in earlier times. During the Renaissance, moreover, "the prevailing view [was] that man had degenerated in the course of the last 1,500 years." J.B. Bury explains:

> From the exaltation of Greek and Roman antiquity to a position of unattainable superiority, especially in the field of knowledge, the degeneration of humanity was an easy and natural inference. If the Greeks in philosophy and science were authoritative guides, if in art and literature, they were unapproachable, if the Roman republic, as Machiavelli thought, was an ideal state, it would seem that the powers of Nature had declined, and she could no longer produce the same quality of brain. [12]

It wasn't until the seventeenth century that anyone even thought to challenge the idea of a "Golden Age." The myth of the Golden Age (or the Garden of Eden) and Human Degeneration (or the Fall of Man) served pre-moderns well in several ways: it lent larger significance to natural feelings of nostalgia, and, more importantly, it imparted cosmic meaning to historical events and human suffering.

RACIAL DEGENERACY

There is another type of de-evolution, that of degeneration from one race of humanity to another, or from man to apes. During the eighteenth and early nineteenth centuries, anthropologists adopted various "Theories of Degeneracy" to explain racial differences, as well as our resemblance to the apes.[13] Degeneracy, in fact, preceded the reverse theory, that of evolution from "primitive" races to Europeans, and from apes to man. For example, Georges-Louis Buffon (1707–1788) hypothesized that man's original color was white, which degenerated over the years into shades of yellow, brown and black. Johann-Friedrich Blumenbach (1752–1840), first to refer to whites as "Caucasians," wrote that white skin "can easily degenerate to a blackish hue." And later, the eugenics movement played on fears that civilization was helping the weakest individuals to survive, causing a general degeneration of the human race.[14]

These theories of degeneration—as well as the religious myths of human decline—finally gave way, in the nineteenth century, to the modernist optimism of progress and evolution. It was only among some occultists, racists and basement metaphysicians that the idea would remain popular.

THE SECRET DOCTRINE

Beginning in the mid-nineteenth century, Madame Blavatsky helped revive the popularity of the cyclic, de-evolutionary view of history in the west, mainly via her tome *The Secret Doctrine* (which also influenced ET Intervention mythology).

The Secret Doctrine, claimed Blavatsky, was based on stanzas from an ancient book of esoteric wisdom called the "Book of Dzyan," which she identified as the source of occult, sacred texts from all over the world. The "sons of Light" in Central Asia who recorded the "Book of Dzyan" from the words of divine beings wanted to show mankind "his rightful place in the scheme of the Universe." This bible of sorts, said Blavatsky, was written in "Senzar," a "secret sacerdotal tongue." It was so secret, in fact, that nobody except Blavatsky had ever heard of it. At one time, though, wrote Blavatsky, it was a universal language, "known to the Initiates of every nation."

Whether she knew it or not, Blavatsky's work was in the spirit—if not the tradition—of the ancient, radically anti-materialist Gnostics. The Gnostic sects thrived, mainly in Egypt, during the early years of Christianity. They believed in one eternal, supreme deity, from which emanated "Aeons," or manifestations of particular attributes of the Godhead. Matter, created by a fallen Aeon called the "Demiurge," was essentially evil. Hence, some Gnostic sects saw the human body in its materiality as evil. The Gnostics differed from other Christians in their belief that Jesus Christ, if he was human, couldn't also have been divine because the divine couldn't unite with the material in the form of a man. He had died, not to save mankind from the wrath of God, but to impart knowledge, or *gnosis*, that would preserve those possessing it for eternity.[15] Blavatsky, like the Gnostics, viewed matter as evil, and devoted her life to transmitting "secret knowledge" to seekers after God.

In Blavatsky's cyclic version of Earth history, humanity proceeded through seven "Root-Races" on seven primeval continents, each Root-Race representing a step down — spiritually — from that which preceded it. In the process, matter attempted to triumph over spirit, but failed, and humanity both "evolved" and de-evolved.

During the first epoch, lasting millions of years, a race of immortal giants with ethereal bodies lived in the Imperishable Sacred Land at the North Pole. The second race — giant androgynous semi-humans — resulted from the first attempt at material nature; they lived on a continent called Hyperborea, south of the North Pole. The third race represented the "fall of man" because they were divided into two sexes; they lived during the Golden Age, 18 million years ago, when the "gods walked on Earth and mixed freely with mortals" on the continent of Lemuria. The fourth race lived on Atlantis, and the fifth, called "Aryans," lived in Europe. Two more races are supposed to follow before the end of this cycle or "Round."

Blavatsky, in agreement with the Judeo-Christian Bible, regards humanity as an inherently higher form than animals. The first humans, the first Root-Race, had no resemblance to "missing links" or "ape-men." Their world "was as ethereal as ours is material." Humans preceded all other mammals: we are not descended from apes, they are descended from us. Humanity, moreover, has the potential to degenerate, or de-evolve, into materialistic, spiritless beasts like the apes, if matter, or unaided nature, attempts to dominate spirit. Clearly stating her anti-Darwin bias, Blavatsky wrote, "Nature unaided fails," producing inferior half-humans and monsters:

> Thus physical Nature, when left to herself in the creation of animal and man, is shown to have failed. She can produce the first two and the lower animal kingdoms, but when it comes to the turn of man, spiritual, independent and intelligent powers are required for his creation, besides the "coats of skin" and the "breath of animal life." The human Monads of preceding Rounds need something higher than purely physical materials to build their personalities with, under the penalty of remaining even below any "Frankenstein" animal.[16]

The right kind of evolution occurs only with the aid of spirits or deities. When the spirits descend, they destroy the inferior products of material evolution; monsters, like something out of H.G. Wells' *The Island of Dr. Moreau*: "two- and four-faced" creatures, "goat-men," "dog-headed men" and "men with fishes' bodies."

Despite Blavatsky's distaste for Darwin, the Root-Races in *The Secret Doctrine* develop according to a roughly evolutionary scheme, from asexual to androgynous to full sexual reproduction. Though "the little ones of the earlier races were entirely sexless," Blavatsky writes, "those of the later races were born androgynous." Finally, "it is in the Third Race that the separation of the sexes occurred." This event in human evolution marks "the fall of Man." Another example of our fall is in physical stature. The Atlanteans (the fourth Root-Race) were giants of physical beauty and strength. But since then man has been dwindling in stature and continues to dwindle.

It was the fourth Root-Race that first acquired intellect. But it was also at this point that we divided into "average humanity" who received their "intellectuality" later, and the "narrow-brained," who had "hardly evolved from the lower animal forms." "The lower races," as seen through Blavatsky's nineteenth century eyes, are savages who are "simply those *latest arrivals* among the human Monads which *were not ready*" for the spark of intellect. They bred with the "she-animals" to beget the "dumb races," and "a race of crooked, red-hair-covered monsters, going on all fours," the great apes. In other words, the chimps, gorillas and orangutans are de-evolved humans. In the following passage, Madame Blavatsky explains the evolutionary, Karmic, and spiritual status of the great apes:

> The apes are millions of years later than the speaking human being, and are the latest contemporaries of our Fifth Race. Thus, it is most important to remember that the Egos of the apes are entities compelled by their Karma to incarnate in the animal forms which resulted from the bestiality of the latest Third and the earliest Fourth Race men. They are entities who had already reached the "human stage" before this Round. Consequently they form an exception to the general rule. They are truly "speechless men," and will become speaking animals (or men of lower order) in the Fifth Round. . . . Karma will lead on the Monads of the unprogressed men of our race and lodge them in the newly evolved human frames of the thus physiologically regenerated baboon.[17]

Theosophy resonated (and continues to resonate in its various contemporary forms) with those who find the material world bankrupt but who find mainstream religions too rigid. Like those who believe our ancestors were ancient astronauts, they want to reinstate humanity as the central focus of the universe—with a definite role to play. It's important for them to believe that man didn't begin as an animal, but as a spiritually perfect being. And, as the wheels of the universe turn, inevitably perfection will reign again.

ARCTIC ORIGINS

Blavatsky saw the history of the world as cyclic, humanity's origins as divine and modern humanity at the trough of a cycle. Our divine and semi-divine ancestors originated in Hyperborea, Atlantis and Lemuria, all of which were ultimately destroyed. The destruction of these continents was concurrent with—and symbolic of—humanity's decline. Metaphysical scholar Joscelyn Godwin, author of *Arktos*, believes this alternative outlook "frees one from the existential anguish of our time."

Blavatsky's successors continue to elaborate on her alternative history. In his version of cyclic history, for example, René Guénon (1886–1951) wrote that each cycle of 64,800 years represents a progressive solidification of the world, which is finally reduced to "mere corporeal entities." Our hyper-materialist age, then, is a degradation of earlier, more spiritually perfect times.

Another modern esotericist, Jean Phaure, attempted to reconcile Guénon's cycles with the Hindu Yugas, astrology, the Bible and the Greek Ages of Man. His timeline is as follows:

1. 62,800–36,880 B.C.: Golden Age—Krita Yuga—(Leo) one precession—earthly paradise before incarnation.
2. 36,880–17,440 B.C.: Silver Age—Treta Yuga—nine astrological cycles—fall—incarnation—Hyperborea—Lemuria.
3. 17,440–4480 B.C.: Bronze Age—Dvapara Yuga—half precessional cycle—end of Atlantis—Atlantis colonies—Noah's flood—writing.
4. 4480 B.C.–2000 A.D.: Iron age—Kali Yuga—classical history—Piscean Age.
5. Millennium—Aquarian Age—Paronisia—Judgment—New Cycle.[18]

In this version humanity wasn't born until the Silver Age, long after the earthly paradise had ceased to exist; these first people, however, who originated in the Arctic, did know better times than their descendants, since they subsisted on spiritual rather than physical sources of energy. Again, earlier races of mankind are depicted as spiritually superior to moderns, stuck in their fallen, materialist hell.

Phaure's conjecture—that the original home of mankind was in the Arctic—is a common theme in de-evolutionary histories. Godwin, in his 1993 book *Arktos*, traced the Arctic origins theme in detail. This tradition is based in part on the idea that the earth at one time spun on its axis vertically, rather than at the present angle of 23 and a half degrees, which produces the seasons. During this Golden Age of a vertical Earth, there were no seasons and the weather at the North Pole was mild. Only after a cataclysm caused the earth's axis to tilt did the

North Pole become cold, forcing its inhabitants to migrate south. (We met this idea in the previous chapter: in some of the human vs. reptoid scenarios, our alien enemies tilt the earth's previously vertical axis during battle.)

According to Godwin, the idea of an Arctic homeland originated in Asia and migrated west via Jesuit missionaries and British colonial administrators. One of the first westerners to formalize a theory of a polar Eden was astronomer, mystic and revolutionary Jean-Sylvain Bailly (1736–1793). Bailly believed that the antediluvian North was the homeland of humanity and of a superior culture, the mother of all the ancient civilizations, including Atlantis. He argued that the fable of the phoenix symbolizes the annual disappearance of the sun in the Arctic. The 300 days of sunlight there each year parallels the 300 days of the phoenix before it takes wing.[19] Bailly—anticipating the methods of modern pseudo-scientists—also found evidence for this theory in the mythologies of Egypt and Syria, which he believed preserve a "racial memory" of our origin in the far North and our migration south.

In the 1885 book *Paradise Found*, Boston University president, Rev. Dr. William F. Warren, submitted a "scientific" theory of polar origins. Though his arguments were neither occult nor Theosophical, they directly opposed Darwin. They also assumed the historical accuracy of the Bible. Warren used scientific findings and comparative mythology to suggest that there was once a country at the North Pole but that it was submerged in Noah's flood. Our ancestors who originated there were the noblest and longest lived people in history. Warren thought that mythological symbols such as Atlas' pillar, the spine of the earth, and the charming stick all referred to our ancestral home in the polar paradise.

These kinds of arguments were not exclusively the domain of Americans and Europeans. Bal Gangadhar Tilak (1856–1920), an Indian, used similar reasoning in his 1903 book *The Arctic Home in the Vedas*. He argued that the (Indian) Vedic hymns to the dawn describe images that make sense only in the Arctic. Where the *Rig Veda* describes darkness sheltering the enemies of Indra, it's really describing the long darkness that grips the poles. The Devayana and the Pitriyana (the two alternative paths that a soul may take upon death) parallel as well the two divisions of day and night at the poles. Godwin states that Tilak's theories, though they had little impact in the West, are very much alive in India. H.S. Spencer's 1965 book, *The Aryan Ecliptic Cycle*, based on Tilak, was endorsed by then-president of India Sir S. Radhakrishnan. Spencer went even further than Tilak in tracing the Aryan migration from the North to India, applied Zoroastrian scriptures and used *Oahspe* as a reference. Godwin's synopsis of the book shows Spencer to be "no conventional scholar":

> The "Aryan ecliptic cycle" of the title runs from 25,628 BCE to 292 CE,
> beginning with the residence of the Aryans in their polar homeland

during the Inter-glacial Age. Spencer insists that they must have been there long before the earliest dates mentioned by Tilak, in order to have made the religious "progress" evident from the Vedic Hymns. Eventually they were forced to leave their happy home of Aryano-Vej by "the presence of huge reptiles and the advent of intense cold and snow," as the Ice-Age spread a "glacial flood" around the Pole. This happened around 10,000 BCE, and was just one of the several results of the natural cataclysms of that time, which destroyed three other ancient civilizations in Atlantis, Lemuria, and around the Gobi Sea. The Aryans gradually battled their way against the forces of nature and the indigenous races of Asia, suffering a period of enslavement to the Turanians, until by about 8,500 BCE they were supreme over all their neighbors, ruling from the seat of their empire at Balkh in Bactria.[20]

Friedrich von Schlegel (1772–1829) first used the term "Aryan" to denote an aristocratic race of ancient Indians, purportedly the ancestors of the Germans. Thus, some of the early freethinkers who rejected the biblical Eden replaced it with an Asian one, populated by Aryans. The Aryan myth, which developed during the first half of the nineteenth century, was first embraced by the German Romantics, then by Theosophists and occultists, and later, by the Nazis.[21]

One influential Aryan vision was that of the nineteenth-century composer Richard Wagner. Historian Léon Poliakov summarizes it in his detailed history of the Aryan myth:

> Long ago, in the Golden Age, men lived in a state of primitive innocence as vegetarians on the high plateaus of Asia. But they were tainted by original sin when they killed the first animal. Ever since then a thirst for blood had taken possession of the human race, so that murders and wars increased and were followed by conquests, exiles and migrations. Christ, who was either Indian or Aryan, had tried to save mankind by showing the way back to the innocence of primitive vegetarianism—whose significance he revealed to men at the Last Supper by changing bread [sic—should probably be "blood"] into wine and flesh into bread. Finally, "He gave up his life to expiate the blood shed by carnivorous men since the beginning of the world." A Church, influenced by Jewry, had perverted the sense of this message, with the result that mankind had continued to degenerate, polluted by animal flesh and by the poison of Jewish blood. The Jew being "the devil incarnate of human decadence" and Western civilization a "Judaeo-barbaric jumble," an apocalyptic end could not be long delayed. Only one hope remained—a new purification, a new receiving of the holy

blood according to the rites of the mystery of Parsifal, the Germanic redeemer.[22]

Jorg Lanz von Liebenfels (1874–1954), founder of "Ariosophy," was among many in pre-Nazi Germany who adhered to more esoteric variations of the Aryan myth. Calling the Aryan homeland Arktogaa, which is Greek for "northern earth," von Liebenfels taught that non-Aryans were the result of bestiality between the ancient Aryans and beasts. One of his disciples lectured that humanity was the result of a forbidden mixture of angels and animals and used the Bible to back it up.[23] Each race, he said, represented a different percentage of angel and beast, the Aryans coming out on top, with one percent angel.

The Nazis adopted their Aryan myth from Alfred Rosenberg, author of the 1930 best-seller *Myth of the 20th Century*, and through the revisionist science of Herman Wirth. In his 1928 book, *The Rise of Mankind*, Wirth wrote that humanity began at the North Pole, having split from the apes millions of years ago. After shifting continents and poles made the nether regions uninhabitable, the Arctic Aryan race wandered south. The remnants of Aryan high culture survive to this day only in the blond, bearded Eskimos found by the Danish "Thule Expedition" of Knud Rasmussen. Implicit in all of these stories is the idea that much of present humanity has degenerated (for various reasons such as mixing with Jewish blood) from its former superiority and purity. Only Aryans retained the former glory.

Julius Evola's (1898–1974) version of the polar/Aryan myth is even more explicitly de-evolutionary. With the strong scent of Blavatsky, Evola suggested in his 1934 *Revolt Against the Modern World* that early in the history of humanity, the "boreal race"—whose icy homeland created warriors and conquerors—migrated from north to south and from east to west. (Evola probably thought humanity originated in the Arctic along the lines of Blavatsky's *Secret Doctrine*, though my sources don't make this clear.) This Nordic-Atlantic race had split into two: the Boreal and the Atlantean. The Atlantean became polluted with the demonic elements of the Lemurians, whose descendants are the dark races; our current age of miscegenation represents the degeneration of mankind. Evola wrote:

> In every historical epoch since the decline of the Boreal races, one can recognize the action of two antagonistic tendencies, repeating in one form or another the fundamental polarity of North and South. In every later civilization we have to recognize the dynamic product of the meeting or collision of these tendencies . . . victory or defeat falling to one or the other of the spiritual poles, with more or less reference to the ethnic streams which originally knew the "Northern Light," or else capitulated to the sorcery of the Mothers and the ecstatic abandon of the South.[24]

Evola continued his commitment to de-evolutionary metaphysics throughout his life. In his 1969 book, *The Metaphysics of Sex*, Evola named his reversal of evolution "involution":

> Our starting point will be not the modern theory of evolution but the traditional doctrine of involution. We do not believe that man is derived from the ape by evolution. We believe that ape is derived from the man by involution. We agree with De Maistre that savage peoples are not primitive peoples, in the sense of original peoples, but rather the degenerating remains of more ancient races that have disappeared. We concur with the various researchers . . . who have rebelled against the evolutionary dogma, asserting that animal species evince the degeneration of primordial man's potential. These unfulfilled or deviant potentials manifest as by-products of the true evolutionary process that man has led since the beginning.[25]

Other esotericists who write about "Thule" usually incorporate UFO and hollow Earth legends as well, glossing over its inherent racism. However, Chilean author and ambassador Miguel Serrano (b. 1917) offered *Adolf Hitler: The Last Avatar* as late as 1984, in which der Führer is shown literally to be a Bodhisattva in the mold of Gautama the Buddha.[26] His take on pre-history also incorporates the Gnostic idea of the Demiurge, the evil entity responsible for the creation of Matter. Serrano wrote that the "First Hyperborea" was founded by beings from outside our galaxy, though their origins have been concealed by an enormous conspiracy that misrepresents them as extraterrestrials in spaceships; were we able to see them, they would appear as disks of light. The inferior Demiurge, evil lord of the planet, was only able to create a low, robotic, Neanderthal type of human. The superior, non-material Hyperboreans made the ultimate sacrifice, incarnating to combat the mechanical universe of the Demiurge. As recorded in Genesis 6:4, where "the sons of God came in unto the daughters of men, and they bore children to them," the Hyperboreans bred with the sub-humans, precipitating the Fall of Man, caused by the earth's collision with a moon or comet, which in turn caused the North and South poles to reverse.

The Hyperboreans subsequently fled to the South Pole and to Europe; they were none other than the refined and artistic Cro-Magnon men. Since then, the Hyperboreans have constantly battled the Demiurge, who threatens to dilute their blood. The Brahmins of India, pure descendants of the Hyperboreans, have wisely prevented this calamity from happening to them. On the other hand, the Demiurge has employed the Jewish people, authors of the Great Conspiracy, to act as his tool. The Thule Society and the SS were valiant efforts to combat the menace of the Demiurge, which resulted in the dilution of Aryan blood and, ultimately, human de-evolution.

Like the "reptoid" vs. human scenarios we saw in the last chapter, the new Arctic-centered myths of human de-evolution meld older mythologies (the Bible, the Golden Age, polar paradise) with new ones (UFOs, aliens, Aryans, hollow Earth) to explain the past as essentially a fight between good and evil entities for the control of spiritual humanity. The confusions of modern life and the "degeneration" of mankind can then be blamed neatly on the spiritually malign entities and those entities' masterpiece: modern materialism.

In The Beginning Was The End, OSCAR KISS MAERTH takes a dim view of humanity

THE BEGINNING WAS THE END

In the early 1970s, Hungarian author Oscar Kiss Maerth presented a unique anti-materialist, de-evolutionary polemic to the world. A wealthy eccentric living in Italy, Maerth entitled his book—originally published in German by Econ-Verlag—*Der Anfang war das Ende*, which translates as "The Beginning Was the End." Econ-Verlag, who had earned handsome profits from Erich von Däniken's ancient astronaut books, hoped that Oscar Kiss Maerth would become the next von Däniken. The book fizzled, says Volker Zotz, a German scholar who corresponded with Maerth for a decade, despite Econ-Verlag's heavy promotion. Maerth appeared on "the most reputed German TV-show on culture," wrote Zotz, which was no easy feat "if you were out of the mainstream." Econ-Verlag "did everything to have him seen, reviewed, interviewed—but the book sold very badly." [27] The publisher's efforts seem to have worked only on English-language reviewers, who were under the erroneous impression that the book was a best-seller.

A year after its publication in Germany, *The Beginning Was the End* was picked up in the United States by Praeger, a press which often publishes books at the request of the CIA.[28] Mocking reviews of Maerth's book appeared in numerous publications. The *Atlantic Monthly* worried that "this bizarre work is reportedly a great best-seller in Europe, which can be taken to imply several things, all sinister." *Library Journal* concluded, "The book has been a best-seller in Italy, and thus might have some demand here; but I cannot recommend it on its own merits. It has none." *Time* appreciated the work's eccentricity, but only up to a point:

> In *The Beginning Was the End* the enthusiasm of author Oscar Kiss Maerth spills over in red ink. The book . . . bears all the markings of pristine eccentricity: a big theme, a closed system of self-perpetuating logic, a disdain for accepted thought, no specific scientific references, no index and no bibliography. Kiss Maerth . . . seems never to have heard of Lamarckian biology, T.D. Lysenko's bogus theory that

Communism could be inherited as an acquired characteristic or even about the lowly planarian worms, which were forced to cannibalize their siblings in hope that their modest laboratory lessons would be passed on to future generations. . . . It is quite a read, though persons on a low cholesterol diet might care to pass it up.

The Times Literary Supplement of London was perhaps the only periodical to find anything positive about it, suggesting that "the book is a collector's gem," adding "for way-out speculation it is unbeatable." The collectors, however, disagreed, and the book was quickly dispatched to the remainder bins.

Maerth doesn't challenge Darwin's theory of natural selection or even our descent from ape-like creatures. Instead, he challenges the idea that our evolution *was natural and good.* Using anthropological rather than esoteric sources, Maerth insists that the evolution of *Homo sapiens* was "unnatural," because *cannibalism*—specifically the eating of brains—caused it. All distinctly human traits—the oversized brain, lack of fur, and bipedalism—were, according to Maerth, a direct result of our ape ancestors' preference for ape brain at the proto-human dinner table.

The de-evolution of humans didn't begin with a Golden Age or a Garden of Eden. Instead we went from bad to worse. "The road from ape to man was made up of a chain of criminal acts contrary to the laws of Nature," Maerth writes. "Man has become the lunatic genius of the universe whose diseased mind with its absurd objectives is necessarily and inevitably becoming his doom." This lunatic genius, however, is ignorant of the basic fact that civilization and progress are the products "of his disturbed mind." Moreover, modern apes, despite their intellectual inferiority to humans, "are still living today in better health and with fewer worries than man."

Maerth's grand idea is that our species deviated from the morally and physically superior apes when our first ancestors "discovered that eating fresh brain of one's own kind increases the sexual impulses." After that it was all downhill. "He and his descendants became addicted to brains," Maerth writes with disgust, "and hunted for them." The result was increased intelligence but also moral and physical degradation, with the dreaded final outcome, *Homo sapiens.*

Maerth presents as evidence for his theory skulls unearthed which were detached from their skeletons, skulls broken at nose level with marks showing that their contents had been scraped out, and skulls broken, like nuts; human skeletons that were not dismembered, except for the skulls. He says they prove "that cannibals did not use an empty skull for some purpose or other, but wanted to get at the brain." Moreover, the brain couldn't have been eaten as a delicacy because it's "devoid of flavour and has the consistency of rubber." He adds, "About 20 hours after such a repast [of eating brain] there is a feeling of warmth in the brain, like a gentle pressure." Maerth knows this because he's tried ape

Separated At Birth?
(from *The Beginning Was The End*)

brain himself. "After about 28 hours the body is flooded by vitality, with increased sexual impulses."

Addiction to brains caused not only an overabundance of cleverness, but also hairlessness. Apparently our forebears' imbalanced diet of gray matter produced a disturbance of the central nervous system. In a cascade of dysfunction, the pituitary gland ceased to produce the coat of fur, as well as the female fertility signs or estrus. Maerth is scandalized that humanity unknowingly calls this diseased condition "progress."

The diseased condition is the key to why, for the most part, our species has given up its old cannibalistic ways. The most obvious downside to an appetite for the grey rubbery stuff is the increase in madness and in diseases such as epilepsy. Despite the early hominids' lust for sex and knowledge, about 50,000 years ago they realized that something was amiss and gave up brain eating. They also began to practice alteration of the skull in an attempt to ease the brain pressure diseases caused by it.

Those alive today who continue to practice cannibalism and brain eating lag behind the rest of humanity; they continue to eat human brain because they had a late start. They are *less* de-evolved, so to speak, than the rest of us:

> The earlier a group of apes turned into cannibals, the sooner its members became men and the farther [sic] the process—which is not yet concluded for any race—has advanced among them. Isolated groups of apes which did not take up cannibalism and become men until later are still today living at an earlier stage of human development and are in part still cannibals today.

The various human types, races and nations developed from different breeds of ape. Maerth provides the "separated at birth?" photos—each human type beside their closest ape relation—to prove it. He placed an orangutan, for example, beside a Southeast Asian face, a gorilla beside an African face, a chimpanzee beside a Near-Eastern face, and several unidentified monkeys next to various peoples from around the globe.

Maerth, moreover, attributes all human differences and problems to the distribution of brain eating, cannibalism and meat-eating among peoples. Woman is presumably less clever than Man because "he gave her no brain to eat." Supposed differences in racial intelligence "depends only on when their ape ancestors were transformed into cannibal human beings and how often they practiced cannibalism." All religions answer

Separated At Birth?
(from *The Beginning Was The End*)

the problems posed by the eating of brains, with the Judeo-Christian Bible a treatise on brain-eating. In Genesis, the fruit of the Tree of Knowledge represents the brain; eating the fruit of the Tree of Knowledge represents eating brain; and Adam and Eve's nakedness represents mankind's loss of fur—which resulted from eating brain.

In Maerth's reductionist view, even *smelly armpits* can be attributed to brain-eating:

> No ape or any animal at all on Earth suffers from smelly armpits: only "God's image" who supposedly developed within the context of natural evolution and in harmony with cosmic order—and began to smell. . . . Most people earn their money by the sweat of their brow, but some do so by the sweat of other people's armpits. This is called the "damages of civilization," but for its origin one must look not in the armpits, but in the head.

Side-effects of brain-eating like smelly armpits, madness and loss of fur pale beside our tragic loss of extra-sensory perception—a trait that we alone, among living things, lack. Though we may have become smarter, "a physical short circuit occurred whereby man lost the animal capacity for Extra-Sensory Perception." This ESP allowed us to "perceive the existence of the immaterial world" and our true selves, "through which the origin and meaning of existence are revealed and life is made worth living." All living things, including plants and protozoa, have this capacity; humans are the only exception. And humans are the only creatures who possess language, because we are the only ones who need it. Lack of ESP, says Maerth, "is the source of [our] spiritual troubles," to which we apply delusionary material measures, which "beget new spiritual and material troubles." Maerth cries passionately for change. "This unending chain of unsuccessful material measures is what man calls progress," and it will eventually destroy us.

We can only glimpse what our capacities used to be through "atavistic throwbacks" who naturally possess clairvoyance and ESP. In the old days we communicated by thought, not only with our own species, but also with intelligent beings on other planets. These beings were the "gods" of yore. Later, after most of us lost our ESP, the "atavistic throwbacks" who still had it were bred as gods in Mesopotamia, India and China. This practice developed into the caste system, Indian philosophy, and yoga, a process whereby ESP may be regained. Maerth— who practiced yoga—believed he had gained supernatural powers from the discipline.[29]

As our ancestors became aware they were losing their ESP, they developed methods to preserve it. "One of the methods," says Maerth, "was to form on the top of the skull a dome shaped like a knot of hair to create more room for the brain." Asian gods such as Shou-Lao are depicted "with an enormous domed bump on the front part of the roof of his skull." This may have helped us at one time, but now progress and civilization threaten these endangered bits of wisdom, possibly our only chance to be delivered from doom.

The mission of the population of the world, therefore, should be to defend against encroaching civilization, by embracing simple, healthy, natural living. Maerth prophesied that *The Beginning Was the End* will cause humanity to wake up to the problem.

Shortly after the publication of *The Beginning Was the End*, Maerth received a letter from a German student, Volker Zotz. Zotz describes his reception from Maerth:

> He answered my first letter because he looked for disciples. Kiss Maerth was a "would like to be guru," eager to find young men in each nation to train them as leaders of the future civilization he dreamed about. In his very first letter he predicted that I would become one of his followers. . . . Forgiving me gently that I was instead going to be a scholar, he found solace in the idea that I would later serve his goal in an indirect way: If I was going to study Asian philosophical and historical sources, he wrote, I could find one day a scientific proof for his ideas about cannibalism and development of intelligence by brain-eating.[30]

Though his arguments are based on physical rather than metaphysical sources, Maerth's conclusions converge with those of the esotericists. And, though it rests on a chain of what most would identify as crazy ideas, the underlying message— that Western culture is bankrupt, progress is a dangerous illusion, and modern humanity is degenerate—conforms to the world view of contemporary alternative culture. Maerth's final words could easily have come from the lips of a crystal-wearing vegetarian, an environmental activist chained to a tree, or an urban flock of pierced, tattooed teenagers.

WE ARE DEVO!

Around the same time Maerth was toiling away on his theory in obscurity, rebel youths from the American industrial heartland were introducing de-evolution to the masses via pop music.

It began with a small group of characteristically decadent art students from Akron, Ohio, who would later become famous as the band called DEVO. They were sitting around speculating on the future of art. "We said there'd been Art Nouveau and Art Deco," recalls DEVO co-founder Gerald Casale, "what could there be next?" They had seen an old EC comic book, like *Weird Science* or *Tales from the Crypt*, "where there was a scientist who had a de-evolution chamber." Casale relishes the memory of the revelatory comic book: "There was a big knob and a big lever, one end said 'evolution,' and one end said 'de-evolution.' And they de-evolved this guy into a half-man half-ape." They laughed very hard, and said, "that's it, de-evolution, Art DEVO."

Jocko-Homo Heaven Bound by B.H. SHADDUCK, an anti-evolution tract. One of the early inspirations for DEVO.

Art DEVO was laughed at, but some of the motivations were serious. Gerald Casale and Mark Mothersbaugh had been students at Kent State in 1970 when the Kent State Massacre occurred: Ohio National Guardsmen fired into a crowd of Kent State students protesting the U.S. invasion of Cambodia, killing four and wounding nine demonstrators. Casale and Mothersbaugh observed how the media and the people in power twisted the story to fit their own agendas. This event only added to their distrust of Akron-style piety and paternalism. Casale recalls that he and Mothersbaugh responded by embracing "anything that would question linear progress and the innate goodness of man and technology, and bring into play an explanation of duplicitous, evil behavior, of avarice, of greed, of brute force over good ideas." He identifies it as the "classic rock and roll rebellion . . . with kind of an intellectual perverse twist." It might have been a comfort to them if they'd known they were living in the Kali Yuga, the Age of Darkness.

As retaliation for life in Akron, practitioners of Art DEVO spouted de-evolutionary doctrine. They asked the rhetorical question, "Art DEVO, how low can you go?" to acknowledge what Casale pinpoints as "the forbidden and the low and the pop and the trash" co-existing "like some kind of Jungian dark side to . . . fine art and literature." They placed themselves in the de-evolution chamber and pulled the lever down as far back on the evolutionary scale as they could go.

One of the results was the primitively repetitive sound of DEVO, the band. Around 1973 Casale and Mothersbaugh asked "What would DEVO music sound like?" With their limited equipment and musical ability, they answered that DEVO music would be minimal, like "the jungle meets outer space." To accomplish this, Casale recounts that they literally tied one hand behind their drummer's back, and that nobody was allowed to play more than one chord. "Everybody had to pick a sound," says Casale, "and use it the whole time." They eschewed the conventional devices of pop music as changes and hooks. And they used cutting edge technology like synthesizers, not to be sophisticated, but to get more primitive.

Intellectual theorizing on culture and art produced lyrics that were "consciously stupid," with titles such as "Be Stiff," "Auto Mowdown" and "I Need a Chick." Their song "Chango" was inspired by an article in *National Geographic* about an African tribe. Their politically incorrect imitations of natives harkened back, in consciously poor taste, to a simpler time when native rituals done in blackface were acceptable entertainment.

DEVO naturally gravitated to strange tomes which would help them build what Casale calls a "reservoir of quack information." Mothersbaugh had come across an anti-evolution pamphlet by preacher B.H. Shadduck, entitled *Jocko-Homo, Heaven Bound*. Casale recalls that Man was shown "scaling the stairway to Hell . . . each stair [labeled] 'Alcohol,' 'Tobacco,' 'Slavery,' 'Usury,' 'Adultery,' . . . ." A monkey pointed to a poem, later immortalized in the DEVO anthem, "Jocko Homo":

> God made man, but he used a monkey to do it.
> Ape's in the plan, and we're here to prove it.
> You can walk like an ape, talk like an ape, do what monkeys do.
> God made man, but a monkey supplied the glue.[31]

The refrain from Jocko Homo, "Are we not men?" was taken from H.G. Wells' tale of evolutionary manipulation gone awry, *The Island of Dr. Moreau*.

Shadduck's book could be viewed as the DEVO "Old Testament." And when in 1974, Casale and Mothersbaugh read a review of Oscar Kiss Maerth's *The Beginning Was the End*, they realized that they'd found their New Testament. Immediately, they began to search for the book, in vain. Two years later, in New York, they visited Samuel Weiser's, a well-known metaphysical bookstore. Casale recounts that he asked for the book, and the guy behind the counter "right away looks at me like I'm Himmler, and says, 'Why do you want *that* book?'" Casale answered, "I read about it in a magazine almost two years ago and I couldn't find it and I want it." The bookseller finally brought two copies out from the back, which Casale and Mothersbaugh bought. Casale adds, "He was disgusted."

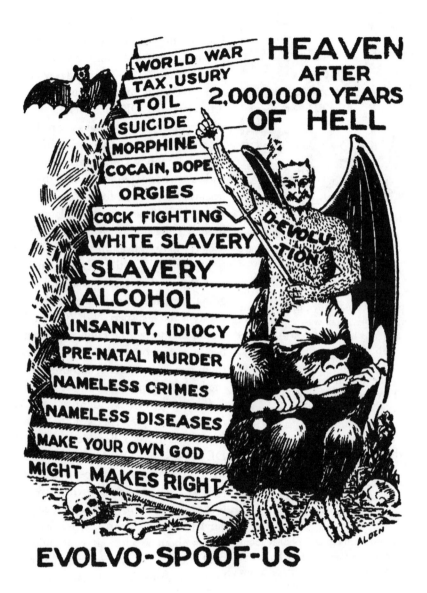

WORLD WAR
TAX, USURY
TOIL
SUICIDE
MORPHINE
COCAIN, DOPE
ORGIES
COCK FIGHTING
WHITE SLAVERY
SLAVERY
ALCOHOL
INSANITY, IDIOCY
PRE-NATAL MURDER
NAMELESS CRIMES
NAMELESS DISEASES
MAKE YOUR OWN GOD
MIGHT MAKES RIGHT

HEAVEN
AFTER
2,000,000 YEARS
OF HELL

D-EVOLU-TION

ALDEN

EVOLVO-SPOOF-US

B.H. SHADDUCK's representation of "De-evolution." This squat "ancestor" with doubtful table manners, is presumed to be the dam or sire of the race. When we found "it" in a magazine this crude poem of our pedigree was only about three drops of ink removed from glorious manhood. They called it "Scientific Symbolism." Elsewhere, this hairy poem is called all sorts of names ending in "-pus." When "Mother Goose" scientists fix up a poultice like this, they omit the details. I have asked the artist to add the brutal facts that put a "D" before evolution. The Bible says, "He that sitteth in the heavens will laught." No wonder! (from *Jocko–Homo Heaven Bound*)

B.H. SHADDUCK's caption reads:
Genealogically speaking, the sub-gentleman (center) and his "cousins" are said to have been in the same hide when our "ancestors" wiggled loose from the shell of a reptile's egg. After continuing as the same sprout on the family tree from some millions of years, there was a split in the family and the more refined learned to use a club and eat the neighbors. According to Theistic-evolution-ism, this was the fortunate beginning of a two-million-year carnival of bloodshed, treachery and cannibalism that would evolve a man who could make the next jump—to angel level—in thirty minutes. Meanwhile, "science" has discovered enough difference between the peace-loving branch of the family and the killer branch to justify keeping one in a cage and letting the other one buy the peanuts.

To keep you from being snobbish about it, they say that before you were born you passed through the monkey stage a few days before you reached human exclusiveness. Believe it if you wish, but to me, the wide range of man's capacity for saintliness or deviltry argues that man fell from God-likeness rather than climed [sic] from reptile level. Science, with all its speed, cannot lift the highest ape to the level of a baby's prayer in a million years.
(from *Jocko-Homo Heaven Bound*)

After DEVO had their new scripture, Casale notes, "everything else just became a mere trifle on the way to finding *the Bible*." DEVO saw de-evolution and Maerth as "cracked" substitutes for orthodoxy. To DEVO, "fucking around with people's idea of what's . . . real," was far more important than scientific truth "because nobody knows what's going on and everybody pretends like they do, because they live in fear." *The Beginning Was the End* "was a better explanation of human behavior as we knew it in the society that we lived in than the Bible." So, to "embed . . . the idea that anybody that thinks they know what the hell is going on and thinks they understand reality is to be suspect," DEVO members would memorize the bold-faced chapter headings and other choice quotes, spout them during interviews, and use them as the basis for song lyrics.

The mysterious identity of *The Beginning Was the End*'s author, Oscar Kiss Maerth, also became part of the DEVO arsenal. DEVO figured that he was a phantom, a made-up character: "'Oscar Kiss My-Ass'—when we saw that we assumed it was a conscious pun," laughs Casale, "'Maerth,' it was so close, it was about as close as you could get. And the picture on the back, where he lived in some Yugoslavian villa, and looked like one of the guys that escaped the Nuremberg trials; well, it was just too *good*." Later they found out from a friend who had some inside information on the book that Maerth was no pun and that he may well have been an old Nazi.

DEVO hadn't realized that their "cracked substitute for orthodoxy" was genuine, and that their own tongue-in-cheek rebellion wasn't far off from more traditional expressions of discontent. DEVO's appeal was only marginally due to their music. It was the ideas, expressed theatrically (in some of the first and finest music videos ever produced) and through lyrics that ignored both the schmaltzy pop music formulas at one extreme and punk rock rage on the other. Moreover, their fans were (and are) comprised of nerd-cool artists and writers, people who appreciate ideas. While DEVO may not have sparked a scientific or even metaphysical revolution, they got a few people talking—and thinking—about de-evolution. And de-evolution illuminates how unusual our Western notion of progress is.

And now, nearly 30 years after the founding of DEVO, the idea of de-evolution seems right at home. Among socially conscious, educated people it's almost axiomatic that progress and technology have failed—and will continue to fail— to bring peace and happiness to mankind; that the excesses of Western civilization are to blame for the problems of the world. Television, print media and the movies regularly lampoon naive faith in "American know-how," technological progress and "our way of life"—often embodied by images from the 1950s. The dangers of progress are more than just a joke to many Americans, from survivalists to radical environmentalists, who choose to unplug themselves from our high-velocity, high-tech society. In short, human efforts to improve life on Earth inspire a rampant cynicism—not unwarranted given the events of the past 60 years. We have seen the dark side of progress in nuclear waste, devastating weapons and the crumbling of individual privacy due to high-tech gizmos. We have also seen the dark side of human nature in genocide after genocide and war after war.

In such a climate, legends of the Golden Age, human decline and de-evolution refuse to go away.

---

1. Lyrics © Devo Music.
2. About a year after my DEVO conversion, I was spooked by an uncanny resemblance between Booji Boy and a regular on the bus I took to work each day.
3. See chap. 4, "Eugenics."
4. See chap. 3, "Race."
5. Bettmann, *Good Old Days*, p. 47.
6. Godwin, Arktos, p. 16. Quoted from *The Encyclopedia of Religion and Ethics*.
7. Eliade, *Myth of the Eternal Return*, p. 117.
8. Bury, *Idea of Progress*, pp. 9–10.
9. Hesiod's quotes detailing the Five Ages of Man were culled from *Works and Days*, translated by Lattimore.
10. Bury, *Idea of Progress*, p. 9.
11. Ibid., p. 10.

12. Ibid., p. 33.
13. See chap. 3, "Race."
14. See chap. 4, "Eugenics."
15. Pike, *Encyclopedia of Religion*, p. 164.
16. Blavatsky, *Secret Doctrine*, p. 161.
17. Ibid., p. 212.
18. Godwin, *Arktos*; source for timeline.
19. In the Arctic, the sun rises on only 300 days each year, alternating with 65 days of complete darkness.
20. Godwin, *Arktos*, p. 34.
21. See chap. 3, "Race," for more on the Aryan myth.
22. Poliakov, *Aryan Myth*, p. 312.
23. As recounted by Ley in "Pseudoscience in Naziland."
24. Evola, quoted in *Arktos*, by Godwin, p. 60.
25. Evola, *The Metaphysics of Sex*, pp. 9–10.
26. Godwin, *Arktos*, p. 70; Godwin writes that Serrano was "Chile's Ambassador to India (1953–62), Yugoslavia (1962–64), and Austria (1964–70), and a member of various international commissions."
27. Private communication from Volker Zotz, a German scholar who corresponded with Oscar Kiss Maerth, on and off, for ten years.
28. Jeff Coplon, "In Search of a Soviet Holocaust," *Village Voice*, 12 January 1988.
29. Private communication from Volker Zotz.
30. Ibid.
31. My copy of *Jocko-Homo, Heaven Bound* doesn't contain this poem; it may have come from one of Shadduck's many other similar pamphlets.

CHAPTER THREE

RACE

How do we recognize one group from the other?
You should have no problem in looking about you and deciding
who are the true descendants of Shem, often fair-haired, fair-skinned,
predominantly blue-eyed, healthy, creative, productive, proud, disdaining
to engage in any dishonest activity, and always fiercely individualistic, these are the
people who remain true to the tradition of the people of Shem. The Canaanites,
on the other hand, are generally shorter, darker, more furtive, and almost
always engaged in some type of criminal activity, usually with special
government approval or license. . . . They are also frequently involved
in some sort of extracurricular sexual activity which can be traced
directly back to the orgies of Baal, human sacrifice,
and obscene sexual rites.
EUSTACE MULLINS, *The Curse of Canaan*

They have blond hair, blue eyes and are known to be killer apes.
The gorilla on the other hand who has been subliminally compared to the
Nubian (Blackman), has thin lips, straight limp hair and underneath all of
the hair, you'll find pale, pinkish flesh. Now who does that remind you of?
BLOND HAIR, THIN LIPS, PALE, PINKISH SKIN AND
A KILLER INSTINCT. This is a typical description of
the Paleman (Canaanite, cursed seed of Canaan,
Physical Devil)!!!
ISSA MUHAMMAD, *The Paleman*

Part — Tribal Supremacy

TRIBE AND MYTH

"Race" is a dead, meaning-less term in physical anthropology even while it survives as a dangerous, often deadly figment of the collective imagination. Whether they are "racists" or not, most people assume that the biological categories of humanity called races actually exist. The American Anthropological Association, in its "Statement on 'Race,'" however, sets the record straight. The statement begins:

In the United States both scholars and the general public have been conditioned to viewing human races as natural and separate divisions within the human species based on visible physical differences. With the vast expansion of scientific knowledge in this century, however, it has become clear that human populations are not unambiguous, clearly demarcated, biologically distinct groups. Evidence from the analysis of genetics (e.g., DNA) indicates that most physical variation, about 94 percent, lies within so-called racial groups. Conventional geographic "racial" groupings differ from one another only in about 6 percent of their genes. This means that there is greater variation within "racial" groups than between them.

Race—as a necessary grouping of physical traits such as skin color, head shape and body size—is a phantom. But you wouldn't know it from the word's constant use by politicians, philanthropists and social scientists, and from the racial fallacies that dominate public discourse. Though we tend to think of race as a primary human characteristic, it's a relatively new concept (aside from its use as a synonym for "nation" or "ethnic group"), first used by European colonists during the sixteenth century upon encountering unfamiliar peoples in the New World and Africa. Through the years, European naturalists searched for a scientific basis for the idea of race, their theories often used to justify the ill treatment of aboriginal Africans, Americans and Australians. But after several centuries of attempting to divide humanity into distinct racial types—coming up with anywhere from three to 400 races—anthropologists gave up. They also abandoned the hope of finding a "pure" race, because there is no such thing.

Race is a purely cultural construct, an extension of the human tribal experience of "us" and "them." Before there were races, there were nations; and before there were nations, there were tribes. What we really mean when we talk about people of another race is "those people over there who are different from us." There is no xenophobia, however, among genes.

In simpler times, the difference between "us" and "them" was often reinforced by a tribe's creation myth. These stories were inherently "racist" in that they told the story of the origin of exactly one tribal group: "ours." And that origin was most likely divine and glorious, while the origin of the other tribes was demonic, ill fated, or merely mundane. As historian Léon Poliakov observed, ethnic egotism, or what we would today identify as racism, "is the simple expression of an urge which is universal among human groups or cultures; namely that of claiming a distinctive origin, an ancestry which is both high-born and glorious." Each tribe, separately, invents history, in its quest for origins. The scenario it finds typically involves descent from a god, a hero or a "divine" animal. And each myth of creation answers a tribe's questions: Where did we come from? (Gods and Heroes.) Who is the Greatest Tribe of All? (We are.)

The Tagalog creation story, from the Philippines, is a perfect example of a "racist" myth:

God carefully shapes a small clay figure but does not know how much heat is needed to bake it. Left too long in the oven, the image comes out burned black. This is the Negro. The next figure is underbaked and comes out pasty white. The Caucasian. The third time God takes His clay from the oven at exactly the right moment, when it is a lovely warm brown. So the brown man, the Malay and Filipino, begins his career by pleasing God.[1]

The Mayan myth from Popul Vuh similarly tells of a series of unsuccessful attempts by the gods to create men, with perfection finally achieved in the creation of the real men of the Quiche tribe. The failures are monkeys:

At first they resort to mud, but these creatures are ugly, stupid and crumble and fall down. The gods are displeased and do away with them. Next they choose wood. These men can chatter and reproduce, but they have no minds and walk on all fours. Disapproving, the gods ordain a deluge which drowns most of them, although a few of these men, made of wood, escape and become monkeys. This is why monkeys look like men. Finally the gods fashion four men out of cornmeal, and these are wonderful beings.[2]

Tribes who feel superior to other tribes are similar to those who feel superior to other species. Depending on their circumstances, a group's natural enemies might be identified as other tribes, other races, or even other primates.

TRIBAL EUROPE AND THE BIBLE

Long before European scholars divided humanity into "races," they divided it into families, guided by genealogies in the Bible. Though Genesis contained creation stories about just one group—the Hebrews—and their tribal god, Yahweh, early Christians adopted it as their own. Europeans read Genesis as a creation myth for all people, not just Hebrews. The Bible told them that the entire human race was descended from Adam and Noah; the human family divided neatly into three branches, one for each of Noah's sons: Japheth, Shem and Ham. Theologians took hints from the Bible to determine which group or nation descended from which son.

Prior to 1492, many in Christian Europe thought Europeans were the descendants of Japheth, Asians of Shem, and Africans of Ham, who bore the curse of slavery. Others surmised that the three sons of Noah corresponded to the feudal social classes: the serfs were descended from Ham, the clerks from Shem and the nobility from Japheth. All agreed, however, that Hebrew was the original language of mankind, and Palestine the cradle of humanity.

Despite the Christian doctrine of brotherly love and the belief that all humanity descended from Adam, there were ethnic political tensions in Europe for centuries. Notions of pure blood and tribal superiority eventually grew into highly sophisticated forms of tribalism, nationalism, and racism. Léon Poliakov has traced how the fledgling nations of Europe provided fertile ground for the cultivation of the nineteenth century "Aryan myth" of Germanic superiority. In each can be seen the tendency to glorify the conquerors, while vilifying the vanquished. Thus, the conquering Germanic tribes were favored during the Middle Ages as coming from "noble" stock while the vanquished indigenous, Celtic, Slavic and Latin tribes were seen as servile and common.

In post-Islamic Spain, beginning in the fifteenth century, the situation was complicated by the prejudice against former Moslems and Jews who had been forced to convert to Christianity or leave the country. These "conversos" were of a lower caste than the "original" Christians were. Poliakov explains that "Spanish theologians worked out a doctrine according to which the false beliefs of both the Moors and the Jews had soiled their blood, and this stain or 'nota' had been transmitted by heredity to their furthest descendants." Their acceptance of Christ was merely nominal; their original "rejection" had forever corrupted them.

In France, the tension between the Germanic Frankish conquerors and the indigenous Latin-Gauls eventually precipitated into a "Controversy about the Two Races," beginning around the sixteenth century. There should have been no delusion about the purity of the Germanic and Latin-Celtic elements in the French population; both were fused—culturally and biologically—beyond recognition by the end of the first millennium. But for centuries French intellectuals debated which culture dominated in their blood—the Gauls or the Franks.

The English, on the other hand, continued to trace their ancestry to Adam. In the early Middle Ages they rejected the lineage through Noah's son Japheth, and instead adopted Noah's eldest son Shem as their ancestor. Shem had traditionally been identified as the father of the Hebrews whereby they acquired the designation "Semites." The English also identified Shem as Melchizedek, a legendary figure identified in Genesis 14 as High Priest of God and King of Salem. The English traced their lineage not only through biblical figures, but also through the British gods and heroes: from Adam to Noah to Shem to Woden to King Alfred to King David.

This uniquely British spin on ancestry later developed into the British-Israelite doctrine, which, in the twentieth century, mutated into a more virulent American strain, Christian Identity. The British-Israelites, which at one time numbered in the hundreds of thousands—including Queen Victoria and King Edward VII—believe that the British are the direct descendants of the Ten Lost Tribes of Israel, making them the true "chosen people" of God. The doctrine began with a friendly nod to the Jews who, to them, represented the direct descendants of the other two tribes of Israel. But later versions, to varying degrees, vilify the present-day Jews as—at best—hapless pretenders to the title of "chosen people," or at worst, Satanic conspirators bent on their own ascendancy at the expense of the righteous Anglo-Saxon race.

The residents of Italy, however, didn't replace their pagan genealogies with biblical ones until the twelfth century. Even after they had traced their ancestry to Adam, they included their pagan gods in the genealogy. Known for their veneration of antiquity, Italians came to see themselves as an ancient, pure race, descended through either the Etruscans or the Romans, who invented civilization. Twentieth century Fascists adopted the same idea—the Italians are one race descended directly from the Romans.

While the Italians venerated antiquity, Germans were suspicious of it. They tended to associate antiquity with decay, disdaining the "old" races as decadent and impure. Their myths venerated youth and pictured the German race as young, and therefore pure. At the same time, many (paradoxically) claimed that the Germans were the original race of mankind. Germans were perhaps even more prone than other Europeans to emphasize race, because what united them were their common tribal heritage and language, rather than a locale. However, like others who had adopted Christianity, the Germans traced their ancestry to Adam and Eve, and through their chosen biblical patriarch, Ashkenaz.

During the 1100s, the mystic Hildegard of Bingen was the first to suggest that Adam and Eve spoke German, which she thought to be the original language of mankind. Three centuries later, this concept was taken a bit further by an anonymous "Revolutionary of the Upper Rhine," who wrote a racial polemic entitled "The Book of a Hundred Chapters" which could sit comfortably on a bookshelf next to *Mein Kampf*. The author claimed that Adam and Eve were German and proposed a millennial Reich, the enslavement of non-Germanics and the massacre of the Roman Catholic clergy. The author suggested that the Germans were a superior race of noble, free rulers, descended directly from Japheth, who, after the flood, settled in Germany, giving birth to an imperial line of the greatest conquerors and kings that the world had ever seen, from Alexander the Great to Tamerlane. Moreover, Adam and his Germanic progeny were free from original sin. The Slavs, on the other hand—who along with the Romans bore the brunt of the anonymous author's wrath—were the descendants of Noah's cursed son Ham.

From about the fifteenth century, not just mystics and wild-eyed revolutionaries, but also eminent German intellectuals, believed that German was the original language of mankind and that the German people had pure blood. At the same time they were reviving pre-Christian mythologies, which had been largely forgotten during the Middle Ages. An Antwerp doctor in the sixteenth century argued, using philological, historical and genealogical evidence, that all the biblical patriarchs spoke a Germanic language, from which Hebrew was derived.

Other scholars claimed that German had preceded Greek and Latin, while new genealogies were proposed whereby the old pagan gods were identified with biblical figures.

During the Enlightenment, it was all the rage in Germany to be skeptical of the Bible—though not of one's own ethnic and national prejudices. The eminent philosopher Leibniz suggested that Germany—not Palestine—was the cradle of humanity. Germans were eager to replace Adam and the Bible with Wotan and their old native myths.

Just as the Slavs were often vilified in Germany, they were revered in Russia. Slow to be Christianized, the Russian people were still worshipping their ancestors in the Middle Ages, and considered themselves the grandsons of the sun god Dajdbog. Later the ruling Romanovs claimed to be of Germanic ancestry, but the veneration of German blood was short-lived and confined to the nobility. During the 1700s, various Russian scholars began claiming the antiquity of Slavic languages, just as the German scholars claimed the antiquity of Germanic languages. Catherine the Great went even further, arguing that the Slavs were racially superior and that their language was the mother of all tongues. She wrote to Grimm in 1784, ". . . and I could show without much trouble that [the Slavs] provided the names of most of the rivers, mountains, valleys, regions, and provinces of France, Spain, Scotland and other places. . . . The Salian Franks and Salic Law, Chilperic I, Clovis and all the Merovingian race were Slav, as well as all the Vandal Kings of Spain."[3] Osiris, Zoroaster and Odin, she claimed, were originally Slav names, and even the Anglo-Saxons were Slavs.

Though the Europeans' arguments were much more sophisticated than the simple creation myths of their ancestors, their conclusion was nearly identical: MY tribe is older, purer, nobler, better, smarter, and more powerful than YOUR tribe.

Part II—Origins of White Supremacy

PRE-ADAMITES

After the discovery of the New World and the deeper exploration of the old one, the biblical genealogies the Christian world had accepted on faith began breaking down. The existence of the Native Americans, the Pacific Islanders and other "savages" puzzled the scholars. If all men had descended from Adam, either these newly discovered tribesmen were not human, or they had migrated from the Holy Land to the South Seas and America, making them lost tribes of Israel. A third, somewhat heretical option was that they were descended not from Adam, but from an earlier creation, making them "pre-Adamites." The fourth option, of rejecting the biblical view of pre-history, was generally not even considered.

In the early sixteenth century, a theological debate ensued which had very material consequences. Were the American Indians sons of Adam, complete with souls? Or were they pre-Adamites, forever lost to God? If they had no souls to save, it would be pointless for missionaries to journey over the Atlantic to try to save them. The Catholic Church solved the problem in 1537. The Holy See proclaimed that the Indians were men capable of receiving the faith, giving the theological go-ahead to tidal waves of New World missionaries.

Some scholars concluded that the Aztecs and Incas were the descendants of Shem, and were therefore Israelites. Variations on this view were supported by Rabbi Manasseh ben Israel, William Penn, and later, the Mormons, who still believe it today. At the same time, the black Africans were considered to be the progeny of Noah's cursed son Ham, which helped justify their enslavement.

The pre-Adamite idea was first proposed before the Christian era; Jewish scholars speculated that there might have been an earlier creation than the one described in Genesis and that angels, demons and men from the earlier creation might continue to exist. In the tenth century, the idea was revived by Arab historian, al-Masudi, who, "in the course of speculating . . . on the 28 letters of the Arab alphabet postulated the existence of 28 nations before Adam."[4] In fourteenth century Europe, Spanish monk Tomas Scotus postulated pre-Adamites in conjunction with his heretical doctrine of Averroism, which assumed the world to be eternal and uncreated. He wrote, "There were men before Adam. Adam was made by these men, whence it follows that the world has existed from all time and that it was inhabited by men all time."[5] But scholars didn't take the pre-Adamite idea seriously until the sixteenth century, when Europeans were still puzzling over the origins of "savages." Paracelsus was the first to suggest that native Americans must be descended from "another Adam." Giordano Bruno proposed that there was not one, but three ancestors of mankind: Enoch, Leviathan and Adam. Adam's only distinction was that he was progenitor of the Jews, the youngest race.

MONOGENY VS. POLYGENY

During the seventeenth and eighteenth centuries, the pre-Adamite debate widened into a debate over "monogeny" versus "polygeny." Enlightenment thinkers asked whether there was just one, or were there many, roots in the human family tree? Or, to put it in modern scientific terms: is there just one or many species of mankind? The monogenists held that people of all races had a common origin, the polygenists that each race developed separately.

The monogenists were a long way, however, from proposing that all men were "equal." Many of them adopted the "Theory of Degeneracy," that "lower" races and apes had developed, or "degenerated," from superior white men. Naturally, inherent in this idea was the assumption that Europeans were biologically superior to darker peoples.

The idea of racial degeneracy—as opposed to the decline of all humanity explored in the de-evolution chapter—stems from a scientific, rather than spiritual tradition. In fact, the idea of degeneracy preceded early theories of human evolution that reversed the process—white men developed or "evolved" from "lower" races and apes. Early monogenists who adopted the "Theory of Degeneracy" to explain racial differences included renowned French scientists Pierre-Louis de Maupertuis (1698–1759) and Georges-Louis Buffon (1707–1788) and the German scientist known as the "father of physical anthropology," Johann-Friedrich Blumenbach (1752–1840).

Buffon's *Natural History* was the standard text on the subject of degeneracy for a century. Buffon claimed the original man was white, and some of his descendants, because of environmental conditions, degenerated into the darker races. In Buffon's view, the inhabitants of the vicinity of the Caspian Sea were the most perfect specimens of humanity, and therefore this region must have been the cradle of mankind. Those who live there now possess the "real and natural color" of man, the original white that eventually degenerated into varying shades of yellow, brown and black. Blumenbach, for his part, preferred the peoples of the Caucasus to Buffon's Caspian Sea dwellers. He was the first to use the word "Caucasian" to describe the white race, because he thought that "the finest race of men" could be found in the Caucasian mountains, which, for "physiological reasons," must have been the cradle of mankind. He explained authoritatively that white skin "can easily degenerate to a blackish hue." Not only the skin degenerated; the skulls were affected as well. Blumenbach spent his days observing the skulls of Mongolian, American, Caucasian, Malay and Ethiopian "races." His judgment as an objective scientist told him that the Caucasian was the loveliest and the most symmetrical of all the skulls "from which, as from a mean and primeval type, the others diverge by most easy gradations on both sides to the two ultimate extremes." [6]

James Cowles Prichard (1786–1848), British anthropologist and medical researcher, was perhaps the only monogenist to propose that the human race was originally black. He opposed the theory of degeneracy and replaced it with a theory of evolutionary progress. He reasoned that since savages were usually dark-skinned, whereas civilized peoples were white, progress and civilization must produce white skin. As people adopted more civilized attitudes and morals, they would

The Five Races of Mankind according to J.F. BLUMENBACH (from *The Death of Adam* by JOHN C. GREENE)

prefer to breed with more aesthetically perfect, beautiful, pale individuals, the perfection of which was reached in the European race.

Though monogeny could easily be reconciled with the Bible, not so polygeny, the doctrine that each race was a separate species. Thus polygeny had the support of the leading thinkers of the day—such as Voltaire—who were eager to free themselves from the intellectual shackles of Scripture.

One influential English polygenist, Edward Long (1734–1813), divided men into three species: Europeans, Negroes, and orangutans. Orangutans, he wrote, "did not seem at all inferior in the intellectual faculties to many of the negroe race; with some of whom it is credible they have the most intimate connexion and consanguinity . . . the negroes themselves bear testimony, that such intercourses actually happen; and it is certain that both races agree perfectly well in lasciviousness of disposition. . . ." [7] Mulattoes, Long proclaimed, are infertile, like mules. They come in two types: first, the offspring who result from the coupling of a Negro and a Caucasian; and second, the offspring of a Negro and an orangutan. The latter are often the result of "the passion the male Orang-Outang has for the Negress."

Another respected polygenist, German philosopher Christoph Meiners (1745–1810), wrote of two lineages of mankind, the fair and beautiful and the dark and ugly. The whites possess courage, love of liberty, and other good qualities, while the dark lack virtue and character and are naturally irritable. Meiners proposed a gradual transition from beasts to men: monkeys, Orang-Outangs, chimps, Negroes of the forest (Hottentots, Bushmen, and Australians), through the copper-colored, "yellow" races, to Slavs and up to the Germanic races.

The nineteenth century French anthropologist and polygenist Jean Baptiste Bory de Saint-Vincent identified as many as 15 distinct, separately created human species and placed them in descending order. At the top was the white "Japhetic" race, that had produced "the greatest geniuses humanity can boast of." In second place came the "Arabic race," the descendants of Adam. Various peoples of Asia, Africa and the Americas were placed underneath, with the Australian aborigines at the very bottom, because they were "the last to be formed by nature, without religion or laws or the arts." [8]

Darwinist Karl Vogt founded the "polyphyletic theory" of human origins, which affiliated each race with a species of anthropoid ape ancestor. Thus, whites are closely related to chimpanzees, Negroes to gorillas, and Asians with orangutans. Though he was vague about which primates fathered each race, DEVO's hero Oscar Kiss Maerth adopted this concept as late as the 1970s. He backed it up with photos pairing people of various unnamed ethnicities with unidentified specimens of monkeys and apes. [9]

These crudely outlined versions of pre-Darwinian evolution were apparently supported by the results of empirical scientists, such as the Dutch anatomist Petrus Camper (1722–1789). Camper was the first to conceive of measuring the facial angle

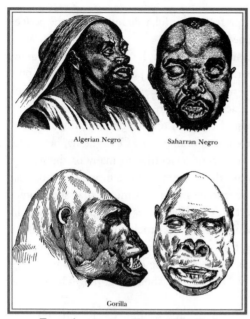

Algerian Negro   Saharran Negro

Gorilla

From the 1854 text *Types of Mankind*
by Nott and Gliddon who wrote:
"The palpable analogies and dissimilitudes
between an inferior type of mankind and a
superior type of monkey require no comment."
(from *The Mismeasure of Man*
by Stephen Jay Gould)

of monkeys, apes and men, to determine their place in the evolutionary line. "Upon placing beside the heads of the Negro and the Calmuck those of the European and the ape," he wrote, "I perceived that a line drawn from the forehead to the upper lip indicates a difference in the physiognomy of these peoples and makes apparent a marked analogy between the head of the Negro and that of the ape. . . ."[10] Though some polygenists concluded that there were several species of men, with the Negro at the bottom, others concluded that the Negro is a hybrid between white men and apes.

Though the theory originated in Europe, polygeny was embraced much more warmly in the United States, with distinguished naturalist Louis Agassiz (1807–1873) as its leading spokesman.

Agassiz, born in Switzerland, immigrated to America in the 1840s. He was a professor at Harvard, founded Harvard's Museum of Comparative Zoology, and directed the museum until the day he died. Stephen Jay Gould estimates that "no man did more to establish and enhance the prestige of American biology during the nineteenth century."[11]

The popular professor apparently converted to polygeny after his move to the U.S., where he encountered blacks for the first time. Though he opposed slavery, Agassiz became convinced that Negroes were a separate, created species. Gould adds that the Swiss naturalist was "first of all, a devout creationist who lived long enough to become the only major scientific opponent of evolution." A letter written to his mother in 1846 (translated by Gould) describes, in detail, the background for his conversion to polygenism:

> It was in Philadelphia that I first found myself in prolonged contact with negroes; all the domestics in my hotel were men of color. I can scarcely express to you the painful impression that I received, especially since the feeling that they inspired in me is contrary to all our ideas about the confraternity of the human type and the unique origin of our

species. But truth before all. Nevertheless, I experienced pity at the sight of this degraded and degenerate race, and their lot inspired compassion in me in thinking that they are really men. Nonetheless, it is impossible for me to repress the feeling that they are not of the same blood as us. In seeing their black faces with their thick lips and grimacing teeth, the wool on their head, their bent knees, their elongated hands, their large curved nails, and especially the livid color of the palm of their hands, I could not take my eyes off their face in order to tell them to stay far away. And when they advanced that hideous hand towards my plate in order to serve me, I wished I were able to depart in order to eat a piece of bread elsewhere, rather than dine with such service. What unhappiness for the white race—to have tied their existence so closely with that of negroes in certain countries! God preserve us from such a contact![12]

Polygeny was a neat solution to the scientist's feelings of revulsion—as well as pity. If Negroes were of another species, then it was much easier to bear their differences and their pitiful plight.

Agassiz denied that the theory of polygeny opposed Scripture, arguing that even if each race is of a separate species, men are still bound together by structure and sympathy; moreover, the story of Adam and Eve only applies to whites. He further elaborated the theory by hypothesizing that each race was created en masse, in its own unique, natural territory:

These races must have originated . . . in the same numerical proportions, and over the same area, in which they now occur. . . . They cannot have originated in single individuals, but must have been created in that numeric harmony which is characteristic of each species; men must have originated in nations, as the bees have originated in swarms.[13]

Though it would seem that polygenists like Agassiz were somehow more "racist" than the monogenists, this was not necessarily the case. In fact, the term as we use it today would have applied to virtually everyone of European descent. The monogenists thought the original superior white race degenerated to form the many darker ones, while the polygenists saw a species hierarchy from the apes to the dark races to the white ones. All who studied the question—even those who opposed slavery—concluded that the darker races were inferior to whites. Therefore, contemporary white supremacists looking for scientific justification for their views can find it easily in any mid-nineteenth century anthropology text.

Part III—White Supremacy

EUROPE: ARYAN AND NARROW-HEADED

During the eighteenth and nineteenth centuries, the monogenist, polygenist, and pre-Adamite debates continued, joined by speculation about the birthplace of humanity. The "Mysterious East" was beginning to open her doors to cultivated Europeans, many of whom became enthralled with all things Oriental. Intellectuals read and translated the sacred Scriptures of Taoists, Hindus and Buddhists for the first time, and credited Asians with the invention of more than just gunpowder. Voltaire and others believed that all civilization had come from the high-caste Brahmins of India. Some scholars even claimed that India was the birthplace of humanity. Kant preferred Tibet, since it was the highest country. He speculated that all European civilization and culture could trace its origins to Tibet, through India. He even went so far as to identify Abraham—of the Bible—with the Indian deity Brahma. Still others preferred central Asia and Scythia—homeland of the ancient nomadic Scythians—near the Black Sea. The Lutheran pastor Johann Gottfried von Herder (1744–1803) was certain that the cradle of humanity was in the "primitive mountains of Asia." At the same time he proposed a racial connection between the Germans, the Persians and the Indians, giving the German people the distinction of a superior racial heritage.

In the 1780s, the English poet and jurist William Jones was surprised to discover a connection between the Asian language Sanskrit and European languages. This connection defined the linguistic category of Indo-European languages. It also had the effect of making the idea that the Europeans originated in Asia much more plausible.

In 1788 Jones published his theory that Greek, Latin and Sanskrit, and possibly Gothic and Celtic have a common source, an ancient language that no longer exists. He also ventured into the area of mythology and found close analogies between Greco-Latin and Indian mythology. There was indeed strong evidence for a connection between Indian and European languages, and European intellectuals swiftly adopted Jones' theories. Despite the purely linguistic nature of the connection, many scholars assumed that this meant that the connection was also racial. The Indo-European theory eventually became the basis for Romantic speculations and fantasies about the supposed speakers of the long-lost Indo-European mother of tongues, the ancestors of both Europeans and Indians, who came to be known as the "Aryans."

Scholar and diplomat Friedrich von Schlegel (1772–1829) first used "Aryan" in this way in 1819. The word had previously been applied to the ancient Persians, but Schlegel connected it to the German word "Ehre" or "honor." Schlegel's Aryans became the people of honor, the aristocracy of all humanity.

Schlegel had studied Indian mythology, and found references to a holy mountain in the north. This led him to the thesis that the Indians had originated in the northern mountains, from which they marched in columns to their destiny as the civilizers of the West. While in Northern India, they mingled with others and became the Aryans. Schlegel believed that all civilization and all higher culture came from India, by way of the noble Aryans.

Many European scholars agreed that India was the birthplace of mankind. Though they used linguistic and other evidence to support this idea, it was frequently expressed in romantic, poetic terms, belying a passion to find more than merely scientific truth. August-Friedrich Pott wrote, "The march of culture, in its general lines, has always followed the sun's course. The people of Europe at first nestled in the bosom of Asia; like small children they played around this mother. . . . [In Asia] were situated the playground and school of the earliest material and spiritual energies of the human race." [14] Léon Poliakov interprets this obsession with India to be "the literary and political expression of a subconscious desire to abolish the social yoke of law and culture by making an appeal to the rights, duties and laws of 'Nature' with all its wide semantic connotations." [15] And in Nature dwelled Human Destiny, personified by the Aryan race. Ernest Renan, a French scientist, imagined that the Aryans shared a common birthplace as well as the distinction of being a "great and noble race" with the Semites. He called the Semites a decadent race in steady decline; it was up to the newly chosen Aryan race to lead the march of human destiny. Of Mount Imaüs, Renan's mythical birthplace of white humanity, he wrote:

> We salute those sacred summits, where the great races, which carried the future of humanity in their hearts, contemplated infinity for the first time and introduced two categories which changed the face of the world, morality and reason. When the Aryan race, after thousands of years of striving, shall have become the masters of the planet which they inhabit, their first duty will be to explore that mysterious region. . . . No place in the world has had a comparable role to that of the nameless mountain or valley where mankind first attained self-consciousness. Let us be proud . . . of the old patriarchs who, at the foot of Imaüs, laid the foundations of what we are and of what we shall become. [16]

The Aryan/Semitic dichotomy began seeping its way into anthropology, among both monogenists and polygenists. By 1860 intellectual Europe accepted the division between Aryan and Semitic races as dogma. Most everyone agreed that Europeans were members of the Aryan race, who had originated in the high plateaus of Asia.

This dichotomy paved the way for the extreme, influential racism of French diplomat and scholar Comte Joseph Arthur de Gobineau (1816–82); in the middle of the nineteenth century he published his "Essay on the Inequality of the Human Races." He analyzed all historical events and persons according to racial differences and, in the pre-Adamite tradition, believed that the book of Genesis provided a genealogy for the white race only. He divided whites into the sons of Ham, Shem and Japheth—father of the superior sub-race of Aryans. The white race, wrote the Count, has "the monopoly of beauty, intelligence and strength."

Gobineau assumed the existence of a "racial instinct" in all peoples, as well as its corollary, "the law of repulsion," which kept the races from crossbreeding. But it is the white race in particular, he argued, which most needs to abide by its racial instinct, because of its vulnerability to infusions of "inferior blood." In short, mixed races, such as the Hamites, and, to a lesser degree, the Semites, are degenerate. By contrast, the sons of Japheth—the Aryans—remained pure until the Christian era, after which they began their racial decline.

Gobineau provided an obsessively detailed racial analysis of history. The Hellenes, he wrote, were "Aryans modified by yellow elements but with a great preponderance of the white essence and some Semitic affinities." Phoenicians were "Black Hamites." Arabs and Hebrews were "very mixed Semites," while Philistines were "Semites perhaps of purer stock." Libyans, on the other hand, were "almost black Hamites."[17] Gobineau concludes his racial analysis of mankind with a de-evolutionary, proto-eugenic prognosis for the decline of the Aryan race. Poliakov summarizes it as follows:

> The final chapters of his book are dedicated to a description of the bastardization of the Aryans; nor is any exception made (as is generally thought) in favour of the Germans, who were also contaminated by residual European blood-types as well as by "Finnish blood." Still more tragic were the prospects in the New World, whose inhabitants "are the products of the detritus of all the ages, of Irishmen and Germans thoroughly cross-bred, of some French who are no less so and of Italians who are more so than all the others." Furthermore, to this mixture would be added before long the blood of Blacks and Indians from which there could only result the "juxtaposition of the most degraded beings."[18]

Gobineau ends on this particularly de-evolutionary note:

> The white species will disappear henceforth from the face of the earth. . . . The portion of Aryan blood, already subdivided so frequently, which still exists in our countries and which alone sustains the edifice of our society, advances daily towards the last frontier before total absorption. When this result is achieved the age of unity will have been reached . . . this state of fusion, far from being a consequence of the direct marriage of the three great archetypes in their

pure state, will be no more than the caput mortuum of an infinite series of mixtures and, consequently, of attenuations. It will be the last stage of mediocrity in all its aspects; mediocrity in physical strength, mediocrity in beauty, mediocrity in intellectual aptitudes, one might almost say annihilation.[19]

It would be only three or four thousand years before "the final spasm of our species, when the lifeless earth will continue, without us, to describe its apathetic orbits in space."

Gobineau and like-minded colleagues saw skin color and other racial traits largely as the superficial packaging for essential, metaphysical forces. Gustav Klemm (1802–1867) developed this concept as the bi-polar principle of races, detailed in his *History of Civilization*, which was considered authoritative. Klemm conceived mankind as divided into an active race, and a passive race, "each necessary to the other" as are male and female. The passive race, who were native to the plains, included dark peoples, Slavs and Russians; the conquering, active race, native to mountains, included German and Latin tribes. Contrary to Gobineau, however, Klemm had no innate horror of race mixing. On the contrary, it was in race mixing that Klemm saw the perfection of humanity.

The active/passive and Aryan/Semitic dichotomies—eagerly adopted by nineteenth century Germans—were joined by the dichotomy between the brachycephalic (round-headed) and the dolichocephalic (narrow-headed) peoples. This division was supported by the brand new quasi-scientific study of heads, "craniometry." The Aryan narrow-heads were said to be tall and blond; they had conquered the darker, stouter round-heads, who included Finns, Slavs, Lapps and Prussians. Georges Vacher de Lapouge (1854–1936) envisioned dark times ahead directly resulting from differences in the "cephalic index":

> The ancestors of the Aryans cultivated wheat when those of the brachycephalics were probably still living like monkeys. . . . The conflict of races is now about to start openly within nations and between nations, and one can only ask oneself if the ideas of the fraternity and equality of man were not against nature. . . . *I am convinced that in the next century people will slaughter each other by the million because of a difference of a degree or two in the cephalic index. It is by this sign, which has replaced the Biblical shibboleth and linguistic affinities, that men will be identified . . . and the last sentimentalists will be able to witness the most massive exterminations of peoples.*[20]

Lapouge's prediction was strangely accurate; millions would soon be slaughtered because of differences no less slippery than "a degree or two in the cephalic index."

AMERICA: WHITE SUPREMACY & THE BIBLE

In the meantime, the "Hamitic Curse" was still being used to justify slavery among Bible-believing Americans. Jefferson Davis, in his 1861 "Inaugural Address as Provisional President of the Confederacy" in Montgomery, Alabama, declared, "[Slavery] was established by decree of Almighty God . . . it is sanctioned in the Bible, in both Testaments, from Genesis to Revelation." [21] Even after the slaves were freed, scientists demonstrated the inferiority of the Negro while preachers invoked the Hamitic curse and other abstruse biblical arguments to prove that Negroes were beasts or the seed of Satan. Scientist and preacher alike cautioned against miscegenation: scholars said it produced inferior offspring while preachers declared it to be a sin against God.

In 1880 Alexander Winchell, a geologist and biologist at the University of Michigan, published *Preadamites: or A Demonstration of the Existence of Man Before Adam*, in which he combined both biblical and evolutionary ideas to support the conventional wisdom of the time. He argued that Adam, who was not the first man, was the ancestor of whites only. Adam's ancestors were Negro and "Oriental" pre-Adamites. Noah's flood destroyed Adam's line (except for Noah and his family) but spared the swarthy pre-Adamites. So, after the flood, Noah's descendants "were everywhere confronted by races of men already in possession of the earth." Winchell believed in evolution for the Adamic race only; they continued to progress, while the non-Adamic races ceased to evolve, and eventually became genetically inferior to their white cousins. Interbreeding with them generated less than perfect offspring.

While Winchell was a monogenist, the creationist preachers tended to be polygenists, believing that Negroes were not even human. They argued that Negroes were neither the sons of Ham nor even of Adam. In such tracts as *The Negro: What Is His Ethnological Status?* by "Ariel" (Rev. Buckner Payne, 1867), *The Missing Link: or The Negro's Ethnological Status* by Gottlieb Hasskarl (1898) and *The Negro: A Beast*, by Charles Carroll (1900) it was argued that the Negro was created in Genesis 1 with the other "beasts of the field" to serve the white race, while "the Adam" was created in Genesis 2. The serpent in the Garden of Eden was a Negro beast. The "sons of God" in Genesis 6:4 were whites, but the "sons of man" were Negroes; when the two interbred, they produced monsters. God sent the flood to destroy the mongrels. The Negroes were spared only because they boarded the Ark with the other beasts. But miscegenation continued after the flood, and it was Christ's mission to end it.

EUROPE: PROTO-NAZI ANTHROPOLOGY

While materialist practitioners of craniometry were applying tape measures to anthropoid skulls, in Germany, the romantic reaction to science, rationalism and modernity was in full swing, with various occultist and *völkisch* [22] movements in ascendance. The Aryans now existed not only in theory, but also in the German imagination. All manner of folk legend began to cling like electrostatically charged lint to the once-theoretical "Aryan" speakers of the ancient Indo-European tongue. This climate gave birth to a host of mystics and fringe characters, each with his own racially charged version of human prehistory. Nazi anthropology became the newest link in an ideological chain that grew from German Romanticism and reached all the way back to the Middle Ages.

Nicholas Goodrick-Clarke's *The Occult Roots of Nazism* traces these Romantically inspired movements with particular emphasis on Ariosophists Guido von List (1848–1919) and Jörg Lanz von Liebenfels (1874–1954). Goodrick-Clarke shows that though they were only peripherally involved in Nazism *per se*, such fringe dwellers as these two "had the imagination and opportunity to describe a dream-world that often underlay the sentiments and actions of more worldly men in positions of power and responsibility."[23] This dream world was no Nazi nightmare, for behind their occult doctrines was the desire to restore mankind, nobility intact, to a central position in the cosmos.

List, a native of Vienna, made a name by combining *völkisch* ideology with occultism and Theosophy. His celebrity stemmed largely from his image as the bearded patriarch whose mystic powers could reveal the forgotten glory of ancient Ario-German state. His pretension to aristocracy was topped by his claim to be the last of the "Armanist" magicians, the demi-gods of the Aryan world.

List's articles, plays and novels depicted a romantic world of an ancient Teutonic priesthood—the *Armanenschaft*—who practiced mystic rites and cast runic spells. He applied Teutonic mythology to Theosophy to create a homegrown antique religion. He adhered to Blavatsky's scheme in the *Secret Doctrine* of seven Root-Races in each "round" or world-cycle.[24] List identified Blavatsky's first four rounds with the four Teutonic realms of Muspilheim (inhabited by fire-dragons), Asgard (inhabited by air-gods), Wanenheim (inhabited by water-giants) and Midgard (inhabited by men). The first four Root-Races in the current round, said List, were Teutonic giants. The fifth and current Root-Race of Ario-Germanic god-men were the highest form of life to evolve in the universe.

List's followers were anything but low-lifes; for the most part, they resided in the world of middle- and upper-class respectability. These men were united in their theosophical, nationalist, anti-Semitic and pan-German beliefs, and in their desire to connect with fantasies of their ancient heritage through ritual. List's *Armanenschaft* provided them with the structure in which to practice their beliefs. List claimed that the *Armanenschaft* was in fact an ancient hierarchy of Ario-German priest-kings that had been suppressed, but whose rituals had been passed down via secret societies such as the Rosicrucians and the Freemasons. Thus, his *Armanenschaft* had more resemblance to a summer camp for Freemasons than a scary coven of bloodthirsty sorcerers.

Jörg Lanz von Liebenfels' Order of the New Templars (ONT)—founded around the same time as the *Armanenschaft*—glorified racial purity far more than Teutonic nostalgia. Some scholars argue that it was the prototype for the Nazi SS. The ONT's members were steeped in Lanz's abstruse "Theozoölogy," which combined Gnostic religion with racial pseudoscience. Lanz's dualistic system identified the pale, yellow-haired Aryan race with Good, and the darker Negroes, Mongols and "mediterraneanoids" with Evil. The Aryans were cosmic entities working for order in the universe, while the Dark Races were cosmic demons working for chaos.

Lanz, like List, hailed from Vienna and harbored spurious claims to German aristocracy; hence the "von Liebenfels." He had begun his career as a Cistercian monk and teacher, but renounced his holy vows at the age of 24. In 1903 he published an article entitled "Anthropozoon biblicum" in a biblical research journal and later published such enduring works as *Theo-Zoology: or The Lore of the Sodom-Apelings and the Electron of the Gods*, as well as the journal *Ostara*, which at its height in 1907 boasted a print-run of 100,000 copies.

Lanz wrote of two separately created races of men: the pygmies or beast-men, and the Aryans or god-men. The beast-men were the spawn of Adam, who wasn't the first man, but the first pygmy. The Aryan god-men, on the other hand, were created at the former polar continent Arktogäa. The Aryans had been naturally endowed with extrasensory organs that they used to transmit and receive electrical signals. Their fall—and the atrophy of their ESP organs—occurred when they began to interbreed with specially bred "love-pygmies" used in satanic rites for some of the Aryans' idolatrous pleasure.

While his interpretation of the Old Testament was strange, Lanz was convinced that the New Testament was a treatise on the mighty struggle between bestial pygmies and electrical Aryans. Christ was "electronic," as witnessed by his miracles, magical powers and transfiguration. The electronic Christ, however, was surrounded by pygmies, who attempted to rape him, cheered on by members of satanic cults devoted to interbreeding with pygmies.

Long after biblical times, the struggle continues. Though the Aryans rule the world, the mixed races produced by Aryan/pygmy bestiality continue to multiply, their numbers threatening the natural order of Aryan world domination. The only hope for restoring the Aryans' power (electrical and otherwise), warned Lanz, would be a universal program of racial segregation:

> The time has come! The old brood of Sodom is degenerate and wretched in the Middle East and all round the Mediterranean. . . . Our bodies are scurfy despite all soaps, they are udumized, pagatized and baziatized [verbs of corruption formed from the Assyrian names for the pygmies]. The life of man has never been so miserable as today in spite of all technical achievements. Demonic beast-men oppress us

from above, slaughtering without conscience millions of people in murderous wars waged for their own personal gain. Wild beast-men shake the pillars of culture from below. . . . Why do you seek a hell in the next world! Is not the hell in which we live and which burns inside us [i.e. the stigma of corrupt blood] sufficiently dreadful?[25]

Lanz further demanded that rather than treat weak and inferior members of the species with compassion, they had to be humanely exterminated through eugenic sterilization programs. Racial purification also demanded that women be strictly subjugated to their Aryan husbands, due to their unfortunate tendency to lust after the demonic beast-men. Brood-mothers would be sent to eugenic convents, where they would be serviced by pureblooded Aryan studs. Inferior races would be deported to Madagascar, used as beasts of burden or simply incinerated as a sacrifice to God. After an apocalyptic battle, the millennium would then usher in a permanent Aryan racial paradise. Lanz's apocalyptic plan would be amusing were it not so similar to the one carried out by the Nazis, about 20 years later.

In 1915 Lanz coined the word "Ariosophy," as a sort of hyper-racist Theosophy. Among its basic tenets was the belief that "pan-psychic" energy, or God, animates the universe and is perfected in the pure Aryan, from whom all cultural achievement originates. Ariosophists would study palmistry, astrology, heraldry and cabala, in order to further understand and analyze the differences between the blondes and the darks.

In 1918, Lanz left Austria for Hungary, where he flourished. After the socialists took over Austria in the '30s, he fled to Switzerland, where he watched Hitler and the Nazis from a distance. He had high hopes for Hitler, but was disappointed by his actual performance in office.

NAZI ANTHROPOLOGY

Of the many racist treatises circulating in Nazi Germany, the most influential was Alfred Rosenberg's best-selling *Myth of the 20th Century*. According to Peter Viereck, author of *The Roots of the Nazi Mind*, Rosenberg wrote that God created humanity not as individuals but as races, the building blocks of history. Races, not individual men, possessed souls. The blond, blue-eyed god-like Aryan race had migrated from Atlantis, to rule over the non-Aryans, dispatching their noble warriors in four waves, all over the globe. The first migration took the Aryans to North Africa. The second went to Persia, India and Greece to create the Hellenic and Roman civilizations. He identified the third migration with the spread of Teutonic tribes over Europe, and the fourth was the colonization of the globe by Germanic Europeans, led by the English. Aryans built all the great empires of history, according to Rosenberg, and fell only because of Aryan interbreeding with inferior races. Rosenberg also revealed that Jesus, generally thought to have been a Jew, was an Aryan, since Galilee was a "Nordic stratum" untainted by Jewry.

Perhaps more influential among the Nazi inner circle and the culture of the SS was "Himmler's Rasputin," Karl Maria Wiligut (1866–1946). Wiligut's paranoia and occult pursuits precipitated his commitment to a lunatic asylum from 1924 to 1927. This episode didn't hinder his later ascendancy, however, in the ranks of the SS. In 1933 he joined the élite organization and was appointed head of the "Department for Pre-History" with the Race and Settlement Office. Goodrick-Clarke writes, "His duties here appear to have consisted in committing examples of his ancestral memory to paper, discussing his family traditions with Himmler, and being generally available to comment on prehistoric subjects." [26]

What he expounded on for Himmler primarily concerned the glorification of Wiligut's own "Irminist" ancestors. He wrote that in 228,000 B.C. there were three suns. Air gods, water gods, giants and dwarves inhabited the earth. Wiligut's ancestors were those wise kings who had descended from the air and water gods. History proper began in 78,000 B.C. when Wiligut's ancestors restored peace to the world, inaugurated the "second Boso culture," and founded the city of Arual-Jöruvallas. Wiligut was also convinced that he personally was the victim of an age-old persecution against his tribe and their "Irminist" religion, perpetrated in modern times by the Catholic Church, the Jews, and Freemasonry.

Whether the pre-historical lore of occultists such as List, Lanz or Wiligut ever appealed to Hitler himself is a matter of dispute. Historians point out that Hitler was a practical man whose main pursuit was politics and who had little time or patience for metaphysical mumbo jumbo, no matter how racist. In *Mein Kampf*, Hitler denounced "*völkisch* wandering scholars" with their antiquarianism and ceremonies, as being ineffectual in the fight for Germany's salvation. However it's likely that early on, Hitler read Lanz's magazine *Ostara*. After the war, Lanz claimed that, in fact, Hitler had visited him at his *Ostara* office in 1909, seeking to buy back issues to complete his collection, and various official records corroborated details in Lanz's story. Though such literature probably influenced Hitler, *der Führer* never acknowledged the debt. And the final insult came in 1942, when the Gestapo suppressed Lanz's ONT.

Though there's only circumstantial evidence of a direct connection between the Ariosophists and the Nazis, their visions were uncannily similar. This vision provided a metaphysical basis for mass murder, which was combined with "racial hygiene," [27] its "scientific" basis.

AMERICA: CHRISTIAN IDENTITY AND NEO-NAZI ANTHROPOLOGY

"Neo-Nazi" is something of a misnomer when applied to current American white separatist and supremacist organizations. Their core ideologies, in fact, come from a long line of American fundamentalist beliefs. Their use of the word

"Aryan" and of the Swastika is only a European costume. At bottom such groups as the Aryan Nations and Church of the Creator are as American as the Ku Klux Klan.

As discussed earlier in this chapter, Anglo-Israelites, Identity Christians and Yahwists believe that Anglo-Saxons (or Whites or Aryans) descended directly from the Ten Lost Tribes of Israel, the chosen people of God, or Yahweh. They usually hold the Jewish people in contempt, as fraudulent pretenders to the title of "chosen people." Since they consider their own race as chosen, they see other races and nations as their natural enemies.

Early in this century, Anglo-Israelite preachers adopted and embellished the standard "Hamitic Curse" and "Negro a beast" arguments used in the past to justify slavery. The influential Anglo-Israelite Howard B. Rand's book, *In the Image of God*, was based directly on Carroll's *Negro a Beast*. During the 1940s and '50s, Anglo-Israelite William Lester Blessing, pastor of Denver's House of Prayer for All People, taught that members of the white race are the true Israelites, and that the Bible teaches white supremacy. In his 1952 book *White Supremacy*, Blessing argued that there were several creations—perhaps billions of years ago—prior to Genesis 1:2. Nonwhites were created on the sixth day; God rested on the seventh, and then created Adam and Eve. Moreover, Jesus was not a Jew but was "Pure White."

Christian Identity's "Two Seed Doctrine" is a newer variation on the pre-Adamite theme. It identifies the serpent in the Garden of Eden as Satan, who, rather than merely offering Eve some fruit, seduced her. Thus Cain was the child of Eve and Satan, while Abel was the child of Eve and Adam. The fraternal twins/half-brothers thus produced two "seedlines," the satanic sons of Cain, and the godly sons of Adam. Furthermore, Cain sullied his already satanic line by marrying a pre-Adamite. The "mongrelized" Jews are of the satanic seedline while the "Adamic" White Race is of the godly seedline, each in an eternal struggle against the other. Moreover, the Jews are engaged in a conspiracy to destroy the White Race, using Negroes (pre-Adamites) to help mongrelize it.

According to Christian Identity author Jeffrey A. Weakley, the Satanic Seed doctrine came to Christian Identity via San Jacinto Capt, Wesley A. Swift (founder of Aryan Nations) and William P. Gale. Capt and Swift, says Weakley, were members of the KKK, which is where they originally heard the Satanic Seed doctrine.

But where did the KKK get it? Weakley speculates that the KKK got it from the Freemasons (whom he associates with ancient Rosicrucians, unseemly Kabbalistic rites and Jewish conspiracies). I find it more likely that the Satanic Seedline doctrine is in fact a bowdlerized version of esoteric and Gnostic teachings, seen through the eyes of literal-minded conspiriologists such as Nesta Webster, who wrote:

> Thus in a book by the leader of [the Rosicrucians] we find it solemn-
> ly stated that according to Max Heindl, Eve cohabited with serpents
> in the garden of Eden, that Cain was the offspring of her union with
> "the Lucifer Samael," and that from this "divine progenitor" the most
> virile portion of the human race descended, the rest being merely the
> "progeny of human parents." [28]

Wherever they obtained it, the Christian Identity preachers twisted the two-seedline story's meaning to confirm their beliefs: Whites are God's Chosen People and God endorses hatred of Jews and Negroes. Though they agree on these basics, each Christian Identity preacher teaches his own version.

For example, KKK Grand Dragon Robert Miles of the Mountain Church of Jesus Christ in Michigan preached the following variation of the Two Seed Doctrine: God created white mankind as "the Adam" on the sixth day, but the false god Satanael created another Adam—a corrupted mixture of heaven and earth—on the eighth day. Cain was the offspring of Eve's coupling with one of Satanael's rebel angels. Genesis 6 is the story of the mating of the women of God's creation with God's angels, which produced the "North Folk." After the flood, the North Folk bred with the descendants of the Second Adam, produc-ing a mongrelized mix of good and evil. Thus racial purification is the moral duty of the white race.

Richard Butler's Christian Identity/Yahwist Church of Jesus Christ Christian (founded by Dr. Wesley Swift), better known as the Aryan Nations, holds to a more traditional Two-Seed Doctrine. Adam, they say, is the father of the White Race only; the twelve tribes of Israel became the "Anglo-Saxon, Germanic, Teutonic, Scandinavian, Celtic peoples of the earth." The natural enemies of Yahweh and the Israelites are Satan and his children, the descendants of Cain, better known as the Jews. "The Jew," they say in their statement of beliefs, "is like a destroying virus that attacks our racial body to destroy our Aryan culture and the purity of our Race," and they cite Scripture as proof. Because they are God's Chosen People, the Aryans' disobedience to "Divine Law" endangers the world. But soon there will be a day of reckoning, the usurper will be thrown out, and Christ's Kingdom will be established on Earth as Yahweh's people, the Aryans, fulfill their special destiny.

BEN KLASSEN, founder of Church of the Creator

While the Aryan Nations and other Christian Identity believers appeal to Divine Law, Ben Klassen of the Church of the Creator summarily rejects Judeo-Christian religion, appealing instead to "Natural Law." He concurs with the Yahwists that each human race is of a different species but doesn't need Scripture to prove it. His 1973 book, *Nature's Eternal Religion*, a raging catechism for the new faith, promises that its principles are "Based on the Eternal Laws of Nature, Based on the Experience of History," and "Based on Logic and Common Sense." Moreover, the book itself is "the most profound and meaningful religious book ever written for the survival of the White Race . . . the noblest creation in Nature's realm." The Church of the Creator, or "Creativity," is so-named for the "characteristic soul of the White Race."

The first chapters of the book concern what Klassen supposes to be the Laws of Nature, a segregationist reading of "survival of the fittest." To Klassen, species' don't merely attempt to survive; they have a "right" to survive. The highest Law of Nature, he writes, "is the right of any species to survival, expansion and advancement of its own kind." And, since to Klassen, the White Race is a species, its "right to survival, expansion and advancement of its own people is . . . the highest Law of Nature," which is threatened by "a flood-tide of colored mongrels." Of course, these mongrels as a species have a right to survival as well, but unlike the White Race, they are not the "pinnacle of [Nature's] creation . . . her most outstanding and most advanced species." Thus, it is up to the White Race to insure its own perfection and purity against pollution by inferior elements.

Appealing to nature, Klassen cites 87 species of kingfishers, 175 species of woodpeckers and 75 species of swallows who only mate "with their own kind." "If this were not so," Klassen warns:

> Then all the species would soon be mongrelized into one mixed-up species. Furthermore, the mongrelized swallow would soon breed with the 75 species of mongrelized larks and we would soon have a swallark. The mongrelized swallark would soon breed with the mongrelized cardinals and bluebirds and the whole process would degenerate into a mongrelized bird. The end result would soon be that birds would lose their own innate, peculiar characteristics that enabled them to survive all these thousands of years.[29]

Humanity, for some reason, has flouted the laws of Nature, and become mongrelized. "Much to our disgust and detriment," writes Klassen, "something unnatural like this has been going on amongst the human races in recent years. If it is not stopped, we, the White Race, will be paying a heavy price for our criminal perversion of Nature's laws."[30]

It's odd that Klassen, who claims to have earned both a B.A. and an Electrical Engineering degree, seems wholly innocent of the basics of biology. He doesn't seem to be aware that the swallow is *unable* to breed with the lark, and that that's what defines them as separate species. Nor does he ask how it is that something as fundamental as a "Natural Law" could be broken or perverted by mere mortals. To Klassen, Nature is not an impersonal machine, but more like a white man, "continually striving to upgrade, to improve, and to find a better breed, a better species, a better specimen."

Thus Klassen resurrects an early concept of evolution, whereby species don't merely survive, but improve, through time. He also revives the nineteenth century biological hierarchy with white humanity at the top.

Yet another white separatist organization, the Nordic Nations, relies on neither Divine nor Natural Law, and instead appeals to archeology and history. Their books *Our Nordic Race*, and *The History of the White Race*, both authored by "Odin" and excerpted on the Nordic Nations website, echo nineteenth century European notions about the Indo-Aryans, updated and simplified for late twentieth century American comprehension.

Odin contends that humankind came originally from neither Africa nor the Middle East, but from Northern Europe, about 40,000 years ago. He then attacks evolutionists for allegedly claiming that *Homo sapiens* evolved directly from *Homo erectus*, ignoring the fact that current paleo-anthropologists view *Homo erectus* as only a *possible* ancestor and that evolution itself does not hinge on this point. He mainly focuses, however, on the achievements throughout history of the tall, yellow-haired, blue-eyed Nordic Race, who supposedly were the authors of every great civilization and achievement in the history of the world. He even claims that the indigenous Japanese Ainu—who physically resemble Europeans—are "that society's highest class." In fact, the Ainu are treated the same as indigenous tribes everywhere, as savage outcasts who barely retain their right even to exist.

Odin's version of the Aryan Myth closely resembles mid-nineteenth century theories. He writes that the Indo-Aryans, who invaded India, Iran and Iraq, were Nordic sun-worshipping tribes who spoke Sanskrit or Sumerian. The words, "India," "Iran" and "Iraq," he states, "are all corruptions of the original word Aryan." The Egyptians, Babylonians and the Greeks as well, were originally tall, blond Nordic Aryans who built everything from the pyramids of Egypt to the first irrigation ditches. In fact, all invention and human achievement can be traced to the White Race, and all the great civilizations in history fell because of interbreeding with darker races. Even obviously non-white civilizations, such as the Chinese and Aztecs, are indebted to a handful of Aryans who got things going for the dumb natives. The downfall of these civilizations, says Odin, should be a lesson to us; if we let the Aryans become mongrelized now, Western Civilization will fall, just like the rest of them.

The so-called "Preadamite" races, according to ALEXANDER WINCHELL,
19th century professor of geology and paleontology at the University of Michigan.
(from *The Origin of Race and Civilization* by Weisman)

The Nordic Nation's message is no less than a wake-up call against the "rising tide of color," which is now destroying not only the purity of the White Race but Western Civilization itself. Ironically, Odin—a supposed super-creative Nordic Aryan—wasn't able come up with anything more original than a rehash of turn-of-the-century bigotry.

Antique anthropology texts provide a treasure trove to current white supremacists of all persuasions. Christian Identity writer Charles A. Weisman, who publishes his own books out of Burnsville, Minnesota, venerates the anthropologists of old such as Blumenbach, Prichard and many others. In *The Origin of Race and Civilization*, published in 1990, Weisman verifies his white supremacy with "science" (outdated anthropology texts), "Scripture" (Christian Identity doctrine), and "history" (the Aryan Myth). Moreover, his three sources, "history, science, and the Bible . . . are immutable." Therefore, "they cannot themselves be illogical, nor can there be any inconsistency between any of them or within any one of them." He claims that unlike evolutionism and creationism—both of which are wrong—his doctrine reconciles science and the Bible.

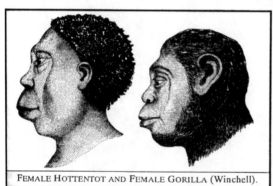

FEMALE HOTTENTOT AND FEMALE GORILLA (Winchell).

WINCHELL's comparison of Hottentot and gorilla, unearthed by WEISMAN (from *The Origin of Race* and *Civilization*)

Weisman is a pre-Adamite polygenist like many of the pre-Darwin anthropologists, and indeed, these men provide him with his scientific proof. He considers Neanderthals and Cro-Magnon men to be of the pre-Adamic creation and quotes an 1878 text comparing the Cro-Magnon with the Negro to prove that "many races living today are descended from these Cro-Magnon people," whereas the white, fully human, Adamic race was created separately. Weisman concludes: "God did not create one generalized 'kind' from which all races are derived, as claimed by creationists regarding Adam. *Neanderthals* were a distinct creation as were Hottentots and Eskimos." Weisman identifies the six separate human species as follows:

1. *Homo europaeus:* Europeans—"This species has the highest facial angle with high forehead. They are active, ingenious and adventurous."

2. *Homo hyperboreus:* Arctic peoples, Eskimos.

3. *Homo columbicus:* American Indians.

4. *Homo afer:* Negroes of central Africa—"The eye often has a

yellowish sclerotic coat over it like that of a gorilla. . . . The ears are roundish, rather small, standing somewhat high and detached thus approaching the simian form. . . . The three curvatures or the spine are less pronounced in the Negro than in the white and thus more characteristic of an ape. . . . The two bones proper of the nose are occasionally united as in apes."

5. *Homo hottentotus:* South African tribes.

6. *Homo australasicus:* Australian aborigines.

Adam "was of the White Race." Therefore, the Bible, which is a chronicle of Adam's lineage, history and destiny, is about the white race only. Weisman backs this up with the "blood in the face" argument: "The name 'Adam' (*aw-dawm*) in Hebrew means a 'ruddy human being' . . . which means '*to show blood* (in the face), i.e. *flush* or turn rosy.' Only the white race has the characteristic of blushing or showing blood in the face or skin."[31] Adam's descendants as well were described variously as "ruddy, and of fair countenance" (King David), "fair" (David's daughter), "very fair" (Sarah and Rebekah), and "exceedingly fair" (Moses). The reason God created Adam as white, says Weisman, was because white symbolizes purity, holiness, cleanliness, eternity, wisdom and right-eousness, while black repre-sents disaster, mourning, suf-fering, evil, wickedness and

Representation of facial angles of different species of man showing the more acute angle in the more primitive species.

CHARLES A. WEISMAN resurrects the methods of 19th century anthropology
(from *The Origin of Race* and *Civilization*)

corruption. God Himself is also white, since he created Adam in his own image.

Weisman also points out that hybrids are a no-no in Nature, because they are sterile or weak. Therefore, crossing Anglo-Saxons with Negroes, for example, is a big mistake. Moreover, it's a sin against God, who in Leviticus 19:19 commanded: "You shall keep my statutes. Thou shall not let thy cattle gender with a diverse kind: thou shalt not sow thy field with mingled seed." Hence, "God has provided in nature factors that inhibits hybrids and a command to man not to induce them." God wasn't just talking about cattle, though. He also insisted that his cho-sen people remain racially pure. When God commanded the Israelites to refrain from marrying, and to smite and cast out Hittites, Amorites and Canaanites, he was talking about races, not nations. Furthermore, in Acts, God expresses his desire to segregate the races, by commanding his people to "separate" from the

Wzur okladki do broszury „W szponach komunizmu".

Po Rosji i Hiszpanji — kolej na Polskę! Trzeba
skąpać we krwi! Zostawić po niej ruiny i zgliszcza! Ży
już wiedzie kostuchę na żniwo do Polski! Baczmy na to
pochód i czuwajmy, bo gorze nam! Gorze!!L...

Nakl. „Samaobrona Narodu" Poznań   Drukarnia Centralna Poznań

A cartoon from a Polish brochure of the thirties, *In The Grip of Communism*. The Jew leads Death to his harvest in Poland, whose fate, according to the caption, will be worse than that of Russia and Spain.

A view of the Jews shared by Polish anti-Semites during the 1930s and current American author CHARLES WEISMAN (from *Who Is Esau-Edom?*)

WHO IS ESAU-EDOM?

By Charles A. Weisman

others. "Thus, segregation," writes Weisman, "is a divinely ordained precept." Moreover, "Christ's parable of the tares and the wheat (Matt. 13:24–30) is actually a parable of segregation."

Though he doesn't invoke the Two-Seed Doctrine, Weisman identifies today's Jews as mongrels who have been bent on the destruction of pure white Christians since biblical times:

> We should now begin to realize why the concepts of racial purity and segregation are attacked and downgraded by the anti-Christian Jews who control much of the media and government. The Jews themselves are mongrels and seem to represent, either racially or figuratively, many of the cursed and rejected individuals in the Bible.[32]

In another book, *Who Is Esau-Edom?* (1991), Weisman specifically identifies the Jews as descendants of Esau, first born of Isaac. Esau was white, but he disobeyed God by marrying pre-Adamites. His mongrelized descendants were converted to Judaism, and lived in the land of Edom. Later, they became the Asiatic Khazars and eventually modern-day Jewry. According to Bible prophecy, in the End-Times the Edomite-Khazarite-Jews will become the enemy of the true Israelites.

Today, the Jews (Esau-Edom) represent anti-Christianism, Communism, bloodshed, sin, Satan, the beast of the apocalypse and banking. Weisman proves this by pointing out that the Hebrew words Esau and Edom mean "red." Thus:

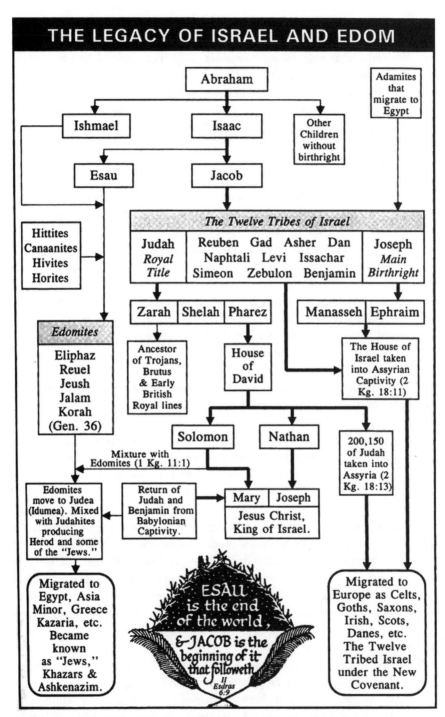

THE LEGACY OF ISRAEL AND EDOM

Bloodlines of the Jews versus the true Israelites, according to
Christian Identity author CHARLES WEISMAN (from *Who Is Esau-Edom?*)

The banking industry, which is a part of red Babylon's economic control over Christendom, is led by the Jewish banking family of Rothschild, which *means "red shield. . . ."* The color of Jewish-Communism is red as indicated by such terms as red nation, red star, "Red Square," etc. The Russian Revolution that brought about "Red Communism" was planned and financed by Jews, and "the revolutionary leaders nearly all belonged to the Jewish race." [33]

Weisman's conclusion:

[The Jews are] the rejected and cursed of Judah, mixed with the cursed lineage of Esau, along with other peoples, and that cursed lineage compels them to act the way they do. Their fruit identifies who they are and who they are not, just as their odd and unpleasant facial features attest to their hybridity (which is also a curse placed upon the Jew). . . .

As mongrels or hybrids, the Jews do have some biological roots extending back to Abraham and the Judah people. But as mongrels, they can never possess the birthright or claim true heritage of the original or pure Adamic race. [34]

While Jews are mongrels, represented in Scripture as a cursed people, the pre-Adamic races don't even rate as villains:

These matters of Scripture do not pertain to the pre-Adamic races. The Negro, Oriental and Tasmanian were not made in the image of God, were not written in the Book of Life, and will never be resurrected. [35]

Weisman, like his predecessors and compatriots in white supremacy, bends the Bible, history, science and whatever is needed, in order to conform to his bigotry. Each writer's version is just a little different, depending on their religious quirks and which ethnic group they hate most, even though they are all supposedly based on the same data. What they have in common, however, is testament to the powerful influence of the Aryan Myth and fundamentalism on garden-variety bigotry.

RACIST CONSPIRIOLOGY

Some racist anthropology seems quaintly anachronistic rather than dangerous. But add a dose of conspiracy theory to otherwise laughable racial assumptions, and you get a poisonous brew of vicious ideology. Eustace Mullins has been writing on conspiracies of all kinds since the 1950s, producing such titles as *Secrets of the Federal Reserve, Murder by Injection, The New World Order* and

The Rape of Justice. His many books and conspiracy theories are tied together by his belief that an anti-white, satanic, secular humanist conspiracy drives all the others.

Mullins considers himself the protegé of Ezra Pound, whom he first met when the poet was incarcerated at St. Elizabeths Hospital. In an interview with Tom Valentine on the shortwave program "Radio Free America," Mullins recounted that Pound lectured him on world history every day for three years, during hospital visits. On one of these visits, Pound suggested that Mullins take a trip to the Library of Congress to find out what he could about the Federal Reserve System. Mullins took the advice, and he's still taking it 50 years later. Pound had opened Mullins' eyes to the truth about the Federal Reserve and all the other conspiracies in our midst.

Later, after Mullins began to study the Bible, he tied all the conspiracies together, concluding that "All con-spiracies are Satanic!" His 1987 title, *The Curse of Canaan: A Demonology of History*, exposes the giant conspiracy behind all the others, perpetrated by the lit-eral children of Satan, whom he identifies as secular humanists, Freemasons, communists, homosexuals, Jews, and the dark-skinned races of the world.

Mullins adopts a pre-Adamite anthropology and a variation of the Two-Seed Doctrine to explain the exis-tence of the Satanic race. "Pre-Adamic [man]" he states, is a "hybrid creature whose origins are described in ancient books," such as the *Book of Enoch*. According to Mullins, these texts are treatises on the continuing struggle between the Satanic, dusky, secular humanists and the people of God.

The Curse of Canaan by EUSTACE MULLINS: the Bible as racist treatise

As described in the *Book of Enoch*, Satan and 200 angels married the daugh-ters of men and became the fallen angels, or the Watchers. The children of that union were a race of giants, the Nephilim. These horrible mutants had abom-inable habits. They murdered and ate one another, introducing cannibalism to the world. They also practiced sodomy, inaugurating the first "unusual lifestyles" in history. One of these demons, who goes by the name Lilith, Mullins identifies as the "patron goddess of the lesbians." God punished the Nephilim by slaugh-tering some and imprisoning others inside the earth, but many of them also sur-vived on the surface. More recently, God has been smiting them with AIDS, just the latest skirmish in a millennia-old war. "The history of mankind since [Satan's] rebellion," writes Mullins, "is the history of the struggle between the people of God and the Cult of Satan."

Noah's flood, in fact, was an attempt by God to flush the dark pre-Adamites from the earth, once and for all. But the plan backfired due to the disobedience of Noah's second son, Ham, who copulated with a pre-Adamite named Naamah, on the Ark. Noah was greatly distressed by Ham's disobedience, and this is why he drank too much wine and lay naked, exposing himself to Canaan, son of Ham and Naamah. When Noah awoke, he realized that Canaan—since he had pre-Adamite blood—might have committed sodomy with him, while he was drunk and naked. So he cursed him, declaring that he would be a slave to his brothers. Subsequently, the Canaanites became "the greatest curse upon humanity" even to this day. "Not only did they originate the practices of demon-worship, occult rites, child sacrifice, and cannibalism," claims Mullins, "but as they went abroad, they brought these obscene practices into every land which they entered."

Since Canaan's mother was "dark-skinned," so was Canaan. But Mullins isn't explicit on this point, perhaps preferring to let the readers come to their own conclusions. He instead emphasizes that Cush, another son of Ham and Naamah, was black and founded the land of Ethiopia. Mullins points out that Cush's blackness was punishment for Ham's intercourse on the Ark. And the black Cushites, notes Mullins, were demon worshippers, just like their cousins, the Canaanites. In fact, it seems as if the Cushites are as bad as, or even worse than the Canaanites, despite the title of the book, *The Curse of Canaan*. Specifically, Cush's son Nimrod "stands unequal for his symbolism of evil and Satanic practices." Mullins reports that he not only built the Tower of Babel, but also founded Freemasonry.

> The legendary symbol for Nimrod is "X." The use of this symbol always denotes witchcraft. When "X" is used as a shortened form meaning Christmas, it actually means "to celebrate the feast of Nimrod." [Nimrod was born on December 25, "the high Sabbath of Babylon."] A double X, which has always meant to double-cross or betray, in its fundamental meaning indicates one's betrayal into the hands of Satan. When American corporations use the "X" in their logo, such as "Exxon," the historic Rockefeller firm of Standard Oil of New Jersey, there can be little doubt of this hidden meaning.
>
> Nimrod also introduced the practice of genocide to the world. . . . Throughout the ensuing centuries, the fair-skinned descendants of Shem, Noah's oldest son, have ritually been slaughtered by the darker descendants of Ham and Nimrod, in the world's most persistent campaign of racial and religious persecution.
>
> Not only did Nimrod kill and eat the fair-skinned descendants of Shem, in his fury and hatred he often burned them alive. The type of human sacrifice involving the eating of the slaughtered human victims derived its name from the combined names of his uncle, Canaan, and the demon god Baal, the two names being combined to form the word "cannibal." [36]

Mullins states proudly that Noah's first son Shem, whose descendants, the "Semites," were white and virtuous, founded Egyptian civilization, built the pyramids, and exemplified all the godly attributes of mankind. Hence those whom we usually think of as "Semites"—Arabs and Jews—are not Semites at all, but evil Canaanites. The "true Semites" says Mullins "are the fair-haired warriors who built one great civilization after another." They are also those who "remain true to Christ." The true Semites today are "often fair-haired, fair-skinned, predominantly blue-eyed, healthy, creative, productive, proud, disdaining to engage in any dishonest activity, and always fiercely individualistic."

The Canaanites, on the other hand, "are generally shorter, darker, more furtive, and almost always engaged in some type of criminal activity, usually with special government approval or license. . . . They are also frequently involved in some sort of extracurricular sexual activity, which can be traced directly back to the orgies of Baal, human sacrifice, and obscene sexual rites. . . . In their communities, they are often found to be leaders in activities advertised as 'compassionate' and 'caring'; they are often found in government offices, in the media, and in the educational institutions."

The victimized people of Shem "have no idea what is going on," and it's time to wake up. "Now time grows short," pleads Mullins. "History will not allow the people of Shem additional centuries, or even decades, to come to their senses and realize what is going on. Just as they have been victims of massacre and genocide for centuries, the people of Shem now face the determination of the Canaanites to exterminate them utterly and finally, a goal which they hope to achieve by the end of this millennium."

It seems the Aryans (a word Mullins is careful not to use) have come full circle, and acquired a biblical heritage. Though he may not realize or admit it, Mullins is in essential agreement with Aryan Nations and Christian Identity; the only difference is in terminology and details of the great white lineage.

Part IV—Black Supremacy

During the twentieth century, African-Americans devised their own racist anthropologies. Since they share the cultural heritage of white Europeans—especially the Bible—many black supremacist anthropologies closely resemble their white counterparts. In some cases they are identical, and only the names have changed. In other cases, they are turned upside-down or inside out. And in the strangest inversions, the story is the same, the names are the same, but only the moral interpretation is reversed. Black Messiah sects originally developed these creation stories to provide themselves with a superior black identity or heritage. More recently, ideas embodied in those stories have taken on a life of their own, becoming the jumping off point for Afrocentric studies: theories of history, anthropology, and even biology, that place Africa,

Africans, and black-hued skin squarely in the center of Western and world civilization.

BLACK MUSLIMS

Elijah Muhammad, who led the Nation of Islam for over 30 years, can be credited for popularizing the epithets "blue-eyed devils" and "white devils."[37] It's easy to mistake these for ordinary racial slurs, but Elijah Muhammad meant them literally. He taught that black people are descended from the original human race, the godly "tribe of Shabazz," while whites are an inferior race of devils created artificially by an evil scientist named Yakub. The full story can be found in his *Message to the Blackman in America*, first published in 1965 and which remains a central text for Black Muslims to this day.

Elijah Muhammad claimed that his story of human origins came straight from Allah himself. Muhammad's story of "Yakub" and his selective breeding of the white race, however, is apparently lifted directly from the biblical story of Jacob and his selective breeding of livestock, in Genesis 30:32–43. The resemblance is uncanny. But in order to transform the Bible story into something a bit more Muslim, Muhammad had to make a few essential changes. The result is a bizarre science fiction tale which begins 66 trillion years ago, elevates black people to semi-divine status, and vilifies whites as the nasty spawn of an evil experiment in genetic engineering.

The "original man," Elijah Muhammad used to say, "is the black man . . . The black man is the first and last, maker and owner of the universe." But 66 trillion years ago, God, whom Muhammad identifies as "one of our scientists," attempted to get everyone to speak one language but failed, so "he decided to kill us by destroying our planet." He caused a great explosion that divided the planet into the earth and the moon. One tribe—the tribe of Shabazz—survived. They were "lucky to be on this part, Earth," writes Muhammad, "which did not lose its water in the mighty blasting away of the part called Moon."

Since they were the first people on Earth, the tribe of Shabazz "were the first to discover the best part of our planet to live on, the rich Nile Valley of Egypt and the present seat of the Holy City, Mecca, Arabia." Kinky hair, however, didn't come with the original tribe; it was created by "one of our dissatisfied scientists, 50,000 years ago, who wanted to make all of us tough and hard in order to endure the life of the jungles of East Asia (Africa) and to overcome the beasts there."

The scientist Yakub changed civilization by producing "a new race of people who would rule the original black nation for 6,000 years." "He learned," wrote

Elijah Muhammad, "from studying the germ of the black man, under the microscope, that there were two people in him, and that one was black, the other brown. He said if he could successfully separate the one from the other he could graft the brown germ into its last stage, which would be white." He realized that he had the knowledge to create a white race that could "rule the black nation for a time." He won converts to this plan by promising them that they could get others to do their work for them. "Naturally," writes Muhammad, "there are always some people around who would like to have others do their work. Those are the ones who fell for Mr. Yakub's teaching, 100 percent." Yakub was arrested and then exiled with 59,999 followers to the island of Patmos on the Aegean Sea. This is where the white race was created through selective breeding and infanticide.

On Yakub's island, whenever two "real black ones" wished to marry, they were told they would have to find other mates. But marriages between those who were less black and more brown were encouraged. If a black baby was born, the nurses were ordered to kill it, but if a brown baby emerged, the nurses would "make much ado over it," telling the mother that it would have a bright future. Thus Yakub and his people created the brown race from the black, in just 200 years. And in another 200 years, using the same method, they created the red-yellow race, and just 200 years after that, the white. The end result after this 600 years of selective breeding was that "the Yakub made devils were really pale white, with really blue eyes; which we think are the ugliest of colors for a human eye. They were all Caucasian—which means, according to some of the Arab scholars, 'One whose evil effect is not confined to one's self alone, but affects others.'"

The white devils were immediately exiled to the hills and caves of "West Asia," better known as Europe. Their level of intelligence was abominably low, and they had to start from scratch:

> They were without anything to start civilization and became savages. They remained in such condition for 2,000 years—no guide or literature.
>
> They lost all knowledge of civilization. The Lord, God of Islam, taught me that some of them tried to graft themselves back into the black nation, but they had nothing to go by. A few were lucky enough to make a start, and got as far as what you call the gorilla. In fact, all of the monkey family are from this 2,000 year history of the white race in Europe. . . . [38]

It then took another 2,000 years for the ape-like whites to create a civilization and to conquer the darker races. But in the end, they remained inferior, morally and intellectually, to the original black man:

[The whites] are in the image and likeness of a human being (black man), but are altogether a different kind of human being than that of the black human beings. . . .

Black people have a heart of gold, love and mercy. Such a heart, nature did not give to the white race. This is where the so-called Negroes are deceived in this devil race. They think they have the same kind of heart; but the white race knows better. They have kept it as a secret among themselves, that they may be able to deceive the black people.[39]

The mission of the Nation of Islam, says Elijah Muhammad, is to wake the black man up to the truth of his identity as "the original man," and to end the rule of the white devils. Thus, his strange tale of ancient scientists "grafting" the white race from the black is essential to the Nation of Islam worldview.

While Elijah Muhammad's tale of racial origins inevitably borrows here and there from white supremacist ideas, another Black Muslim leader, Issa Muhammad, lifts many such ideas verbatim. Issa has a long history as leader of various Black Muslim sects, which have gone by a succession of names and theologies.[40] His treatise on race, *The Paleman*, is uncannily similar to Christian Identity and white supremacist literature; only the names have changed. In fact, *The Paleman* is almost a mirror image of Eustace Mullins' *The Curse of Canaan*. Like Mullins, Issa reinterprets the tale of Noah's drunkenness and the curse on his grandson Canaan to his own ends. And, both Issa and Mullins agree on at least one point: Jews are satanic.

Pale skin is caused by the biblical curse of leprosy says Nubian Islamic Hebrew Mission founder Issa Muhammad

Like Elijah Muhammad, Issa maintains that the original people of the earth were black. He writes, "The Prophet Adam was created of black mud and his progeny were also Nubian (Black)." Like Christian Identity preachers, Issa interprets biblical genealogy as racial genealogy:

The Nubian (Black) man is Asiatic through the Apostle Noah. The Apostle Noah lived in Asia and moved his family into Sudan the land of two blacks. The Greeks and Romans were responsible for changing its name to Africa. . . . His sons Shem, Ham and Japheth fathered the tribes throughout the land of Nubia. There are also Asiatic Pale men (the descendants of Canaan) who lived in the caves of Asia, and Asiatic Red man (red and yellow races of the Orientals, called Edomites) who descended from Esau the twin brother of Jacob.[41]

The full story of the white race began, says Issa, when the Devil appeared as a snake in the Garden of Eden. "This was a sign from the Almighty for you to reflect on and realize that these Canaanites (Pale race), like reptiles, who also shed (lose) skin and peel easily are as I've stated, mutants." The story continues after the flood, when Noah got drunk and went to sleep naked. Noah's son Ham had been arguing with his wife and became possessed by the Devil. When he entered Noah's tent he mocked his nakedness and looked at him with the thought of sodomy; through him 200 fallen angels were able to return to Earth. Hence Allah cursed Ham's fourth son Canaan with leprosy; this caused him to be born as an albino, becoming the first "Paleman."

The story continues:

> Because Canaan was an albino, he lacked the normal eye coloring which caused his eyes to weaken and become sensitive to direct and indirect sunlight. So Canaan took his sister Salhah (who was Nubian) and sought refuge in the mountains, where the light was dim. The cold climate of the mountains was also conducive to their leprous condition because it stopped the leprosy from spreading. Canaan's descendants were the original cavemen.

Issa continues the story of the Canaanites, whom he also calls "Amorites":

> When they fled to the mountains, Canaan and his wife began reproducing and remained there for 309 years, with their progeny, while no one knew that they existed. . . .
>
> Many inscriptions have been found in the caves of Europe. At the time of the Exodus of the Israelites, these people inhabited the land of Canaan. Before this, several hundred years had passed during which time the families of the Amorites had experienced several states of advancement to the point where they could be considered civilized. They had to be raised from the degenerate, diseased state that they were in, in the mountains and caves. In time, they descended to the level of animals, eating raw carcasses, walking on all fours and mingling freely with the animals, mainly dog-like animals.
>
> Once the salts in their bodies reached a dangerous low, they lost their ability to reproduce. It was at this point that the lepers went down from the mountains, kidnapped and raped clean Nubian women. The mixture produced an offspring with black skin and straight, black hair.

Issa's version of de-evolution applies only to the Canaanites:

> The lepers that did not mix (predominately the women) were pushed further back up into the mountains and fell so low as to mate with the dog-like animals. The result of this mixture were ape-like animals. They had sexual intercourse with the jackal (the original dog) and through this intercourse the offspring that was brought forth was an ape-like man. They loved the dog so much that they turned his name around to worship it, DOG = GOD. The phrase, "A Dog is Man's Best Friend" came out of this situation. The dog would lick the festered sores of the leper and clean the sores for them.
>
> Even to this day it's a common belief that if a dog licks your sores, it will make it better. This is where venereal disease came from. The curse (leprosy) caused many of the lepers and their ape-like offspring to die, leaving their rotten flesh to pollute the area with still more disease (since these creatures had no knowledge of embalming or burying).

Issa goes on to say that the Canaanites finally left the mountains in 3691 B.C., for Germany; these were the original Neanderthals. And, those who ended up in southern Europe and Central Asia were the Cro-Magnons. He doesn't seem to be aware that his dates for these early humans are off by about 30,000 years.

Issa takes his racial interpretation of the Bible even further, by reading the story of Abraham's son Esau as the origin of the "Mongoloids." (White supremacist Charles A. Weisman used the same story for the origin of the Jews.)

SONS OF CANAAN

- They Dwelled In The Dark Caves Of The Caucasus Mountains.
- They Walked On All Fours And Ate Raw Flesh.
- They Were An Abomination, Laying With Dogs And Contracting Diseases.

WHO WERE THESE LOATHSOME BEINGS AND WHO ARE THEIR DESCENDANTS TODAY?

The descendants of Canaan were pale-skinned brutes according to ISSA MUHAMMAD (from *The Paleman*)

Abraham had forbidden the mixing of his seed with the Canaanites, but his son Esau disobeyed and married a Canaanite. The result was that Esau became the father of a new cursed race, the Edomites. Japanese, Koreans, Eskimos and Indonesians are their descendants. When blacks intermarried with the Edomites, they became the American Indians. The "slanted eyes" of all these people are a mark of Allah's curse. "When

Allah places a curse on someone," explains Issa, "it appears in the genes of man." Like the Canaanites, who were cursed with leprosy, the Edomites were cursed with mongolism, or Down's syndrome:

> One clear example of the curse placed on Esau by Allah is the disease known as "Mongolism" (Down's Syndrome). Now ask yourself why is it that any mongoloid or retarded child born to any race always has the same appearance, they look Asian. They are always born with slanted eyes, broad heads, large tongues, no matter what race their parents are from. How can this be possible? The answer is very simple. As we previously stated, when Allah places a curse on a people, He places the curse in their genes.

The Bible, cited by mainstream Christians for its message of brotherly love, provides white and black supremacists with as many justifications for their racial views as they need.

AFROCENTRISM: ICE PEOPLE AND SUN PEOPLE

Afrocentric scholarship began as a way to correct the Eurocentric bias of Western scholarship, but has instead replaced a white bias with a black one. With its current emphasis on melanin and the dichotomy between "Ice People" and "Sun People" it simply parrots the biological determinism of nineteenth century white racism. The Afrocentric extremists don't yet claim that there's a "curse" on white genes, but they do claim that whites are at a spiritual disadvantage solely because of their genetic heritage, which amounts to the same thing. Their methods might be more sophisticated than the revelations of Elijah Muhammad, but their conclusions are the same.

Afrocentrists assume that because of their racism, western scholars haven't given credit to the contributions of non-white peoples, especially black Africans, to Western civilization. They also assume an exaggerated black African contribution to Western civilization. Thus, the Afrocentric historians seek to uncover the truths about the African origins of Western civilization that have been concealed by white scholars for generations. They conclude that

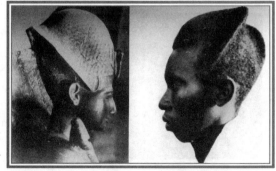

Pharaoh Ramses II and a Modern Watusi. CHEIKH ANTA DIOP writes: "The Watusi hair-do can be conceived only for woolly hair. The small circles on the Pharoah's helmet represent frizzy hair." (from *The African Origin of Civilization: Myth or Reality*)

though it may be intellectually and technologically advanced, Western civilization is, at bottom, morally bankrupt. Thus Afrocentrists claim credit for Western civilization in one breath and vilify it in the next.

Cheikh Anta Diop (1923–1986), born in Diourbel, Senegal, was one of the first to suggest that Africa played a central part in the history of civilization, though he never claimed racial superiority of blacks. Diop, a man of letters, is a major hero for Afrocentrists. He argued, beginning in the 1950s, that Egypt was the center of Africa's culture and language, that Egypt received its main influence from central Africa and that blacks created Egyptian civilization. Hence, blacks were responsible for one of the most ancient, highly developed and influential civilizations in the world. Diop also developed a chemical process to test the melanin content of the skin of Egyptian mummies in order to establish their black ancestry. But, as he was unable to complete his research, the results were inconclusive.

Another early Afrocentrist was George G.M. James, author of the 1954 book *Stolen Legacy*, popular among some African-Americans. James, through specious logic and questionable scholarship, argued that the Greeks, who "did not possess the native ability essential to the development of philosophy," stole Greek philosophy from the black Egyptians. He claimed that the Greek philosophers had studied the "Egyptian Mystery System" in Egypt with Egyptian priests and then turned around and plagiarized their philosophy. Greek scholar Mary Lefkowitz notes that what James identifies as the "Egyptian" Mystery system is, in fact, a product of eighteenth century French neo-Platonism, which used some Egyptian elements. Thus, what James thought the Greeks stole from Egyptians didn't even exist until two millennia later and was itself based on Greek philosophy.[42]

Leonard Jeffries, notorious professor at the City College of New York, is responsible for popularizing Afrocentrism and the Sun People/Ice People thesis. Jeffries and others developed the theme that black "Sun People"—because melanin allows them "to negotiate the vibrations of the universe"—are cooperative, collective and peaceful, while non-black "Ice People" are competitive, individualist and

exploitative. Wasn't that the same thing the nineteenth century Europeans were saying about the Aryans and the non-Aryans, or the Narrow-heads and the Round-heads? For the Afrocentrists, the values are reversed. Whereas white racists see "competitive" and "individualistic" as good qualities and "passivity" as bad, for black racists it's the reverse: passivity or "cooperation" is good, while competitiveness, or "exploitativeness" is bad.

Psychiatrist Frances Cress Welsing goes even further. She believes that whites are not only genetically programmed to be competitive or individualistic, but also *genocidal* towards non-whites. In 1969 she developed the

"Cress Theory of Color-Confrontation," the thesis that the "recessive" whites have maintained a "global white supremacy system" to prevent "white genetic annihilation" by "genetically dominant" non-whites.[43] In her 1991 book, *The Isis Papers: The Keys to the Colors*, she reduces all global problems to the white fear of genetic annihilation. Even the Nazi destruction of the European Jews during World War II—which would appear to be the genocide of one white people by another—stems from global white supremacy. According to Welsing, the Semitic Jews are non-white mulattos. The word "Semite," she says, is

from the Latin prefix "semi," which means "half." Thus the word "Semite" means half black, half white. She ignores the well-known derivation of "Semite" from the Hebrew "Shem," son of Noah.

Welsing uses the Cress Theory as a reductionist tool for reading all artifacts of Western civilization as symbols of the whites' fear of genetic annihilation. The Washington Monument is a symbol for white male genitals that tower over a city of non-whites. The Christian cross symbolizes black male genitals—castrated:

> I submit that the cross, as an important and provocative symbol in the white supremacy system/culture, is none other than a brain-computer distillate of the white collective's fear-induced obsession with the genitals of all non-white men (of Black men in particular), who have the potential to genetically annihilate the white race. Furthermore, the cross represents the Black male's genitals removed from the Black male's body—meaning castrated genitals. Thus the cross is a critical symbol in the thought processes of the white supremacy system, beginning its evolution almost 2,000 years ago during early white aggression against Blacks in Africa and Asia.[44]

The best-selling book, *The Exorcist*, and the movie of the same name, says Welsing, are also rife with racial symbolism:

> The [white] female used the cross to masturbate herself when she was possessed by the devil (i.e., the black monster). This symbolic portrayal emerged during a time period in which increasing numbers of white females were selecting Black males as "mates" or, more correctly stated, white females began sexually aggressing against socially powerless Black males to gain possession of the Black phallus.

Even *King Kong* expresses the desire the white female has for the black male, as represented by a giant black ape, who is slaughtered in the end. Welsing also reads racial symbolism in the prevalence of white female scientists such as Jane Goodall and Dian Fossey, who have lived among apes:

> Some of these white females actually have attempted to get very, very close to these great black apes so that they can touch the apes and, perhaps unconsciously, so that the great black apes can touch them!

This is presumably caused by their forbidden desire for black genes that would impart dark pigmentation to their children.

Welsing identifies the whites' drive for dominance as a "reaction-formation." In other words, it stems from a deep sense of inferiority. She goes a step further, straying from Freudian analysis, to claim that the whites feel inferior because they *are* inferior. They lack melanin, the chemical that could turn their pale skin dark. Because most people in the world "are not so afflicted" with a lack of melanin, this is an "abnormal" condition. Furthermore, whites' lack of melanin is "the neurochemical basis of evil":

> [The absence of melanin] critically impairs the depth sensitivity of the nervous system and the ability to tune in to the total spectrum of energy frequencies in the universe. This deficiency of sensory aware-ness sets the stage for the absence of harmony (the chaos and destruc-tion), which is evil. . . . White supremacy is the greatest known evil on Earth. Likewise, racism (white supremacy) is the unified force field that encompasses all of the lesser evils we now recognize.

In contrast, those with high concentration of melanin are more sensitive, have more rhythm, and are more religious. They have a "sixth sense" for the unseen energy currents around them and possess "soul." Hence, the dark pigmentation of the African-American scientist George Washington Carver (who studied peanuts) enabled him to "communicate with the energy frequencies emanating from plants [and to] learn their secrets and purposes."

Polymer chemist Carol Barnes, author of the 1988 book, *Melanin: The Chemical Key to Black Greatness*, concurs that it is melanin itself that is directly responsible for behavior. He argues that the "expressive, flamboyant and cocky" behavior of blacks is caused by melanin. Melanin, he asserts, is made up of gran-ules that are "Central Computers" that analyze and initiate bodily reactions. Moreover, melanin is responsible for the existence of civilization, religion, truth, justice and righteousness.

Another psychiatrist, Richard King, is author of *The African Origin of Biological Psychiatry* (1990), which argues that early African scientists were experts in brain functioning and consciousness. King considers melanin to be ". . . the black seed of all humanity, archetype of humanity, the hidden doorway to the collective unconscious-darkness, the shadow, primeval ocean, chaos, the womb, doorway of life." Furthermore, "the chemical key to life and the brain itself was found to be centered around black neuromelanin." King adopts the "ancient African concept" that the locus coeruleus in the brain "is a Black Dot doorway to the collective unconscious."

For extreme Afrocentrists, melanin imparts more than just pigment; it is, for them, the biological key to the black soul.

T. Owens Moore defends the study of melanin in his 1995 book, *The Science of Melanin: Dispelling the Myths*. A professor of psychology (his Ph.D. is in physiological psychology), Moore has been studying melanin since 1987. His book is an attempt to separate the wheat from the chaff in melanin research by criticizing the theories of his predecessors and then offering some of his own. His summaries and criticisms of the melanin scholars are helpful, but his skepticism is only skin-deep.

Moore's own theories seem to be based on a combination of popular prejudices, Afrocentrism, New Age metaphysics, and a fallacious understanding of evolution. He repeats the Sun People/Ice People thesis: "Nonwhite people are generally believed to be more in tune with nature by living in peace and harmony with the world and its inhabitants (leading to spiritualism). White people, however, have generally been more inclined to control and dominate nature (leading to materialism)." This is because: "Some people have evolved from cold and resource-limited environments, whereas others have evolved from tropical and resource-plentiful environments. Depending on the environment, one can develop thought patterns centered around materialism or spiritualism." And it's all because of melanin, "the molecule, both in the human body and in the universe, which acts as a conduit between the visible (material) and the unseen (spiritual) world. . . . There is an intricate connection between the material-spiritual planes, and the melanin in the skin and nervous system helps to provide metaphysical experiences."

Kinky hair, as well, helps those of black African descent tune into the universe:

> African people naturally have kinky or wiry hair. Non-African people have matted or animal-like hair. In other words, kinky or wire-like hair is an evolutionary advance since very few animals (sheep, buffalo, yak etc.) have hair similar to African people. Kinky or wire-like hair is constructed like an antenna to absorb more readily those naturally occurring electromagnetic waves in nature. The "conscious waves" we mentioned earlier are also more attracted to kinky or wire-like hair. Matted or animal-like hair may generate electricity in the

form of static; however, it is matted and limits the conversion of radiant energy into other forms of energy.[45]

And the reason that the "dark matter" in the universe confounds the white scientists is because it is, in fact, melanin:

> In sum, the special bioelectric properties of melanin are critical for the energy that is constantly transmitted to and from outer space. It is this dark matter (melanin) that maximizes the connection of melinated human bodies to the spirit of the universe. Through the elaborate world of electromagnetism, our skin and nervous system link our internal melanin to the cosmic melanin to allow us to tune in with cosmic nature.

And finally:

> Melanin in the surface of the skin, in the internal organs and the nervous system, can enhance a person's connection to the spiritual world and act as a battery charger for the chakra system.

Though most Afrocentric scholars are, as you might expect, black, Michael Bradley, author of such Afrocentric titles as *The Iceman Inheritance* (1978) and *Dawn Voyage: The Black Discovery of America* (1981), is white. He claims, however, to be a descendant of the first non-white postmaster general, Andrew Jackson Hunt, and a distant relative of Sequoia, the Cherokee Indian chief. Born in Talladega, Alabama in 1944, Bradley has been a freelance writer with a social conscience since the late 1960s. In addition to writing books, Bradley has written radio, television and movie scripts and has been a columnist and feature writer for Canadian papers. He also taught African History at Dalhousie University in Canada. He is one of those few journalists who is sincerely dedicated to incorporating "genuine moral and uplifting messages" into all his work.

MICHAEL BRADLEY, author of *The Iceman Inheritance*

The Iceman Inheritance: Prehistoric Sources of Western Man's Racism, Sexism and Aggression fits squarely inside the Afrocentric belief system and shares its assumptions about the inherent immorality of white people and the black African origin of civilization. It seeks to provide hard anthropological evidence for the "Ice People" half of the Sun People/Ice People Thesis, but delivers polemics instead. Ironically, Bradley relies on anthropologists branded as "racist" by their colleagues to support his thesis. In fact, he adopts the theories and terminology of Carleton S. Coon whose text *The Origin of Races* (1962) has been denounced by Ashley Montague and others for its racist slant.

Bradley's thesis is that "the problem with the world is white men," who are congenitally racist, sexist and aggressive. Furthermore, their destructive tendency to "rampant progress" is the result of the unique evolution of the "Caucasoid" race in northern, ice-bound climates; "rampant progress," he writes, "seems to be a racial inclination." Thus, Bradley, who is dedicated to ending social injustice and racism, is in essential agreement with Neo-Nazis.

The aggressions and wars of white people, says Bradley, are more "intellectual" and "abnormal" than those of non-whites:

> It is in the sphere of "abnormal" violence that we Caucasoids excel among races. The Caucasoid domain has witnessed far more than its fair share of philosophical and religious conflict . . . waves of competing belief sweeping from the Urals to the Atlantic, from the Sahara to the Baltic, clashing in dins of merciless racial fratricide, and leaving flotsam of broken bodies and swirling eddies of blood testifying to the violence of Caucasoid intellectual paroxysms. Intellectual violence is statistically rare among other races. Intellectual violence is typical of Caucasoids. Our wars of religion, our Inquisition, our philosophical conflicts have no parallel among yellow, brown or black men.[46]

Apparently, "the swirling eddies of blood" and "merciless racial fratricide" of the Hutus against Tutsis, or of Japanese against Chinese, or of the Mongol Hordes against Europeans, are "normal" because they were perpetrated by non-whites. Bradley seeks to blame white skin and Western culture for all the injustice and oppression in the world, and for evil itself. He sees "progress" as a Caucasoid disease that is spreading to the rest of the world:

> Progress as we have institutionalized it, and as Caucasoids understand it, is a symptom of undisplaced aggression resulting from Caucasoid psychosexual maladaptation: the maladaptation happened long ago. In spite of its terrible and ever-escalating costs to our health and security, progress provides one absolutely invaluable commodity, one utterly priceless necessity: biological and psychological identity. Mankind as a whole wistfully longs for it, but the Caucasoid racial need for it borders on metabolic addiction.

Bradley recounts Chief Scientist of the Third Reich Hans Hörbiger's theory of Fire and Ice, because he believes that there is a germ of truth in it. This is the theory, based on Germanic myth, that the earth once had four moons, three of which crashed to Earth. During this period, organisms grew large and men were gods; the Aryans are remnants of this time and will someday evolve into "new men." Bradley states that this theory is a "racial memory" of real history, that Caucasoids did indeed evolve amid fire and ice, i.e. camp fires and glaciers. "Almost all European peoples," he claims, "preserve some memory of coming from the East and traditions of 'originating' in the vicinity of the Caucasus-Pamir chain of mountains." Bradley doesn't cite a reference for this claim, but it rests on Blumenbach's nineteenth century assumption that white people originated in the Caucasus Mountains.

Bradley also agrees with the eighteenth and nineteenth century polygenists who believed that each race evolved from a different species of ape. And, like ultra-white supremacist Ben Klassen, he sees the struggle of evolution as a struggle between races. He cites the displacement of the African Bushmen by other Africans as an example of the mechanism of evolution, which favors stronger races over weaker ones. In other words, genocide is merely a natural product of human evolution. But when practiced by whites, it's "pathological":

> Not intelligence, nor morality, nor "spirit," but aggression, is responsible for the white man's "superiority." Aggression is responsible for the expansion of Caucasoids, both geographically and culturally, at the expense of other races. We witness the final act of this expansion in our own time. It began when the glaciers retreated, when Würm released the white race from its tutelage under fire and ice, when pathological temporal aggression was unleashed upon the world.

Bradley adopts Carleton S. Coon's theory that the various races of man crossed the "sapiens threshold"—that is, became smart, modern humans—at different times. In Bradley's view, the Caucasoids alone crossed the sapiens threshold in a glacial environment. This, he says, traumatized them and made them pathologically aggressive.

Bradley also contends that Caucasoids are more "sexist" than non-whites, probably the most absurd of his many absurd statements. This, he says, is a result of the greater sexual dimorphism in the Caucasoid race, which they inherited from the Neanderthals. This rests on his equally absurd contention that Caucasoid women have larger hips than non-Caucasoid women do. Bradley believes that the supposed greater sexual dimorphism in "Neanderthal-Caucasoids" resulted in greater sensitivity to physical differences between groups, which led to sexism and racism.

For someone who has dedicated his career to defending non-western peoples, Bradley seems to be deeply ignorant of their cultures and histories. His claim that the status of women in pre-revolutionary China was higher than in England is exceeded in absurdity by his assumption that Egyptian and Chinese civilizations were "environmentally supportable." In fact, all civilizations ancient, modern, white, and black, are and were devastating to the environment. Presently the Chinese are some of the worst devastators on Earth, sacrificing endangered birds and mammals in the hope that their powdered remains will enhance male virility. It seems Bradley's presupposition of the moral superiority of non-western cultures has prevented him from finding out how they actually work.

It's unlikely that *The Iceman Inheritance* has converted any anthropologists to the Afrocentric cause. Instead, it provides the Afrocentrists with another mishmash of speculation and polemics (with a few hard facts thrown in) that confirm their belief system. Like the conspiriologists who blame Jews for the problems of the world, it makes the Afrocentrists feel better to blame the white race for the problems of the world.

Bradley and the extreme Afrocentrists—though their intentions are different—are in essential agreement with their white racist predecessors. The "superior" qualities for the white supremacists—aggression, creativity and individuality—are for the Afrocentrists negative qualities, and vice versa. To the White Supremacists, whites are creative, noble warriors, whereas to the Afrocentrists, they are psychologically damaged controllers.

We have come full circle in the game of Which Tribe is Best? Nobody plays that game unless they know the answer before they start.

—◆—

1. Freund, *Myths of Creation*, p. 126.
2. Ibid., p. 143.
3. Catherine the Great quoted in *Aryan Myth*, by Poliakov, p. 121.
4. Poliakov, *Aryan Myth*, p. 131.
5. Scotus quoted in *Aryan Myth*, by Poliakov, p. 131.
6. Blumenbach quoted in *Death of Adam*, by Greene, p. 224.
7. Long quoted in *Aryan Myth*, by Poliakov, p. 178.
8. Bory de Saint-Vincent quoted in *Aryan Myth*, by Poliakov, p. 220. His hierarchy seems to contradict biblical genealogy, since Japheth descended from Adam.
9. See chap. 2, "De-evolution."
10. Camper quoted in *Death of Adam*, by Greene, p. 190.
11. Gould, *Mismeasure of Man*, p. 43.
12. Agassiz quoted in *Mismeasure of Man*, by Gould, p. 45.
13. Ibid., p. 46.
14. Pott quoted in *Aryan Myth*, by Poliakov, p. 197.
15. Poliakov, *Aryan Myth*, p. 204.
16. Renan quoted in *Aryan Myth*, by Poliakov, p. 208.
17. Gobineau quoted in *Aryan Myth*, by Poliakov, p. 236.

18. Poliakov, *Aryan Myth*, pp. 236–37.

19. Gobineau quoted in *Aryan Myth*, by Poliakov, p. 237.

20. Lapouge quoted in *Aryan Myth*, by Poliakov, p. 270.

21. From Dunbar Rowland, *Jefferson Davis*, 1:286; and quoted on the following website: <http://www.religioustolerance.org>.

22. "Folk," with an emphasis on the native German soul.

23. Goodrick-Clarke, *Occult Roots of Nazism*, p. 1.

24. See chap. 2, "De-evolution."

25. Lanz quoted in *Occult Roots of Nazism*, by Goodrick-Clarke, p. 96.

26. Goodrick-Clarke, *Occult Roots of Nazism*, p. 183.

27. See chap. 4; "racial hygiene" was the German name for eugenics.

28. Nesta H. Webster, *Secret Societies and Subversive Movements*, 1924.

29. Klassen, *Nature's Eternal Religion*, p. 13.

30. Ibid.

31. Weisman, *Origin of Race*, p. 57.

32. Ibid., p. 77.

33. Weisman, *Who Is Esau-Edom?* pp. 20–21.

34. Ibid., pp. 127–29.

35. Weisman, *Origin of Race*, p. 82.

36. Mullins, *Curse of Canaan*, p. 11.

37. See *Kooks*, by Kossy for more details.

38. Muhammad, *Blackman in America*, p. 119.

39. Ibid., pp. 121–22.

40. See *Kooks*, by Kossy, and chap. 1, "Extraterrestrial Origins."

41. Issa, *Paleman*, p. 10. The following four excerpts in the text are also from *Paleman*; p. 70, p. 71, p. 77 and p. 193, respectively.

42. See *Not Out of Africa*, by Mary Lefkowitz, for a scholarly critique of Afrocentrism.

43. When used correctly, the genetic terms "dominant" and "recessive" apply to traits, not people; e.g., blue eyes are a recessive trait and brown eyes a dominant trait. But blue-eyed people are not recessive; nor are brown-eyed people dominant.

44. Welsing, *Isis Papers*, p. 64. The following three excerpts in the text are also from *Isis Papers*; p. 65, p. 66, and p. 238, respectively.

45. Moore, *Science of Melanin*, p. 107. The following two excerpts in the text are also from *Science of Melanin*; p. 109, and p. 114, respectively.

46. Bradley, *Iceman Inheritance*, p. 14. The following two excerpts in the text are also from *Iceman Inheritance*; p. 12, and p. 26, respectively.

Chapter Four

Eugenics

Racial impoverishment is the plague of civilization.
This insidious disease, with its twin symptoms the extirpation of superior
strains and the multiplication of inferiors, has ravaged humanity like a consuming
fire, reducing the proudest societies to charred and squalid ruin.
Lothrop Stoddard, *The Revolt Against Civilization*

We can have almost any kind of a race of human beings we want.
We can have a race that is beautiful or ugly, wise or foolish,
strong or weak, moral or immoral.
Albert Edward Wiggam, *The Fruit of the Family Tree*

*I*n the year 1920—the end of the second decade of the brave new twentieth century—the prospects for the human race never looked better. In Kansas, along with its traditional steer, hog and sheep stock competitions, the State Fair added a "human stock" section. That year, genetically superior human specimens and families would be rewarded at the Fitter Families Contest. A brochure for the contest proclaimed: "The time has come when the science of human husbandry must be developed, based on the principles now followed by scientific agriculture, if the better elements of our civilization are to dominate or even survive." The winners would be certified "Grade A Individuals." All over the country, progress-minded ladies and

JOHN HUMPHREY NOYES, founder of the Oneida Community

gentlemen lectured on the scientific propagation of the human race, sex education, and the emancipation of women. Men of letters, scientists and socialists debated the finer points of improvement of the human race through better breeding, while state legislatures argued over whether to sterilize imbeciles and drunks. In Virginia, when the high court approved a state-ordered sterilization, Justice Holmes proclaimed, "Three generations of imbeciles are enough." Asians could no longer immigrate to the United States and others were required to pass a literacy test. In the meantime, Germany prepared for the rule of "racial hygiene," when the unfit and the useless would be mercifully put to sleep in the name of public health.

Such an atmosphere seems unthinkable today, but the ideas that made it possible remain. We may shudder at the Nazi "euthanasia" chambers—where mental patients and other "unfit" specimens of humanity were gassed with carbon monoxide and then cremated—but we must also acknowledge that they didn't spring ready-made from the imagination of the Third Reich. From the late 1800s to the end of World War II, the educated classes all over the western world—particularly in the United States and Britain—found the lure of eugenics irresistible.

Victorian gentleman FRANCIS GALTON, who coined the word "eugenics"

English gentleman-scientist Francis Galton coined the word "eugenics" in the nineteenth century to mean improvement of the human race by better breeding. Though Galton—Charles Darwin's first cousin—was the first to devote his career to it, the concept is ancient. Plato first suggested that the race might be improved by state regulation of marriages to prevent the birth of biologically inferior individuals. Plato, of course, knew nothing of genetic science or evolutionary theory or anything resembling our modern notion of human progress. These concepts later became indispensable to eugenics crusaders.

Such a scheme for the material perfection of the human race hadn't a chance in the Christian world of the dark ages, when human improvement was supposed to be in the hands of God alone. Philosopher John Passmore, in his book *The Perfectibility of Man*, explains: "Christianity . . . did not encourage Platonic Utopianism. It was even less attracted by the idea of genetic controls. If men's moral improvement is dependent on the exercise of divine grace, then it was impious to suggest that they might, by more careful breeding, improve the moral character of their descendants."[1] Any scientific attempts to uplift the race would have amounted to blasphemy. Thus, the originally pagan idea lay dormant until the classically-inspired Renaissance when Campanella's "City of the Sun" described a eugenic utopia where:

> Love is foremost in attending to the charge of the race. [The wise ruler] sees that men and women are so joined together, that they bring forth the best offspring. Indeed they laugh at us who exhibit a studious care for our breed of horses and dogs, but neglect the breeding of human beings.[2]

But aside from the occasional utopian thinker, eugenics didn't come into its own until the path was cleared by the ideas of human progress, biological evolution, natural selection and Social Darwinism in the eighteenth and nineteenth centuries.

SURVIVAL OF THE FITTEST

The phrase "survival of the fittest," which became synonymous with Darwinism, wasn't coined by Darwin but by the English Social Darwinist philosopher Herbert Spencer. Intellectuals overlook Spencer today, but at the time Spencer's fame in the United States far surpassed Darwin's. He was immeasurably influential among philosophers, biologists, eugenists, fascists, and the captains of American industry.

Spencer believed that the biological process of natural selection extended to social life. (Natural selection, briefly, is the *mechanism* of evolution—discovered concurrently by both Darwin and Alfred Russell Wallace—whereby environmental pressures and genetic variation influence an organism's ability to survive, produce offspring and propagate their own traits.) Spencer equated the poor with the "unfit" who would be eliminated by the inexorable laws of evolution, ensuring the continual improvement of society, culminating in the disappearance of evil and the perfection of humanity. To Spencer, biological evolution implied moral progress. "Progress," he wrote, "is not an accident, but a necessity. Instead of civilization being artificial, it is a part of nature; all of a piece with the development of the embryo or the unfolding of a flower."[3] Thus, the state was foolish in supporting welfare for the poor and diseased, tampering with the natural process of evolution. Instead, the unfit should be eliminated: "The whole effort of nature is to get rid of such, to clear the world of them, and make room for better."[4]

Spencer's popularity in the United States peaked just after the Civil War, and by 1903, sales of his works totaled 350,000 volumes, unprecedented for works of philosophy and sociology. Political conservatives and business tycoons eagerly ingested the ideas of Spencer and other Social Darwinists, elevating laissez-faire economics to biological law. To them, the free market would bring about more than just a healthy economy; it would also unmercifully weed out the unfit, inefficient and incompetent.

The leading U.S. spokesman for Social Darwinism, Yale professor William Graham Sumner (1840–1910) went so far as to claim that millionaires, due to their proven success in the free market, were the fittest individuals of society "naturally selected in the crucible of competition." Millionaires like Andrew Carnegie and John D. Rockefeller agreed. Carnegie and Rockefeller, in fact, joined Sumner in his scientific defense of big business. In a Sunday-school address, Rockefeller compared the seemingly ruthless growth of big business to the creation of the American Beauty rose, whose "splendor and fragrance brings cheer to its beholder only by sacrificing the early buds which grow up around it." Rockefeller explained that rampant capitalism is not "an evil tendency in business," but "merely the working-out of a law of nature and a law of God."[5]

Carnegie, in an 1889 article entitled, "Wealth," in the *North American Review*, wrote that the Law of Competition "is here; we cannot evade it; no substitutes for it have been found; and while the law may sometimes be hard for the individual, it is best for the race, because it insures [sic] the survival of the fittest in every department."[6] This line of argument was the first of many attempts on the part of ruling elites to persuade poor people that "our excessive wealth and power is not only good for us, but it's good for you too!" (It was succeeded almost a century later during the Reagan administration in the early 1980s by the slightly more tactful "trickle-down" theory of economics whereby the enormous wealth of successful corporations eventually "trickles down" to everybody else.)

The old-style business tycoons perhaps slept easier, knowing that their pursuit of power was morally and scientifically sanctioned by the best minds of the Western World—and God. Social Darwinism likened the social environment to a jungle where only the fittest survive. But, as supreme beneficiaries of civilization, their philosophy stopped short of celebrating the savage state of pure human nature. Carnegie or Rockefeller would be the last to return to any real jungle. To their way of thinking, the fittest like themselves survived by blind, mechanistic forces of evolution, not by personal force or cruelty. They were likely deceiving themselves. Perhaps it would have been more honest to admit that the logical conclusion of Social Darwinism is that "might is right," and that they themselves took their booty by whatever means necessary. Their refinement or goodness had not gotten them where they were; their fighting determination had, along with their sharp claws.

Most likely, neither Rockefeller nor Carnegie had read *Might is Right: or Survival of the Fittest* by the pseudonymous Ragnar Redbeard, first published in 1896.[7] Ragnar Redbeard's vision of Earth, "this circling planet-ball," was as "a vast whirling star-lit Valhalla, where victorious battlers quaff the foaming heartsblood of their smashed-up adversaries, from the scooped-out skull goblets of the slain in neverending war." It was hardly the sort of literature a cultivated man of the world would seek out. *Might is Right* soups up the "survival of the fittest" doctrine—The Philosophy of Power—in order to attack Christian morality and the democratic status quo. More raging rant than reasoned argument, it seeks to expose the many layers of lies about human nature that underlie Western civilization. In its place, Ragnar Redbeard pines for the olden days of masculine valor, when warriors made no apologies for their bloodlust:

> Mankind is aweary, aweary of its sham prophets; its demagogues and its statesmen. It crieth out for kings and heroes. It demands a nobility—a nobility that cannot be hired with money, like slaves or beasts of burden. The world awaits the coming of mighty men of valor, great destroyers (destroyers of all that is vile, angels of death). We are sick unto nausea of the "good Lord Jesus," terror-stricken under the executive of priest, mob and proconsul. We are tired to death of "Equality." Gods are at a discount, devils are in demand. He who would rule the coming age, must be hard, cruel, and deliberately intrepid, for softness

assails not successfully the idols of the multitude. Those idols must be smashed into fragments, burnt into ashes, and that cannot be done by the gospel of love.[8]

Ragnar Redbeard's gospel has room only for the truth of "cruel and merciless" nature, who "does not love the wrong-doer, but endeavors in every possible way to destroy him." In contrast to the praying dupes of organized religion, "strong men are not deterred from pursuing their aim by anything," but "go straight to the goal, and that goal is Beauty, Wealth, and Material Power." Moreover, "The mission of Power is to control and exploit the powerless, for to be powerless is to be criminal." In short, "Human rights and wrongs are not determined by Justice, but by Might." Obviously, I might add, the rich and powerful didn't get where they are by being good people. Though we might think humanity has progressed far from our barbarous past, Redbeard knows in his gut that "disguise it as you may, the naked sword is still king-maker and king-breaker, as of yore."

Might is Right,
RAGNAR REDBEARD'S
polemic on "The
Survival of the Fittest"

Spencer had reasoned that due to survival of the fittest, human society would evolve just as the human organism had evolved, and that the result would be a morally superior society. But to Ragnar Redbeard, nature—and therefore society—will always value power alone. The mightiest will always survive, and survival is the highest moral value. There can be no moral progress, because nature—including human nature—doesn't need improvement.

Redbeard exhorted civilized men to stop wasting their energy on improving society and, instead, heed the call of nature, where "each molecule, each animal, fights for its life." Rather than loving mankind, they should make sure that their "beaks and spurs, fangs and claws are as sharp as steel, and as effective as science can make them"[9] because in nature, gooey doctrines like the "brotherhood of man" are useless.

Because all men are *not* created equal, our world is teeming with poor genetic specimens, waiting to be weeded out. The majority of farmhands, factory workers, seamen and salesmen alike, wrote Redbeard, "are extremely poor specimens of humanity." One need only look at them: "Their heads are to a large extent unsymetrical [sic], their features distorted, ape-like, unintelligent. Their bodies are out of all proportion, dwarfed, stunted, diseased, malformed, cretinous. Their movements are contracted, artificial, ungainly, and their minds (outside of routine) are utter vacuums."[11] Providing welfare or charity for these weaklings, defies nature and "the proper home for incurables is—the grave."[11]

Though Ragnar Redbeard's Philosophy of Power diverged in many respects from the more reputable brands of Social Darwinism, they agreed in essentials;

that "survival of the fittest" applied to human society, that the unfortunates among us were biologically unfit, and that it was an edict of Nature that they be eliminated to make room for the strong. Spencer thought this process would create a higher civilization, Ragnar Redbeard thought it would create a race of valiant warriors.

Redbeard's conclusions seemed closer to those of the eminent German biologist Ernst Haeckel (1834–1919) who wrote, "Passion and selfishness . . . is everywhere the motive force of life. Man . . . forms no exception to the rest of the animal world. . . . The whole history of nations . . . must therefore be [a physio-chemical process] explicable by means of natural selection."[12]

Haeckel was originally trained as a physician but found his true calling after reading Darwin's *Origin of Species*. Darwin's theory of natural selection provided the young Haeckel with the answer to everything. It also inspired him to begin a new career in zoology. By the end of his career "the ape-professor of Jena" had conducted many successful expeditions abroad in search of new creatures, described 4,000 new species of marine invertebrates, wrote monographs on sponges, worms and medusae, and coined the word "ecology." He also invented the oft-repeated phrase "ontogeny recapitulates phylogeny"[13] which he thought the most basic law of evolution. Haeckel idolized Darwin, and after meeting him in 1866 wrote: "It was as if some exalted sage of Hellenic antiquity . . . stood in the flesh before me."

Haeckel was a leading force in German Social Darwinism. In 1906 he co-founded the Monist League to organize scientific and political support for the unification of life, politics, culture, religion and morality under the principles of natural selection. The League advocated German social policies that assumed the German *völk* to be the culmination of evolution. As a respected zoologist, Haeckel freely compared human racial differences to those between animal species in defense of social policies that would maintain the purity of the *völk*:

> The morphological differences between two generally recognized species—for example, sheep and goats—are much less important than those . . . between a Hottentot and a man of the Teutonic race. . . . [The German völk have] deviated furthest from the common form of ape-like men [and] outstrip all others in the career of civilization. . . . Woolly-haired [races are] incapable of a true inner culture or of a higher mental development. . . . No woolly-haired nation has ever had an important history. . . . [Because] the lower races—such as the Veddahs or Australian Negroes—are psychologically nearer to the mammals—apes and dogs—than to civilized Europeans, we must, therefore, assign a totally different value to their lives.[14]

Haeckel worried that social policies kept inferior stock safe from natural selection, causing "domestication-induced degeneracy." The solution would be to institute the destruction of "useless lives." Haeckel became a national hero, even though his ideas were eventually discredited. Scores of Germans listened when he implored them to accept evolutionary destiny by surpassing their biological inferiors, because in the end, only the fittest nations would survive. "Politics," he wrote, anticipating the racial hygiene edicts of the Third Reich, "is applied biology."

BETTER BREEDING

Sir Francis Galton (1822–1911), the tireless crusader for better breeding and founder of modern eugenics, dedicated himself in other areas as well. He authored some 200 scientific publications, including: "Statistical Inquiries into the Efficacy of Prayer" (1872), "Measurement of Character" (1884), "Head Growth in Students at the University of Cambridge" (1889), "Arithmetic by Smell" (1894), and "Three Generations of Lunatic Cats" (1896). Galton was particularly fond of applying numbers, measurement and statistics to living things.

The youngest child of a wealthy English family, Galton's career took a circuitous route before settling into his life's work. By the age of 22 he had earned degrees in both medicine and mathematics, but after the death of his father brought him a large inheritance, he quit his studies and set out for the Middle East. No mere holiday, Galton's travels took him up the Nile and through the desert on camelback to Khartoum, Beirut and Jerusalem. He learned to speak Arabic and settled in Damascus with two Sudan monkeys and a mongoose. By his late 20s, Galton had explored and mapped 1,700 miles of the African interior. Upon his return, he was awarded a Gold Medal from the Royal Geographical Society.

While in Africa, Galton began to muse upon—and measure—human differences. In a letter to his brother he wrote:

> [Hottentot women are] endowed with that shape which European milliners so vainly attempt to imitate. . . . I have seen figures that would drive the females of our native land desperate—figures that could afford to scoff at Crinoline. . . . As the ladies turned themselves about, as women always do, to be admired, I surveyed them in every way and subsequently measured the distance of the spot where they stood—worked out and tabulated the results at my leisure.[15]

Twenty years later Galton constructed a "beauty map" of Great Britain by carefully recording the frequency with which he saw attractive women in various towns and regions of the nation.

After reading his cousin's magnum opus, *Origin of Species*, Galton—much like Haeckel—knew that he'd found his life's work. He recalled that he "devoured its contents and assimilated them [quickly and easily], which perhaps may be ascribed to an hereditary bent of mind that both its illustrious author and myself have inherited from our common grandfather."[16] Galton immediately set out to probe the "heredity and the possible improvement of the Human Race."

Galton gathered information on 1,000 talented Cambridge students from 300 families. The results appeared in his first eugenics book, *Hereditary Genius* (1869). Galton found that talent was concentrated in certain families, each of which produced an unusually large number of scientists, musicians, artists and statesmen. Galton concluded that intelligence and character are inherited, rather than acquired through social advantage, education or wealth. Producing talented people, and hence, a better society, would only be a matter of better breeding, or what Galton dubbed "eugenics." Henceforth eugenics became an obsession for him. He strongly believed improving the race was a supremely noble aim that "ought to become one of the dominant motives in a civilized nation."[17]

Galton shared the Social Darwinists' faith in the power of heredity over culture, including their assumption that only white people—who were biologically superior to others—could have produced something as complex as Western civilization. Galton differed, however, from the Social Darwinists in at least one important respect. He saw nothing sacrosanct about nature or natural selection. He wrote of natural selection, in fact, as an unnecessarily cruel and wasteful process that "displays the awe-inspiring spectacle of a vast eddy of organic turmoil."[19] Instead, he advocated eugenics—a kinder, gentler process of selection. "Its first object," he wrote, "is to check the birth-rate of the Unfit . . . [and] the improvement of the race by furthering the productivity of the Fit by early marriages . . . of the best stock."[19]

In contrast to what the race might become through eugenics, Galton believed that the Dark Ages were the result of the anti-eugenic, or "dysgenic" practice of religious celibacy. He wrote as if this period of history was an insult against him, personally:

> Whenever a man or woman was possessed of gentle nature that fitted him or her to deeds of charity, to meditation, to literature or to art, the social condition of the time was such that they had no refuge elsewhere than in the bosom of the Church. But the Church chose to preach and exact celibacy, and the consequence was that these gentle natures had no continuance, and thus, by a policy so singularly unwise and suicidal that I am hardly able to speak of it without impatience, the Church brutalized the breed of our forefathers. . . . She practiced the arts which breeders would use, who aimed at creating ferocious, currish, and stupid natures. . . .[20]

Galton's eugenic vision was articulated further in his utopian novel Kantsaywhere, finished in 1911. Though Galton destroyed the manuscript when it was rejected by his publisher, bits and pieces survive. Philosopher John Passmore, in *The Perfectibility of Man*, describes the novel as "a somewhat remarkable Utopia . . . in which, for example, only those who receive sufficiently high marks at public examinations are permitted to marry. Those who fail their examinations have the option of emigrating, or living under a constant surveillance designed to ensure that they do not propagate their kind."

Galton himself suffered from an infertile marriage. As far as we know, he was unable to contribute his superior genes to future generations. This might account for the fervor with which he encouraged other well-bred specimens to produce as many offspring as possible. He advocated awarding a Certificate of Merit and financial support to capable men and women, to encourage superior individuals to breed early and often. In 1904 he offered £1500 to University College in London, for a research fellowship in eugenics. He also upgraded the Eugenics Record Office in London, that was in the business of collecting pedigrees, for a National Eugenics Laboratory. His will ensured that upon his death, £45,000 would be set aside for a eugenics professorship.

Galton converted many socially progressive ladies and gentlemen to his cause in Great Britain, Europe and the United States. Darwin paid homage to his cousin in *Descent of Man*, reporting that, "We now know, through the admirable labours of Mr. Galton, that genius . . . tends to be inherited."[21] But there were critics as well. Some attacked eugenics because of its "hereditarian" stance in the nature/nurture debate, and others because of its anti-clerical implications. But, according to historian Daniel Kevles, most hereditarians took no notice of eugenics at all. Though they shared the same aims as eugenists, the Social Darwinists thought that eugenic coercion was unnecessary because the unfit would die out anyway. In its infancy, eugenics appealed most to social reformers on the left, rather than Social Darwinists on the right. Asylum superintendents, prison wardens, prison doctors, sociologists and social workers imagined that better breeding would eventually eliminate the problems of poverty, mental illness, feeblemindedness, and crime. Women's emancipation would also follow from "the scientific propagation of the human race."

EUGENIC GUINEA PIGS AT ONEIDA

During the mid-1800s, the controlled environment of John Humphrey Noyes' Oneida Community provided fertile soil for social, sexual and eugenic experimentation. Inspired by the Bible and Francis Galton, Noyes was able to realize his dreams of putting into practice "complex marriage," elimination of the male orgasm, and a selective breeding program called "Stirpiculture." The experiment yielded 58 "scientifically" produced offspring but was eventually abandoned, partly due to pressure from the disapproving moralists of the outside world.

John Humphrey Noyes, born in 1811 in Brattleboro, Vt., was the product of a reserved, upper-crust New England family who were conservative when it came to religion. The Noyes' were scandalized when young John, who had been a top student at Dartmouth and was studying law, became caught up in the religious frenzy of the time. During this "Great Awakening" of religious faith in the "Burnt-over District"[22] of upper New York state, revivalists saved souls by the thousands. In 1830 alone, an estimated 100,000 people were converted to Christ. In 1831 a revival tent came to Putney, Vt., home of the Noyes. Mrs. Noyes probably thought a revival meeting would be a good influence on her introverted, skeptical son John. He reluctantly attended the revival, but the well-meaning mom got more than she'd bargained for. After the meeting, young Noyes spent four days wrestling with Satan, until "light gleamed upon his soul." At that moment he knew his true calling. He decided to abandon law and devote himself full time to the ministry of the Lord.

Noyes began his ministerial studies at Andover Theological Seminary and continued at Yale Divinity School. In 1833 he obtained his license to preach in the Congregational Church. It soon became clear, however, to both his teachers and his classmates that Noyes was no ordinary minister. He was disgusted, for one, by the "guilt-ridden Christianity" of sin. He gravitated to Perfectionism, which taught that sinless perfection for mankind was attainable—not just in Heaven—but on Earth. Perfectionists preached "the way of perfect holiness" but didn't expect their members to be entirely free of sin. Noyes, however, knew that he was without sin and that those who "committeth sin" were "of the devil." His fellow students concluded that he was crazy. His teachers agreed, and his license to preach was revoked. The date Noyes lost his license later became an Oneida holy day.

Noyes took this utter rejection by his friends and colleagues not as defeat, but as a rebirth. He began wandering around New York and New England, preaching his own brand of Perfectionism. He published Perfectionist newspapers, first *The Perfectionist*, then *The Witness*.

These newspapers became a forum for Noyes' unorthodox views. Noyes was no fool, however, and after his experiences at divinity school knew to keep his more radical views—about marriage, for instance—private. He advocated the complete elimination of marriage. He had written to a correspondent that marriage bred the ungodly traits of exclusiveness, jealousy and quarreling, which had no place "in the

Oneida Mansion, 1867 (from *Heavens on Earth*)

marriage supper of the Lamb." Unfortunately, Noyes' remarks became public and caused an immediate furor. It was one thing to eliminate sin, but quite another to eliminate marriage. For most, this was tantamount to advocating immorality, whoring and "free love." Noyes lost most of his subscribers and nearly lost his newspaper.

John Noyes, like others in his taciturn Yankee family, had always been shy of women. According to a family legend, the Noyes men were so bashful that they could only muster the courage to propose to their own cousins. They even had a name for this problem, the "Atkinson Difficulty" after the town of Atkinson, Mass. where they had lived. It must have occurred to John that if marriage were eliminated, he wouldn't have to grapple with this family problem.

As it turned out, practical considerations overcame both Noyes' beliefs and his shyness. He saw a way out of his money problems when a plain but rich Perfectionist, Miss Harriet Holton, fell in love with him. He proposed marriage to her in writing, and she accepted. Noyes wrote to a friend, "By this marriage, besides herself, and a good social position which she held as belonging to the first families of Vermont, I attained money enough to build me a house and a printing office and to buy a press and type."

Noyes' proposal to Miss Holton was frank and unromantic. He honestly summarized what they could expect from one another:

> We can enter into no engagement with each other which shall limit the range of our affections as they are limited in matrimonial engagements by the fashions of the world. I desire and expect my yokefellow will love all who love God, whether man or woman . . . as freely as if she stood in no particular connection with me.[23]

The high-minded couple were married in June of 1838. They spent their honeymoon in Albany, buying a printing press. When they returned home to Putney they taught themselves to set type and printed the new issue of *The Witness*.

The Noyes were soon joined in their faith by a small community of believers who became known as the Putney Perfectionists. In 1846 the community became a commune when the upstanding group of "Bible Communists" agreed to consolidate their households and belongings, with Noyes as "father and overseer."

The group's intimate domestic arrangements got them in constant trouble with the outside world. Because they renounced traditional "simple" marriage and replaced it with "complex" marriage where "each was married to all," the group became known as libertines. Rumors of a "free love" cult spread throughout Vermont and beyond. In fact, members were at least as chaste, and often more so, than the citizens in the outside world.

The term "complex marriage" and its definition were from the Bible. Noyes wrote:

> In the kingdom of heaven, the institution of marriage which assigns
> the exclusive possession of one woman to one man, does not exist
> (Matt. 22:23-30). In the kingdom of heaven, the intimate union of life
> and interests, which in the world is limited to pairs, extends through
> the whole body of believers; i.e., complex marriage takes the place of
> simple (John 17:21). The abolishment of sexual exclusiveness is
> involved in the love-relation required between all believers by the
> express injunction of Christ and the apostles and by the whole tenor
> of the New Testament. "The new commandment is that we love one
> another," and that not by pairs, as in the world, but en masse. . . .[24]

This "marriage" of each to all was an unusually sterile one. Whenever a bride
and a groom wished to consummate their vows, they had to consult with an older
intermediary first. Any lovemaking had to stop short of ejaculation. No wonder
some members remained celibate their whole lives.

Avoidance of ejaculation was known as "male continence." More than just a
birth control measure, male continence was a cornerstone of Bible Communism.
Noyes recognized that love between men and women involved two separate
functions: the social, and the propagative. He wanted to keep them separate. The
joint practices of complex marriage and male continence would prevent propagation from intruding into the social bonds of marriage.

Local villagers did not take kindly to this kind of experimentation. *The
Vermont Phoenix* expressed the conventional wisdom about sect:

> When such notorious doctrines as these are promulgated and prac-
> ticed, and when there is such indubitable evidence as the history of
> the sect has furnished us to prove that the young, the innocent, and
> the unsuspicious are entitled to disgrace and ruin by them, and that
> systematic seduction and licentiousness are practiced under the spe-
> cious garb of religion . . . it is time . . . to expose the true character of
> its principles, and warn the young and credulous . . . of the snares that
> are spread for them.[25]

Noyes was arrested on charges of adultery in October, 1847, and was released
on bail, with a trial set for the following April. A month later warrants were
issued for two more Putney Perfectionists. Noyes and his brethren decided to
leave the state rather than face a criminal trial by small-minded villagers, or
worse, an angry mob. In 1848 they abandoned Putney for Oneida, N.Y., where
they flourished. By 1853, the group had grown to 130 residents on 250 acres, and
to 306 residents by 1878.

The Oneida Community was now free to practice their version of righteousness
in the privacy of their own commune. Or so they thought. Articles continued to

condemn Oneida's "impure and shocking practices." A story in the scandal-mongering *Police Gazette* was illustrated with a picture of an "innocent young man being led by a leering matron into a community bed in which three naked Oneida maidens lasciviously awaited his defloration." The caption read, "Please, M'am, is your marriage as complex as *that?*"[26] To counter such bad publicity, the masthead of their Circular announced: "The O.C. and Branches are not 'Free Lovers' in the popular sense of the term. They call their social system *Bible Communism or Complex Marriage*, and hold freedom to love only within their own families, subject to Free Criticism and Male Continence."

In 1869, Oneida had saved enough money to begin propagating new Oneidans. Propagation remained a separate function, and all procreation would be achieved scientifically and eugenically by Stirpiculture.

Stirpiculture was a word invented by the Oneidans, from the word "stirpes," which is Latin for "race," and "culture," as in cultivation for improvement. The products of Stirpiculture would be called "Stirpicults" or "Stirps," for short.

Fifty-three young women and 38 young men agreed to become queens and studs for God and Science. Before they began propagating, they were required to sign written statements. The statement signed by the women stipulated:

1. That we do not belong to ourselves in any respect, but that we belong first to God, and second to Mr. Noyes as God's true representative.

2. That we have no rights or personal feelings in regard to child-bearing which shall in the least degree oppose or embarrass him in his choice of scientific combinations.

3. That we will put aside all envy, childishness, and self-seeking, and rejoice with those who are chosen candidates; that we will, if necessary, become martyrs to science, and cheerfully renounce all desire to become mothers, if for any reason Mr. Noyes deem us unfit material for propagation. Above all, we offer ourselves "living sacrifices" to God and true Communism.

The statements signed by the men were far simpler:

The undersigned desire you may feel that we most heartily sympathize with your purpose in regard to scientific propagation, and offer ourselves to be used in forming any combinations that may seem to you desirable. We claim no rights. We ask no privileges. We desire to be servants of the truth. With a prayer that the grace of God will help us in this resolution, we are your true soldiers.

Over the next ten years, whenever a couple wished to become parents, they applied to a Stirpicultural Committee who either approved or vetoed the request. Occasionally the committee would make its own selections. Out of 51 applications, 42 couples were deemed fit, and nine were deemed unfit. The result was 58 bouncing baby Stirpicults. Noyes, who was in his 60s at the time, sired at least nine of them.

While Galton and others only discussed eugenics, the Oneidans boldly ventured into the unknown realm of "scientific procreation." Moralists were quick to denounce them yet again, this time for introducing "barnyard ethics" (deliberate breeding principles) to the bedroom. The gossips ignored the fact that the stirps were better cared for than many "normal" children. Though the Oneidans probably didn't breed genetically superior overmen, their rates of disease and death were far below the national average, due to the superior care they received. Constance Noyes Robertson, both of whose parents were Stirpicults, wrote that they were "a crop of fine, healthy children, most of them beyond the average in stature and many of them beyond the average in intellect and character. . . . The later lives and careers of this class, so far as they are known, suggest that the experiment was at least a successful beginning."[27] Though she could hardly be called an objective observer, Robertson's writings show that she was immensely proud of her scientifically bred forebears.

The experiment was to end prematurely, when the first crop of stirps had reached about ten years of age. In 1879, due to internal problems and the strains of bad publicity, Noyes fled to Niagara Falls, Canada. This put an end to complex marriage, and two years later, to communal living. In 1881 the Oneidans incorporated as the Oneida Community, Ltd., and still exists today as a manufacturer of silverware.

THE DEGENERATE IN OUR MIDST

Outside of religion, eugenics most caught the imagination of those who ran asylums, prisons and hospitals. Rather than the "positive eugenics" schemes for encouraging breeding among better people, those in charge of our public institutions concentrated on the "negative eugenics" of marriage restriction, sterilization and custody of defective individuals. At first, they were motivated less by some fantasy of a perfect race than by their reformist desire to ease the pain of their charges.

But as brightly-clad immigrants speaking exotic tongues flocked to our cities, sympathy for outsiders of all types—the poor, the foreign-born, the insane and the feebleminded—declined. Less tolerant attitudes were also fueled by the new studies of human degeneracy, criminal anthropology, craniometry and biometrics. In 1857 the French physician Bénédict-Augustin Morel's influential text on human degeneracy proposed that alcoholism, criminal insanity, epilepsy and feeblemindedness were all manifestations of "hereditary degeneration." In 1876, the Italian professor of legal medicine Cesare Lombroso came out with the definitive study of criminal anthropology, *Criminal Man*. Lombroso believed that criminals are born and not made, that they are throwbacks to our savage past, easily identified by their small eyes, thick eyebrows and crooked noses.

In 1875, Richard L. Dugdale's study of the degenerate and prolific "Juke" family became an instant eugenics classic.[28] After noticing that six relatives were all held in the same New York state jail, Dugdale decided to trace their family history in hopes of finding the causes of crime and poverty. The family records told a story of degraded humanity. Out of 709 Jukes in six generations, 18 had kept brothels, 128 had been prostitutes, over 200 had been on relief and over 75 had been convicted criminals. The total cost to the public, Dugdale estimated, had been almost $1.5 million. Eugenists were quick to conclude that the continued multiplication of Jukes, and others like them, would cost many millions more, in prison, police, hospital and court expenses. Despite Dugdale's reluctance to draw purely hereditarian conclusions, his book provided generations of eugenics crusaders a graphic picture of degenerate breeding out of control.

Statistician Karl Pearson—Galton's devoted disciple—feared the fertility of the lower classes and clung to eugenics with a religious fervor. He co-invented the science of biometry—the application of statistics to living populations—with zoologist Walter F.R. Weldon, to help in the fight against the spread of degeneracy. As Director of the National Eugenics Laboratory, Pearson gathered statistics on the inheritance of legal and commercial abilities, hermaphroditism, hemophilia, cleft palate, harelip, tuberculosis, insanity, mental deficiency, and other human maladies. The results were compiled into *The Treasury of Human Inheritance*, a pioneering effort in preserving data on human heredity. The lab also produced studies on the relationship between physique and intelligence, the resemblance of cousins, the role of heredity in alcoholism, the effects of occupation on birthrate, and "Studies in National Deterioration." Pearson concluded that because the most prolific breeders were the unfit; "the habitual criminal, the professional tramp, the tuberculous, the insane, the mentally defective, the alcoholic, the diseased," Britain was "ceasing as a nation to breed intelligence." Pearson and others hoped that measurements—of skulls, brains and intelligence—would scientifically identify the defectives in our midst.

When H.H. Goddard, director of research at the Vineland Training School for Feebleminded Girls and Boys in New Jersey, brought the IQ test to the United States, identification of mental defectives became much easier. While the French inventor of the IQ test, Binet, never claimed that his test measured a single inborn entity, Goddard was less cautious. He translated the tests into English, gave them to his charges, and interpreted the results as a measure of one inherited quality: human intelligence. Goddard also created a numerical classification scale of feeblemindedness that ranged from "idiots," to "imbeciles," and up to "morons," a term he invented for "high-grade defectives." Idiots and imbeciles had already been classified: idiots were those who were unable to develop speech; imbeciles were those incapable of learning to read or write. The morons worried Goddard most, because among them were the criminals, alcoholics, prostitutes, sociopaths, and those who were simply "incapable of adapting themselves to their environment and living up to the conventions of society or acting sensibly." Like Pearson, Goddard worried that as the highest of the defectives, the ne'er-do-well moron was a great threat to the health of the race:

> The idiot is not our great problem. He is indeed loathsome. . . . Nevertheless, he lives his life and is done. He does not continue the race with a line of children like himself. . . . It is the moron type that makes for us our great problem.[29]

Goddard believed that there was a single gene for mental ability, and thus it would be a simple matter to eliminate feeblemindedness, through eugenics. Matings between two feebleminded individuals should be forbidden, and enforced by "the intelligent part of society," by either sterilization or "colonization."

But morons entered our country not only through the womb, but also through our seaports and borders. Thus, Goddard began placing himself at Ellis Island, to help weed them out by applying his IQ test to those who were just off the boat. On his first foray he picked out a young man, and gave him the IQ test. Because the man tested at the mental age of eight, Goddard concluded that he was "defec-

Members of the infamous Kallikak clan, as pictured in H. H. GODDARD's book, *The Kallikak Family*, with mouths and eyebrows altered to accentuate evil or stupidity

tive." This youth was only the first of hundreds to be so tested, fresh from steerage. What's astonishing is that it never occurred to Goddard that the test results would likely reflect whether the subjects were familiar with American customs, whether they'd attended school, and their level of fatigue, not to mention their command of English. Many arriving peasants had never held a pen or pencil in their hands before taking Goddard's test. Goddard concluded that the immigrants "were of surprisingly low intelligence" because they were unable to tell him the month, day and year, or to come up with 60 words in three minutes. This, he lamented, could only reflect the changing character of the immigrants who were arriving at our borders. In contrast to the earliest years of our nation, he wrote, "we are now getting the poorest of each race," whose average intelligence was "of the moron grade." The morons, feared Goddard, were arriving at our borders daily by the hundreds and thousands.

While Goddard tirelessly promoted intelligence testing and tightening of immigration standards, state legislatures began to pass sterilization laws. In 1907, Indiana passed the first such law, which ordered mandatory sterilization of criminals, idiots, imbeciles and rapists, reflecting the popular perception that the feebleminded were a menace to society.

In 1912, Goddard produced his own variation on Dugdale's Jukes study, *The Kallikak Family: A Study in the Heredity of Feeblemindedness*, which is cited almost as often as *The Jukes*. Albert Wiggam devoted several pages to the Kallikaks in his popular 1925 pro-eugenics book, *The Fruit of the Family Tree*, using it as a cautionary tale to young men and women:

> Martin Kallikak was a young soldier of the Revolutionary War. His ancestry was excellent. But one wild night up the Hudson River, Martin forgot his noble blood. In this night of dissipation he met a physically attractive, feebleminded girl. The result of that meeting was a feebleminded boy. This boy grew up and married a woman of whose mentality Doctor Goddard could secure no record. But she was evidently of the same ilk. They produced a numerous progeny with a large percentage of feeblemindedness. These grew up lazy, thriftless, shiftless, trifling, thieving people. Marrying into their own kind, another generation of the same general character came upon the human scene. This has gone on now for some six generations. . . .
>
> However, on the other side of the canvas, blood has painted a different and wonderful story. Later in his life, Martin married a young Quaker woman of splendid talents and heroic ancestry. . . . This line has given us 496 direct descendants. All have been normal people. . . .[30]

During the period before World War I, this kind of story became kind of a fad, spawning a whole genre of imitations, including such titles as: *The Tribe of Ismael, The Pineys, Sam Sixty, The Happy Hickory Family, The Nam Family, Hill Folk* and *The Dack Family*. Magazine articles, tracts, committees and lectures also contributed to the public crusade against what became known as the "Menace of the Feebleminded." The Committee to Study and Report on the Best Practical Means of Cutting Off the Defective Germ-Plasm in the American Population, for example, pushed for mandatory sterilization of defectives. "Society must look," the committee reported, "upon germ-plasm [genetic material] as belonging to society and not solely to the individual who carries it."

State legislators were listening. By 1931, a total of 30 states had passed sterilization laws applying to institutionalized mental defectives. By the mid-'30s, 41 states had laws forbidding marriage of insane or feebleminded individuals, 17 states prohibited the marriage of epileptics, and four states made it a crime for

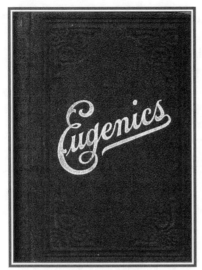

Eugenics by T.W. SHANNON, one of many family health books during the early 20th century, touting the new science of eugenics

confirmed drunkards to marry. The marriage laws were of course very difficult to enforce, and rarely were. However, the sterilization laws did have their effect: 60,926 "imbeciles," "morons," and "idiots" had been sterilized nationwide by 1958.

THE EUGENICS ERA

During most of Francis Galton's life, only a handful of idealistic reformers and scientists were concerned with eugenics. But in the first few years of the twentieth century it gained popularity, and during the teens and twenties became something of a fad. In 1907, Pearson wrote to Galton, "You would be amused to hear how general is now the use of your word *Eugenics!* I hear most respectable middle-class matrons saying if children are weakly, 'Ah, that was not a eugenic marriage!'"[31] Galton was knighted in 1909. In 1913, the first official "eugenic baby" was born to a London woman, who named the girl "Eugenette." In 1914, Princeton undergraduate F. Scott Fitzgerald wrote a song entitled "Love or Eugenics" for the college's Triangle Show. It asked the musical question: "Men, which would you like to come and pour your tea/Kisses that set your heart aflame/Or love from a prophylactic dame."

Romantics had good reason to worry, for prophylactic dames, sensible marriages and family pedigrees were being funded by no less than the Carnegie Institution. In 1904, the biologist Charles Benedict Davenport had persuaded the Carnegie Institution to establish a laboratory for the study of evolution—in essence, a eugenics laboratory—at Cold Spring Harbor, Long Island. In 1910 a Eugenic Records Office was added. The main business at Cold Spring Harbor was the collection of extended family pedigrees. The 1911 book, *Heredity in Relation to Eugenics* reported the results of the pedigree studies. The book concluded that inherited "unit characters" are responsible for physical defects such as hemophilia, otosclerosis, polydactyly and albinism. It also concluded that insanity, alcoholism, pauperism, criminality, nomadism, shiftlessness, feeblemindedness and various national and racial traits were heritable as well. Thalassophilia (love of the sea), Davenport reasoned, was a sex-linked recessive trait because, like color-blindness, it was only expressed in males. Poles were "independent and self-reliant though clannish." Italians tended to "crimes of personal violence." Hebrews were "intermediate between the slovenly Serbians and Greeks." "The tidy Swedes, Germans, and Bohemians," were given to thieving but were rarely involved in personal violence. "The great influx of blood from southeastern Europe" was less prone to burglary, drunkenness and vagrancy than native blood, and "more attached to music and art." Thus the foreign blood that was pouring into the United States would make the population "darker in pigmentation, smaller in stature, more mercurial . . . more given to crimes of larceny, kidnapping, assault, murder, rape, and sex-immorality." In order to prevent defective germ-plasm from tainting our stock, Davenport recommended that immigration be restricted for families with a "poor hereditary history."[32]

The only difference between Davenport's studies and the prejudices of common people was that Davenport had credentials. He also had a knack for inventing new terminology. He coined the term "feebly inhibited," a heritable trait that causes people to be sexually licentious. Davenport explained: "In normal people, the erotic center [in the brain] would be of moderate strength and inhibited by a genetically determined governor; in abnormal people, the erotic center would be excessively energetic and would lack the inhibiting mechanism."[33] Jews in particular were prone to this malady; they showed "the greatest proportion of offenses against chastity and in connection with prostitution, the lowest of crimes."[34]

Young people could spend their summers at Cold Spring Harbor for training as Eugenic Field Workers. The students learned the principles of heredity and how to collect family histories, took field trips to asylums and the homes of defective families, and were trained in heredity counseling for prospective mates.

Meanwhile, magazine and newspaper articles on the art and science of better breeding proliferated, and full-length pro-eugenics tracts hit the bestseller lists. The fad peaked when a huge number of health, marriage and self-help guides included the word "eugenics" on their covers. Many of these books devoted only a few pages to the subject; it seems the word was used as a selling point, much like "internet" and "Generation X" are today.

These quaint texts are relatively easy to find, and at least one—*Nature's Secrets Revealed: Scientific Knowledge of The Laws of Sex Life and Heredity, or EUGENICS*—was reprinted in 1970 by Doubleday and Company. It was originally published by the S.A. Mullikin Co. of Marietta, Ohio in 1917. Essentially a compendium of old wives' tales and superstition, it was peddled as a scientific health book. Its frontispiece advertised that inside can be found "Vital Information for the Married and Marriageable of All Ages; a Word at the Right Time to the Boy, Girl, Young Man, Young Woman, Husband, Wife, Father and Mother; also, Timely Help, Counsel and Instruction for Every Member of Every Home— Together with Important Hints on Social Purity, Heredity, Physical Manhood and Womanhood by Noted Specialists—Embracing a Department on Ethics of the Unmarried by Prof. T.W. Shannon, A.M.: International Lecturer; Editor of Eugenics Department, Uplift magazine; President, Single Standard Eugenic Movement; Author of *Self-Knowledge, Perfect Manhood, Perfect Womanhood, Heredity Explained, Guide to Sex Instruction*, etc." I can almost imagine "professor"

Shannon as an itinerant mountebank hawking his new, scientific eugenics book to local rubes.

Though its abbreviated title is *Eugenics,* the book contains nothing on genetics or eugenics except a photo of a congenital paraplegic with the caption, "Results of conception when the father was intoxicated." Instead, Shannon repeats the popular wisdom on morality, character, etiquette and ethics of the time. His warning against bad books and bad pictures is like a snapshot of nineteenth century morality:

> Bad Books—One-half of the youth in our prisons and houses of correction started on their evil careers by reading bad books, or at best, worthless novels. These books are the nicotine and alcohol of literature; they poison, and burn, and blast the head and heart as surely as their cousins do the stomach. . . .[35]

From *Eugenics*—the caption reads: "Results of Conception when the Father was Intoxicated"

Another text, the 1922 *Ethical Sex Relations, or The New Eugenics: A Safe Guide for Young Men—Young Women* by C.S. Whitehead, M.D. and Charles A. Hoff, M.D., from The John Hertel Co. of Chicago, is a little more truthful about its contents and actually contains a couple of chapters on practical eugenics for young people. The dedication reads: "Designed in particular for fathers and mothers, young men and young women with the earnest hope that millions yet unborn may have the inalienable right of being *well born,* this volume is affectionately dedicated by the authors." The first chapter is devoted to eugenics, but the rest are on practical topics such as the Genito-Urinary System, Menstruation, Love and Marriage, and Childbirth. Such books as these seem to use eugenics as a code-word for sex education, or as the very least, as an excuse to offer frank discussions on sex to teenagers and young adults.

The New Eugenics advises young people to choose one's spouse prudently and never to marry someone with VD, or who is physically or mentally defective. In case there's any doubt about whether or not someone is a complete idiot, or merely feebleminded, it describes the four grades of feeblemindedness: "1) Complete idiots, who live a merely negative existence; 2) incomplete idiots with few rudimentary ideas; 3) imbeciles with limited and often perverted ideas, but capable of being taught by special methods to read and write; and 4) feebleminded persons." By contrast, "A normal person is one who shows by his life and actions, his successes, even his failures, that he possesses that degree of mental power characteristic of the average man."

Those young people who were undaunted by circular logic were treated to an entire chapter on the evils of masturbation entitled "The Solitary Vice," which seeks to clear away the falsities and misconceptions about this "revolting and disgusting" topic. The signs of "self-abuse," the medical authorities tell us, are pimples, idleness, and "fondness for being alone and of going into water closets and other solitary places." Worst of all, the psychiatrists are sure that it's "one of the great causes of insanity," causing thousands to become "irresolute, languid, unfit for business pursuits, and inefficient for any of the high purposes of life." It's clear from such passages that though eugenics may have given such books an aura of scientific authority, their primary purpose was to provide old-fashioned moral instruction; in effect they promoted a confusion between religious morality and science.

Indeed, many scientists, educators and authors believed in eugenics with a religious faith: they replaced Jesus Christ with Charles Darwin, brotherly love with better breeding, and the Second Coming of Christ with the prospect of a perfect race. Though many mainstream clergymen—especially Catholics—bristled at this new religion, some accepted, and even embraced it. In 1926 the American Eugenics Society sponsored a eugenics sermon contest. Three hundred sermons of various denominations were inspired by the contest, and 60 were submitted for judging. Protestants reinterpreted the Bible as a eugenics book, claiming that Jesus was born into a family resulting from "a long process of religious and moral selection." Jews accepted eugenics as just another commandment of God: as one Rabbi put it, "May we do nothing to permit our blood to be adulterated by infusion of inferior grade."

British educator Caleb Williams Saleeby's 1909 book *Parenthood and Race Culture: An Outline of Eugenics* reads like a sermon for the new faith. From his pulpit, Saleeby preached that eugenics "must be instilled into the conscience of civilization like a new religion . . . which sets before it a sublime ideal, terrestrial indeed in its chosen theater, but celestial in its theme, human in its means, but literally superhuman in its goal." [36] He further proclaimed eugenics to be "the final and only judge of all proposals and principles, however labeled, new or old, orthodox or heterodox." Moreover, education "must culminate in preparation for the supreme duty of parenthood." Young people must be instructed in "those bodily functions which exist not for the body nor for the present at all, but for the future life of mankind." Though he might have been preaching a new "scientific" religion, Saleeby taught—like the Christians—that sex exists not for pleasure, but for procreation. Chastity was no longer merely a religious duty, but also a scientific one; one night of wanton behavior, and you were damning not only your soul, but the future of the human race as well. It was all-important to instill in young people the desire to fulfill Man's destiny by ensuring that the *finest*, rather than the fittest, reproduce.

Author, journalist and Chautauqua lecturer Albert Wiggam shared Saleeby's faith in eugenics. Wiggam spoke of eugenics in religious tones in his

1923 best-seller, *The New Decalogue of Science*. Wiggam wrote that eugenics is a new religious creed, which is "simply the projection of the Golden Rule down the stream of protoplasm." Wiggam likened the principles of eugenics to the Ten Commandments given to Moses on Mount Sinai:

> [I]n our day, instead of using table of stone, burning bushes, prophecies and dreams to reveal His will, [God] has given men the microscope, the telescope, the chemist's test tube and the statistician's curve in order to enable men to make their own revelations. These instruments of divine revelation have not only added an enormous range of new commandments—and entirely new Decalogue—to man's moral codes, but they have supplied him with the technique for putting the old ones into effect.[37]

Wiggam's 1925 book, *The Fruit of the Family Tree*, put those God-given techniques—especially the gathering of human pedigrees—to work for "the health, intelligence and beauty of the unborn."

Wiggam believed that "an enormous proportion of . . . undesirable citizens are descended from undesirable blood overseas," that "America's immigration problem is mainly a problem of blood," and that "the low foreigner . . . constitutes our chief national problem." Wiggam's creed was explicitly aristocratic; his data on the nobility came from Galton's *Hereditary Genius*, while his data on the serfs, from Goddard's *The Kallikak Family*.

Wiggam presented the pedigrees of prominent American families as if they were the pedigrees of prize spaniels or thoroughbred horses:

> [T]he union of two streams of great blood of *similar character* begets great blood. The son of the first marriage [of Richard Edwards] was Timothy Edwards, one of the founders of Yale University. He was the father of Jonathan Edwards. From Jonathan Edwards, who married also a wonderful woman, Sarah Pierpont, have descended 12 college presidents, 265 college graduates, 65 college professors, 60 physicians, 100 clergymen, 75 army officers, 60 prominent authors, 100 lawyers, 30 judges, 80 public officers—state governors, city mayors and state officials—three congressmen, two senators and one vice-president of the United States. Compare this with the worthless descendants of Martin Kallikak.[38]

Wiggam went beyond mere textbook eugenics, which might produce a *better* race, to his own heart's desire: a more *beautiful* race. He devoted an entire chapter to the question, "Can We Make the Human Race More Beautiful?" Wiggam said we could. "We can have almost any kind of a race of human beings we want," he wrote. "We can have a race that is beautiful or ugly, wise or foolish, strong or weak, moral or immoral."[39] While Galton produced a beauty map of Britain, Wiggam's beauty map spanned the history of Western civilization:

> Greece wanted beautiful women and got them. Rome did the same thing. The Dark Ages wanted ugly women and got them. Cromwell's Roundheads wanted ugly men and women and got them. The Renaissance wanted beautiful human beings and got them. We want ugly women in America and we are getting them in millions. . . .[40]

If only marriage selection were in the hands of aesthetes, like Wiggam:

> Yes, we can have any kind of a race we want, provided we will but give our artists and educators a chance to guide our ideals of marriage selection. . . . Husbands and wives and likewise their children will be beautiful and intelligent if the ideals of beauty and intelligence are in the minds of our young people beforehand so that they unconsciously reject the ugly and stupid, and find their happiness only in people that are lovely and of good report.[41]

Though many people were reading Wiggam's books, most were continuing to select their mates as unscientifically as they always had. Converting the masses—who were busy with their own problems—to the eugenics cause proved difficult. Soon, even the eugenics prophets themselves would wake up from their dream of a more beautiful, kind and intelligent race to the stinging realities of depression and war.

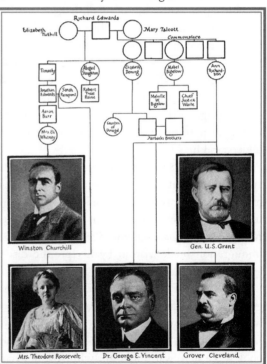

Eugenics author ALBERT E. WIGGAM's pedigree chart of the Edwards Family, of which Winston Churchill, Ulysses S. Grant, Mrs. Theodore Roosevelt, Grover Cleveland, and 1,400 persons "of great social worth" were members (from *The Fruit of the Family Tree*)

WORLD EUGENICS

The ugly, the insane, the criminal and the feebleminded were easy targets; who could argue that the world would be a better place if fewer of them were born? But it was more difficult to convince legislators that Hungarians, Jews, Chinese and Italians were a congenital menace. For decades, Anglo-Saxonists lobbied for immigration restriction without success, believing that inferior stock was contaminating the American bloodstream.

Some argued that it was simply a matter of biology. Closely related races could safely interbreed, but when you crossed a Mediterranean with a Nordic, or a White with a Negro, the offspring would be—as Henry Pratt Fairchild put it— "a reversion, atavism, or throwback." Davenport said that "a hybridized people are a badly put together people and a dissatisfied, restless, ineffective people." [42] In his 1916 book, *The Passing of the Great Race*, Madison Grant argued that the Nordics constituted a "native aristocracy" which rests upon "layer after layer of immigrants of lower races," but that the "great race" was in decline. Neither ruffian nor crackpot, Grant was a wealthy and distinguished New York attorney voicing the private thoughts of many of his class. He was merely trying to preserve what he'd been brought up to expect out of life: privilege based on inherited wealth, good breeding and superior manners. He worried that New York would produce "many amazing racial hybrids and some ethnic horrors that will be beyond the powers of future anthropologists to unravel." The individual of better stock, wrote Grant, "is to-day being literally driven off the streets of New York City by the swarms of Polish Jews," and others of foreign blood. "These immigrants," he warned, "adopt the language of the native American; they wear his clothes; they steal his name; and they are beginning to take his women, but they seldom adopt his religion or understand his ideas." [43]

During the 1890s, laws restricting immigration were repeatedly introduced and defeated. But in 1917, one year after Grant's book came out, an immigration restriction law was finally passed—over Wilson's veto—that required a literacy test and which excluded Asians entirely. Grant wrote the introduction to *The Rising Tide of Color Against White World-Supremacy*, the best-selling 1920 anti-immigration book written by his prolific disciple, Lothrop Stoddard, lawyer, journalist and Harvard Ph.D.

Stoddard, like Grant, abhorred contamination of white stock by inferior immigrants; he also feared that the overcrowding and rebellion of colored nations would threaten white hegemony, and ultimately destroy civilization. "The basic factor in human affairs," wrote Stoddard, "is not politics, but race." Stoddard's book was a stern warning to the white overlords: the racial map of the world could change radically, favoring not the whites but the browns, reds, yellows and blacks. The yellows were preparing to expand their territories into white man's land; the blacks had begun to reject white domination; the browns continued to emigrate to white lands and poison their blood; and the reds had already interbred with

whites, with disastrous results. Whites, he urged, must guard against mongreliza-
tion because like a blood stain, "black blood, once entering a human stock, seems
never really bred out again." The proof of this could be found in Latin America,
where miscegenation had produced "the most extraordinary ethnic combinations"
and grotesque "unheard-of fusions of races," and, ultimately, the degeneration of
white stock, with a profusion of unhappy, confused mongrels, whose every cell was
"a battle-ground of jarring heredities."

The racial crème de la crème, the Nordics, said Stoddard, were being crowd-
ed out in the United States by "swarming, prolific aliens" and by mongrels. And,
because "the melting-pot may mix but does not melt," the mongrel is "a walking
chaos, so consumed by his jarring hereditities that he is quite worthless." To make
matters worse, the Nordics in Europe were decimated during the Great War.
Instead of coming together in white solidarity, the white nations fought among
themselves, killing off their best stocks, while sparing the weaklings and degenerates. The prognosis was grim:

> Here is the truth of the matter: The white world to-day stands at the
> crossroads of life and death. It stands where the Greek world stood
> at the close of the Peloponnesian War. A fever has racked the white
> frame and undermined its constitution. The unsound therapeutics of
> its diplomatic practitioners retard convalescence and endanger real
> recovery. Worst of all, the instinct of race-solidarity has partially
> atrophied.[44]

Stoddard's solution was "world-eugenics," a Nazi-like plan for the preservation of white supremacy, with hints of genocide. Stoddard quoted Prescott Hall
who argued, "Just as we isolate bacterial invasions, and starve out the bacteria by
limiting the area and amount of their food-supply, so we can compel an inferi-
or race to remain in its native habitat, where its own multiplication in a limited
area will, as with all organisms, eventually limit its numbers and therefore its
influence."[45]

Stoddard expanded his plea for world eugenics in his 1922 polemic, *The
Revolt Against Civilization: The Menace of the Under Man*, which warned of the
congenital degenerate in our midst, who not only comes in black, brown, red or
yellow, but in white as well:

> The truth is that as a civilization advances it leaves behind multitudes
> of human beings who have not the capacity to keep pace. . . . Some
> are congenital savages or barbarians; men who could not fit into any
> civilization and who consequently fall behind from the start. . . . They
> must be clearly distinguished from the true degenerates: the imbecile,
> the feebleminded, the neurotic, the insane—all those melancholy

waste-products which every living species excretes but which are promptly extirpated in the state of nature, whereas in human societies they are too often preserved.[46]

According to Stoddard, these inferiors—the Under-Men—cannot adapt to complex society and are in a state of "instinctive and natural revolt against civilization." We might control them by force or coercion, but society must be ever-vigilant because "he remains; he multiplies; he bides his time. And, now and then, his time comes."[47] Via such poisonous doctrines as egalitarianism, democracy and Bolshevism, the Under-Man threatens to destroy the very civilization that allows him to exist:

> The Under-Man is unconvertible. He will not bow to the new truth, because he knows that the new truth is not for him. . . . What the Under-Man wants is, not progress, but regress—regress to more primitive conditions in which he would be at home. In fact, the more he grasps the significance of the new eugenic truth, the uglier grows his mood. So long as all men believed all men potentially equal, the Under-Man could delude himself into thinking that changed circumstances might raise him to the top. Now that nature herself proclaims him irremediably inferior, his hatred of superiority knows no bounds.[48]

Stoddard saw the white world as a new Roman Empire threatened by barbarians from without and by degenerates from within. But, unlike the Romans, we have a chance to preserve our civilization through science. The choice, proclaimed Stoddard, is clear; we can follow either Biology, "the hope of a progressive future," or Bolshevism, "the incarnation of the atavistic past."

Stoddard, no biologist, equated biology with race betterment, which consists of two phases: multiplication of superiors, or race building, and elimination of inferiors, or race cleansing. By "race cleansing," Stoddard did not mean killing off undesirables, but rather the segregation of the insane and feebleminded in institutions. However, his choice of words was prophetic, if not influential. His main concern was that unfit individuals be eliminated.

Even scientists who were sympathetic to eugenics considered the blatant racism of Grant and Stoddard too extreme. Like many who had been early advocates of eugenics, Ernest A. Hooton, Professor of Anthropology at Harvard, became disillusioned with the idea due to its increasingly racist spin. In his 1937 popularization of human evolution, *Apes, Men & Morons*, Hooton wrote candidly of "The Eugenics Bogy":

A good many years ago I attended an International Eugenics Congress, the president of which was one of our most celebrated public scientists, an aristogenist if there ever was one. At the formal banquet which is an inevitable and depressing feature of scientific congresses, this genial, erudite, and justly famous scientist made an introduction of the foreign speaker of the evening in terms which I recall as follows:

"Twenty thousand years ago, when the ice sheet had retreated sufficiently to lay bare a coastal strip of Scandinavia, there landed upon those frigid shores a band of intrepid adventurers, who have remained there to this day, who have pioneered in all of the arts of civilization and yet have maintained the purity and integrity of their Nordic racial blood and physical heritage. And tonight, I am privileged to introduce to you one of the most famous scientists of this Nordic race, who is foremost in research upon racial hygiene and in the promotion of measures to insure racial integrity."

From my obscure and remote table of uncelebrities, I peered myopically to catch a glimpse of this dolichocephalic, blond Viking who was to embody the physical, intellectual, and scientific ideals of the "Great Race." At first I got the elevation of my sight too high and saw no one standing at the speaker's table except the blandly smiling president who had made the eloquent introduction. Then I heard sounds of broken English, and, lowering my gaze a foot or two, I was able to discern its source. It was a sawed-off, rotund person with a head round as a bullet, black hair, a blobby nose and a face reminiscent of the full moon—in short, the complete Alpine. I thereupon decided that every man is his own Nordic, and I am afraid that I leaped to the conclusion that eugenics is a lay form of ancestor worship. . . .[49]

In *Apes, Men & Morons*, anthropologist ERNEST A. HOOTON takes a cautious approach to eugenics.

Those ancestor worshippers were keenest on eliminating "inferior" human specimens by preventing their birth. Though Grant and Stoddard likened them to vermin, few advocated eliminating the unfit by killing them. But a handful did, and euthanasia became a hot topic for debate.

Nobel Prize winning physiologist Alexis Carrel weighed in on the side of euthanasia in the closing pages of his 1935 international best-seller, *Man, the*

Unknown. Carrel, who was French, conducted much of his research at the U.S. Rockefeller Institute for Medical Research. While investigating cell and tissue cultivation, he discovered how to maintain living cells *in vitro*, for which he was awarded the Nobel Prize in 1912. Carrel also invented the iron lung and was the first to maintain whole organs alive, outside the body.

Already well-known, Carrel became even more so through his close association with Charles Lindbergh, with whom he collaborated on the invention of a sterile glass pump that circulated fluids in the life-support system of tissues and organs. Newspapers began circulating rumors that Carrel was a real-life Dr. Frankenstein, who was developing an artificial human being in his secret laboratories. A 1936 Hearst syndicate article read:

> Dr. Carel [sic] is now working in his closely guarded laboratory at Rockefeller Institute on the problem of the relation of cells to those of vegetables and plants, with the hope that some time in the future he can build in his laboratory an artificial human being.
>
> This robot—with blood coursing through his veins, heart beating, brain vibrating, lungs breathing—would be an assembled man; he would have the heart of one dead man, the brain of another corpse, the lungs of a third.[50]

The previous year, Carrel's *Man, the Unknown* had appeared, with phenomenal success: over 100,000 copies were sold in the first year, mostly in France and the United States. By 1936, it had been translated into 13 languages. The book explained the latest developments in the human sciences and contained speculations on telepathy and the power of prayer in healing, as well as quirky passages on eugenics and how excessive exposure to sunlight caused the degeneration of the human race. The critics attacked the book for mixing religion with science— the very combination that made eugenics popular.

Carrel's eugenic speculations took aim not only at imbeciles and criminals, but at "most civilized men" as well, who "manifest only an elementary form of consciousness." Industrial progress had caused their degeneration, damning them to prefer only lowbrow entertainment like "athletic spectacles" and "childish and vulgar moving pictures." Even worse, they had "engendered a vast herd of children whose intelligence remains rudimentary." The common degenerates constituted no less than "three million criminals living in freedom," wrote Carrel, as well as the criminals in jail, the "feebleminded, the morons," and "the insane who overflow from asylums and specialized hospitals."[51]

Eugenics, cautioned the physiologist, was no panacea. *Unaided*, it would *not* guarantee the production of superior individuals. It had to be supplanted with sterner measures:

There remains the unsolved problem of the immense number of defectives and criminals. . . . Why do we preserve these useless and harmful beings? . . . Why should society not dispose of the criminals and the insane in a more economical manner? . . . Perhaps prisons should be abolished. They could be replaced by smaller and less expensive institutions. The conditioning of petty criminals with the whip, or some more scientific procedure, followed by a short stay in hospital, would probably suffice to insure order. Those who have murdered, robbed while armed with automatic pistol or machine gun, kidnapped children, despoiled the poor of their savings, misled the public in important matters, should be humanely and economically disposed of in small euthanistic institutions supplied with proper gases. A similar treatment could be advantageously applied to the insane, guilty of criminal acts. . . .[52]

Some thought Carrel was a Nazi sympathizer, but he probably was not.[53] Nevertheless, he anticipated the Nazi gas chambers by only four years. Were German doctors who murdered their patients propelled by motives and ideas that prevailed, not only in Germany, but also in the United States and Britain, and throughout the Western world?

GERMANY: RACIAL HYGIENE

In Germany, the term "racial hygiene" was preferred over "eugenics." Though in the beginning, the German racial hygiene movement much resembled the eugenics movement, by the time it was adopted by the Nazis with Adolf Hitler as "the great doctor of the German people," the United States eugenics movement had lost much of its steam. This didn't stop the Nazis, however, from modeling their own sterilization laws after laws passed a decade earlier here, in the Land of the Free. In his thought-provoking book *Racial Hygiene: Medicine Under the Nazis* (1988) Robert N. Proctor traces the history of this movement, from its nineteenth century Social Darwinist beginnings to Third Reich orthodoxy. Proctor's history is less a tale of evil Nazi doctors than of the smooth transition made by ordinary people from eugenics to euthanasia to state sanctioned murder in the name of public health.

During the nineteenth century, German Social Darwinism lacked the optimistic, free-market element that dominated in the U.S. When they looked at the human race, all the German Social Darwinists saw was degeneration. About 1895, biologist Alfred Ploetz coined the term *Rassenhygiene* or "racial hygiene" which would reverse the trend of degeneration: by withdrawing medical care from the weak; withdrawing support to the poor of child bearing age; avoiding war, revolution and alcohol; and discouraging inbreeding. Ploetz derived inspiration from American eugenics, and even traveled to Iowa in the 1890s, to conduct a eugenic experiment at the Icarus utopian community. The experiment failed, but Ploetz held fast to racial hygiene. In 1904 he founded the *Journal of Racial and Social Biology* to investigate "the principles of the optimal conditions for the maintenance and development of the race." The following year he co-founded the Society for Racial Hygiene, which by 1930 had grown to 1,300 members. Membership in the Society required a promise not to marry if your potential spouse was in any way unfit.

To some, racial hygiene required not only preventing the unfit from being born, but destroying those that already were. Euthanasia became a hot topic for debate in Germany. In 1920, in *Destruction of Lives Not Worth Living*, Dr. Alfred Hoche and law professor Rudolf Binding argued the incurably sick, physically or mentally, should be mercifully killed, and that the right to live must be earned and justified. The lives of those in mental institutions, which they described as empty human husks, were "lives not worth living." In 1922 Ernst Mann went much further when he published a novel that portrayed the destruction of the poor as a way to eliminate poverty.

The meaning of the word "race" in "racial hygiene" was debated as well. In the beginning, the racial hygiene movement, though nationalist, was neither racist nor anti-Semitic. Ploetz himself argued against the idea of pure races and had no problem with "race mixing." Wilhelm Schallmayer, another early racial hygienist, criticized the idea of Nordic superiority as "vulgar race propaganda" which threatens the goals of true racial science. However, racial hygiene attracted the Nordic racists, just as eugenics attracted the Anglo-Saxonists. Beginning in 1909, the Society for Racial Hygiene barred membership to non-Nordics. By the mid-'20s, the non-Nordic faction had seceded and formed their own organization, the German Association for Völkish Improvement and Genetics.

In the end, the Nordic supremacists dominated. Foremost among them was the geneticist Fritz Lenz. Lenz looked to racial hygiene for no less than the solution to the problem of good and evil, through the "ultimate principle of value," which was race. Lenz was a believer in the Aryan Myth, with the Nordic as the hero of history. His textbook, *Outline of Human Genetics and Racial Hygiene*, first published in 1923, was the most prestigious genetics text for more than 20 years and was considered the standard work in the field. It also won international critical acclaim. In the United States, the *Journal of Heredity* hailed it as "encyclopedic" and "worthy of the best traditions of German scholarship," and five years later as the "standard textbook of human genetics." It also received rave reviews from many U.S. and British sociological journals.

Lenz's acclaimed textbook included summaries of the genetic traits of various races. The Australian Aborigines, wrote Lenz, lack imagination, and "are certainly closest to our own apish ancestors." The Negro, who is somewhat higher than the Aborigine, lacks foresight, is inclined toward crime and poverty, is "more strongly influenced than Europeans by the immediate impressions of the senses" and is thus "less inclined to work hard in the present in order to provide for well-being in a distant future." Mongols, for their part, exceed Nordics in mental development but have more capacity "for imitation than invention." In fact, the Chinese may not have been the inventors of Chinese civilization, for "in modern China, there are millions of persons having a slender build, a narrow head, a narrow face, and a narrow prominent nose, whose general type, therefore, suggests a European origin." Jews, as well, are "a mental race," but are especially interested in sexual life. They're precocious and witty but lack genuine creativity. Thus, Einstein and Spinoza, Lenz concluded, were not actually Jews. Since most Jews have had to adapt to foreign surroundings, they are shrewd, alert, diligent, persevering, and also have an unusual sense of empathy. "The Near Easterner in general," wrote Lenz, "and the Jew in particular, has been selected not for the control and exploitation of nature, but for the control and exploitation of other men." Thus they make their living from the clothing trade, theater, the press, publishing and the law. "The Jew knows what pleases and convinces people," wrote Lenz. "The 'hysterical Jew' has played a great part in revolutionary movements. The Jew outdoes the Gentile in the arts of oratory and persuasion; the Jew is 'a born actor.'" Industrial production and agriculture, however, are completely foreign to the Jews, and "owing to their deficient talent or inclination for the primary work of production, it would seem that a state consisting entirely of Jews would be impossible." [54]

Perhaps the strangest Jewish genetic trait identified by Lenz was the tendency towards Lamarckism. Lenz believed that the process of natural selection had weeded out Jews who believed in Darwinian natural selection, while sparing those who believed in the less cruel process of the inheritance of acquired characteristics. He explained this as a side-effect of the Jewish desire to become German. "If acquired characters could be inherited," he wrote "then, by living in a Teutonic environment and by adopting a Teutonic culture, the Jews [think they] could become transformed into genuine Teutons." [55]

Nordics, predictably, possess many superior traits: they are industrious, imaginative, intelligent, organized, artistic, individualist, meditative, and they are willing to obey orders. They exhibit self-control and self-respect, and show respect for life and property; they're unusually curious, possess a wandering instinct, as well as a fondness for the sea; they love order, cleanliness, sport, danger and war. Moreover, "objectivity," according to Lenz, "is a Nordic racial trait."

Amazingly, Lenz denied that he believed in any kind of racial hierarchy. He claimed that his book contained purely scientific, objective descriptions, but no moral judgments. He also denied being an anti-Semite, adding that the Jew had played a constructive role in history, is a good family man, and has a natural business sense. "Next to Teutonic," wrote Lenz, "the Jewish spirit is the chief motive force of modern Western history."

In 1926, perhaps inspired by the Fitter Families contests in the United States, the Nordic faction held a contest to find the best Nordic head, one male and one female. The competition was conducted by mail, via photographs; 793 male Nordic heads and 506 female Nordic heads were sent in. The judges based their decision on which head they thought best represented the ideal Nordic type.

Through the '20s, beliefs in Nordic supremacy, Nazism, and racial hygiene increasingly overlapped. And, by the mid-'30s, Nazi propaganda had become indistinguishable from the rhetoric of racial hygiene. With jargon borrowed from racial hygiene, SS journals began calling for selection to replace counterselection. And National Socialism became synonymous with "applied biology" and "applied racial science."

The propaganda filtered down from the Nazis to the medical world to the patients via popular medical magazines placed in hospital and clinic waiting rooms. Racial questions dominated the pages of *People's Health Watch*, for example, with a circulation of over 100,000 copies. A 1934 issue contained the article, "Blood and Race: New Research Results" by Dr. Eugen Stähle, in which the author reported that besides external racial differences, there are "deeper, physiological differences among the races," like "racial smell." Careful research had led the doctor to conclude that "Europeans find the smell not only of Negroes, but of East Asians to be repulsive, even when they are clean," and that "the Oriental himself will of course make similar claims." Dr. Stähle then speculated on racial differences in musculature, nervous sensitivity, longevity and blood. Blood, he wrote, is "not merely symbolic, but has also a physical, material meaning." He cited a Russian professor who could identify chemically, with 90 percent accuracy, whether a blood sample came from a Jew or a Russian. "Think what it might mean," he enthused, "if we could identify non-Aryans in the test tube! Then neither deception, nor baptism, nor name change, nor citizenship, and not even nasal surgery could help [the Jew escape detection]. One cannot change one's blood." [56]

The German education system was also injected with a healthy dose of racial hygiene propaganda. "No boy or girl must leave school," suggested Walthur Schultze, the Bavarian Health Inspector, "without being made aware of the essence of blood unity." Needless to say, racial hygiene was a required course for medical students.

While German society was being inundated with racial hygiene propaganda, Americans were beginning to forget eugenics. But the American legacy was well appreciated by the Germans, who often cited the Jukes and Kallikaks studies, translated the works of Madison Grant and Lothrop Stoddard into German, and took inspiration from our immigration, sterilization and anti-miscegenation laws. In 1932 Walter Schultze wrote in the *Journal of the Nazi Physician's League* that Racial Hygienists must learn from the United States, a nation where "racial policy and thinking have become much more popular than in other countries," and where the influx of Jews, Poles and southern Europeans was already restricted by law.

In 1933 the Nazis enacted their own sterilization edict, the Law for the Prevention of Genetically Diseased Offspring. It established a Genetic Health Court to help separate the fit from the defective. Under the law, a person could be sterilized if found by the Genetic Health Court to be feebleminded, schizophrenic, manic-depressive, epileptic, blind, deaf, or severely alcoholic. If someone refused a court-ordered sterilization, they risked being sent to a concentration camp. By the end of the Nazi era, approximately 400,000 people—most of them "feebleminded"—had been sterilized under the law.

To help sort out the finer points of their new genetic duties, members of the medical profession read a new journal entitled *The Genetic Doctor*. It contained an advice column for physicians, who would write in with questions on how to determine genetic fitness, when to sterilize, and how to administer eugenic counseling. Its publisher, Dr. Verschuer, wanted to transform medicine from treatment of the individual to treatment of the race. Every doctor, he proclaimed, must be a "genetic doctor."

The Nuremberg Laws, sold to the German people as public health measures, were enacted in 1935 to further cleanse the German population of bad blood: The Reich Citizenship Law defined citizens as those "of German or related blood who through their behavior make it evident that they are willing and able faithfully to serve the German people and nation." Jews and single women, for example, were merely residents.

The Law for the Protection of German Blood and German Honor (Blood Protection Law) prohibited marriage and sexual relations between Jews and non-Jews, and later between Aryans and non-Aryans. Under this law, a "Full Jew" was anyone with at least three Jewish grandparents. For those with one or two Jewish grandparents—the dreaded mongrels—things got a little sticky. Those of one-quarter Jewish ancestry were considered German and were allowed to marry other Germans. However, one-quarter-Jews weren't allowed to marry one another, because of the supposed danger that their offspring might be half-Jewish.

The Law for the Protection of the Genetic Health of the German People (Marital Health Law) required a medical exam before marriage to check for racial damage, and prohibited marriage to someone with VD, feeblemindedness, epilepsy, or some other genetic infirmity. Couples who were both "genetically ill" were allowed to marry, but only after being sterilized.

The enforcement of the Nuremberg Laws required that the genetic courts determine some of the thornier racial issues. Physicians and anthropologists showed authorities how to identify race by looking at the shapes of the forehead, brow, eyelids, nose, eyes and ears. Hitler claimed he could identify a Jew by looking at whether or not his earlobes were attached to his neck. He ordered photographs of Stalin's ears, in order to determine whether or not he was Jewish.

This kind of logic was codified for mass consumption in such publications as the 1937 *Handbook for Hitler Youth*. Through this required text, seven million children learned that Nordics are "uncommonly gifted mentally," are "outstanding for truthfulness and energy," and that Nordic men possess "a great power of judgement." Members of the Western race found in England and France were "much more ready to talk, lively, even loquacious . . . have much less patience [and] act more by feeling than by reason" than the Nordic. Other races were similarly lacking in comparison to the Nordic.

The *Handbook* also provided an outline of genetics to help the student understand the necessity for racial consciousness, which was simply a matter of public health. It warned against "pollution and injury" of the heredity stream by "diseased elements" and by "racially foreign" blood. It also explained the Sterilization and Nuremberg Laws, which prevented the births of "unfortunate, restless" hybrids with a "split personality," and that the National Socialist racial outlook was essentially "humanitarian."

Hitler proclaimed 1939 as the year of "the duty to be healthy." What this meant—though unofficially—was that it was the duty of those who were not healthy to die. In secret memos, Hitler authorized the destruction of incurably sick patients, deformed and retarded children, and mental patients. "The Committee for the Scientific Treatment of Severe, Genetically Determined Illness" administered the euthanasia programs. The destruction of mental patients followed the formula 1000:10:5:1, which meant that for every 1,000 Germans, ten needed psychiatric care; five of those ten needed continuous care; and one of those five should be destroyed. When they administered poison, or gas, or slowly starved their patients, physicians knew they were only doing their duty as a genetic doctor to disinfect the race. Nevertheless, they made sure that the bodies of the unfit were cremated to hide the evidence, before the arrival of curious relatives.

Doctors began to experiment with extermination by carbon monoxide gas in 1940. Trial runs were carried out at the Brandenburg Hospital on 20 people. After the patients undressed, nurses led them into a shower room and closed the doors. An observer wrote that when the gas began to come into the room, "there was no great disturbance or commotion" and the patients simply laid or fell down. Afterwards, their bodies were taken to the crematoria to be burned. The experiment was deemed successful; soon other hospitals were outfitted with their own gassing apparatus, "shower rooms," and crematoria.

Apparently, those who participated in the euthanasia programs enjoyed their work. Proctor reports that "in 1941 the psychiatric institution at Hadamar celebrated the cremation of its ten-thousandth patient in a special ceremony, where everyone in attendance—secretaries, nurses, and psychiatrists—received a bottle of beer for the occasion." [57] The relatives of the victims, however, became suspicious that their loved ones were being killed and began to complain about the gassings. The killing of incurables continued, but through lethal injection, starvation and slow poisoning, which were easier to hide than mass killings in gas chambers.

On the other hand, some German parents, eager to be rid of their retarded children, had no objections to euthanasia. A 1920 survey had found that 73 percent of parents of handicapped children stated that they would agree to euthanasia, under varying circumstances.

Nazi policy encouraged Nordic women to stay home and breed as many Nordic babies as possible. In 1938 Hitler established the Honor Cross of German Motherhood: bronze for four children; silver for six; gold for eight. Lucrative loans were offered to married men whose wives gave up their jobs. It's been estimated that a total of three million additional German babies were produced as a direct result of these policies.

Meanwhile, propaganda had transformed political anti-Semitism into medical policy. In his 1935 treatise *Racial Mixing and Disease*, for example, Wilhelm Hildebrandt had argued that because each race has a distinct life span, their organs mature and degenerate at different rates. Race mixing produces diseased mongrels whose organs are out of sync with one another, and who lack the "equilibrium" of the pure races. After the war broke out, the danger of the spread of disease was used to separate Jews from the non-Jews in occupied territories. Propaganda explained the separation of Germans and Poles on Warsaw streetcars as "a hygienic necessity." When Jews were banned from unauthorized railway travel in occupied Poland, newspaper headlines read, "Germ-carriers Banned from Railways." Nazi officials considered the walled Jewish ghettos in Poland as a hygienic necessity, like quarantines. Radio stations reported that the Jews in the ghettos were "ulcers which must be cut away from the body of the European nations." If the Jews hadn't been walled in, the "whole of Europe would be poisoned."

Proposals for the ultimate quarantine of Jews, a.k.a. "The Final Solution," abounded: deport all Jews to Madagascar; establish a Jewish reservation near Lublin; sterilize by X-ray Jews capable of work, and exterminate the rest. It was finally decided to gas them in concentration camps, because this method had already worked so well on mental patients.

Jews were not the only out-group stigmatized as genetically ill. Gypsies, Communists, homosexuals, the feebleminded, tuberculars, alcoholics, prostitutes, drug addicts, the homeless and others were also considered hygienic menaces. Homosexuality, for example, was treated as an epidemic, and homosexuals were exterminated so they wouldn't infect healthy Germans. Likewise, fear of the "Gypsy Plague" condemned thousands of Gypsies to the gas chamber.

The rhetoric of eugenics and racial hygiene was indispensable to the Nazis in justifying the mass murder of Jews, Gypsies and homosexuals, as well as the traditionally "unfit." The question remains, however: Did they consciously use racial hygiene as an "excuse" for politically motivated murder—or did they really believe that killing people was hygienically necessary? It seems likely that the physicians, and many of the top Nazis as well, really did believe that they were valiant fumigators, cleansing humanity of disease and filth.

EUGENICS IS A DIRTY WORD, BUT ...

After the war, the racial hygienists continued their careers as professors of human genetics at German universities. Their texts were altered to remove all references to National Socialism and racial hygiene. Elsewhere, support for anything remotely resembling eugenics or racial hygiene vanished. The dream of controlling the development of the human race through breeding was now seen as, at best, unethical, or, at worst, a sure path to genocide.

Eugenics temporarily disappeared not only because of the bad example of the Nazis. It was also rejected because it rested on outdated beliefs and assumptions, some of which had fallen out of fashion and others which had been scientifically discredited. Eugenics belonged in a world in which everyone agreed about which human traits were "desirable" and which were "undesirable," where it was assumed that objectively identifying those traits was possible, and where intelligence and other behavioral traits were believed to be inherited. Eugenics also required the ethical stance that "defective" people have fewer rights than others.

The would-be manipulators of the human race were forced to try their hand in fields other than genetics. In 1942 Dr. Foster Kennedy, professor of neurology at Cornell, in an article published in the Journal of the American Psychiatric Association, called for the killing of retarded children aged five and over, whom he described as "those hopeless ones who should never have been born—nature's mistakes." Almost imperceptibly, the flame of scientifically sanctioned human manipulation was being passed from the racial hygienists to the psychiatrists, who would soon justify using humans as guinea pigs for lobotomies and electroshock therapy with appeals to improving the human condition.

During the past 30 years, however, eugenic practices—if not eugenic philosophies—have returned, fueled by breakthroughs in genetics, medicine and reproductive technology. Lori B. Andrews, an expert in legal and ethical implications of reproductive technologies (such as in-vitro fertilization, the use of fertility drugs and surrogate motherhood) documents the controversies surrounding these practices in her 1999 book, *The Clone Age: Adventures in the New World of Reproductive Technology.*

Many of the players in those controversies—though not necessarily familiar with the word and its history—harbor eugenic motives. Cyndy Imhof, for example, an early egg donor, told Andrews in 1984 that she agreed to donate eggs to infertile women because "I come from an extremely healthy background without cancer, diabetics, disfigurements, or catastrophic diseases. I couldn't see why I should just waste these wonderful genes I was blessed with."[58] Imhof's feelings are natural, but her underlying assumption is that "good genes" make better babies. That assumption works in reverse as well. Andrews knew a law professor who had been rejected by an agency to be a surrogate mother. The woman, crosseyed and slightly overweight, concluded she wasn't "commercially viable"—in other words, no one would want her genes in their children.[59]

For years women have been able to check their fetuses for maladies such as Down's Syndrome and spina bifida using amniocentesis and ultrasound. While many decide to abort their genetically ill fetuses, it's a painful decision, and abortion is never easy. But now that genetic testing can be done on embryos outside the womb, eliminating genetic defects is much easier. Couples using in-vitro fertilization, for example, can easily practice eugenics if they so choose. After an ovary has been fertilized, the resulting embryo can be tested for a number of genetic defects and traits. Typically, the couple can choose from among several or a dozen embryos to implant in the woman's womb. Naturally, they choose those with the traits they want, eliminating those with genetic defects or "negative" traits. Princeton biologist Lee Silver realized the eugenic potential of this practice saying, "In a very literal sense, IVF [in-vitro fertilization] allows us to hold the future of our species in our own hands." [60]

Overtly eugenic rhetoric has returned as well. Francis Galton would have been proud of Robert Klark Graham, who established the Repository for Germinal Choice sperm bank in Escondido, Calif., available only to "geniuses." When he opened his clinic in 1979, the sperm in his bank came from Nobel prize-winning scientists only. The women using the bank also had to be of high intelligence. Soon, however, Graham had difficulty finding Nobelists who were as eugenics-minded as he was, so he opened up his bank to other "geniuses"—specifically, members of Mensa.[61]

Graham spouts ideas that are practically indistinguishable from the eugenics writings of a century ago. Andrews posed as a candidate for Graham's clinic, and during her application process Graham told her:

> "Intelligence is the only thing that sets man apart from the beast. For many years, man evolved through the survival of the fittest so that only the most intelligent lived to bear children, but now technology lets those with genetic defects live and reproduce. And while bright women are postponing having children or not having children at all, we're financing poor women to have them." [62]

Graham's genius sperm bank would be only the first step in the race to outbreed those of presumably lower IQ. He also advocated—as did eugenicists of old—using economic and social incentives to encourage "worthwhile" couples to have more children. The government, he said, should build special low-rent suburban housing developments for high-IQ couples only, who would agree to bear at least one child every two years.[63]

The generations that remember the heyday of eugenics and the horrors of Nazism are almost gone, and with them will go a visceral distaste for anything smacking of eugenics. Eugenics was a dirty word for 50 years but it's making a comeback, due not only to advances in technology but also the perennial desire to improve the human condition by better breeding. Though it's never been scientifically confirmed that humanity can be improved using eugenics, or even that such traits as intelligence are solely the result of genes, the eugenic hope will never go away.

———◆———

1. Passmore, *The Perfectibility of Man*, p. 186.
2. Campanella, "City of the Sun," p. 281.
3. Spencer, "Social Statics" quoted in Hofstadter, *Social Darwinism*, p. 27.
4. Ibid.
5. Rockefeller, in *Our Benevolent Feudalism* by William J. Ghent; quoted in Hofstadter, *Social Darwinism*, p. 31.
6. Carnegie, "Wealth," quoted in Hofstadter, *Social Darwinism*, p. 32.
7. One cannot help imagining Ragnar Redbeard as a wild-eyed red-head bedecked with Viking headgear typing madly, while laughing lustily, swigging from an oversized beer stein and ripping off pieces of raw meat with his teeth. On the other hand, he may well have been a hen-pecked, frustrated Walter Mitty type.
8. Redbeard, *Might is Right*, p. 4.
9. Ibid., p. 12.
10. Ibid., pp. 52–53.
11. Ibid., p. 89.
12. Haeckel quoted in *Encyclopedia of Evolution* by Milner.
13. "Ontogeny recapitulates phylogeny," is the now discredited theory that the growth of the embryo parallels the evolution of the species.
14. Haeckel quoted in *Final Solutions* by Lerner, p. 25. Original source; *Haeckel, The History of Creation: or, The Development of the Earth and its Inhabitants by the Action of Natural Causes*, n.p., 1876.
15. Galton quoted in *In the Name of Eugenics*, by Kevles, p. 7.
16. Galton quoted in *Encyclopedia of Evolution*, by Milner.
17. Ibid.
18. Galton quoted in *Parenthood and Race Culture*, by Saleeby, pp. 45–46. Originally from *Sociological Papers*, 1905.
19. Galton quoted in *Encyclopedia of Evolution*, by Milner.
20. Galton quoted in *Hereditary Genius*, by Saleeby, p. 132.
21. Kevles, *In the Name of Eugenics*, p. 20.
22. So called because it was "burnt over" with religious fervor.
23. Orrmont, "John Humphrey Noyes: Communist of Love," and Robertson, *Oneida Community*.
24. Robertson, *Oneida Community*, pp. 267–68.

25. Orrmont, "John Humphrey Noyes: Communist of Love," p. 30.
26. Ibid., p. 46.
27. Robertson, *Oneida Community*, p. 337.
28. Dugdale, "The Jukes: A Study in Crime, Pauperism, and Heredity."
29. Gould, *Mismeasure of Man*, p. 162.
30. Wiggam, *Fruit of the Family Tree*, pp. 8–10.
31. Kevles, *In the Name of Eugenics*, p. 57.
32. Davenport quoted in *In the Name of Eugenics*, by Kevles.
33. Ibid., p. 53.
34. Ibid.
35. Shannon, *Eugenics*, p. 20.
36. Saleeby, *Parenthood and Race Culture*, pp. 17–18.
37. Wiggam quoted in *In the Name of Eugenics*, by Kevles, p. 68.
38. Wiggam, *Fruit of the Family Tree*, p. 17.
39. Ibid., p. 262.
40. Ibid.
41. Ibid., p. 275.
42. Haller, *Eugenics*, p. 148.
43. Ibid., Grant quoted in *Eugenics*, by Haller, p. 149.
44. Stoddard, *Rising Tide of Color*, p. 196.
45. Hall, "Immigration Restriction and World Eugenics," *The Journal of Heredity*, 1919, in *Rising Tide of Color*, by Stoddard, pp. 259–60.
46. Stoddard, *Menace of the Under Man*, p. 22.
47. Ibid., p. 25.
48. Ibid., p. 86.
49. Hooton, *Apes, Men, and Morons*, p. 231.
50. Schneider, *Quality and Quantity*, p. 274.
51. Carrel, *Man, The Unknown*, p. 139.
52. Ibid., pp. 318–19.
53. Schneider, *Quality and Quantity*, pp. 276–80.
54. Lenz quoted in *Racial Hygiene*, by Proctor pp. 53–55.
55. Ibid., p. 55.
56. Stähle quoted in *Racial Hygiene*, by Proctor, p. 78.
57. Proctor, *Racial Hygiene*, p. 191.
58. Andrews, *Clone Age*, p. 37.
59. Ibid., pp. 95–96.
60. Ibid., p. 145.
61. Admittance to Mensa is based on IQ, which must be in the top two percent.
62. Andrews, *Clone Age*, p. 129.
63. Ibid., pp. 132–33.

CHAPTER FIVE

CREATIONISM

*We would rather a thousand times trace our descent up
to God through Adam than down to a sea jelly through wormy
ancestors whose children were apes!*

REV. HARRY RIMMER

*Adam had a computer-like mind that was far superior to
ours today. It was created a perfect brain with computer-memory
circuits unaffected by decay, breakdown, aging, deterioration, death.*

REV. EMIL GAVERLUK

C reationists believe God created the universe, life and mankind the way the Bible tells us. Some take the Bible more literally than others, but all appeal to biblical authority for answers about the origins of our world. As such, creationism is just one tenet of Protestant fundamentalism, whose defining principle is the inerrancy of Scripture.

Modern American creationists, as frontliners in the fundamentalist war on secularism, present themselves as mainstream, conservative defenders of the faith. Certainly, they are the most mainstream of Darwin's challengers; as recently as 1982, a Gallup poll found 44 percent of Americans agreed with the statement, "God created man pretty much in his present form at one time within the last 10,000 years."

GEORGE MCCREEDY PRICE, an early modern creationist (from *A History of Modern Creationism*)

Creationists, however, have much in common with believers in alien intervention and de-evolution. Modernism, materialism and scientific authority threaten creationists, just as they threaten their more far-out cousins.

CREATION MYTHS & GENESIS

Though they would probably deny it, modern creationists share some fundamental beliefs with such people as the Ewes of western Africa, Hindus, and Apaches, all of whom believe in the special creation of the universe, and mankind. In the Ewe story, which resembles the creation of man and then woman in Genesis 2, "God fashioned a man and set him on the earth; after that he fashioned a woman. The two looked at each other and began to laugh, whereupon God sent them into the world."[1] The Ewes believe that God made people out of clay, just as the biblical god Yahweh made man from the dust. The creation story of the Jicarilla Apache of New Mexico centered also on the theme of creating mankind from the earth. In this story, the world creator, Black Hactcin, mixed a drop of rain with the earth to fashion a bird from the mud, along with some bird and animal companions. The creatures told Black Hactcin that they wanted a new companion, in the form of a man:

> And so [Black Hactcin] told them to gather objects from all directions. They brought pollen, . . . and they added red ocher, white clay, white stone, jet, turquoise, red stone, opal, abalone, and assorted valuable stones. And when they put these before Black Hactcin, he told them to withdraw to a distance. . . . He took pollen and traced with it the outline of a figure on the ground, an outline just like that of his own body. Then he placed the precious stones and other objects inside this outline, and they became flesh and bones. The veins were of turquoise, the blood of red ocher, the skin of coral, the bones of white rock; the fingernails were of Mexican opal, the pupil of the eye of jet, the whites of the eyes of abalone, the marrow in the bones of white clay, and the teeth too were of opal. He took a dark cloud and out of it fashioned the hair. It becomes a white cloud when you are old.[2]

The Indian Upanishads contains a quite different variation of the special creation of mankind:

> In the beginning this universe was but the Self in the form of a man. He looked around and saw nothing but himself. . . .
> . . . He desired a second. He was just as large as a man and woman embracing. This Self then divided himself in two parts; and with that, there were a master and a mistress. . . . He united with her, and from that mankind arose.
> She, however, reflected: "How can he unite with me, who am produced from himself? Well then, let me hide!" She became a cow, he a bull and united with her; and from that cattle arose. She became a mare, he a stallion; she an ass, he a donkey and united with her; Thus he poured forth all pairing things, down to the ants. . . .[3]

In at least one respect, those who hold to such creation legends are one step behind today's current crop of biblical creationists: we have yet to hear of Apaches conducting chemical analysis to prove that man was made by Black Hactcin out of precious stones, or Ewes insisting that their story of God creating man and woman out of clay is "scientific." Today's fundamentalists seek to convince themselves and others that their conception of natural history—which relies entirely on a literalistic reading of one sacred text—is consistent with current observations of the natural world. Scripture is the creationists' anchor in a tumultuous world—and they'll do anything to defend it. Rather than endure a soul-testing crisis of faith, fundamentalists prefer to think that their creation myth is somehow different from all the other creation myths in the world. It's unique, it's literally true, and what's more, it's scientific.

The new-wave creationists also prefer to ignore evidence that the Judeo-Christian Bible shares many themes with earlier, Mesopotamian texts. Scholars agree that Babylonian, Sumerian and Egyptian myths all had a strong influence on the Bible, especially the book of Genesis, which may be read as a collection of not necessarily consistent Middle Eastern creation myths. According to the Babylonians, mankind was created from the body of a rebellious god, to serve the rest of the gods as slaves.[4] In Genesis 2, written about 1,500 years later, the first man, Adam, was created from dust to serve the One God, Yahweh, by tending a garden:

> And [Yahweh] formed man of the dust of the ground, and breathed into his nostrils the breath of life; and man became a living soul. And [Yahweh] planted a garden eastward in Eden; and there he put the man whom he had formed. And out of the ground [Yahweh] made to grow every tree that is pleasant to the sight, and good for food; the tree of life also in the midst of the garden, and the tree of knowledge of good and evil. And a river went out of Eden to water the garden; and from thence it was parted, and became into four heads. . . . And [Yahweh] took the man, and put him into the garden of Eden to dress it and to keep it. And [Yahweh] commanded the man, saying, "Of every tree of the garden thou mayest freely eat: but of the tree of the knowledge of good and evil, thou shalt not eat of it: for in the day that thou eatest thereof thou shalt surely die." And out of the ground [Yahweh] formed every beast of the field, and every fowl of the air. And [Yahweh] caused a deep sleep to fall upon Adam, and he slept: and he took one of his ribs, and closed up the flesh. . . . And the rib, which [Yahweh] had taken from man, made he a woman, and brought her unto the man. (King James Version)

The sequence of creation here, found in the second chapter of Genesis, is that first God creates man (Gen. 2:7), then animals (Gen. 2:19) and then woman (Gen. 2:22-23) from Adam's rib. The creator deity is called Yahweh, translated in the King James Version as "Lord God." Joseph Campbell writes that this "charming fairy tale" is essentially a re-working of a Sumerian myth, characteristic of planting cultures: "We recognize the old Sumerian garden, but with two trees now instead of one, which the man is appointed to guard and tend. . . . And, finally, . . . one of the chief characteristics of Levantine mythology . . . is that of man created to be God's slave or servant. . . . As a whole, this early Judean myth—which has seared deeply the soul of Western man—is of the general category . . . common to the planting cultures of the tropics. . . ." [5]

Though it's placed in the second chapter of Genesis, the Garden of Eden story, which dates from the ninth century B.C., predates the other creation myth in the first chapter. This very different tale—with inklings of evolution—was written about five centuries later. Here, the creator is called "Elohim," which means "the gods":

> In the beginning [Elohim] created the heaven and the earth. And the earth was without form, and void; and darkness was upon the face of the deep. And the Spirit of [Elohim] moved upon the face of the waters. And [Elohim] said, "Let there be light," and there was light. . . . And [Elohim] said, "Let the waters bring forth abundantly the moving creature that hath life, and fowl that may fly above the earth in the open firmament of heaven. . . ." And [Elohim] made the beast of the earth after his kind, and cattle after their kind, and every thing that creepeth upon the earth after his kind; and [Elohim] saw that it was good. And [Elohim] said, "Let us make man in our image, after our likeness; and let them have dominion over the fish of the sea, and over the fowl of the air, and over the cattle, and over all the earth, and over every creeping thing that creepeth upon the earth." So [Elohim] created man in his own image . . . male and female created he them. (King James Version)

Here, the sequence is the reverse of the Garden of Eden story. Animals are made first (Gen. 1:20–25), and then man and woman together, in God's image (Gen. 1:26–27). Campbell categorizes this as a more primitive story of creation "from the power of the word."

Popular translations of the Bible, including the King James Version cherished by fundamentalists, create much confusion by translating Yahweh from the second chapter as "Lord God," and Elohim from the first chapter as "God," thus making it look like the two deities are one and the same. Similarly, placing the later story first, and the earlier story second, makes it look as if one is a continuation of the other, when, in fact, they are two separate myths, originating at different times from different people. It would be like presenting *Mutiny on the Bounty* as part two of *Moby Dick*—as if *Moby Dick* were the inerrant word of God. Because of their reliance on the Bible for absolute truth, current fundamentalists—like many Christians before them—are reluctant to face its inconsistencies. The confusion between the two creation stories of Genesis, however, has unduly influenced Western religious thought, and will probably do so for many years to come.

THE CREATION AND THE CHURCH

According to Andrew Dixon White, author of the classic study *A History of the Warfare of Science with Theology in Christendom* (1896), church fathers did their best to reconcile the two conflicting creation stories of Genesis. St. Augustine (354–430), the prolific author and monastic who many view as the founder of Christian theology, was skeptical of a literal interpretation of Genesis. He observed, for example, that it's nonsense to speak of God creating "days" when it's night on the other side of the globe. "How can we possibly confine God to one spot," he asked, "where he will be in night, while somewhere else the light has departed from him?" [6] Rather than take Genesis literally, Augustine saw it as a cloak for the mystery of creation. The Bible, nonetheless, was still the last word. "Nothing is to be accepted save on the authority of Scripture," he wrote, "since greater is that authority than all the powers of the human mind." This view held firmly through the Middle Ages, despite the growing domination—in the real world—of church authority over that of Scripture. Literalism received a boost, however, when leaders of the Protestant Reformation replaced the authority of the church with the authority of Scripture. Martin Luther (1483–1546), German leader of the Reformation, rejected all mystical or allegorical interpretations in favor of a literal acceptance of Scripture as the authority on the natural world. French Protestant theologian John Calvin (1509–1564), as well, contended that all creatures were created in six days, and that no new species had appeared since.

Andrew Dixon White remarks that the literal conception of creation "can scarcely be imagined" in this enlightened age. He wrote a century ago, when it seemed that "progress" had defeated religion. Fundamentalism as we understand it today hadn't yet been invented. White would be aghast if he knew how many Americans at the end of the twentieth century believe that the universe was created in six days. In a simpler era, he notes, "the Almighty was represented in theological literature, in the pictured Bibles, and in works of art generally, as a sort of enlarged and venerable Nuremberg toymaker." Or, "The Creator was shown as a tailor, seated, needle in hand, diligently sewing together skins of beasts into coats for Adam and Eve."

In this cozy little world fossils posed no quandaries. According to White, scholars saw them simply as "models of his works approved or rejected by the great Artificer," as "outlines of future creations," as "sports of Nature," or as "objects placed in the strata to bring to naught human curiosity." Mankind was literally the center of the universe. No organism could be imagined apart from its connection to ourselves. God created some creatures to help us, others to instruct us, and still others only to chastise us. Noxious beasts were thought to exist as punishment for sin. Before the fall of man, they simply did not exist. "I confess I am ignorant why mice and frogs were created, or flies and worms," wrote Augustine. "All creatures are either useful, hurtful, or superfluous to us. . . . As for the hurtful creatures, we are either punished, or disciplined, or terrified by them, so that we may not cherish and love this life." Likewise, Luther thought that an annoying fly was sent by the Devil to vex him while reading. Theologians from St. Basil (329 B.C.–79) to St. Augustine stressed that man was fashioned separately and directly by the Creator's hand, while beasts came into being *en masse*, by the Creator's voice. No wonder the suggestion that we're related to beasts would later cause such a scandal.

Natural history was a sacred science during the Middle Ages. Rather than using observations in the natural world to back up Scripture, as creation scientists do today, theologians used Scripture to reveal truths about the natural world. "Naturalists"—whose only observations were made in between the pages of a book—found that "the basilisk kills serpents by his breath and men by his glance, that the lion when pursued effaces his tracks with the end of his tail, that the pelican nourishes her young with her own blood, and that serpents lay aside their venom before drinking, that the salamander quenches fire, that the hyena can talk with shepherds, that certain birds are born of the fruit of a certain tree when it happens to fall into water, with other masses of science equally valuable."[7]

Their quandary about a Hebrew word found in the book of Job, translated as "ant-lion," led Church scientists to a tortured conclusion. "As to the ant-lion, his father hath the shape of a lion, his mother that of an ant; the father liveth upon flesh and the mother upon herbs; these bring forth the ant-lion, a compound of both and in part like to either; for his fore part is like that of a lion and his hind part like that of an ant. Being thus composed, he is neither able to eat flesh like his father nor herbs like his mother, and so he perisheth."[8]

Questions about the antiquity and chronology of the world and of mankind were likewise answered by Scripture. During the first three centuries of the Christian Era, church fathers reasoned that because there were six days before the appearance of "first Adam," that there were 6,000 years before the appearance of "second Adam," Christ. Thus Man was created in 6,000 B.C. Theophilus, Bishop of Antioch wrote in the second century, "One day is with the Lord as a thousand years." Hence, each day of creation in Genesis corresponds to 1,000 years. This idea came from a passage in the New Testament: "But, beloved, be not ignorant of this one thing, that one day is with the Lord as a thousand years, and a thousand years as one day" (II Peter 3:8). The meaning of the passage is that God-time and human-time are incommensurable. The chapter where it is found concerns the return of Lord Jesus Christ and has nothing to do with Yahweh or the Elohim of the Old Testament. The Bishop was only the first of a long line of theologians who would take this passage out of context in order to calculate biblical dates. This sort of "day-age" reasoning has endured; some theologians use it to predict the precise year of the second coming of Christ—others to reconcile scientific evidence for an old Earth with Scripture.

St. Jerome posited another view in the fourth century, one that would dominate Western Europe through the Middle Ages. From calculations based on passages in the Old Testament he concluded that Adam was created some time between 4000 and 6000 B.C. Because of his authority as Latin Church Father and as a revered Christian scholar, to doubt his conclusions was to risk eternal damnation. St. Augustine, for example, considered such doubt a deadly heresy.[9]

Pinpointing the precise date of creation became an obsession for many theologians. Around 1580 the Roman Church published a declaration stating that the creation of Man took place in exactly 5199 B.C. But when Archbishop Ussher published *Annals of Ancient* and *New Testaments* 70 years later, the official date of creation was pushed up to 4004 B.C., and stuck there. Ussher had spent years of careful study to arrive at this date, and the Church authorities received it as the final word on the subject. They promptly added his dates to the margins of the authorized version of the English Bible. Ussher's marginal notes were regarded with as much piety as the sacred text itself. In the seventeenth century Dr. John Lightfoot, the Vice-Chancellor of the University of Cambridge, pinpointed the date even more precisely, declaring that the creation took place "on the twenty-third of October, 4004 B.C., at nine o'clock in the morning."

The mid-seventeenth-century Christian scholar La Peyrère attempted to reconcile the existence of various native peoples with Scripture by proposing that they were pre-Adamites.[10] "He was taken in hand at once; great theologians rushed forward to attack him from all parts of Europe; within 50 years 36 different refutations of his arguments had appeared; the Parliament of Paris burned the book, and the Grand Vicar of the archdiocese of Mechlin threw him into prison and kept him there until he was forced, not only to retract his statements, but to abjure his Protestantism." The cracks in the old edifice of Bible belief were only just beginning to appear.

CREATION BEFORE DARWIN

Though modern creationists pick on evolution in general, and Darwin in particular, the Scriptural theory of the natural world was already in trouble, long before Darwin. It all started with the exploration of the New World beginning in the late fifteenth century.

Because new species—or Scripturally, "kinds"—were being discovered by the boatload, theologians were required to claim that 160 distinct, miraculous interventions by the Creator produced the 160 species of land shells that were found in Madeira, and that 1,400 miraculous interventions produced the 1,400 species of one well-known shell. By the mid-nineteenth century, wrote White, "the whole theological theory of creation—though still preached everywhere as a matter of form—was clearly seen by all thinking men to be hopelessly lost."[12]

The germ of the theory of evolution didn't generate overnight. It was lurking in, of all places, the first chapter of Genesis, for millennia. God created first the fishes, then the land animals, then the birds, and so on, until he created man and woman. Though tacitly creationist it hints at evolution from cruder to more complex forms of life. Theories suggesting evolution, though overshadowed by the idea of instantaneous creation, continued their minute influence. Finally, in the eighteenth and nineteenth centuries, the weight of evidence gathered from distant shores began tipping the scales in evolution's favor.

Those who devised these new theories were frequently pious individuals with no bone to pick with the theologians. The eight Bridgewater Treatises, for example, a scientific series commissioned in 1829 by the will of the Rev. Francis Henry Egerton, eighth Earl of Bridgewater, appeared, dedicated to "the Power, Wisdom, and Goodness of God, as Manifested in the Creation." [13]

But theologians continued reading radical impiety, immorality and heresy into scientific work. In 1844, an intense firestorm erupted over a book entitled *Vestiges of the Natural History of Creation* written anonymously—but whose author was later discovered to be a gentleman geologist from Edinburgh, Robert Chambers. Among other, more dubious theories, Chambers proposed evolution. "The simplest and most primitive type, under a law to which that of like-production is subordinate," he wrote, "gave birth to the type next above it, that this again produced the next higher, and so on to the very highest, the stages of advance being in all cases very small—namely, from one species only to another; so that the phenomena has always been of a simple and modest character." Chambers' implications were too strong for even some other scientists to bear. Geologist Adam Sedgwick, for example, was provoked, by *Vestiges*, to moralistic ranting:

> The world cannot bear to be turned upside down; and we are ready to wage an internecine war with any violation of our modest principles and social manners. . . . If our glorious maidens and matrons may not soil their fingers with the dirty knife of the anatomist, neither may they poison the springs of joyous thought and modest feeling, by listening to the seductions of this author; . . . who tells them—that their Bible is a fable when it teaches them that they were made in the image of God—that they are the children of apes and the breeders of monsters—that he has annulled all distinction between physical and moral (p. 315). . . . If the book be true, the labours of sober induction are in vain; religion is a lie; human law is a mass of folly, and a base injustice; morality is moonshine; our labours for the black people of Africa were works of madmen; and man and woman are only better beasts! [14]

Chambers wrote *Vestiges* within the framework of natural theology, including reassurance that "God created animated beings, as well as the terraqueous theatre of their being, is a fact so powerfully evidenced, and so universally received, that I at once take it for granted." He emphasized mechanistic, natural processes, however, over those of the Creator. He criticized the prevailing notion "that the Almighty Author produced the progenitors of all existing species by some sort of personal or immediate exertion," as absurd and superstitious. It was more logical, he argued, to consider organic creation as a single event. In so many words, God created the world, gave it a little kick, and it's been rolling ever since. Similar reconciliations of creation and evolution, by the way, are still popular among Catholics and non-fundamentalist Protestants.

Critics attacked the *Vestiges* not merely as incorrect, but also as "dangerous." Readers, apparently hungry for a bit of philosophical danger, were drawn to it like moths to a flame. It went through four editions in less than two years, and 11 by 1860. Because of his anonymity, it became a game at high society dinner parties as well as scientific meetings, to attempt to identify the author. Leading candidates were Thackeray, Lady Lovelace, Sir Richard Vyvyan, Sir Charles Lyell, George Combe and Prince Albert. But the scientifically inferior *Vestiges* would soon be forgotten in favor of weightier fare.

As if anticipating the decline of natural theology, a popular author named Philip Gosse produced a reconciliation of science and Scripture entitled *Omphalos* (the Greek word for navel), in 1857, only two years before the appearance of *Origin of Species*. If God created Adam and Eve complete with navels, hair and fingernails, reasoned Gosse, then he must also have created the earth complete with fossils and geologic strata. Rather than as evidence for a long process of change and evolution, Gosse wrote, the geologic features, fashioned by the Creator in an instant, haven't changed in 6,000 years. This attempt to combine science with Scripture was ridiculed by both scientists and clerics alike. Little did they realize that this kind of logic would return in creationist writings of the twentieth century.

REACTIONS TO DARWIN

The clerical outrage vented on the *Vestiges* . . . was only practice for Darwin's *Origin of Species*, a decade later, which introduced Darwin's theory—that new species arise by the mechanism of "natural selection"—to the scientific world. "Yearly more [organisms] are bred than can survive," wrote Darwin of natural selection. "The smallest grain in the balance, in the long run, must tell on which death shall fall, and which shall survive. Let this work of selection, on the one hand, and death on the other, go on for a thousand generations; who would pretend to affirm that it would produce no effect, when we remember what in a few years [Robert] Bakewell effected in cattle and [Lord] Western in sheep, by this identical principle of selection."[15] Clergy and scientists alike perceived the implications immediately: if the blind mechanism of natural selection creates new species, who needs an all-powerful Creator? Further, if new species arise naturally and gradually, humans arose naturally and gradually from a similar species, probably an "ape-man."

Almost immediately upon the first appearance of *Origin of Species* in 1859, "reviews, sermons, books light and heavy, came flying at the new thinker [Darwin] from all sides." First out of the gate was Samuel Wilberforce, Bishop of Oxford. In 1860, the Bishop's famed eloquence drew 700 people to a meeting of the British Association for the Advancement of Science at Oxford. Wilberforce had been complaining, in the *Quarterly Review*, that Darwin dishonored nature, and moreover, was guilty of limiting God's glory in creation. This legendary meeting pitted Bishop Wilberforce for the Church, against Darwin's "bulldog," the biologist and agnostic Thomas Henry Huxley (1825–1895) for evolution. By all accounts, the meeting was every bit as dramatic as the Scopes Monkey Trial 65 years later.

According to an eyewitness, the Bishop spoke "for full half an hour with inimitable spirit, emptiness and unfairness. . . . In a light, scoffing tone, florid and fluent, he assured us there was nothing in the idea of evolution; rock-pigeons were what rock-pigeons had always been. Then, turning to his antagonist with a smiling insolence, he begged to know, was it through his grandfather or his grandmother that he claimed his descent from a monkey?"[16]

Huxley immediately saw his opportunity to answer the blow in kind, and "slowly and deliberately arose." He was "a slight tall figure, stern and pale, very quiet and very grave." He replied, "If this question is treated, not as a matter for the calm investigation of science, but as a matter of sentiment, and if I am asked whether I would choose to be descended from the poor animal of low intelligence and stooping gait, who grins and chatters as we pass, or from a man, endowed with great ability and a splendid position, who should use these gifts"—at this point there was a great outburst of applause—"to discredit and crush humble seekers after truth, I hesitate what answer to make."[17]

The debate between the traditionalists and "humble seekers after truth" continued after the 1871 appearance of Darwin's *Descent of Man*. In 1877, an eminent French Catholic physician, Dr. Constantin James, called Darwin's latest offering a "fantastic and burlesque . . . fairy tale." The Catholic hierarchy received Dr. James' book, entitled *On Darwinism, or the Man-Ape*, enthusiastically. Pope Pius IX liked it so much that he wrote a long letter to the author, and appointed him an officer of the Papal Order of St. Sylvester. The zealous pope also suggested a new title: *Moses and Darwin: The Man of Genesis compared with the Man-Ape, or Religious Education opposed to Atheistic*. Dr. James heeded the pope's advice and adopted the cumbersome title.

According to some, creation by divine fiat applied not only to natural products like plants, animals and men, but also to civilizations. In 1875, a Mr. Southall published a work entitled, *The Recent Origin of the World*, in which he sought to show that recent archeological finds were consistent with Scripture. Southall proposed—in an argument much like Gosse's—that the hands of the Creator Himself had fashioned the high civilization of Egypt, complete with its classes, institutions, written language and monuments. "The Egyptians," Southall argued, "had no Stone age, and were born civilized." This argument would later be echoed in the ancient astronaut books, with the "Creator" as a band of extra-terrestrial scientists.[18]

GOD—OR GORILLA

Although believers in Genesis cried out against Darwinism, the theory's crit-ics were not all literalists. Alfred Watterson McCann, LL.D., author of the 1922 anti-evolution rant *God—or Gorilla*, was a lawyer rather than a Bible thumper. He wrote numerous health books including *Starving America, The Failure of the Calory in Medicine, This Famishing World and The Science of Eating*. He boasted that he'd been involved in 204 libel suits—and won them all.

McCann never declares his religious affiliation in the pages of *God—or Gorilla*, but there can be no doubt that he was an anti-Modernist. The 350-page volume, subtitled, "How the Monkey Theory of Evolution Exposes Its Own Methods, Refutes Its Own Principles, Denies Its Own Inferences, Disproves Its Own Case" reads like a legal brief, with evolutionists, anthropologists and pale-ontologists as defendants, and McCann as prosecutor. Unfortunately, there's no judge to keep the arguments fair or the proceedings reasonable. The cover blurb reads:

> The author of God—or Gorilla does not argue with the popular idea of evolution, unless ripping the heart out of a thing can be called argument. He pretends to no gentleness as he shows the "intellectual" victims of scientific superstition that the very thing they profess to hate has possession of their souls. . . . No sane man or woman, despite former convictions on the subject of evolution, can ignore the astounding facts, which the author of God—or Gorilla has marshalled against the most spectacular hoax of a hun-dred years.

The "astounding facts" demolish "Darwinism, Wellsism," and "barnyard materialism—Evolution." The blurb on the inner sleeve continues:

> Colleges, Academies and Schools the country over—many of them religious—are teaching Evolution, teaching your children that they and you are come from a gorilla. . . .
>
> When your children insistently and trustingly ask you "Who made us?"—your answer must not be evasive, it must be truthful and you must choose for their maker either God—or a Gorilla.

God—or Gorilla overflows with anti-evolutionary zeal. Darwinism, McCann tells us in his introduction, is the "ape-man hoax now scattering its corruptions throughout the world and impressing its deceptions upon the world's 'best minds.'" He argues—as many creationists argue to this day—that evidence used by scientists to support evolution is faulty, and that the "missing link" between apes and humans doesn't exist. Deluded, God-hating scientists try to cover up the fact that all the evidence really supports creationism, not evolution. McCann and his successors dwell on well-known hoaxes, outdated controversies and blind alleys, rather than on high-quality evidence.[19] They also employ another popular tactic: to present a series of contradictory quotations from scientists. It greatly distresses McCann that the anthropologists couldn't agree on what Java Man, a supposed link in the evolution from ape to man, actually looked like:

GOD—OR GORILLA

Alfred W. McCann, LL.D.

THE author of GOD—OR GORILLA does not argue with the popular idea of evolution, unless ripping the heart out of a thing can be called argument. He pretends to no gentleness as he shows the "intellectual" victims of scientific superstition that the very thing they profess to hate has possession of their souls.

Perhaps the most disturbing feature of GOD —OR GORILLA is that it proves its case out of the mouths of the very professors and educators who tell us that evolution is the only real thing left in the world. That this is their pity and their shame the author makes clear, for he is merciless in his vivisection of their inventions, subterfuges and shams. To their despair he points out that they are in too deep to wade out, and cannot swim.

No sane man or woman, despite former convictions on the subject of evolution, can ignore the astounding facts which the author of GOD—OR GORILLA has marshalled against the most spectacular hoax of a hundred years.

God-or Gorilla?, ALFRED W. McCANN's entertaining anti-evolution polemic.

> The MacGregor bust [of Java Man] represents a short-haired, hideous creature suggesting a slightly improved gorilla, whereas the Rutot bust is that of a long-haired, heavily-bearded, somewhat pious creature, looking heavenward with no expression of squat ferocity but rather with a soft sweetness, emphasized by two armsful of gorgeous vegetation, palm leaves, fern and other symbols of docility and peace. . . .[20]

Because the anthropologists did not agree on details, McCann believed the entire edifice of human evolution was in danger. When researchers expressed honest, scientific doubts about their own theories, these were taken to be a sign of weakness rather than of healthy scientific debate. He quoted scientists' doubts out of context, and then identified them as "admissions" and "confessions." Rather than evaluating the *evidence*, McCann and others evaluated the *words* of scientists, as if it were Scripture—or testimonial evidence in court.

McCann ignored the good evidence and concentrated on the bad, claiming that because some of the evidence was faulty the entire case was lost. In lawyerly fashion McCann made Professor Osborn and other anthropologists look like liars covering up for their guilty friend Darwin, whose hastily concocted alibi had just unraveled during cross-examination:

> Professor Osborn admits that no living ape belongs to the pedigree of man. He also admits that no fossil ape belongs to the pedigree of man. His witnesses Schwalbe and Klaatsch admit that the Trinil monster does not belong to the pedigree of man. They do admit that the Trinil monster [a Pithecanthropus fossil found in Trinil, Java in 1891] does belong to the pedigree of the modern apes, but as modern man and modern apes are admitted to have no relation to each other, Professor Osborn can't bring in the Trinil monster without bringing in the modern apes, and precisely that he confesses he cannot do.[21]

McCann didn't rest his case until he presented Neanderthal Man as a clear refutation of human evolution because his brain was larger than that of modern humans. According to McCann's understanding, evolution entails that humans become smarter and their brains grow, through time. This argument—surprisingly popular among modern creationists who should know better—rests on a simplistic, outdated and fallacious understanding of evolution where all creatures progress from small to large, from stupid to smart, and from lower to higher—an idea that went out with Spencer about a century ago. Emotionally-based attacks on evolution underlie the creationist method as pioneered by Mr. McCann, whose arguments could be mistaken for those presented by a fundamentalist in the 1990s.

Evolution or Special Creation?
a booklet published in 1963
by Seventh-Day Adventists

THE FIRST CREATIONISTS

American Bible believers first spelled out fundamentalism between 1910 and 1915 in a twelve-volume paperback anthology entitled *Fundamentals.* The contributors to the widely distributed, anti-Modernist series interpreted Scripture literally. They believed that human history could be explained as a series of seven dispensations, that the current dispensation is the sixth, or church age, and that Christ would return soon. This "dispensationalist" theology had developed as a result of increased interest in biblical prophecy following the Civil War. In 1920 the word "fundamentalist" first appeared.

Fundamentalists were those who wanted to preserve the "five fundamental truths" of Christianity: 1) The inerrancy of Scripture; 2) The virgin birth of Jesus; 3) That Jesus died for our sins (the "substitutionary atonement"); 4) The bodily resurrection of Jesus; 5) The second coming of Christ.

While some contributors to *Fundamentals* were creationists, others were not. The creationists, *per se*, first appeared among the even more extreme Second-Coming-of-Christ crowd: Seventh-Day Adventists (SDA), Jehovah's Witnesses and other sects. In 1906, the SDA schoolteacher George McCreedy Price published *Illogical Geology: The Weakest Point in the Evolution Theory* that would set the tone for creationist polemics in years to come. Price was notorious among scientists for his "creationist geology," which sought to prove that the SDA prophetess Ellen G. White was right when she said that geological features were the result of Noah's flood. By the 1920s, Price, who characterized Darwinism as "a most gigantic hoax," was receiving national attention. In 1925—the year of the Scopes Monkey Trial—he wrote that evolution is "essentially pagan or atheistic." He declared that "the whole of evolution is crumbling to pieces, and that a literal Creation of all the great primal types of plants and animals, including man, is the only fact left for men who are acquainted with the progress of scientific discoveries in modern times." [22]

The Scopes Monkey Trial in 1925 set back the creationist cause. John T. Scopes, a high school biology teacher in Dayton, Tennessee, confessed to teaching evolution, which violated a new state law forbidding the teaching of human evolution in public schools. Scopes' confession and trial arose as a challenge to the law. The American Civil Liberties Union (ACLU), looking for someone to challenge the new law, found Scopes by chance, and he reluctantly agreed to confess to teaching evolution. As Scopes pointed out at the time, most other Tennessee biology teachers—if they used the standard textbook—taught evolution as well.

Dayton, barely a dot on the map deep in the Bible Belt, became the scene of a media circus. The popular three-time presidential candidate William Jennings Bryan pitted himself against the brilliant criminal defense lawyer Clarence Darrow, with a young H.L. Mencken covering the events from the peanut gallery for the *Baltimore Evening Sun*.

Bryan—depicted by Mencken as a pompous old fool—eloquently defended his beliefs and those of the creationists, declaring that he was not interested in the age or rocks, but in the Rock of Ages. In his pious courtroom speech, he attacked evolution as immoral:

> There is no place for the miracle in this train of evolution and the Old Testament and the New are filled with miracles. . . . [Evolutionists] eliminate the virgin birth . . . the resurrection of the body . . . the doctrine of atonement. . . . [Scientists] believe man has been rising all the

time, that man never fell; that when the Savior came there was not any
reason for His coming. . . . [Outsiders] force upon the children of the
taxpayers of this state a doctrine that refutes . . . their belief in a Savior
and . . . heaven, and takes from them every moral standard that the
Bible gives us. . . .[23]

Darrow's passionate commitment to liberalism, free speech and free thought,
however, surpassed Bryan's piety:

Bigotry and ignorance are ever active. . . . Always it is feeding. Today
it is the public school teachers, tomorrow the private. The next day the
preachers . . . the magazines, the books, the newspapers. After a while,
your Honor, it is the setting of man against man and creed against
creed, until with flying banners and beating drums we are marching
backward to the glorious ages of the sixteenth century, when bigots
lighted fagots to burn the men who dared to bring any intelligence
and enlightenment and culture to the human mind.[24]

HARRY RIMMER,
an early modern
creationist (from *A
History of Modern
Creationism*)

Technically, the creationists won: Scopes was convicted and fined $100 for breaking the law. But they had lost
their standing with the American public when the press
painted them as backwoods bigots and the image stuck.
Then their champion fell; soon after the trial Bryan,
whose health had been failing, died in his sleep. Even the
creationists' legal victory evaporated when the verdict was
overturned on a technicality.

Tennessee's law against teaching evolution still stood,
however, and remained in the books for another 42 years.
Mississippi and Arkansas soon passed anti-evolution bills
of their own. And, as author Garry Wills points out, there
was no need to enforce the law because textbook publishers
were quietly expunging Darwin from textbooks not just in
Tennessee, but all over the country. The creationist cause had taken a public blow,
but it still wielded power on school boards and in state legislatures.

The Scopes Trial, though thought by most as a setback, was also a boon to creationists because it forced them to re-examine their public image. Soon they
would evolve from "backwoods bible thumpers" to "Creation Scientists." Harry
Rimmer, a Presbyterian minister and an admirer of creation geologist Price,
emerged from the ashes of the Scopes Trial as a leading advocate for creationism.
Rimmer called himself a research scientist; he thought he deserved the title
because of his one term at a small homeopathic medical school. His homemade
laboratory for embryological research became the foundation for the Research

Science Bureau, which Rimmer established in the early '20s to prove that biology, paleontology and anthropology were compatible with a literal interpretation of Scripture. He even planned an expedition to Africa to prove that gorillas were not related to humans, but the expedition never materialized. Rimmer popularized the creationist cause via lectures and debates throughout the United States, and by offering a $100 reward for anyone who could find a scientific error in the Bible. He was never compelled to pay up.

Examples of Rimmer's writing can be found in his anthology, *The Theory of Evolution and the Facts of Science*, published by the Research Science Bureau, Inc. in Duluth, Minn. The collection includes five pamphlets, written between 1926 and 1945, including "The Theories of Evolution and the Facts of Human Antiquity," "The Facts of Paleontology," and "Monkeyshines!" written in the aftermath of the Scopes Monkey Trial. Rimmer claims that the little volume reconciles science with religion by presenting scientific facts that back up the Bible. Creationists, he says, rely on scientific facts while evolutionists believe in the great antiquity of man, on faith. What the paleontologists present as evidence of the evolution of mankind, is, in fact, "purely hypothetical, entirely erroneous . . . and manufactured out of the imagination of the sponsor of such evidence." With echoes of *God—or Gorilla* (described by Rimmer as a "thorough, scientific, scholarly discussion of the question for advanced students"), Rimmer picks apart the words of the experts to find inconsistencies and disagreements. Since scientists, for example, can't agree on whether a fossil is one million or one and a quarter million years old, it's proof enough that the fossil is actually neither: it's 6,000 years old. While none of the minutiae of scientific debate over dating escapes Rimmer, he ignores the problems with his own dating method, which relies entirely on one particular interpretation of the words of one collection of religious stories.

Rimmer, like McCann, has a crude, erroneous conception of evolution, which he takes to mean progression from the small to the large:

> The largest creature of the genus Elephas the earth has ever harbored is not the familiar "Jumbo" of the modern circus, but the mighty Elephus imperator of the past geological age. This mighty monster dwarfs the modern elephant into a veritable pygmy in size, and is the largest of its genus yet known. . . . At any rate, here is a notable refutation of the so-called law of evolution; the elephant is proceeding from the **large** to the **small**![25]

Rimmer's misconstrual goes one step further than McCann's:

> How startling it is to the unprejudiced thinker to realize that, although the great creatures of the past ages are remembered only by

their fossil bones, and countless hundreds of species and genera have perished from the face of the earth in the course of "evolution," The One-celled Ancestors Still Remain! . . . This is an anomaly, indeed, that evolution cannot explain.[26]

Rimmer seems to think that according to evolution, once a new species emerges from an old one, the old one has to die. If that were the case, there could be only one species in existence at any given time. It's not Rimmer's intention to figure out what scientists are really saying. Instead, true to scriptural literalism, he takes his own flawed understanding of evolution as "gospel," and then refutes it by finding contradictions.

In the end, for Rimmer it all comes down to preference: he doesn't want a monkey, or a sea jelly, or a worm, for an ancestor:

> We would rather a thousand times trace our descent up to God through Adam than down to a sea jelly through wormy ancestors whose children were apes! . . . No worm ever gave life to any progeny except worms; no dinosaur ever gave birth to anything but another dinosaur (and we are well acquainted with Archeopteryx). And no monkey ever gave birth to any creature that in time became man![27]

Though most of the first anti-evolutionists, like Bishop Wilberforce, had attacked evolution because of its inherent opposition to Scripture, McCann and Rimmer claimed to attack evolution on scientific grounds, even though their underlying motivations were obviously religious. For both, evolution was a symbol of atheism, materialism and immorality, and, as such, must be defeated by any means necessary. As members of the new generation of creationists, they took their fight a step further than their predecessors by using the weapons of their enemy: scientific jargon.

A NATION OF CREATIONISTS

After the Scopes trial mainstream scientists—confident that they were not a threat—ignored the creationists. In the late 1950s, however, cold war fears in the U.S. spurred a national effort to upgrade science education; by the 1960s evolution had returned to textbooks and the American classroom. Evolution in the classroom was just one of many phenomena—the decreasing popularity of old-style religion, the legalization of abortion, the birth control pill, increased sex and violence on television, to name just a few—that would, during the '60s and '70s, frighten fundamentalists into political action. Creationism was just one of the causes that would be taken up by the "religious right" in the coming decades.

By the 1980s, a new wave of "scientific" creationists had emerged, with allies in high places. Campaigning for the presidency in 1980, Ronald Reagan told a group of evangelicals:

> [Evolution] is a theory, it is a scientific theory only, and it has in recent
> years been challenged in the world of science and it is not yet believed
> in the scientific community to be as infallible as it was once believed.
> But if it was going to be taught in the schools then I think that also
> the biblical theory of creation, which is not a theory but the biblical
> story of creation, should also be taught.[28]

The scientists slowly noticed that science education was under attack, and
have been actively combating the creationists ever since. While the Tennessee law
challenged by Scopes forbidding the teaching of evolution was obviously a dra-
conian measure, the legislation introduced by creationists in the '80s, looks much
more benign. All they want, they say, is "equal time." If you teach evolution, they
argue, then to be fair, the public schools should also teach creation. By this argument, the Aquatic Ape theory, various alien intervention theories, de-evolution,
and countless creation myths and alternative theories of evolution should also be
given "equal time" in the classroom. "Equal time," in fact, is just a device creationists use to ensure their own voices are heard over the threatening sounds of
secularism they hear in the schools, on television and at the movies.

The "equal time" device works: creationists convinced many Southern state
legislators to support their cause. In 1981 both Arkansas and Louisiana passed
bills allowing equal time for creation science in the public schools. The Arkansas
law was immediately challenged in a court scene that might have been dubbed
Monkey Trial, Act II. In the end, the court overturned the law, stating that "the
evidence is overwhelming that both the purpose and the effect of Act 590 is the
advancement of religion in the public schools." The U.S. Supreme Court overturned the Louisiana Law as well, in 1987.

The American public—easily swayed by simplistic arguments, emotionalism
and faulty logic—has been kinder to the creationist cause than the courts.
Creationists, who are often talented speakers and evangelists, appeal at an emotional level, charging scientists and educators with the crimes of materialism,
atheism, immorality and dishonesty. In public debates between creationists and
scientists, local church groups bussed in for the occasion fill high school and college auditoriums with pro-creationist sentiment. Joyce Arthur, writing in *Skeptic
Magazine*, points out, "Debates are a poor forum for imparting the complexities
of science and evolution, and a good forum for delivering the simplistic and often
eloquent rhetoric of creationism. Having a debate implies that creation and evolution are on equal terms and that the question of which one is right is an open
issue that can be won or lost, and confidently decided, by a nonscientific audience
in one evening." Explaining the subtleties of current evolutionary theory to people who get their history from docudramas and their science from the Discovery
Channel isn't easy; evolutionists might do better if they simply accused creationists of molesting children.

Two surveys taken in the 1980s, one by Gallup, and the other as part of an academic study, confirm the creationists' success, as well as the failure of science education. A 1982 Gallup Poll found that 44 percent of the U.S. population believe in strict, biblical creationism: "God created man pretty much in his present form at one time within the last 10,000 years." An embarrassingly low number—9 percent—believe that "Man has developed over millions of years from less advanced forms of life. God had no part in this process." And 38 percent of Americans believe that God guided man in his evolution, that "Man has developed over millions of years from less advanced forms of life, but God guided this process, including man's creation." The remaining 9 percent were undecided on the question of human evolution. Needless to say, the poll didn't provide for any of the alternative theories of human origins covered in this book.

In a similar survey, conducted by professors Francis B. Harrold and Raymond A. Eve and published in 1987, a large sample of college students in Texas, California and Connecticut were asked a series of questions regarding their views on evolution and creation. For supposedly college-educated people, the results were astonishing. When asked if dinosaurs and humans lived at the same time, over 35 percent of the students in Texas answered yes, and over 30 percent didn't know. The minority, less than 30 percent, answered that dinosaurs and humans did not live at the same time. Even in Connecticut, about 30 percent answered yes, 25 percent didn't know and over 40 percent answered no. When asked if God created Man in his present form within the last 10,000 years, over 25 percent of the Texan students answered yes, 30 percent didn't know, and 40 percent answered no. Californians, despite their notorious spaciness, were less prone to creationism, with only 20 percent answering yes, 20 percent undecided and 60 percent answering no. The results in Connecticut were similar to those in California.

A historian quoted in the *Encyclopedia of Evolution* estimated that possibly a quarter of all Americans "live in a universe created miraculously only a few thousand years ago, and on an earth tenanted only by those fixed organic kinds that survived a global Flood." But creationists, evangelicals that they are, aren't satisfied with only a quarter of the U.S. population. They want to utterly squash the theory of evolution, which they consider to be, at best, a dangerous godless philosophy, and, at worst, evil and Satanic.

WHAT CREATIONISTS BELIEVE

While possibly a quarter of all Americans inhabit the simple universe of Genesis, others adhere to lesser-known variations on the creationist theme. The book Bones of Contention written by a Marvin L. Lubenow, a young-earth creationist, contains a useful summary of the creationist views that contrast with his own. These "old-earth" creationists seek to accommodate the scientific interpretation of the fossil record, rather than combat it, integrating geological, evolutionary timeframes into their theology much like the natural theologians of the eighteenth and nineteenth centuries. Lubenow divides the old-earth creationists into two categories: 1) old earth/old Adam, and 2) old earth/young Adam. The first group believes that the biblical Adam—perhaps a million years old—was the first human, and thus preceded all human fossils. The second group believes that Adam lived around 10,000 years ago, and that the fossils of earlier humans are those of pre-Adamites.

Bernard Ramm, in his 1954 treatise *The Christian View of Science and Scripture*, argues for an old earth/old Adam view he calls Progressive Creationism. Ramm's type of creationism highly displeases Lubenow because of the "demolition job" it does on Genesis. Ramm argues that because the events in Genesis do not agree with the fossil record, that creation was *revealed* in six days, not *performed* in six days. Moreover, he allows for both creation and evolution: evolutionary change comes from within an organism while creation comes from outside, by a direct act of God. Creation of the universe wasn't an instantaneous act, but a process guided by natural law over billions of years. Humans were created—on a family level—by fiat about a half million years ago. Another variation of the old earth/old Adam view can be found in geologist Davis A. Young's 1977 book, *Creation and the Flood*. He solves the six days of creation problem with the Day-Age theory that each day of creation represents an age, rather than a literal, 24-hour day. He also allows that Adam may have been an early human like an Australopithecine or a Neanderthal.

To old earth/young Adam creationists, Adam could not have been something like an Australopithecine, because these creatures were not fully human. As pre-Adamites, they possessed only animal intelligence, and were not bound to God by the Adamic covenant. Gleason L. Archer, who dates Adam to 200,000 years ago or earlier, thought the pre-Adamites "may have been exterminated by God for reasons unknown," before the creation of Adam.[29]

A slightly different view, "Theistic Evolution" as put forth by Derek Kidner, enjoys the best of both worlds: Adam, says Kidner, evolved, but Eve was created. He also uses the (to some) oxymoronic phrase, "creation by evolution," and believes that "God initially shaped man by a process of evolution." In other words, God breathed spirit into the evolved creature Adam; then God created Eve; finally, the divine image and the Fall were extended to include the other evolved, pre-Adamites. This view is strangely similar to the type of evolution detailed in the *Urantia Book*.[30]

The strict literalists solve the anomalies and absurdities of such views by rejecting modern dating methods altogether, and, as Henry Morris has stated, by using only the Bible as their "textbook on the science of Creationism." Duane Gish defines creationism as the belief that the supernatural creator brought "into being the basic kinds of plants and animals by the process of sudden, or fiat creation." The strict literalists can be divided into two categories, the Biblical Creationists and the Scientific Creationists, which represent a difference in approach, not of belief. According to creationists themselves, the difference is that Biblical Creationists openly use biblical authority to defend their beliefs, while Scientific Creationists make use only of non-religious, scientific evidence.

A leading creationist organization, the Institute for Creation Research (ICR) near San Diego embraces both approaches:

The ICR Tenets of Biblical Creationism specify (along with standard tenets of fundamentalism) that: the Bible is the word of God; it's infallible and completely authoritative, and God created the Universe in six literal days. Evolution is false; and Adam and Eve were the first human beings, specially created by God to dominate all other created organisms.

The ICR Tenets of Scientific Creationism do not mention the Bible, but they do mention a "transcendent personal Creator" who supernaturally created the Universe. Biological life didn't develop by natural processes but was "specially and supernaturally created by the Creator." Each major "kind" of organism "was created functionally complete from the beginning and did not evolve from some

other kind of organism." The first humans (Adam and Eve are not mentioned by name) "did not evolve from an animal ancestry, but were specially created in fully human form from the start." Furthermore, "there are many scientific evidences for a relatively recent creation of the earth and the universe, in addition to strong scientific evidence that most of the earth's fossiliferous sedimentary rocks were formed in an even more recent global hydraulic cataclysm." (Noah's flood isn't mentioned by name.)

Leading modern creationist HENRY M. MORRIS (from *A History of Modern Creationism*)

Creationism has come a long way since the pious oratory of William Jennings Bryan at the Scopes Monkey Trial. Scientific Creationism is an attempt to translate Biblical Creationism into scientific language, to remove creationists from the pulpit and place them in the laboratory. It amounts to a new strategy for inserting Christian belief into public institutions. There is no real difference between Biblical and Scientific Creationism. It's no coincidence that all Scientific Creationists also happen to be fundamentalist Christians.

THE NEW WAVE

The creationist cause is currently led by fundamentalists Dr. Henry M. Morris and Dr. Duane T. Gish, both credentialed scientists: Morris in hydrology, Gish in biochemistry. This new wave began in the late 1950s and was, in part, a reaction to the science boom spurred by the Cold War, when evolution more prominently entered the public school curriculum. In 1959, at the centennial celebration for the *Origin of Species* held at the University of Chicago, Julian Huxley, in an address to the assembled evolutionary biologists, declared, "There is no longer need or room for the supernatural . . . the earth was not created; it evolved." This audacious statement of unbelief infuriated Morris, a believer who had been inspired by George McCreedy Price's books in the 1940s. Morris set to work (with John C. Whitcomb Jr.) on his 500-page magnum opus, *The Genesis Flood: The Biblical Record and its Scientific Implications*, published in 1961. It is still in print, and considered a basic creationist text to this day.

Though it purports to be scientific, *The Genesis Flood* is essentially a theological argument for a literal interpretation of Genesis, using fancy words like "Biblical catastrophism" for the belief that Noah's flood was worldwide. The scientific part is where they use technical geological data in theological discussions. For example, numerical graphs show the drop in the patriarchs' longevity after the flood.

The authors argue—"scientifically"—that Noah's flood was universal. Because the ages of the patriarchs steeply declined after Noah's flood (which presumably existed because it's in the Bible), then "something significant happened to the earth and to man at the time of the flood":

> It would seem that whatever this was, it probably removed the dominant factor for the long life of the patriarchs. . . . Could some antediluvian climatic or other condition have been extremely favorable for long life in man? Perhaps future scientific research will cast some light on this. . . .
>
> The record in Genesis 5 clearly implies that men had large families in those days. . . . Furthermore, the age of the fathers at the birth of each of the named sons ranged from 65 years . . . to 500 years. . . . Consequently the Bible implies that: 1) men typically lived for hundreds of years, 2) their procreative powers persisted over hundreds of years also, and 3) through the combined effects of long lives and large families, mankind was rapidly "filling the earth." [31]

At least a billion people thus lived at the time of the flood. This large population would then have spread all over the earth, beyond the biblical lands of the Middle East, implying that the flood was worldwide. The human fossils that have been found all over the world are their remains. Hence, if you believe in Noah's flood, then you also must believe that Noah's flood was universal. But, contrary to their promises, Morris and Whitcomb fail to give any non-biblical reasons to believe that Noah's flood occurred in the first place.

In answer to physical anthropology, the authors say, "On the basis of overwhelming Biblical evidence . . . every fossil man that has ever been discovered, or ever will be discovered, is a *descendant* of the *supernaturally created* Adam and Eve. . . . This is absolutely essential to the entire edifice of Christian theology, and there can simply be no true Christianity without it." [32] Then they reveal the honest bottom line for creationists:

The true reason why Christians have been willing . . . to take their stand upon a Biblical anthropology, in opposition to an evolutionary anthropology is that they enjoy a vital spiritual relationship with Jesus Christ and accept His authority. It was none other than the Son of God Himself who taught Christians to accept the historical accuracy of the Old Testament in general . . . and the Book of Genesis in particular. . . . Standing upon this infallible foundation, the Christian is perfectly confident that modern scientific theories (colored as they are by the presuppositions of finite and fallible men) cannot possibly constitute the final word on the subject of the origin and early history of man. . . .[33]

Morris, despite his conclusion that evidence is irrelevant, co-founded in 1963 the Creation Research Society (CRS) to collect evidence for creation. He also sought to establish a creationist university. Morris met Tim LaHaye of San Diego's Scott Memorial Baptist Church (who had similar goals), and in 1970 the two co-founded Christian Heritage College (CHC) and the Creation-Science Research Center (CSRC). LaHaye was also co-founder of the Moral Majority, who had mainstreamed the notion that secular humanism is a Satanic plot. In 1972 Morris founded a new organization, the Institute for Creation Research (ICR). Because of a doctrinal split, ICR broke from CHC in 1980 and in 1985 moved to Santee, Calif.

The ICR, obviously a religious rather than a scientific organization, requires a statement of faith from all members. It might surprise some people that the ICR is currently approved by the state of California as an institute and graduate school; students there can obtain Master of Science degrees in science education, geology, astrophysics, geophysics and biology approved by the California State Board of Education. Since it's not accredited by the Western Association of Schools and Colleges, however, such a degree would be considered worthless by most secular institutions.

Morris authored other books for the creationist cause since *The Genesis Flood*, including *The Twilight of Evolution* (1963), *Biblical Cosmology and Modern Science* (1970), *The Troubled Waters of Evolution* (1974), *The Scientific Case for Creation* (1977) and *History of Modern Creationism* (1984).

In a CSRC paperback entitled *Science and Creation* (1973), Morris and co-authors William W. Boardman Jr. (industrial chemist) and Robert F. Koontz (entomologist) explain creationism to a popular audience. The authors begin by stating the "creation-evolution issue is not an argument between religion and science," and both creation and evolution are philosophical frameworks, each impossible to prove scientifically, each consistent with the facts. Evolution, they charge, is as much a religious faith as creation. If evolution is a religious faith, it won't be proved or disproved by evidence. The same goes for creation.

The authors then claim to gather evidence that supports creation and disproves evolution.

The creationists want to have it both ways: when defending creationism, it's just a matter of philosophy, but when attacking evolution or demanding "equal time" in science education, it's a matter of scientific evidence. The authors are chained to Scripture, but refuse to admit it.

Because the Bible is their authority, the authors of *Science and Creation* interpret all fossil hominids as either men or apes, but never an "ape-man," performing logical contortions in the process. They dispose of fossils that are clearly neither man nor ape, like the Australopithecine, as "fragmentary and questionable." But fossils that turn out to be genuine after all are not allowed as evidence for evolution, but instead "might well represent disease or degeneracy." [34] And, if that argument doesn't convince you to abandon evolution, try this one: evolution causes racism. "It is important to recognize," say the authors, "that racism in its virulent forms is mainly a product of evolutionary thinking," because even recent history can be shaped to fit the creationist mold:

> Nietzsche, Hitler, Mussolini, and some other fascistic-type leaders were and are ardent evolutionists. Karl Marx, Friedrich Engels, and practically all other leaders of Communist thought, past and present, have been racists in the tradition of Charles Darwin, in spite of the cynical modern-day incitement of black revolution by Communist cadres.... A much more realistic and salutary approach to racial problems is that of the creationist. In the creationist theory, all present-day men are descendants of the first man and woman, who were brought into being by special creation several thousand years ago.... In fact, the very concept of "race" is strictly and solely a category of evolutionary biology.[35]

The authors might have difficulty explaining biblical arguments for slavery, the Hamitic Curse, Christian Identity, and the fact that racism was alive and well in Europe and America long before 1859. But facts are not critical because the creationists are fighting a war, not just between truth and error, but between good and evil. "This conflict [between creation and evolution] is intimately involved in a 'conflict of the ages,'" wrote leading creationist Henry M. Morris, "[The battle for creation] is not a simple question of democracy, or constitutionality, or scientific evidence—all of which would support creation if allowed to speak honestly. This is a spiritual battle, and the battle plans and tactics can only really be understood in spiritual terms. The primeval war against God the Creator still continues and may well be entering its final critical phases." [36]

Biochemist Duane T. Gish of the Institute for Creation Research put himself in the front lines of that war, popularizing creationism by conducting lively

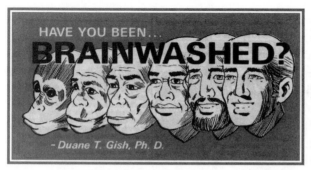

HAVE YOU BEEN...
BRAINWASHED?

- Duane T. Gish, Ph. D.

Anti-evolution tract written by DUANE GISH and published by Creation-Life Publishers in San Diego, California.

public debates and slick, persuasive lectures. Writing in *Skeptic* magazine, Joyce Arthur accuses Gish of using "questionable tactics and misleading arguments, the majority of which are a morass of errors, omissions, misquotes, old data, distortions, and non sequiturs." Even after scientists publicly corrected Gish's errors, "he continues to repeat the same errors in subsequent debates and writings." [37] And when all else fails, Gish simply lies to make his case—or attacks his opponents' credibility, because ethics are irrelevant when you're defending the word of God.

A sample of Gish's writing reveals that he considers evidence supporting evolution as fair game for the most rigorous critique. But he accepts the flimsiest of creationist "evidence." In his 1985 book, *Evolution: The Challenge of the Fossil Record*, after a detailed and sophisticated critique of evolution, Gish concludes that cavemen were descendants of Noah, a statement that apparently needs no evidence:

> Where did cavemen, such as the Neanderthal, Cro-Magnon, and Swanscombe men come from? They were descendants of Noah's family, scattered throughout parts of Africa, Europe, Asia, and elsewhere, as they dispersed from the site of their ancestral home. . . .[38]

In answer to smart-aleck evolutionists who ask, "Where did Cain and Abel get their wives?" Gish answers with a purely theological solution:

> Let us go back now to the very beginning of the human race to answer a question that is often asked: Where did Cain and Abel, as well as Seth, get their wives? From among their sisters of course—where else? This intermarriage was an absolute necessity to propagate the human species. It was ordained of God, or else He would have created more than a single couple. Furthermore, since Adam and Eve were genetically perfect when created, and harmful, crippling mutations had not yet had time to form, at least to a significant extent when such intermarriage was necessary, no harmful biological results would occur from such intermarriage. . . .[39]

Even while skeptics and scientists debate and refute the likes of Morris and Gish, younger and slicker creationists are ever on the horizon. When I first glanced at the 1992 book *Bones of Contention*, I assumed it was just another pop science entry about the current debates on human evolution. Because of its dry, reasonable presentation, this book, written by Marvin L. Lubenow, gives the impression that creation science is respectable. The large, brightly-lit Christian bookstore where I purchased the book was full of similarly bland, inoffensive-looking materials.

Lubenow, who teaches at Christian Heritage College in El Cajon, Calif., does his best to make his work look like a textbook, complete with clear definitions of technical terms. But his true colors glow brightly, if you read the definitions closely. For example:

> **Paleoanthropology**: *Anthropology* is the Greek word for "the study of man." Paleo means "old." Paleoanthropology is the study of fossil humans. The term replaces the older term human paleontology.[40]
>
> **Homo**: Humans are the only living forms in the genus *Homo*. Biblically, there are no creatures past or present who would qualify for the genus *Homo* or "true humans," other than descendants of Adam.[41]

Like Gish and every other creationist author, Lubenow inspects the evolutionary evidence with a fine-toothed comb, but when it comes to his own beliefs, they pass without any scrutiny at all. At its core, *Bones of Contention* is an updated version of *God—or Gorilla*.

Given its sophisticated veneer, some of the errors in *Bones of Contention* are surprising. Though he's familiar with technical terms like "paleoanthropology," Lubenow appears unaware that evolution has changed since the days of Spencer. His challenge to this theory is anachronistic because it hinges on a garbled interpretation of Spencer's outdated phrase, "survival of the fittest."

> The "survival of the fittest" has a flip side. It is the death of the less fit. For evolution to proceed, it is as essential that the less fit die as it is that the more fit survive. If the unfit survived indefinitely, they would continue to "infect" the fit with their less fit genes. The result is that the more fit genes would be diluted and compromised by the less fit genes, and evolution could not take place. The concept of evolution demands death. Death is thus as *natural* to evolution as it is *foreign* to biblical creation.[42]

He fails to realize that the very definition of "fit"—as it relates to natural selection—is the ability to survive. It is therefore oxymoronic to worry about the "survival of the unfit" in the natural world. Lubenow applies the century-old rhetoric of social Darwinism to twentieth century biology, with nonsensical results.

Lubenow's worst blunder, however, is revealed when he writes that evolution is false because "*Homo erectus* people persisted long after they should have died out or changed into *Homo sapiens*." Like his predecessors, Lubenow misunderstands evolution as a simple, linear progression from one species to another:

> We have the right to expect, if evolution were true, that the hominid fossil record would faithfully follow the time and morphology sequence set forth by evolutionists. Since humans are supposed to have evolved from something very different from what they look like today, we have a right to expect that very modern-looking fossils would not show up in Lucy times, or that primitive or archaic fossils would not embarrass the evolutionist by showing up in modern times.[43]

It would indeed be a blow to evolutionary theory if modern human fossils were found in Lucy (australopithecine) times. But it's no "embarrassment" to evolutionists that archaic creatures (amoebas, sharks, cockroaches) exist in modern times; subgroups of species often survive and change, while other subgroups stay the same, or change in a different way. But in Lubenow's version of evolution, there can be no branching—only one species can exist at a time.

Lubenow also claims that modern human fossils exist which are as old as the australopithecine "Lucy," i.e., that a species (modern humans) lived earlier than its supposed ancestor (australopithecines), thus disproving evolution. But, according to Jim Foley, an amateur researcher who has studied creationist arguments for 20 years, the fragments Lubenow identifies as *Homo sapiens*, are examples of australopithecines well known to paleoanthropologists.

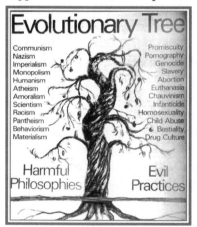

Evolutionary Tree, from which all bad things come, from The Museum of Creation and Earth History in San Diego, California.

Though they've changed their name from creationists to creation scientists, those who produce "disproofs" of evolution are true to their creed, for their arguments haven't —pardon the expression—evolved since the days of the Scopes Monkey Trial. Their presentation, however, has changed. Whereas formerly creationists were associated with the backwoods of Tennessee, now they're behind slickly produced books and videos, institutions of higher learning and popular museums.

In 1977, a creationist museum was founded by the Institute for Creation Research. Writing in *Skeptic* magazine,[44] Tom McIver paints a picture of a well-funded creationist teaching device that rivals secular museums in popularity and execution. The museum is currently situated in Santee, Calif. along with the headquarters of the ICR. After it was remodeled in 1992, it drew 60,000 visitors in two years.

Creationist Tree

True Christology
True Evangelism
True Missions
True Fellowship
True Gospel
True Faith
True Morality
True Hope

True Americanism
True Government
True Family Life
True Education
True History
True Science

Genuine
Christianity

Correct
Practices

Creationist Tree, from which all good things come, from The Museum of Creation and Earth History in San Diego, California.

McIver's descriptions of the exhibits are, in turns, hysterically funny or disturbing. The Museum of Creation and Earth History might be dubbed the "bizarro" version of a traditional science museum:

> Moving past Creation itself we are next confronted by the tragedy of the entry of sin into the Garden of Eden. The fall of Adam, bringing on the curse of sin, is equated with the Second Law of Thermodynamics, which describes the inevitable increase of disorder in the universe and (conversely) the decrease of available energy....
>
> ... The museum dismisses *Australopithecus*, the ape-like but upright-walking fossil hominid, as merely an extinct ape. Regarding *Homo erectus*, clearly transitional between apes and humans, it says that some specimens are true humans while others may be apes.[45]

Unlike conventional science museums, the Museum of Creation and Earth History attempts to teach morality. A prominent display contrasts an "Evolutionary Tree" with a "Creationist Tree." The Evolutionary Tree sprouts Communism, Nazism, Imperialism, Monopolism, Humanism, Atheism, Amoralism, Scientism, Racism, Pantheism, Behaviorism, Materialism (Harmful Philosophies), Promiscuity, Pornography, Genocide, Slavery, Abortion, Euthanasia, Chauvinism, Infanticide, Homosexuality, Child Abuse, Bestiality, and Drug Culture (Evil Practices). The Creationist Tree sprouts True Christology, True Evangelism, True Missions, True Fellowship, True Gospel, True Faith, True Morality, True Hope (Genuine Christianity), True Americanism, True Government, True Family Life, True Education, True History, and True Science (Correct Practices).

Evolution isn't merely a scientific theory; otherwise, why bother spending millions of dollars and entire careers to defeat it? Evolution is no less than a product of the Devil, as manifested in modern times by Materialism and Humanism. To the ICR, evolutionism didn't begin with Darwin, but went back at least as far as the Tower of Babel. Twentieth century manifestations of Satanic evolution include Materialism and Humanism — and Hitler, who carried evolutionism to its logical conclusion.

Mainstream "creation scientists" devote themselves almost exclusively to "education," rather than research. Christian bookstores stock entire shelves full of creationist teaching materials, most published by the ICR, and written by Morris, Gish and a few others. Their enterprise advertises their expertise in technical subjects (usually unrelated to evolution) in an attempt to convince our science-worshipping society to listen. It has been increasingly successful.

Dinosaurs and Men, Walking Together

Why do one-third of college students in Texas believe that dinosaurs and humans lived at the same time? Is it because they grew up watching *The Flintstones* on TV? Or is it because their state is home to the famous giant "man tracks" found near dinosaur footprints?

Glen J. Kuban, an expert on dinosaur footprints, has been studying both the dinosaur footprints and the "man tracks" found in the Paluxy Riverbed, for almost 20 years. Kuban is also a Christian, open to both creation and evolution. For this reason, his objectivity seems impeccable. In a 1996 document entitled "On the Heels of Dinosaurs," posted on the internet, Kuban details the story of the allegedly human footprints, his own findings, and his conclusions.

In the summer of 1909 a teenager, Ernest "Bull" Adams, happened upon a series of large three-toed footprints in the limestone floor of a tributary of the Paluxy River, near Glen Rose, Texas. A local schoolteacher identified the tracks as dinosaur footprints, later confirmed by geologists as belonging to bipedal, carnivorous dinosaurs known as theropods. A few years later another youth from the area, Charlie Moss, found another trail of three-toed dinosaur tracks near a series of strange, oblong tracks that resembled human footprints. However, they were much larger than human footprints (15–18 inches long) so Charlie dubbed them "giant man tracks." The locals accepted this identification for years, not realizing that the discovery of man tracks with dinosaur tracks would be a monumental scientific discovery, since it would contradict the accepted chronology that the last dinosaurs became extinct about 60 million years before the first humans ever appeared.

But genuine curiosities soon made way for profiteering fakers. During the Great Depression, several residents of the area began selling homemade dinosaur and human tracks to tourists. Despite the fact that they were anatomically incorrect ("misplaced ball and arch, and excessively long, misshapen toes"), these fakes took hold of the popular imagination. The area became famous for its Giant Man Tracks.

During the late 1930s and '40s, the "man tracks" lured paleontologist Roland T. Bird to the area; he wondered why someone would bother to carve them. Bird's investigations yielded a windfall of dinosaur tracks of all sorts, including the first brontosaurus tracks ever found, which he described in articles for both *National Geographic* and *Natural History*. In the articles, Bird described how rumors of giant man tracks had led him to Glen Rose. He also recounted that he was shown something he dubbed a "mystery track." This was the 15-inch elongated genuine track found by Charlie Moss. Bird speculated that it was not a giant man track, but was probably made by a "hith-erto unknown dinosaur or reptile."

The creationists—eager for evidence—began to take interest in the man track story. If indeed humans and dinosaurs had walked together (they reasoned) then dinosaurs were much younger than previously supposed. (They didn't consider the other possibility: that humans were much older than previously supposed.) During the '50s, creationist Clifford Burdick, who had founded the "Deluge Society," embraced the man tracks. He visited the Paluxy site and published a pro-man-track article in the Seventh-Day Adventist magazine *Signs of the Times*. He believed the man tracks were real, they demolished evolution in one fell swoop, and they proved that the fossil record was formed during Noah's flood. In the article, Burdick implied falsely that Bird had personally excavated the tracks, and identified them as human.

MRS. MCFALL (on whose property BAUGH'S excavations took place) with giant "mantrack."

By the early '60s, the Paluxy man tracks had become a *cause celebre* for creationists. Morris and Whitcomb's *The Genesis Flood* included photographs of "man tracks" alongside dinosaur tracks, with the caption:

> These tracks were both cut from the Paluxy River Bed near Glen Rose, Texas, in supposedly Cretaceous strata, plainly disproving the evolutionist's contention that the dinosaurs were extinct some 70 million years before man "evolved." Geologists have rejected this evidence, however, preferring to believe that the human footprints were carved by some modern artist, while at the same time accepting the dinosaur prints as genuine. If anything, the dinosaur prints look more "artificial" than the human, but the genuineness of neither would be

questioned at all were it not for the geologically sacrosanct evolutionary time-scale.[46]

By the late '60s and early '70s, creationist expeditions to Paluxy had begun.
Baptist minister Stanley Taylor who owned a company called Films for Christ
visited Paluxy and documented his findings in the 1972 16mm film, *Footprints in
Stone*, which soon became a creationist teaching tool.

But not all creationists were convinced that the man tracks were genuine. A
creationist team from Loma Linda University studied the tracks in 1970 and concluded that some of the "man tracks" were made by three-toed dinosaurs, that
others were the result of erosion, and that still others were homemade carvings.
Increasingly, however, creationists used the Paluxy man tracks as evidence. The
Institute for Creation Research, the Bible-Science Association and other groups
also embraced the tracks. In 1980, John Morris (son of Henry M.) published the
"definitive" pro-man track book, *Tracking Those Incredible Dinosaurs*.

Kuban writes that his own interest began around 1979, after reading about the
tracks during his senior year in college as a biology major. The next summer he
and an associate traveled to the site so that they could study the tracks themselves.
When they began, they were open to creationism and hoped to confirm that the
man tracks were genuine. However, they "resolved to examine and record whatever we found as thoroughly and carefully as possible. . . . We soon concluded,"
writes Kuban, "that some of the alleged human tracks, such as those on the 'State
Park Shelf' were merely erosional features and random irregularities of the rock
surface." However, there were still the mysterious elongated prints to resolve.

After removing sediment and debris from the site, it became clear that the
shapes "were more compatible with dinosaur toes than human ones" and that
they were "some type of unusual dinosaur tracks with elongate 'heels.'" Further
investigation revealed that the elongated prints were not the result of an unusually shaped foot, but of an unusual, flat-footed way of walking. Moreover, "the
anterior impressions definitely indicated long, tridactyl digit patterns compatible with dinosaur feet and inconsistent with human ones. The 'man track'
advocates had apparently overlooked these anterior features, and instead
focused on the oblong, roughly-humanlike metatarsal section at the rear."
Kuban subsequently published his findings, which have been supported by
other researchers in the field, and they convinced many creationists to reverse
their position on the man tracks.

But in 1982, just as the controversy was dying down, another group of creationists led by former Baptist minister (now director of the Creation Evidences
Museum in Glen Rose) Carl Baugh, revived it with new evidence. Baugh's 1987
book, *Dinosaur: Scientific Evidence that Dinosaurs and Men Walked Together* may
be beating a dead dinosaur, but it's still in print ten years later; I purchased my
copy at a mainstream Christian bookstore in 1997.

Baugh identifies himself on the cover of *Dinosaur* as Carl E. Baugh, Ph.D. According to Kuban, however, Baugh never earned advanced degrees in anything, even theology. His perspective is purely that of a Baptist Minister wishing to prove that his strongly held beliefs can be backed up by evidence. In the foreword to Baugh's book, Robert L. Whitelaw writes:

> With the map and pictures of the Paluxy sites before him, the serious archeologist can picture those days only some 5,000 years ago when men and dinosaurs roamed the valley together and fled in terror from the inundating ocean that sealed their tracks and buried them as God opened the fountains of the great deep and the windows of heaven to end forever "the world that was."

In March of 1982 a group of Baptist ministers led by Baugh began their own excavation at Paluxy. Their findings, unlike those of Kuban or the group from Loma Linda, were spectacular. On just the second day they found "a clearly defined human track among 19 dinosaur tracks" under the limestone. Then they found another human print underneath a dinosaur print. By the end of the third day, they'd uncovered four human footprints and 23 dinosaur prints, some within inches of one another. More expeditions followed with similar results. Baugh writes: "The footmarks were every bit as convincing as some others claimed as human footprints by anthropologists in other parts of the world. However, there was one difference; these finds had relevance to the Bible, and to biblical creation." Soon, the press became interested, and stood by, when the group found a human footprint at the same level as that of a Tyrannosaurus Rex, to report the news in the *Fort Worth Star-Telegram*.

Baugh also claims that a couple years later, the group was directed to a giant human skeleton in the possession of Wayland "Slim" Adams, son of Ernest "Bull" Adams (the teenager who'd found dinosaur tracks in 1909) whom Baugh describes as a "highly respected researcher in years gone by." Slim went to his deep freeze chest and assembled a human skeleton, a "seven-foot woman who was believed to have died giving birth to a child because the skeleton of a very young infant was

CARL BAUGH'S *Dinosaur: Scientific Evidence That Dinosaurs and Men Walked Together*, closer to mainstream creationism than one might think.

CARL BAUGH's restructuring of man's descent, from *Panorama of Creation*, published in 1989 by the Southwest Radio Church.

found with her." Baugh ties the skeleton to the giant man tracks, and to Genesis 6:4: "There were giants in the earth" in those days. He also claims that one of the man tracks was made by a sandal-type shoe. But one of his loopiest claims is that he found a fossilized human finger in the Cretaceous layers. The photograph shows a stone, roughly in the shape of a finger, with the caption that it "compares favorably with the modern human finger." His other finds included "out-of-order" fossils, including "giant cat prints," a "human tooth," a "hammer," and a Cretaceous "trilobite." All these finds were later refuted by other researchers.

But Baugh is undaunted, because his biblically-fueled fancy gives rise to a wonder-world, where dinosaurs are friendly—and domesticated:

> Imagine a pre-flood world with giant ferns, plants and trees dominating the land. Unless they were regularly harvested, these giant plants and vines would soon leave man in submission to a dark jungle. Dinosaurs appear to be the perfect master harvester for man's domination of the planet with his beastly friends grazing nearby![48]

Baugh established a small "Creation Evidences Museum" in the Paluxy area, a few years after his first excavations, which he now uses as the base for his creationist crusade.

Kuban studied Baugh's sites shortly after they were excavated and, not too surprisingly, "found that none of the 'man tracks' there closely resembled real human prints." Instead, they were "poorly preserved specimens" of dinosaur tracks, or long, "incompletely cleaned grooves" near dinosaur tracks, that may have been made by the dinosaur's tail, snout or other body part. Others of Baugh's "man tracks," says Kuban, were "vague, shallow, often isolated depressions . . . with only a remote resemblance to human footprints." Kuban also charges Baugh's team with selectively abrading portions of the prints to make them look more like human toes, under the pretense of "uncovering" toes, as witnessed by visitors to the site. Baugh is apparently unaware that this practice is improper, because it can also be clearly seen on Baugh's own videotapes. Kuban's conclusion, corroborated by paleontologists is: "Despite Baugh's creative efforts, none of the markings on his excavations closely resembled real human footprints."

In 1985 Kuban gave creationist leaders, including John Morris of ICR, a guided tour of the Paluxy sites, during which they realized their error in promoting the man tracks as genuine. Morris told Kuban that day that he'd probably stop selling his book, *Tracking Those Incredible Dinosaurs*. Paul Taylor, who was also present, decided to stop distributing his film, *Footprints in Stone*. However, their published statements fell short of full retraction and misrepresented the evidence. Instead, they deemed the man track claims as "questionable," rather than false. In any event, most creationist groups have largely backed off from their previous full embrace, while Baugh and a few others continue to promote and excavate the amazing "man tracks."

DID GENESIS MAN CONQUER SPACE?

Though there does seem to be a time-worn "party line" for creationists, as represented by Henry Morris, Duane Gish and the ICR, some creationists, such as Emil Gaverluk, deviate wildly. Gaverluk's 1974 *Did Genesis Man Conquer Space?* profusely illustrated by Jack Hamm, is a refreshing change from the garden variety anti-evolution tract.

Gaverluk, a North Carolina minister and author of such end-times classics as *The Rapture Before the Russian Invasion, The Oil of Israel and The Church in Space Heading for Isaiah 14:13* always signs his name followed by a "Ph.D. Ed. D." and identifies himself as a "Professional Science Lecturer." (He doesn't divulge where he received his degrees or in what field he earned his Ph.D.) His specialty, rather than astrophysics or biology, seems to be the resurrection of the faithful, in outer space. In one of his promotional pamphlets, he writes that millions will be "caught up into space in the resurrection-rapture," traveling faster than the speed of light. Then, "with heightened senses they [will be] astonished to see the light of the sun bouncing off the earth with every person's 3D motion pictures on the light waves." Next, they will "see the history of the world and [their]

An illustration of a neanderthal from EMIL GAVERLUK's fringe creationist treatise, *Did Genesis Man Conquer Space?*

EMIL GAVERLUK suggests God spoke to Israel via laser beams (from *Did Genesis Man Conquer Space?*)

family too." After seeing the crucifixion of Jesus they will "fly to Isaiah 14:13," a "Judgement Seat," which is "two billion light years wide," and "over 50 million light years from Earth," where they will receive their crowns. After the "wedding," they will "return to Earth in the biggest space ship made of gold, crystal." All this, on the authority of Scripture —an interpretation not shared by Gaverluk's colleagues at the ICR.

Gaverluk contends in Did *Genesis Man Conquer Space?* that the long lives of the patriarchs "enabled Genesis Man to develop a civilization superior to ours—a civilization capable of conquering space and producing technological marvels superior to our own (exotic energy sources for example)." Rather than painstakingly presenting the errors of evolutionists the way the more reputable creationists do, Gaverluk refutes evolution by simply declaring it a "big lie":

> The myth to which modern society has succumbed is that early life on Planet Earth was "simple, on the way to the complex," that it was "primitive" and thus far below our present "developed" civilization. Those who hold to this lie, picture early men as "cave-dwellers, naked savages, sub-humanoids." In such eyes, early man is mere "waste material" put together by "chance forces"—an "experiment" that ultimately produced our own "superior" race.
>
> I deny passionately that I am "waste material" being experimented with for the benefit of future supermen. Who are the "gods" who play with my soul? I resent being told that I will die, my body decompose in the ground, and thus I will not evolve into a "superman." I experience love fiercely for my loved ones. What cruel "gods" dare dictate that I have this but for a moment, and then carelessly throw my loved ones into oblivion? . . .[49]

Humans today are a far cry from the first men, who were biologically superior beings, not beetle-browed brutes:

> Adam had a computer-like mind that was far superior to ours today. It was created a perfect brain with computer-memory circuits unaffected by decay, breakdown, aging, deterioration, death. . . .
>
> When Adam experimentally broke the laws of the universe by his own actions he knew he was being disobedient by his own will. He had no excuse. A perfect brain had made a wrong decision. Death came to that brain. Death came to succeeding brains because they were now imperfect.

As repeated in many creationist books, Gaverluk believes that the pre-flood life spans were literally centuries long, as reported in Genesis. Unlike his colleagues, though, he speculates that because of the longer life spans, that the patriarchs had more time to study science and technology, and to sustain complex projects:

> Certainly when men lived to be almost 1,000 years old with the awesome knowledge they began with as sons of Adam that knowledge of Earth and the heavens was prevalent and they were able to harness the laws of that universe. If scientists could live to be almost 1,000 today, they would be willing to give up 500 or 600 years in space travel to reach planets around the visible stars with the hope of finding another perfect world as there once was.

The patriarchs also had more time to learn—from space aliens:

> The ancients' lives overlapped. Methusaleh knew Adam personally. . . . Methusaleh was able to visit the site of the Garden of Eden. He could hear from Adam what happened there. . . .
>
> . . . They lived on an exceedingly rich planet endowed with awesome beauty and prolific life. They had a knowledge of chemistry and understood the properties of matter. Some perhaps were killed as they playfully brought together the right combination of uranium. They knew the structure of matter, If Not Directly From Adam, Then From Space. Not from physical space aliens as we would think of them; instead, I believe, these aliens had the ability either to assume bodies of men, inhabit them, or actually be able to impregnate females of the human species.

Gaverluk's interpretation of Genesis provides a kind of "missing link" between the mainstream creationists and the alien interventionists who interpret supernatural events in the Bible as the acts of extraterrestrials. If like the fundamentalists you want the Bible to emphasize archaic morality and the second coming of Christ then it will; if like the New Age prophets you want it to emphasize technology then it will.

Literalism, it seems, is all a matter of interpretation.

FAITH AND CREATIONISM

The fundamentalist/creationist rejection of evolution does not simply quibble about the course of prehistoric events. It revolts against the "humanistic" world that dares to question the Bible—the "word of God." To question the Bible—the center of the fundamentalists' existence—is to attack the fundamentalists themselves, their world-view and their God. As they see it, only the forces of evil would attack God. Hence, humanists, secular scientists and most members of modern Western society are in league with the Devil. The creation story in the Bible is just one of many Bible beliefs under attack. Though the creationists voice fury when scientists claim apes and sea-jellies should be included in their family trees, their true fury is directed not towards the apes and the sea-jellies, but towards the culture of non-belief.

Those who accept evolution, then, are lost souls. If they could only hear and understand the truth, they would accept Jesus Christ and the Bible and renounce evolution and its attendant evils. What better way to win over secular scientists than to prove to them "scientifically" that the Bible is true and evolution is false? While it's easy to interpret the rise of "creation science"—creationists adopting the tools and jargon of science—as a naive attempt by amateurs to gain acceptance by the "big boys," it might also be seen as a calculated attempt to win souls. Creationists hope that by beating evolutionists at their own game, their mechanical view of the world will be replaced with one that is based on faith. If they triumph, all will agree that humanity was no accident, but molded from clay by Our Father, the Divine Being.

It is easy to forget that creationists were not always "aberrant anthropologists." The current scientific viewpoint is the real aberration when compared to the beliefs of the larger portion of humanity, past and present. And, even in contemporary society, it will always be a minority who values hard evidence over human purpose. Despite the advances of science and paleoanthropology, there will always be those who find their way back to faith and some form of creationism.

1. Montagu, *Science and Creationism*, originally from Frazer, *Creation and Evolution in Primitive Cosmogonies*, 1935.
2. Campbell, *Primitive Mythology*, p. 235.
3. Ibid., p. 105.
4. This is the same myth cited by Zecharia Sitchin; see chap. 1, "Extraterrestrial Origins."
5. Campbell, *Primitive Mythology*, pp. 103–5.
6. Augustine quoted *Under God*, by Wills, p. 129; from St. Augustine, *Genesis Taken Literally*.
7. White, *Science with Theology*, p. 33.
8. White, quoted from *Physiologus*.
9. White, *Science with Theology*, p. 250.
10. See chap. 3, "Race," for various pre-Adamite views.
11. White, *Science with Theology*, p. 255.
12. Ibid., p. 49.
13. Gillispie, *Genesis and Geology*, p. 152.
14. Sedgwick quoted in *Genesis and Geology*, by Gillispie, pp. 149–50 & 165; from *Edinburgh Review*, 1845.
15. Darwin quoted *Death of Adam*, by Greene, pp. 265–56. Originally from Charles Darwin, edited by Francis Darwin (Cambridge, 1909) *The Foundations of the Origin of Species: Two Essays Written in 1842 and 1844.*
16. Huxley, *Life and Letters of Thomas H. Huxley* (1901), p. 197.
17. Ibid., p. 199.
18. See chap. 1, "Extraterrestrial Origins."
19. To McCann's credit, he called Piltdown Man a hoax long before it was identified as such by scientists.
20. McCann, *God—or Gorilla*, p. 19.
21. Ibid., pp. 27–28.
22. Price quoted in, "Modern Botany and the Theory of Organic Evolution," by Livingstone, *Princeton Theological Review* (1925), p. 156.
23. Milner, *Encyclopedia of Evolution*, p. 397.
24. Ibid., p. 398.
25. Rimmer, "The Theories of Evolution and the Facts of Paleontology," in *Theory of Evolution*, pp. 14–16.
26. Rimmer, "The Facts of Biology and the Theories of Evolution," in *Theory of Evolution*, p. 12.
27. Rimmer, "Monkeyshines," in *Theory of Evolution*, pp. 3–4.
28. Reagan quoted *Under God*, by Wills, p. 120.
29. Archer quoted *Bones of Contention*, by Lubenow, p. 236; originally from *A Survey of Old Testament Introduction*, by Gleason L. Archer (1964).

30. See the Urantia Book section in chap. 7.

31. Morris and Whitcomb, *Genesis Flood*, p. 25.

32. Ibid., p. 457.

33. Ibid., p. 458.

34. Morris, et al., *Science and Creation*, p. 42.

35. Ibid., p. 44.

36. Morris, *Modern Creationism*, pp. 307–11.

37. Arthur, "Creationism."

38. Gish, *Evolution*, pp. 212–13.

39. Ibid., p. 221.

40. Lubenow, *Bones of Contention*, p. 14.

41. Ibid., p. 22.

42. Ibid., p. 47.

43. Ibid., p. 49.

44. McIver, "Walk through Earth History."

45. Ibid., pp. 33–34.

46. Morris and Whitcomb, *Genesis Flood*, p. 174.

47. Baugh, *Dinosaur*, p. 27.

48. Ibid., p. 82.

49. Gaverluk, *Genesis Man*, p. 10. The following three excerpts in the text are also from *Genesis Man*; p. 23, p. 16 and p. 29, respectively.

CHAPTER SIX

THE AQUATIC APE THEORY

*For guardians of the conventional wisdom
of human evolution, the notion that humanity's
immediate ancestors may have been aquatic is only slightly
less bizarre than the fact that the idea is being championed by
a grandmother, now 72, without formal scientific
qualification, whose main claim to fame is as a
writer of TV docudramas.*
PAT COYNE, *New Statesman & Society*

I first encountered the Aquatic Ape theory of human evolution via a "kook" flyer sent to me by an outfit called "Cloud 247 Studios." At the top, was the question "Was the 'Missing Link' an Aquatic Ape???" The flyer promoted the "Cloud 247" Theory of Aquatic Intelligence, which proposed a deep kinship between ourselves and the whales and dolphins. I assumed that the Aquatic Ape must be some kind of dolphin and that the people at Cloud 247 Studios believed we had evolved from dolphins. The flyer made reference to a book entitled *The Aquatic Ape* by Elaine Morgan; I vaguely recalled that Elaine Morgan was a feminist—she was the author of *The Descent of Woman*—so her involvement in what seemed to be some kind of new age dolphin-mania

ELAINE MORGAN,
champion of the
Aquatic Ape

confused me. I reprinted the flyer in the "Kooks Pages" of my 'zine, and then filed it away (see page 210).

Years later I chanced upon Elaine Morgan's book *The Aquatic Ape* at the public library. To my surprise, the Aquatic Ape theory (AAT) didn't suggest we had evolved from dolphins; it didn't even remotely hint at any kind of dolphin-mania. The thin volume was, however, logical and fun to read. Its ideas were irresistible. *The Aquatic Ape* turned out to be one of those books—one of those theories—that fits everything together so well that you feel it just has to be true. For weeks after reading it, I pondered the theory. Soon I found myself preaching the gospel of the Aquatic Ape to my friends.

The Aquatic Ape theory observes that various human traits, such as bipedality, speech, lack of body hair, subcutaneous (under the skin) fat, weeping, face-to-face copulation and sweating, are unique among primates and therefore hard to account for by conventional theories of human evolution. But if humanity was at one time aquatic or semi-aquatic, these traits could be easily explained. The AAT tells us that we share many traits with aquatic mammals which we don't share with our closer relatives, the primates. Therefore, says the AAT, we acquired those traits in an aquatic environment. The beauty of this theory is that it seems to solve, in one fell swoop, all the mysteries of human uniqueness. It's also championed by a skilled writer, unencumbered by the stringent guidelines of scientific research.

When I first became enchanted with the AAT, I knew that Elaine Morgan— a journalist and television writer—was no anthropologist, but I still expected that the theory would be discussed in the current literature, if only to be refuted. In fact, I was dying to know why it might *not* be right. I checked the index of every recent book on human evolution I could, and found *nothing* on the Aquatic Ape theory.

What in the hell was going on?

Little by little, I realized that those most prone to favor the AAT were people like me: non-scientists. The scientific community knew about the AAT but chose to ignore it. This only served to strengthen my own feeling that the AAT must be right: since I hadn't seen any arguments against it, maybe there were no arguments against it. I couldn't help teetering between the two extreme positions that would explain all this: either there was a sinister conspiracy afoot by egotistical scientists to squelch the truth about the AAT because they couldn't bear to be proved wrong by an outsider, or I had been bamboozled by a crackpot myth on the order of Ancient Astronauts and Pyramid Power. In actuality, the explanation was a bit more complicated.

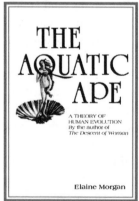

The Aquatic Ape by Elaine Morgan was the first book devoted exclusively to exploring this unorthodox theory.

AQUATIC APE AS MOTHER GODDESS

The Aquatic Ape began as an essentially female vision of human evolution, an antidote to what Elaine Morgan then called "The Mighty Hunter"—a brutish ape-man who used to dominate popular stories of human evolution. The Aquatic Ape, by contrast, emerges from the sea, like Venus or an aquatic Madonna-and-child. Some of the appeal of the AAT might stem from Morgan's colorful depictions of what is essentially a mother goddess.

Freudians identify water-origin myths as essentially female and water as a symbol of the womb. We emerged from a watery womb, so our world emerged from a watery womb as well. The many deluge myths from widely diverging cultures depict the world, and the primal couple, emerging from water and then spawning humanity.

In *Occidental Mythology*, Joseph Campbell notes that water universally symbolizes fertility—because of the obvious connection between rain and the growth of crops. Psychologist C.G. Jung also identified water as an elemental mother symbol, along with earth and wood. Even the Garden of Eden story connects to water, as the serpent was traditionally seen as the Lord of Waters. "Dwelling in the earth, among the roots of trees, frequenting springs, marshes, and water courses," writes Campbell, the Serpent "glides with a motion of waves. . . . When imagined as biting its tail, as the mythological uroboros, it suggests the waters that in all archaic cosmologies surround—as well as lie beneath and permeate—the floating circular island Earth."[1]

The human being compared to whales, dolphins, seals, and other aquatic animals who began on land. ELAINE MORGAN writes: "Time after time throughout evolutionary history, this process has taken place." (From *The Aquatic Ape*)

So, aside from its scientific or explanatory merits, the Aquatic Ape theory also has the archetypes of watery creation on its side that contribute both to its popular appeal and to the scientific community's perception of the AAT as mythological pseudoscience. It seems no accident that the AAT's most dedicated advocate is a woman—and mother of three. The first to propose the Aquatic Ape theory, however, were men.

ORIGINS OF THE AQUATIC APE THEORY

On March 5, 1960 marine biologist Alister Hardy addressed the British Sub-Aqua Club on the topic of "Aquatic Man: Past, Present and Future." In his speech, Hardy suggested that aquatic man represented a crucial phase of evolution in the past, and that "sub-aqua man" would revolutionize the fishing industry in the future. The press loved it, printing garbled versions of Hardy's address in the Sunday papers. But Hardy soon had the opportunity to clarify his position by writing a series of articles for *New Scientist*. In the April issue, Hardy introduced the real Aquatic Ape theory to the general public:

> The suggestion I am about to make may at first seem farfetched, yet I think it may best explain the striking physical differences that separate Man's immediate ancestors (the Hominidae) from the more

ape-like forms (Pongidae) which have each diverged from a common stock of more primitive ape-like creatures which had clearly developed for a time as tree-living forms.

My thesis is that a branch of this primitive ape-stock was forced by competition from life in the trees to feed on the seashores and to hunt for food, shell fish, sea-urchins, etc., in the shallow waters of the coast. I suppose that they were forced into the water just as we have seen happen in so many other groups of terrestrial animals. I am imagining this happening in the warmer parts of the world, in the tropical seas where Man could stand being in the water for relatively long periods, that is, several hours at a stretch. I imagine him wading, at first perhaps still crouching, almost on all fours, groping about in the water, digging for shellfish, but becoming gradually more adept at swimming. Then, in time, I see him becoming more and more of an aquatic animal going further out from the shore; I see him diving for shell fish, prising out worms, burrowing crabs and bivalves from the sands at the bottom of shallow seas, and breaking open sea-urchins, and then, with increasing skill, capturing fish with his hands.[2]

Hardy first conceived the theory in 1927, after a two-year expedition to the Antarctic to study marine life. He came across a passage in Wood Jones' *Man's Place Among the Mammals* that described the layer of subcutaneous fat peculiar to humans that is "familiar to everyone who has repeatedly skinned both human subjects and [other] Primates." "It is difficult to see why," wrote Jones, "there should be such a basal difference between Man and Chimpanzee." Hardy, fresh from his marine voyage, was immediately reminded of whalers and sealers whose first cut into their victims' flesh always yields fat, rather than muscle. Surgeons who cut into humans have a similar experience. Other land mammals' fat is located not under their skin, but in the membranes between the viscera and around the kidneys. Hardy reasoned that our layer of fat might have evolved during an aquatic phase of human pre-history. But he kept his mouth shut, he later admitted, because, he "wanted to get a good professorship [and] to be a Fellow of the Royal Society." Finally, in 1960, he felt secure enough in his professional life to tell it to the world.

Unbeknownst to Hardy, Max Westenhöfer, a professor at the University of Berlin, had proposed the Aquatic Ape theory in his book *The Unique Road to Man* in 1942. He didn't claim to have originated this theory; it's possible that Hardy's private speculations to colleagues and students over the years had reached Germany. Moreover, Westenhöfer hadn't made up his mind about the AAT; he merely suggested it as a promising hypothesis that warranted further study. Because World War II was raging, the German scientist's comments became buried in the literature; the Aquatic Ape had to wait another 20 years before anyone took notice.

After Hardy's 1960 speech to the Sub-Aqua Club, the press and public briefly became interested in the AAT. But his colleagues politely ignored the old prof's "indiscretion" as one of those eccentric aberrations allowed now and then to distinguished scientists in their waning years. Some even thought that Hardy's speech had been a prank. But an interview caught on film (*Water Babies, Australia*) during the last year of Hardy's life testified to his devotion to what he thought was a truly revolutionary view of human evolution.

After Hardy's brief fame, aquatic man was forgotten yet again for nearly a decade.[3] Then, in 1967, Desmond Morris mentioned the Aquatic Ape theory in his best-seller *The Naked Ape*. He remarked that "despite its most appealing indirect evidence, the aquatic theory lacks solid support." But Morris had planted the idea in the mind of at least one reader, who subsequently became the AAT's greatest champion.

THE DESCENT OF WOMAN

To some, Elaine Morgan seems an unlikely candidate for a promoter of unorthodox theories of human evolution. Now a grandmother in her 70s, Morgan was born in Wales, graduated from Oxford and leads a very successful career as a freelance writer. She is most noted for her many television scripts produced by the BBC beginning in the 1950s, several of them award winners.

Morgan's moment of illumination came in 1970. When she read about the Aquatic Ape theory in *The Naked Ape* she felt "as if the whole evolutionary landscape had been transformed by a blinding flash of light." She searched in vain for further information on the AAT and was "astonished that after this key had been put into their hands, people were still going on writing about the move from the trees to the plains as if nothing had happened." Morgan wrote to Hardy, telling him of her plan to write a book about the AAT. The arrival of the letter was "a bit of a shock" to the aging biologist, since he had one day hoped to write a book about the AAT himself. But he gave her his blessing, and urged Morgan to "press on with it as hard as you can." In just two years, Morgan had her own best-seller, *The Descent of Woman*.

The success of *The Descent of Woman* owes probably as much to the book's open defiance of male-centered anthropology as it does to the theory itself. In this, her first AAT book, Morgan wrote about the story of human evolution with woman, not man, as protagonist. Indeed, until *The Descent of Woman* was written, women were scarcely mentioned in books about human evolution at all. Male anthropologists, it seemed, ignored both the importance of females and the Aquatic Ape theory equally. Morgan saw it as her job to rectify this situation "because I thought the then-current scenarios of human evolution were macho and unbelievable." Some of Morgan's wittiest passages describe her skepticism about the then-current scenarios of human evolution, starring "The Mighty Hunter":

> Almost everything about us is held to have derived from [hunting.] If
> we walk erect it was because the Mighty Hunter had to stand tall to
> scan the distance for his prey. If we lived in caves it was because
> hunters need a base to come home to. If we learned to speak it was
> because hunters need to plan the next safari and boast about the last.
> Desmond Morris, pondering on the shape of woman's breasts,
> instantly deduces that they evolved because her mate became a
> Mighty Hunter, and defends this preposterous proposition with the
> greatest ingenuity. There's something about the Tarzan figure which
> has them all mesmerized.[4]

Morgan's antidote to the Mighty Hunter were several small, vegetarian,
not-too-bright, hairy ape-women, faced with a dwindling food supply and a
diminishing forest, who were forced into the dry savannah:

> She knew at once she wasn't going to like it there. She had four
> hands better adapted for gripping than walking and she wasn't very
> fast on the ground. She was a fruit eater and as far as she could see
> there wasn't any fruit. . . . She never thought of digging for roots—
> she wasn't very bright. She got thirsty, too, and the water holes were
> death traps with large cats lurking hopefully around them. She got
> horribly skinny and scruffy-looking.
>   . . . The only thing she had going for her was the fact that she was
> one of a community, so that if they all ran away together a predator
> would be satisfied with catching the slowest and the rest would sur-
> vive a little longer.
>   What then, did she do? Did she take a crash course in walking erect,
> convince some male overnight that he must now be the breadwinner,
> and back him up by agreeing to go hairless and thus constituting an
> even more vulnerable and conspicuous target for any passing carni-
> vore? Did she turn into the Naked Ape?
>   Of course, she did nothing of the kind. There simply wasn't time. In
> the circumstances, there was only one thing she could possibly turn
> into, and she promptly did it. She turned into a leopard's dinner.[5]

This unlucky ape-woman's sister had just a bit more courage and intelligence.
Rather than a leopard's dinner, she became the mother of all aquatic apes:

> With piercing squeals of terror she ran straight into the sea. The
> carnivore was a species of cat and didn't like wetting his feet; and
> moreover, though he had twice her body weight, she was accus-
> tomed like most tree-dwellers to adopting an upright posture, even

though she used four legs for locomotion. She was thus able to go farther into the water than he could without drowning. She went right in up to her neck and waited there clutching her baby until the cat got fed up with waiting and went back to the grasslands. . . .

. . . One idle afternoon after a good deal of trial and error she picked up a pebble—this required no luck at all because the beach was covered with thousands of pebbles—and hit one of the shells with it, and the shell cracked. She tried it again, and it worked every time. So she became a tool user, and the male watched her and imitated her. (This doesn't mean that she was any smarter than he was—only that necessity is the mother of invention. Later his necessities, and therefore his inventiveness, outstripped hers.)

. . . She began to turn into a naked ape for the same reason as the porpoise turned into a naked cetacean, the hippopotamus into a naked ungulate, the walrus into a naked pinniped, and the manatee into a naked sirenian.[6]

Morgan adapted Hardy's arguments to her story and added some of her own as well. Hardy had argued:

1. The hairs on the human body followed the lines that would be formed by a flow of water over a swimmer, distinct from the hair arrangement of other primates.
2. The cracking open of shellfish by an aquatic primate could easily lead to the use of tools.
3. Wading could explain both our erect posture and the increased sensitivity of human fingertips, since the aquatic primate would need to grope underwater for unseen objects.
4. The aquatic primate would have had to keep warm with a layer of subcutaneous fat.
5. The Aquatic Ape theory could explain the ten-million-year hominid fossil gap because the remains of the aquatic apes would have been swept out to sea.

Morgan amended Hardy's theory—and charmed her readers—by drawing from her experiences as a mother. Hardy had explained hair on the aquatic ape's head as protection from the sun while wading, but Morgan explained it as a way for the aquatic ape baby to cling to its otherwise naked mother. "It would be a powerful advantage for a baby if its mother's hair was long enough for his fingers to twine into," wrote Morgan. "[I]f the hair floated around her for a yard or so on the surface he wouldn't have to make so accurate a beeline in swimming toward her when he wanted a rest." This also explained male pattern baldness because "in communities where the males took no part in the bringing up of the offspring there would be nothing to prevent their heads going bald as their bodies. . . ." Female human breasts, which Morgan noted are proportionately larger than chimp breasts, could also be explained by envisioning the lives of the aquatic Madonna and child: larger breasts were easier for nursing water babies to cling to.

Though Morgan would refine her arguments in later books, it was the *Descent of Woman* that defined the Aquatic Ape theory for the reading public. It became a best-seller and was eventually translated into ten languages. It put the AAT on the map, not only for the public but for science as well. The reviews were mixed, however, depending on whether or not the reviewer was a scientist. Anthropologist Ian Tattersal objected to the AAT on the grounds that humans never adapted to underwater breathing as did other aquatic mammals, and because there's evidence that humans have been land creatures for at least 15 million years. A reviewer for *Time* magazine described Morgan's ideas as "fanciful notions," and equated *The Descent of Woman* with "another largely fictional work," Clifford Irving's discredited biography of Howard Hughes. This comparison almost prompted a libel suit from Morgan's publisher.

Another typical dismissal came from Robert Claiborne in *God or Beast: Evolution and Human Nature*, published in 1974. Claiborne charged that Morgan's theory was made up of "fact, folklore and fiction," based on "a fantasy of Sir Alister Hardy . . . that nobody with any experience in any of these fields takes seriously." A dissenting reviewer, Carolyn Riley, echoed the reading public's enchantment with the theory. "Never, I think, will the reader have encountered before a theory," she wrote, "which is so thrillingly convincing, which 'feels so right' when applied to conditions and characteristics observable in the twentieth century." Morgan later summed up the response to the book, noting that both the media and the public were enthusiastic, while only the scientists were contemptuous.

The critics didn't deter Morgan because she really had nothing to lose. Moreover, she claims that she was ready to be proved wrong, if indeed she was wrong. "Writing the book, I did have periods of feeling that it was the most outrageous cheek," Morgan confessed. "Perhaps it was easier for me because I had nothing to lose, no high academic position to think of. If you talk about flying saucers, you're branded as a kook. I don't believe in flying saucers but I suppose this kind of thing looks flying-saucerish to the Establishment." [7]

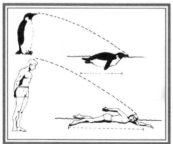

Man and penguin.
ELAINE MORGAN writes: "The penguin's perpendicular stance is unlike that of any other bird as our is unlike any other mammal." (From *The Aquatic Ape*)

Even though most of them disdained even to mention the Aquatic Ape theory, some scientists brought up valid objections, the most important one being the lack of hard evidence. Even if the AAT makes sense as an explanation, it will be nothing more than conjecture until some hard evidence of mankind's aquatic past turns up. As Frank E. Poirier wrote in 1973, "Unless some spectacular evidence is uncovered, the aquatic theory is merely an oddity."

In 1977, Alister Hardy wrote he was convinced that evidence "almost as conclusive as fossil evidence" had actually been found:

> It has been found experimentally that man has the remarkable adaptation which is found only among mammals and birds that dive under water. It is called the diving reflex and now solves the puzzle of how sponge and pearl divers can remain below so long. It only happens if a man's face is submerged; it won't occur if he wears a mask. If he dives under water and his face exposed, there is an immediate reaction cutting down blood supply to most of the body, but leaving a good supply to both the brain and the muscles of the heart. This reaction is typical of whales, seals, penguins, and even diving ducks: I cannot believe that it could have been evolved by natural selection unless man had taken to diving under water some considerable period of his past history. The only remaining test to be made is to persuade some physiologists to do simple experiments with all the known apes. They merely have to be put in a bath of water with their faces submerged for a short time whilst an electro-cardiograph records the changes in the circulation of their blood. If man is really unique in this I am home and dry! But in addition it would be very pleasant in my old age to have a bit of fossil *Homo aquaticus*—or a cast of it—on my mantelpiece; so perhaps the Oxford Exploration Club might think of pandering to my eccentricity.[8]

Hardy's certitude was not shared by his colleagues, who continued to be silent on the subject of the AAT. One scientist later defended this silence by remarking that there was so much evidence against the AAT that nobody thought it necessary to publish a refutation. Instead, it was much easier to dismiss the AAT as Mary Leakey did in 1980 "as nothing more than the outcome of an over-fertile imagination without any possible bearing on the research on human evolution."

THE MATURING AQUATIC APE

In her subsequent books, *The Aquatic Ape* (1982) and *Scars of Evolution* (1990), Elaine Morgan incorporated the diving reflex into her arguments. She also addressed some of the criticisms and offered suggestions for locating fossil evidence.

Man and seal. ELAINE MORGAN writes: "A more finely attuned sense of balance and a more flexible spine." (From *The Aquatic Ape*)

The Aquatic Ape focused on the theory itself, rather than on colorful stories of our first ancestors. Over the ten years since her last book, Morgan had clearly become fluent in the terminology of paleoanthropology, anatomy, physiology, evolutionary theory and marine biology. Now that she was speaking their language, scientists might be more inclined to listen to the uppity author. Morgan says she "used a deliberately non-best-seller style in hope of eliciting a serious response from scientists." But the book, according to Morgan, had "almost no impact" with scientists, and even the media ignored it.

Though she was writing in a drier style, Morgan hadn't lost any of her "cheek." She continued to make bold claims, not yet backed up by hard evidence. She did point out, however, that the AAT was just as consistent with the fossil evidence as the scientifically sanctioned "Savannah" theory that our first ancestors went straight from the trees to the savannah.

Morgan refined her arguments and adopted a less prejudicial strategy for getting them across. Instead of ridiculing "The Mighty Hunter," she compared the Savannah theory and the AAT point by point. Morgan addressed each human characteristic that the AAT allegedly explains better than the Savannah theory: loss of body hair; a layer of subcutaneous fat; salty tears; walking erect; face-to-face copulation; diving reflex; aquatic babies; and speech. She also made it clear that the Savannah theory and the AAT are not mutually exclusive. Morgan's contention was that our first ancestors left the trees for the water, and then returned to the savannah.

Where, exactly, might this have happened? In *The Aquatic Ape* Morgan suggested that flooding in the Danakil Alps in the Afar triangle—an area in Ethiopia between the Blue Nile and the Red Sea—caused our ancestors to become isolated on islands and in swamps. Only after this aquatic sojourn did they migrate to the African Rift Valley (in East Africa and Ethiopia) where so many hominid fossils have been found. She backed up this conjecture with a paper by Leon P. LaLumiere Jr. of the Naval Research Lab in Washington, D.C., who provided evidence that the Danakil Alps region was cut off from the rest of Africa during the period in question. Thus, if someone wanted to find aquatic ape skeletons, Morgan suggested, their best bet would be to try looking in the Danakil Alps. Because of political difficulties in the region, as well as the expense, this has yet to happen.

Even after the success of *The Descent of Woman*, and the refinement of the AAT in *The Aquatic Ape*, the theory remained relatively obscure. But by the late '80s and early '90s Morgan had caught the interest of a handful of scientists, some of whom gathered for an AAT conference in 1987 (discussed below). Morgan continued to refine her arguments and attempted to approach the theory from yet another angle with her 1990 book, *The Scars of Evolution*. Here, she focused not on what we've *gained* by our adaptations but on what we've lost—on our evolutionary scars and defects. Morgan argues that there had to be a very good reason for adaptations like walking erect and losing our fur, otherwise we never would have survived their crippling side effects.

Morgan claims that a diverse range of medical problems and anatomical defects are the direct result of unique human features. This includes lower back pain, obesity, enlarged adenoids, acne, varicose veins, sudden infant death syndrome, sunburn, sleep apnea, sexual malfunction, dandruff, inguinal hernia and hemorrhoids. Obesity is the "cost" of keeping warm with a layer of subcutaneous fat. Crippling back problems and varicose veins are the "cost" of walking on two legs rather than four. Sunburn is the "cost" of losing our fur. And, because the cost was so high, the initial cause must have been severe, dramatic, life-threatening. In other words, no creature would begin to walk on his hind legs—an unnatural posture that would initially slow him down—unless doing so could save his life. As Morgan puts it:

> For absolute beginners [in walking erect] the difficulties were very much greater [than for us.] This is what the orthodox theory asks us to believe: that millions of years ago a population of apes on the savannah chose to walk on two limbs, instead of running rapidly and easily on four like a baboon or a chimpanzee. They stood up, with their unmodified pelves, their inappropriate single-arched spines, their absurdly under-muscled thighs and buttocks, and their heads stuck on at the wrong angle, and they doggedly shuffled along on the sides of their long-toed, ill-adapted feet.[9]

By once again providing detailed anatomical and physiological arguments, Morgan proved herself to be a clever and convincing, if not ingenious, writer. But she still couldn't persuade the scientists. In a *New Scientist* review of *The Scars of Evolution* (the journal in which Hardy introduced the AAT in 1960), Adrienne Zihlman remained unconvinced by Morgan's latest effort. She pointed out in detail the major flaw of the AAT: that it's not supported by evidence. She noted that the three-million-year-old hominid specimens which we have on hand, according to the AAT, should show aquatic adaptations such as "streamlining and reduction of limbs . . . characteristic of . . . aquatic mammals." But they don't. The oldest hominids, including the australopithecine Lucy, "have curved hand and foot bones that bespeak a recent descent from the trees rather than an ascent from the depths." The critic also pointed out that Morgan skirts the issue of hard evidence completely by emphasizing such "soft" features as fat, skin and tear ducts, which cannot be preserved in the fossil record and are "impossible to validate." She also lamented that the AAT holds an attraction for her students, because it "explains everything," making it "unnecessary to learn all that tedious stuff about fossils, anatomy and DNA—if I weren't so unreasonable as to insist on their learning it." In addition to being the friend of the lazy, armchair anthropologist, the AAT, according to Zihlman, is no more than "an entertaining fantasy, with intimations of the origin of life in the Precambrian sea and our prenatal float in the amniotic sac." [10]

THE AQUATIC APE DEBATE

In his 1986 book *The River that Flows Uphill: A Journey from the Big Bang to the Big Brain* William H. Calvin commented, "Anthropologists have been hesitant to discuss the aquatic theory, almost as if they were Victorians standing on ceremony, not having been properly introduced," even though "physiologists keep adding weight to Hardy's theory . . . as they discover more and more about aquatic mammals." Anthropologists, he charged, are "addicted" to hard evidence. Just a year later, that introduction would finally take place, and the hard evidence junkies were given a chance to duke it out with AAT advocates at the first scientific conference devoted solely to the Aquatic Ape theory.

The conference was held in 1987 at Valkenburg, the Netherlands, sponsored jointly by the European Sociobiological Society and the Dutch Association of Physical Anthropology. Papers were presented by Elaine Morgan and other AAT advocates such as physician Marc Verhaegen, as well as AAT skeptics and experts in physiology, biology and psychology. Those looking for a serious discussion of the theory among experts can find it in the book that resulted from the conference, *The Aquatic Ape: Fact or Fiction?* (Souvenir Press, 1991). The book's scientific papers have titles like "Is an Aquatic Ape Viable in Terms of Marine Ecology and Primate Behaviour?" and "The Burden of Locomotion in Water: Could the Aquatic Ape Have Overcome It?" Reading it gives the overall impression that even after close scrutiny of the evidence—soft and hard—the experts found the AAT lacking.

For example, Martin Pickford of the Institut de Paléontologie in Paris, in "Does the Geological Evidence Support the Aquatic Ape Theory?" finds that "the geological record does not provide convincing evidence from which the AAT could benefit." He points out—contrary to what Elaine Morgan has claimed—that if the aquatic ape existed then it would have been in the best possible environment for its preservation as a fossil. But rather than in wet environments, pre-hominid fossils are found "in sediments which accumulated subaerially, well away from lakes" and in wooded and forested plains. Pickford's conclusion:

> If the geological evidence is to be a source of support for the AAT, then all the positive evidence as to palaeo-environments that is currently available has to be discarded or discounted, and recourse taken to what the geological record "might" yield. . . . The only conclusion to be drawn on the basis of available evidence . . . is that apes and hominids avoided lakes and seas throughout the Miocene and

Plio-Pleistocene, just as they do today. Any other conclusion, including the suggestion that we have not looked in the right place, must come under the heading of "special pleading."

In "Adaptation and the Aquatic Ape," Alan Turner of the Hominid Paleontology Research Group at the University of Liverpool criticizes the AAT on the basis of its logic, which he brands a "Just So Story." The AAT, he says, relies on "adaptationist" arguments—*ad hoc* arguments based solely on a trait's current utility. For example, the AAT tells us that we lost our fur and acquired a layer of subcutaneous fat to help us keep warm in the water. Turner points out features don't arise solely because of their future utility, but out of a far more complex process. "We might as well argue," writes Turner, "that the fine balance controls and other characteristics that enable us to ride bicycles must have been developed during a bicycle-riding phase in the Pliocene—perhaps with tandems as reinforcing devices for ensuring monogamous coupling." Morgan has countered this charge by claiming that the Savannah theory relies on "Just So Stories" as well. Morgan may have gotten this impression, falsely, from reading pop anthropology books (like *The Naked Ape*) that typically use adaptationist arguments, while scientific papers do not.

Similarly, Holger and Signe Preuschoft (professors of physiology and anatomy in Germany and the Netherlands) find that the AAT doesn't explain human evolution better, doesn't integrate more facts, and is no more consistent than the other theories. For example, take our nakedness: the Preuschofts point out that counter to the impression given by Morgan, gorillas, chimps and orangutans have lower hair density (300–500 hairs/cm2) than other apes and monkeys (2000–3000 hairs/cm2). Thus our relative hairlessness is on a continuum with the other primates and need not be explained by an aquatic phase in human evolution. The Preuschofts claim—counter to Hardy and Morgan—that our layer of subcutaneous fat is arranged not much differently than in other terrestrial mammals, including primates. And, finally, on the issue of bipedality, the Preuschofts point out that most primates are already "hindlimb-dominated" and have a tendency to sit upright. While they're standing and walking, most primates carry the greater part of their weight on their hindlimbs, rather than on their forelimbs. So, again, humans are on a continuum with the other primates, and there is no need to hypothesize an aquatic phase to account for these features. The Preuschofts also criticize AAT because it's too vague: it provides no detailed causal explanations for the origins of the traits that it explains. (This criticism matches the "Just So Story" charge.) Their conclusion: "Although we feel attracted and, more so, challenged by some of the arguments derived from the Aquatic Ape theory, we regret to conclude that we cannot offer any support to it."

Even the editors of the anthology can't support the AAT, concluding, "While there are a number of arguments favouring the AAT, they are not sufficiently convincing to counteract the arguments against it." But the fact that the conference took place meant that at the very least the AAT was beginning to get the close scientific scrutiny that it deserved. The 1992 conference of the British Association for the Advancement of Science spent one day on the aquatic theory, and in 1993 the American Association for the Advancement of Science followed suit. The Fall 1995 issue of the humanistic psychology journal *ReVision* was devoted solely to the AAT. As Elaine Morgan says, the AAT "is becoming more popular with scientists by the week."

THE AQUATIC APE INVADES CYBERSPACE

The internet now makes basic information about the AAT, arguments pro and con, and spontaneous discussions between Elaine Morgan and her opponents easily accessible. Anyone looking for information on the AAT these days should have no problem whatsoever. In fact, discussions of the AAT at times dominate the Usenet news group sci.anthropology.paleo—to the chagrin of some of the anthropologists. The AAT's appeal to the non-expert makes it a perfect topic for debate in Usenet discussion groups, since these groups are open to scientists and laypeople alike. The tension between the experts and curious laypeople is particularly transparent in these discussions. Non-scientists often enter them looking for information on the AAT, without realizing that the topic was already discussed in detail when someone else went looking for information. Those with a negative opinion of the AAT grow understandably impatient when they must raise the same objections again and again to the uninitiated. Morgan et al. annoy the research scientists; they see her and her defenders as maybe one notch above creationists or alien abductees. The AAT enthusiasts, on the other hand, are never satisfied with the experts' objections. The discussion goes around and around, and then dies down, to be rekindled when someone new enters the group and posts the message "I'm looking for information on the AAT."

The eternal conflict between expert and public is well illustrated by some reactions to a recent pro-AAT appearance by Desmond Morris (who had originally dismissed it in *The Naked Ape*) on British television. Several years ago, scientists posted the following messages to the Usenet group sci.bio.evolution:

> Last night, Desmond Morris went to great lengths to describe the basis of the aquatic ape theory, as an intermediate transitional stage between the forest and the savannah. . . . There is a glaring discrepancy not to say yawning chasm of blithe apathy, apparently on the scientific community's side, between accepted science and that which is shown on our TV screens. This isn't (can't be) good for anybody. So why don't we get better confrontation and categorical dismissal of AA[T] as quackery, or else a reasoned discussion of it?

Desmond Morris or no Desmond Morris, [in my opinion] this aquatic ape nonsense is only a couple steps above Ludwig Plutonium [a
well-known internet crackpot.] I have better things to do than waste
my time rebutting crackpots.

I for one was horrified to see Des peddling the Aquatic Ape theory
on British TV at peak time. All the AA[T] puff with a throw-away
"no fossil evidence" line at the end. I for one don't believe a word of
his pop evolution stories.

There are also several World Wide Web sites devoted to the AAT, both pro
and con, and an AAT "FAQ."[11] Jim Moore, for example, a researcher with
informal training in human evolution devotes several web pages to defending an
anti- AAT position, using an easy-to-understand question-and-answer format.
He also provides a list of AAT claims, and refutes them, one by one. This is
indeed more helpful for non-scientists than wading through technical papers,
looking for a reason to reject the AAT. Here is an excerpt from Moore's list:

Claim: "Human hairlessness is explained by an aquatic past."
Fact: Humans' relative hairlessness is unlike aquatic mammals,
because A) most aquatic mammals aren't hairless; and B) those that
are have skin that's radically different from humans.

Claim: "Only humans and aquatic animals exhibit the 'diving reflex.'"
Fact: The "diving reflex" is found in all mammals.

Claim: "Only humans and aquatic animals can hold their breath."
Fact: Non-human, non-aquatic animals can and do hold their breath.

Claim: "The pattern of human hair alignment is strikingly different
from apes and indicates streamlining for swimming."
Fact: The pattern of human hair alignment is only very slightly different from apes. Also, in order for this pattern to indicate streamlining
for swimming we would have to be swimming with the crown of the
head facing straight forward and your arms held at your sides.

Claim: "Our ancestors wouldn't have changed from quadrupedalism
to bipedalism, because initially bipedalism would be less efficient than
quadrupedalism."
Fact: Actual tests with chimpanzees has shown that bipedalism is no
less efficient for them than quadrupedalism. It wouldn't be for our
ancestors, even if they evolved from knuckle-walking apes such as

chimps. Also, the consensus over the last couple of decades has been that the LCA ["last common ancestor" of the chimpanzees and humans] was far more likely to have been a brachiating (swinging from branches) ape rather than a knuckle-walker, which makes it even less of a problem to be bipedal. In fact, brachiating apes—such as gibbons—always walk bipedally when they are on the ground.

Claim: "Humans have subcutaneous fat which is bonded to the skin rather than anchored within the body, unlike non-aquatic mammals."
Fact: Human fat deposits are anchored to underlying depots, just as those of all mammals are. Human fat deposits are found in the same places, and are anchored the same way, as those of other primates.

Even after five aquatic ape books—most recently *Descent of the Child* (Oxford University Press, 1995) and *The Aquatic Ape Hypothesis* (Souvenir Press, 1997)—Elaine Morgan continues promoting the AAT with admirable energy. Her answers to refutations such as the above can be seen regularly on the internet news group sci.anthropology.paleo. She considers her latest book, *The Aquatic Ape Hypothesis*, "the definitive book on this subject." As increasing numbers of people discover this attractive theory—via Morgan's books or on-line—it is likely that the debate will continue as a beautiful illustration of the largely unacknowledged tension between scientists and laypeople, causing scientists to dismiss outsiders as ignorant and outsiders to dismiss scientists as arrogant.

Aside from its merits, the perception of the AAT as the underdog—a smart, persistent outsider's challenge to mighty scientific orthodoxy—accounts for the theory's appeal among feminists, leftists and humanistic psychologists. The image of the watery, female ape Elaine Morgan evoked during the 1970s in the *Descent of Woman* (even though she has since discarded the image) can't help but appeal to men and women who wish to replace hard-edged male-dominated culture with what they hope will be a softer, female-centered culture. Leftist and New Age critics of Western science and culture, who would reject the alien intervention theory of human origins because it's too irrational, would naturally gravitate to the Aquatic Ape theory. The AAT—though it's shaky as a scientific theory—is elegantly rational compared to competing aberrant anthropologies, and politically correct as well.

No matter the outcome of the "Aquatic Ape Debate," the aquatic ape vision is here to stay. The peaceful, feminine water ape has already joined civilized dolphins, ancient astronauts and serpent people in the pantheon of the modern mythos.

BEYOND THE AQUATIC APE

The following is an excerpt from the "Cloud 247 Studios" flyer, circa mid-'80s, out of Bellingham, Wash.:

WAS THE "MISSING LINK" AN AQUATIC APE???

The "Cloud 247 Theory of Aquatic Intelligence" carries the [Aquatic Ape] hypothesis into the realm of consciousness evolution by stating: The tremendous growth in the hominid neo-cortex (frontal brain) prior to Australopithecus and Homo habilis was stimulated by the inherent pressures of ocean-based survival combined with a long-term relationship with Cetacean beings (dolphins, whales), whose brains and social interaction had already been highly developed for many millions of years. The latest morphogenetic field theories testify to the profound effect of psychic energy-fields upon biological evolution, and anyone who has observed "man's best friend" (Canis familiaris) absorbing the human personality can testify to the profound effect of transspecies relations. Did Cetacean "gurus" allow Homo to become sapiens?

According to the Cloud 247 Theory, over a period of many thousands of generations of ocean-based existence, as our neo-cortex expanded and folded upon itself, our higher-reasoning abilities and communications skills made a quantum leap in complexity comparable to a dicot seedling when it finally breaks the soil surface, greeting the fires of the SUN*RA. In the grand perspective of terrestrial ecology, however, we are yet a species in the "seedling" stage, stubbornly testing our limits and denying long-term responsibility for our actions as "Earthlings." We are an infant soiling its bed, our immature immediacy becoming a raging tantrum of industrial devastation. And, as a baby playing with a box of "strike everywhere" matches threatens to destroy itself in a blazing housefire, we are a species on the brink of self-infanticide, our cleverness racing far ahead of our real-I-zation.

Perhaps the wisest among us have realized that the "E.T." being which we collectively envision as "savior" will not arrive on our doorstep in some sort of high-tech spacecraft; the extra-dimensional source of our "enlightenment" has been with us from the beginning, as close as our nearest seashore. And they swim and dance in the waves yet, those who haven't been murdered for eyeshadow and hair-oil, still gasping for breath and exhaling mist between gummy clots of our industrial waste, still transmitting songs on a broad spectrum of frequency to brains we haven't begun to comprehend, though each Sun-cycle it becomes more difficult to avoid the rude, ugly sounds of internal-combustion machines and the ceaseless traffic of "those-who-bring-fear." Our Ocean-Selves, "those-who-are-truly-free," the whales, dolphins and porpoises, have been singing and socializing and saving drowning humans since the days of the first human. And long before that, when hominids had not yet been a dream in a lemur's restless sleep, the Cetacean beings were already swimming and communicating in complexities we haven't begun to imagine. One can only wonder and intuit the songs of today's Cetaceans, and lament at the sad, tragic story of ourselves as seen through our fellow Earthling's eyes, eyes much older and wiser than we can ever begin to realize, even if we give ourselves the chance. . . .

Current projects at Cloud 247 Studios include a picture book depicting the human-dolphin relationship and the aquatic ape theory, for children of all ages, and observation-feedback studies of the Orca pods in Puget Sound and the Inside Passage. . . .

1. Campbell, *Occidental Mythology*, p. 10.
2. Reprinted in *Aquatic Ape*, by Morgan, pp. 139–40.
3. Unless you count the 1965 film *Curse of the Swamp Creature*, by Larry Buchanan— "bad-film" director of *Zontar: The Thing from Venus*—the film was reported to involve "extras dressed in rubber suits with ping-pong eyeballs and exposed zippers." A mad scientist credits the "Oceana Theory of Evolution" for his work, and a drunken John Agar replies, "You mean the theory that man rose from the sea?"
4. Morgan, *Descent of Woman*, pp. 4–5.
5. Ibid., pp. 15–17.
6. Ibid., pp. 19–21.
7. Morgan quoted in Contemporary Authors CD-ROM.
8. Hardy, "Was there a Homo aquaticus?"
9. Morgan, *Scars of Evolution*, p. 34.
10. Zihlman, "Evolution, a Suitable Case for Treatment."
11. FAQ stands for "frequently asked questions," a file available on the internet which provides an overview of the topic in question.

CHAPTER SEVEN

THE URANTIA BOOK, SZUKALSKI AND H.I.M.

HERE ARE A FEW

ABERRANT

ANTHROPOLOGIES

THAT DON'T EASILY FIT

INTO ANY SINGLE CATEGORY.

Part I—Aberrant Anthropology in The Urantia Book

*T*he Urantia Book (UB) is a channeled bible of colossal proportions, describing the entire history of the earth (called Urantia) and the cosmos. In 2,097 pages it covers every conceivable topic from "The Evolution of Local Universes" and "The Seraphic Hosts" to "Social Problems of Religion" and "The Mind-Gravity Circuit." In print since 1955, *The Urantia Book* has been translated into Spanish, Finnish and French and will soon be translated into Dutch, Russian, Korean, German, Swedish, Hungarian and Italian. Three hundred thousand copies have been printed. Bigger and stranger than *Oahspe, The Urantia Book* is also far more coherent. However, as it's devoted to the intricate organization of such beings as "Omniaphim," "Seconaphim," "Susatia," and "Univatia" in "local" and

DR. WILLIAM S. SADLER, key figure in the production of *The Urantia Book*

"super" universes with names like "Nebadon" and "Vorondadek," plowing through the book can be a major challenge. Over and above the mystery of how anyone could possibly read it is the mystery of how anyone could write it. When I first saw *The Urantia Book*, I had no doubt that only alien intelligences could have come up with such a product. Its mere existence defied all probability.

Indeed, those who compiled and published the book, The Urantia Foundation of Chicago, compounded the mystery by keeping the identity of their "channel" a secret. But, as a result of the sleuthing of master debunker Martin Gardner, the identity of Urantia's channel, as well as the history of the Urantia Foundation are no longer in doubt.

In his book *Urantia: The Great Cult Mystery*, Gardner produces strong evidence that *The Urantia Book* is essentially a Seventh-Day Adventist

(SDA) spin-off.[1] Dr. William S. Sadler (1875–1969) and his brother-in-law Wilfred Custer Kellogg (1876–1956), who were central to the production of UB, both had strong ties to the sect. Sadler, a famous psychiatrist, was the front-man responsible for the Urantia Foundation and for UB's publication, while Kellogg, a shy, unassuming businessman was, according to Gardner, "The man who in his sleep . . . was the conduit through whom the supermortals first communicated their revelations to Sadler."

Those who knew him, writes Gardner, described Sadler as "a rotund little man with a keen sense of humor, snow-white hair, thick gold-rimmed spectacles, heavy jowls (one student likened his appearance to Alfred Hitchcock), a man who usually wore baggy gray suits, white shirts, and out-of-style neckties." He had been a Seventh-Day Adventist since the age of 11. As a teenager, he worked in the kitchen of Dr. John H. Kellogg's (1852–1943) famous Battle Creek Sanitarium (nicknamed "The San") which began as an SDA institution. Sadler soon became a close friend of the influential doctor and health crusader.

In 1897 Sadler married Dr. Kellogg's niece, Lena Celestia Kellogg (1875–1939); both husband and wife would pursue careers in medicine. In 1901 Sadler was ordained as an SDA "elder," or minister.

In the meantime, after a long power struggle with SDA prophetess Ellen G. White over the Battle Creek Sanitarium, Dr. Kellogg was "disfellowshipped" by the SDA Church. It was around that time that the Sadlers quit SDA as well.

But the Sadlers had created their own brand of evangelism, a self-help doctrine which blended the Bible, mental hygiene, health remedies and eugenics. In 1906, Sadler founded the Chicago Institute of Physiologic Therapeutics (later called the Chicago Therapeutic Institute). In 1909 his first self-help book, *Self-Winning Texts*, or *Bible Helps For Personal Work*, appeared, published by Chicago's Central Bible Supply Co. Many popular books followed, including *Mind at Mischief* (1929) which became a best-seller. Husband and wife would also make names for themselves lecturing on the Chautauqua circuit on such topics as unorthodox health remedies, hydrotherapy and eugenics.

Between 1901 and 1952 William Sadler authored over 30 books, including: *Worry and Nervousness, or the Science of Self-Mastery* (1914); *Measuring Men* (1917); *Long Heads and Round Heads, or, What's the Matter with Germany?* (1918); *Race Decadence: An Examination of the Causes of Racial Degeneracy in the United States* (1922); *The Truth About Spiritualism* (1923); *The Elements of Pep: A Talk on Health and Efficiency* (1925); *The Truth About Mind Cure* (1928); *Modern Psychiatry* (1945); and *Courtship and Love* (1952).

DR. LENA SADLER, eugenically-minded wife of DR. WILLIAM S. SADLER (from *Urantia: The Great Cult Mystery*)

Far less is known about Wilfred Custer Kellogg of the famous and somewhat in-bred Battle Creek Kelloggs.

Wilfred Kellogg grew up in the SDA church; both his father and grandfather were SDA elders, and his uncle, Moses Eastman Kellogg, was a prominent SDA editor and writer. Wilfred became business manager of the W.K. Kellogg's Toasted Corn Flake Company[2] and stayed on there until 1910.

The Kellogg family tree is confusing, since many family members married their cousins. Wilfred married his first cousin, Anna Bell Kellogg (1877–1960) the sister of Lena Kellogg Sadler. Thus, he was both cousin and brother-in-law to Mrs. Sadler. Anna, like Lena, was Dr. John Kellogg's niece.[3]

Wilfred and Anna's wedding took place in the home of the Sadlers, near Chicago. Soon after, the Sadlers moved to the Near North Side of Chicago where their building at 533 Diversey Parkway would serve as both their home and headquarters of their Chicago Institute of Physiologic Therapeutics. It later became headquarters of the Urantia Foundation. Wilfred and Anna soon moved into the Sadlers' building; Wilfred became the Institute's business manager.

Gardner's research shows that the channeling activities that evolved into *The Urantia Book* probably began in 1912. One evening Anna Kellogg knocked on the Sadlers' door. She told them that something strange was happening to her husband. The Sadlers rushed downstairs to the Kelloggs' apartment, where they found Wilfred in a deep sleep. But this was no ordinary sleep, as their medically informed probings revealed. He would hold his breath for long periods. His body lurched about. They jabbed him with pins, but he couldn't be aroused. Wilfred awoke an hour later, feeling fine, and remembering nothing.

A few weeks later, the conservative businessman began having similar episodes on a regular basis. During one such spell, Mrs. Sadler asked Wilfred a question. In a voice not his own, he replied that he was a "student visitor" from a distant planet; then he began to converse with the Sadlers on matters of philosophy and religion.

A growing number of alien visitors used Wilfred as their voice. The Sadlers quickly grasped that they had a unique opportunity before them and began asking the celestial intelligences important questions. The conversations that ensued lasted for the next ten years. Wilfred, however, could remember none of the goings-on, even under hypnosis.

In 1923 the Sadlers began hosting afternoon teas to discuss religion, attended by 20 to 30 friends. After a few of these get-togethers, Sadler broke the news about the channeled revelations. Soon, the guests—thereafter known as the Forum—began coming up with their own cosmic inquiries and brought them to the meetings. One night, presumably without knowing what was going on, Wilfred wrote a manuscript, 472 pages long, in answer to the Forum's many questions. Sadler calculated that it would have taken eight hours, writing as fast as possible, to produce that many pages. Even so, the next day, Wilfred's arms weren't even fatigued. Nobody at the Forum doubted that the manuscript had been authored by a non-human intelligence.

Sadler later recounted to a new Forum member how the original Urantia manuscript was written:

> We found there seemed to be an organized group of high intelligences on "the other side," prepared to present to us the whole astounding story of the universe, leading from God, the Universal Father, down to the origin of the human creature, man, and his ultimate glorious destiny beyond the reaches of time and space.
>
> This continued for perhaps seven or eight years when what we considered the first edition of the papers was finished. At that time, the Forum received its first direct message, and its members were advised that now, since their knowledge had been expanded, they should be able to ask more intelligent questions and that if they would do so, as they commenced a rereading of each paper, these intelligences would completely revise the entire, tremendous manuscript.[4]

Eventually, other Forum members—though most often Sadler himself—tried their hand at channeling the Celestial Intelligences. But through it all, Sadler insisted the identity of the initial channel remain a secret. Not even the Forum knew who it was. In the end, *The Urantia Book* was a joint project between Wilfred Kellogg, the Sadlers, the Forum, and the Celestial Intelligences.

After its publication in 1955, *The Urantia Book*'s devotees extended beyond The Forum. UB was never promoted much, the foundation preferring to keep the group small, with belief spread by word of mouth. Believers, which today total no more than a few thousand, are organized into study groups and Urantia societies, each society consisting of ten or more believers. Currently, there are about 200 Urantia study groups and 20 Urantia societies. One current member characterizes Urantia readers as "fairly iconoclastic" people who "keep to themselves." They do not consider their belief in *The Urantia Book* a religion.

In 1989 copyright and trademark problems caused a rift in the organization. The Urantia Foundation split into two organizations: the International Urantia Association and the Fellowship of Urantia Book Readers, both remaining in Chicago. A judge eventually ruled that rights to *The Urantia Book* are in the public domain. Hence, new editions of UB have begun to appear.

COSMOLOGY AND HUMAN ORIGINS IN THE URANTIA BOOK

The Urantia Book's cast of characters sound as if they belong in *Flash Gordon*. But many of them, like Adam and Eve, come straight from the Bible. Many place names sound biblical ("Jerusem," "Bethsaida," "Capernaum," "Satania," "Edentia") but are not. The UB reads as an amendment to the Bible, not a replacement for it.

Traces of Seventh-Day Adventist doctrine and jargon can be found all over the book. Gardner points out that both UB and SDA universes are teeming with inhabited worlds; UB and SDA agree that the otherworldly intelligences are deeply interested in earthly goings-on. Only on Earth is there "A Great Controversy" between Christ/Michael and Satan, and both agree on the doctrine of "soul sleeping," that at death, the soul literally goes to sleep, and that the body is reconstituted at resurrection.

The Urantian universe borrows SDA doctrine from Sister Ellen G. White but also rebels against it by incorporating foreign elements: the metaphysical I AM concept, early- and mid-twentieth century science and eugenics, endless organizational hierarchies, as well as what can only be identified as unique products of imagination.

The UB's cosmology reads like the constitution for a surprisingly well-organized Universe. The UB is simultaneously redolent of bureaucracy and the Bible, filling in all the Bible's blank spaces with copious, organized detail. What the Bible takes a few paragraphs to describe—the creation of mankind for instance—the *Urantia Book* tells in hundreds of pages. It's what the Bible would have been like if it had been written by lawyers and businessmen, rather than priests, prophets and poets.

In the UB, all of creation is known as The Master Universe, a perfectly organized structure. At the center of the Master Universe is Paradise, containing the great I AM. Paradise, the largest body in the Master Universe, is beyond our time and space, elliptical, flat and motionless. Orbiting Paradise is the universe of Havona, which consists of three groups of seven worlds each; and around those 21 worlds are seven elliptical rings, each of those rings containing a billion perfect, unique and timeless worlds.

Outside Havona are two elliptical rings of dark gravity bodies that hold the interior universes in balance. There are universes outside Havona as well: beyond the gravity bodies are seven *imperfect* superuniverses which continue to evolve. Each will eventually contain 100,000 local universes, and each local universe will contain ten million inhabited worlds.

Earth/Urantia is located in the seventh superuniverse, the 606th world in the planetary group of Satania, which contains 619 inhabited worlds and 200 worlds that are currently evolving towards habitation. The headquarters of Satania is the world of Jerusem. One can't help but notice the choice of names here: Satania and Jerusem. Those familiar with the Bible (the ex-SDA members who make up UB's readership, for instance) may easily incorporate these familiar-sounding names. Though the name "Satania" sounds evil, its identity as the planetary group in which Earth/Urantia happens to reside neutralizes that impression, assuring readers that perhaps evil is an accident rather than an inevitability.

Satania resides in a constellation of 100 systems called Norlatiadek, with headquarters on the planet Edentia, another suggestive name which, as we'll see, lent its name to the Garden of Eden. Norlatiadek is itself the 70th world of the universe Nebadon, the 84th universe in the minor sector Ensa, which is the third minor sector in the major sector of Splandon, which is the fifth major sector of the seventh sector superuniverse Orvonton.

Like its cosmology, UB's story of the creation and evolution of life is strangely bureaucratic in flavor. Life and evolution are carried out by beings following master plans devised by their superiors. Members of the cosmic hierarchy always follow strict rules that cause the universe, with all its sectors, sub-universes and worlds to run properly. Urantia is no different from any of the other worlds except for one thing: those in charge of seeding and inhabiting Urantia failed to adhere to the master plan—with tragic consequences.

UB describes the process whereby life is designed and carried to all the evolving worlds—not just Urantia—all according to plans formulated by the Architects of Being:

> Life does not originate spontaneously. Life is constructed according to plans formulated by the (unrevealed) Architects of Being and appears on the inhabited planets either by direct importation or as a result of the operations of the Life Carriers of the local universes.[5]

In the universe of Nebadon, 100 million life carriers described as an "efficient corps of life disseminators," were created, who all answer to their superiors: Gabriel, Father Melchizedek and Nambia. They are efficient, and highly organized:

> Life Carriers are graded into three grand divisions: The first division is the senior Life Carriers, the second, assistants, and the third, custodians. The primary division is subdivided into 12 groups of specialists in the various forms of life manifestation. The segregation of these three divisions was effected by the Melchizedeks, who conducted tests for such purposes on the Life Carriers' headquarters sphere. The Melchizedeks have ever since been closely associated with the Life Carriers and always accompany them when they go forth to establish life on a new planet.

The College of Life Planning on World Number One is devoted to the study of universal life, with teachers and advisors from Uversa and Havona in Paradise. Life Designing—an inordinately technical process—takes place on World Number Two:

> There are over one million fundamental or cosmic chemical formulas which constitute the parent patterns and the numerous basic func-

tional variations of life manifestations. Satellite number one of the life-planning sphere is the realm of the universe physicists and electrochemists who serve as technical assistants to the Life Carriers in the work of capturing, organizing, and manipulating the essential units of energy which are employed in building up the material vehicles of life transmission, the so-called germ plasm.

After life has been successfully transplanted onto a world by the Senior Life Carriers, evolution begins. Eventually the process of evolution reaches its pinnacle: primitive man. Evolution on millions of worlds always has roughly the same outcome: primitive man splits into six races, each a different color: red, orange, yellow, green, blue and indigo, red being the earliest race and indigo (black) the latest. Evolution is anything but a random process. These colored races appear during the development of language and creativity, after mankind learns to stand erect. These colors correspond to the known human "races" here on Earth: unsurprisingly, the red race corresponds to Native Americans, the yellow race to Asians, the indigo/black race to Africans. Somewhat less obvious is that the blue race corresponds to Europeans.

In UB, not all the races are equal, as the "earlier races are somewhat superior to the later; the red man stands far above the indigo—black—race." Life Carriers impart the "full bestowal of the life energies" to the red race, but "each succeeding evolutionary manifestation of a distinct group of mortals represents variation at the expense of the original endowment." Hence, generally, the red race is tallest, for example, and the indigo race is shortest. Furthermore, the first, third and fifth races: red, yellow and blue, are superior to the second, fourth and sixth: orange, green and indigo, who are "somewhat less endowed." Here, UB provides an embellishment to physical anthropology, rather than the Bible.

According to UB, it's quite natural that the superior races enslave the others. For example, "The orange men are usually subdued by the red and reduced to the status of servants." Likewise, "The yellow race usually enslaves the green, while the blue man subdues the indigo." Sometimes the orange and green races are exterminated, as they were here on Urantia. Because we aren't familiar with the orange or the green races, this "natural" enslavement seems benign; what's more, the blue race isn't the only one engaged in it, the yellow and red races do it too. The only reason they're off the hook here on Earth/Urantia is that the orange and green races are no longer here to complain about it.

The development of the first human beings on Urantia went according to plan, as on most other worlds. About one million years ago, when "Urantia was registered as an *inhabited world*," a mutation occurred in the stock of evolving primates, which "*suddenly* produced two primitive human beings, the actual ancestors of mankind." This occurred during the "third glacial advance." The sole survivors of the original "Urantia aborigines" were the Eskimos, who "even now prefer to dwell in frigid northern climes."

The first human beings were a pair, though they were not Adam and Eve. (Adam and Eve did exist but were sent to Earth after mankind evolved to "uplift" the race, as we'll see.) They were prodigy twins, Andon and Fonta, born to primate parents who were far less advanced than they were. They had black eyes and a swarthy complexion, presumably like the Eskimos. Unlike their parents they were able to communicate with each other in an abstract verbal language. After losing patience with their dumb relatives, the twins left home to found the human race:

> The twins *did migrate*, and because of our supervision they migrated northward to a secluded region where they escaped the possibility of biologic degradation through admixture with their inferior relatives of the Primates tribes.
>
> Shortly before their departure from the home forests they lost their mother in a gibbon raid. While she did not possess their intelligence, she did have a worthy mammalian affection of a high order for her offspring, and she fearlessly gave her life in the attempt to save the wonderful pair.

Two years after their departure, Andon and Fonta had a child, named Sontad, the first of 19. This first human family lived in four adjoining rock shelters and made their living by hunting in groups. Andon and Fonta both lived until age 42, when they were both killed by a falling rock during an earthquake.

About 500,000 years later, mutations occurred which produced the colored races, according to the master plan described above. This first mutation took place among the Badonan tribes of Northwest India, when a couple "suddenly" produced a family of unusually intelligent children, whose skins had a tendency to turn various colors when exposed to the sun. Five were red, two orange, four yellow, two green, four blue and two indigo. As they grew, the colors intensified.

UB's story of the human races on Earth/Urantia conform to the prejudices of mid-twentieth century North Americans. The red race, though they were the most intelligent, had problems with the yellow race and also warred among themselves. They migrated from Asia to North America 85,000 years ago. The orange race had the urge to build anything and everything. They began migrating towards Africa but were exterminated by the green race about 100,000 years ago. The yellow race was the first to establish settled communities with a home life based on agriculture. They were peaceful among themselves. The green race was less able than the others; they split into three groups: Northern, Southern and Eastern. The Northern group was enslaved and absorbed by the yellow and blue races. The Eastern group amalgamated with the Indians. The Southern group entered Africa where they wiped out the orange race. Many of their leaders were giants, eight and nine feet tall; their remnants absorbed by the Indigo race. The blue race invented the spear; they had the brainpower of the red race and the soul of the yellow race, but they fought among themselves. The white races are descendants of the blue race with yellow and red mixed in. The indigo race, or the black men, were the least progressive and the last to migrate from their home territory—they settled in Africa.

As on other worlds, it was only after the evolution of the six races that the "Planetary Adams" in the form of Adam and Eve arrived, to "upstep" the human race. Adam and Eve and their descendants were of the Adamic, violet race. UB explains this as a plan that utilizes the variations and endowments of all the races to their fullest—but only if carried out correctly. Apparently, in the case of Urantia, it wasn't:

> These modifications [of the colored races] are beneficial to the progress of mankind as a whole provided they are subsequently upstepped by the imported Adamic or violet race. On Urantia this usual plan of amalgamation was not extensively carried out, and this failure to execute the plan of race evolution makes it impossible for you to understand very much about the status of these peoples on an average inhabited planet by observing the remnants of these early races on your world. . . .
>
> These six evolutionary races are destined to be blended and exalted by amalgamation with the progeny of the Adamic uplifters. But before these peoples are blended, the inferior and unfit are largely eliminated. The Planetary Prince and the Material Son, with other suitable planetary authorities, pass upon the fitness of the reproducing strains. The difficulty of executing such a radical program on Urantia consists in the absence of competent judges to pass upon the biologic fitness or unfitness of the individuals of your world races. Notwithstanding this obstacle, it seems that you ought to be able to agree upon the biologic disfellowshiping of your more markedly unfit, defective, degenerate, and antisocial stocks.

The Planetary Prince usually arrives within 100,000 years of the time mankind begins to walk erect:

> These Sons, for there are two of them—the Material Son and Daughter—are usually known on a planet as Adam and Eve. . . .
> These Sons are the material gift of the Creator Son to the inhabited worlds. Together with the Planetary Prince, they remain on their planet of assignment throughout the evolutionary course of such a sphere. . . .

... While there was a miscarriage of the ideal plans for improving your native races, still, Adam's mission was not in vain; Urantia has profited immeasurably from the gift of Adam and Eve, and among their fellows and in the councils on high their work is not reckoned as a total loss.

Because the material sons'—Adam and Eve's—bodies' glow with violet radiant light, they are called the violet race. The violet race's bodies ranged in height from eight to ten feet tall. And, should they fail in their mission, they are cut off from the "connection with the universe source of light and life." Thereafter they become material beings, "destined to take the course of material life on the world of their assignment." "Material death" will eventually terminate their "planetary career." This, of course, is just what happened on Urantia. It also conforms to the story of the Fall of Man in Genesis.

The Adams and Eves on each inhabited world always construct "garden homes" each named the Garden of Eden in honor of Edentia, the capital of their constellation. Their express mission is to "multiply and to uplift the children of time," by interbreeding with the evolutionary races. But they wait many generations in biological segregation while they build up their own, violet race. UB details this plan for "racial upliftment":

> Usually the violet peoples do not begin to amalgamate with the planetary natives until their own group numbers over one million. . . .
>
> On normal worlds the Planetary Adam and Eve never mate with the evolutionary races. This work of biologic betterment is a function of the Adamic progeny. But these Adamites do not go out among the races; the prince's staff bring to the Garden of Eden the superior men and women for voluntary mating with the Adamic offspring. And on most worlds it is considered the highest honor to be selected as a candidate for mating with the sons and daughters of the garden.
>
> For the first time the racial wars and other tribal struggles are diminished, while the world races increasingly strive to qualify for recognition and admission to the garden.

On Urantia however, race improvement was an uphill battle. The "Caligastia Rebellion," an illegal attempt "to achieve planetary advancement independently of the divine plan of progression," through "unbridled personal liberty," left the planet in chaos. As a result, the planet was cut off from the other planets in the vicinity.

Adam and Eve arrived on Urantia 37,848 years before 1934:

At the time Adam was chosen to come to Urantia, he was employed, with his mate, in the trial-and-testing physical laboratories of Jerusem. For more than 15,000 years they had been directors of the division of experimental energy as applied to the modification of living forms. Long before this they had been teachers in the citizenship schools for new arrivals on Jerusem.

Adam and Eve each stood approximately eight feet high, with blue eyes, and bodies that shimmered with light. They were vegetarians. They founded the "violet race," whose members had white skin and blue eyes, and could communicate with each other through telepathy. "This thought exchange was effected by means of the delicate gas chambers located in close proximity to their brain structures. By this mechanism they could send and receive thought oscillations." They ultimately lost this power, however, due to "the mind's surrender to the discord and disruption of evil."

Why then, does the Bible tell a different story? UB's explanation is that the legends we all grew up with are confused and inaccurate versions of real events:

> The story of the creation of Urantia in six days was based on the tradition that Adam and Eve had spent just six days in their initial survey of the Garden. . . .
> The legend of the making of the world in six days was an afterthought, in fact, more than 30,000 years afterward. . . .
> The story of creating Eve out of Adam's rib is a confused condensation of the Adamic arrival and the celestial surgery connected with the interchange of living substances associated with the coming of the corporeal staff of the Planetary Prince more than 450 thousand years previously.

The creation story found in *The Urantia Book* seems fantastically ludicrous, because it synthesizes the conflicting traditions of Seventh-Day Adventism, Darwinian evolution and racial assumptions of the time, as well as a penchant for intricately bureaucratic hierarchies. But the plot is entirely consistent (even if subconsciously) with the known beliefs of its probable authors: the Sadlers and Kelloggs.

EUGENICS IN THE URANTIA BOOK

The Sadlers and Dr. John Kellogg, like many of their social class, pinned their hopes for mankind on eugenics. In 1906 Dr. Kellogg founded the eugenically-minded Race Betterment Foundation to "call attention to the dangers which threaten the race," to research the "causes of race deterioration," and to promote "biologic living." William and Lena Sadler were active eugenics crusaders as well.

William Sadler authored at least three pro-eugenics books: *Long Heads and Round Heads, or, What's the Matter with Germany?* (1918), *Race Decadence: An Examination of the Causes of Racial Degeneration in the United States* (1922) and *The Truth About Heredity* (1927). In *Race Decadence*, Sadler repeated the eugenic gospel that our American genetic heritage is in jeopardy due to the fecundity of blacks and the influx of inferior racial stocks from abroad, concluding that "morality is hereditary" and that "some races are more moral than others." As documented in the Eugenics chapter, this view was well within the mainstream of the eugenics movement at the time. Lena Sadler, too, cut a swath in the eugenics movement, authoring a paper entitled "Is the Abnormal to Become Normal?" read at the Third International Congress of Eugenics in 1932. Its thesis was that severe eugenic measures are necessary to stem the tide of racial degeneration in America. She pleaded:

> Here we are coddling, feeding, training, and protecting this viper of degeneracy in our midst, all the while laying the flattering unction to our souls that we are a philanthropic, charitable, and thoroughly Christianized people. We presume to protect the weak and lavish charity with a free hand upon these defectives, all the while seemingly ignorant and unmindful of the fact that ultimately this monster will grow to such hideous proportions that it will strike us down, that the future descendants of the army of the unfit will increase to such numbers that they will overwhelm the posterity of superior humans and eventually wipe out the civilization we bequeath our descendants; and all this will certainly come to pass if we do not heed the handwriting on the wall and do something effectively to stay the march of racial degeneracy, for it is said that even now three-fourths of the next generation are being produced by the inferior one-fourth of this one.[6]

She advocated a federal sterilization law, which she predicted would eventually eliminate most crime, insanity, feeblemindedness, moronism, abnormal sex, and many other types of "degeneracy."

In his 1918 book, *Long Heads and Round Heads, or What's the Matter with Germany?* Sadler speculated about the effects of genetics on world politics, along the lines of racist eugenicists Lothrop Stoddard and Madison Grant. He hypothesized that Germany is dominated by two main races: the Nordic/Teutonics and the Alpines. The blonde-haired blue-eyed fair Nordics were blessed with long heads and high intelligence. The world's greatest leaders, including Cyrus, Alexander, Caesar, Charlemagne and Napoleon were all Nordics. The genetically inferior Alpines, on the other hand, were round-headed and dark eyed, like the primitive men and the apes. They were stupid and brutish, and were farmers. Sadler concluded that Germany was threatened by inferior stock: not Jews, but round-headed Alpines. Therefore, the war that the United States was then fighting (WWI) against Germany was necessary in order to defeat the round heads. According to Gardner, Sadler's ideas were directly pilfered from the writings of Madison Grant.[7]

By an amazing coincidence, the entities who wrote *The Urantia Book* were as vehement about eugenics as the Sadlers. Though eugenics would seem out of place in other sacred texts, UB is saturated with eugenic doctrine. In UB, the eugenic principles of race betterment guide the Life Carriers and uplifters throughout the universe. When eugenic instructions are not carried out properly, the result is chaos. On most planets—object lessons in world eugenics—after Adam and Eve found the violet race, the unfit are eliminated and the violet race (except Adam and Eve themselves) uplift the remaining, superior strains of mankind:

> This age usually witnesses the completion of the elimination of the unfit and the still further purification of the racial strains; on normal worlds the defective bestial tendencies are very nearly eliminated from the reproducing stocks of the realm.
>
> The Adamic progeny never amalgamate with the inferior strains of the evolutionary races. Neither is it the divine plan for the Planetary Adam or Eve to mate, personally, with the evolutionary peoples. This race-improvement project is the task of their progeny. But the offspring of the Material Son and Daughter are mobilized for generations before the racial-amalgamation ministry is inaugurated.[8]

The result is spiritual and mental improvement of the evolutionary races because of the "gift of the Adamic life plasm," usually accompanied by physical improvement, invention, energy control, mechanical development, the control of nature, exploration and "the final subduing of the planet." At the end of this period, all races are blended to one color, "somewhat of an olive shade of the violet hue, the racial 'white' of the spheres."

On Urantia, however, we are "a full dispensation and more behind the average planetary schedule," because of "miscarriage of the ordained plans" for race improvement. Eugenics, according to UB, is not only scientific, it's universal law. The reason that our world fell behind was the Caligastia Rebellion and the failure to eliminate the unfit. One can't help reading this as a divinely sanctioned mandate for aggressive eugenic policies.

The "default" of Adam and Eve followed the Caligastia Rebellion:

> [When Adam and Eve] addressed themselves to the all-important work of eliminating the defectives and degenerates from among the human strains, they were quite dismayed. They could see no way out

of the dilemma, and they could not take counsel with their superiors on either Jerusem or Edentia. Here they were, isolated and day by day confronted with some new and complicated tangle, some problem that seemed to be unsolvable.

Under normal conditions the first work of a Planetary Adam and Eve would be the co-ordination and blending of the races. But on Urantia such a project seemed just about hopeless, for the races, while biologically fit, had never been purged of their retarded and defective strains.[9]

To carry out their mission of "upstepping" the mortal races more quickly, Eve consented to mating with a member of the Nodites, a mixed race. Adam followed suit, by mating with a Nodite woman. Though their descendants were allowed to interbreed with the mortals, it was strictly forbidden that Adam and Eve do so. Because they violated the divine plan to never themselves mate with a mortal, they were found to be in "default." Thus, Adamic blood became more diffused than on other worlds, hindering the uplift of mankind. While Adam and Eve patched up their work via last-minute eugenic controls, others were breeding haphazardly, producing mongrelized races such as the current inhabitants of Mexico, Central and South America and India. Even now, interbreeding between higher races (whites, with more Adamic blood) and lower races is ill-advised:

> While the pure-line children of a planetary Garden of Eden can bestow themselves upon the superior members of the evolutionary races and thereby upstep the biologic level of mankind, it would not prove beneficial for the higher strains of Urantia mortals to mate with the lower races; such an unwise procedure would jeopardize all civilization on your world. . . .[10]

When mere mortals advocate "elimination of the unfit" and race purification, they risk being accused of racism and selfishness as were the leaders of the eugenics movement. When the same message comes from a celestial entity being channeled by an unknown conduit, couched in bureaucratic space jargon, the risk diminishes. Though they were not all that uncommon during the teens and '20s, after that time the Sadlers' and Kelloggs' deepest-held beliefs—that the human race must be improved by elimination of the supposed unfit—had to be re-packaged.

It remains a mystery, though, how the subconscious minds of Mr. Wilfred Kellogg and others responded so perfectly to the task of encoding the new belief system.

Part II—Stanislav Szukalski: Raped by the Apes

Pessimists and de-evolutionists see humanity on an ever-descending spiral, but for some, like the late artist Stanislav Szukalski (1893–1987), the damage has already been done. According to Szukalski, our blood has already been mixed; not with inferior human blood but with that of apes—human history is the story of the struggle between the true humans and the a-human Yetinsyny, who even now live among us in human society. They speak our language and they sometimes even take over our nations, but a few of their physical features give them away as the gluttonous anthropoids that they are. We humans are too busy, too foolish and too gullible to notice. Only Szukalski—distinguished artist, discoverer of Protong, founder of Zermatism—was sharp enough to point out the apes among us.

Szukalski was born in Warta, Poland and quickly distinguished himself as a major artistic talent; he first exhibited his work when he was only 14. He emigrated to the United States with his blacksmith father and ended up in Chicago, home of a sizable Polish community. Szukalski met with favor on this side of the Atlantic, and was soon keeping company with such luminaries as Ben Hecht, Carl Sandburg,

STANISLAV SZUKALSKI at work
(from *Behold!!! The Protong*)

Sherwood Anderson and Clarence Darrow. In 1936 Szukalski, who was not soon forgotten by his countrymen, was summoned back to the old country to create monuments to Polish glory on government commission. This was to be the pinnacle of his artistic career, for it was then that he was hailed as Poland's greatest living artist. But his tenure as Polish national artist came to an abrupt halt with the advent of World War II. Nazi bombs obliterated his studio that had doubled as the Szukalski National Museum. Szukalski returned to the United States, settling in Southern California. There he began researching the origins of language and became a familiar face at the public library. His studies of pictographs and illustrations of archeological finds culminated in the discovery of what he called "Protong," or the "proto-tongue." Protong, claimed Szukalski, is the mother of all languages, a pictographic language common to all cultures before the Tower of Babel. He toiled away the rest of his years working out the complexities of such theories, an embittered, ever-busy, unappreciated genius, in what he dubbed the "cultural Siberia" of Burbank, Calif. He died at age 93.

A few years before his death, Szukalski was discovered by underground artists—the first to appreciate his genius in over 30 years. The Polish artist's biggest break came when art patron Glenn Bray founded Archives Szukalski. Through Archives Szukalski, Bray sponsored belated exhibitions of the genius' work—sculptures, paintings, drawings—and published portions of his magnum opus on the science of what he called "Zermatism," in a series of books.

The anthropoid Yetinsyny figure prominently in one such book *Behold!!! The Protong*, a partial reprinting of Szukalski's 1980 publication, *Troughful of Pearls/Behold!!! The Protong*. This incredible work contains an outline of Zermatism as well as a small portion of the 40,000 illustrations Szukalski produced on that subject.

Szukalski's apes are not the gentle, vulnerable, near-extinct cousins described by Dian Fossey in *Gorillas in the Mist*. Instead, Szukalski depicts gorillas as syphilitic, rapacious, cowardly brutes, whose numbers threaten to overrun the earth. And their relation to us is closer than we think:

> Due to our ignorance of our bastardly past, our inbreeding with the apes, we carry the Burden of History, which actually is the struggle between Humans and a-Humans. The a-Humans, however, because they are born in our own countries and communicate in our languages, are not recognized and are taken to be Poles in Poland, Englishmen in England, Russians in Russia.
>
> The gigantic abdomen that gorillas have to keep on filling all day long was inherited by their bastardly descendants, which physical trait was sublimated into avarice for everything in sight.[11]

The history of our intimate connection to these monsters can be found in ancient artifacts from all over the world. For example, the "Pans" of Greek legend, who are depicted on Greek vases are in fact a "species of large apes that attacked human women and raped them." Szukalski notes that "all the wart-nosed Greek philosophers, the pot-bellied, waddling pygmoids, were actually descendants of such interspecies bastardy" between humans and apes. And the bastardy went in the other direction as well. Apparently, some of the female Yeti were enticing enough to attract human males, who willingly copulated with them, and produced "Manape" offspring.[12] Szukalski enthusiastically identifies the descendants of these couplings by such

BEHOLD !!! THE PROTONG

STANISLAV SZUKALSKI's illustrated treatise on the hidden history of Earth and mankind, *Behold!!! The Prontong*

traits as an "undercut nose," long upper lip, long torso, short upper arm, wart nose, pot belly and sometimes even a tail. These bastards typically end up as dictators, political subversives, and communist agents in all nations. Their compulsive opposition to human decency is the cause of all our troubles, past, present and future:

> The history of mankind up to this moment is the enumeration of Struggles caused by the elemental foes of mankind, the results of the rapes of human women by Manapes who, having been born among us and speaking our languages, are mistakenly taken for our own countrymen. But it is these hateful, deadly and fiendishly exterminatory descendants of the Yeti that, on having been thoroughly admixed with the Humans, think up all the ideological Isms that create subversion, treason, revolutions, wars, and the eventual downfall of all Civilization and Culture.[13]

According to Szukalski, these Yetinsyny, once identified, should never be allowed to enter politics or the military service, for they are "devoid of all the genteel traits of [humanity] but retained all avaricious, vengeful, ferocious traits." They only enter public service "for the purpose of attaining positions that allow them to gloat in Vengeance for their obsessive psychosis of Inferiority." And there they bide their time until they get a chance to "exterminate Handsome mankind by the millions." Politically dangerous Yeti have lately included such historically influential characters as Karl Marx, Mao Tse Tung, Nietszche, Bakunin and Kropotkin.

One can't help being reminded of Lothrop Stoddard's Under-Men and Jörg Lanz von Liebenfels' pygmies. However, unlike Lanz and Stoddard, Szukalski feels that the beasts would do well in, of all fields—the arts. He pleads his case that the Yeti rabble rousers should be encouraged to partake in the arts and literature, to which they would excel, due to their unique inferiority complex:

> As frightfully inferiority-obsessed males and females who Never get beautiful human women and men into their beds, they persistently dream of the Impossible. To endure their mental hardships they develop extraordinary patience and such perfect Imagination that almost anything they dream of, they are capable of contriving. Thus, patience and imagination, together with their Animal vitality, make them capable to contribute miracles of inventions in every sphere of interest. They are the nibelungs, the little pixies, the fairies of the legends of every country. Politically, they forever remain ... socialists and therefore, potential communists, because they cannot forgive humankind its popularity with the opposite sex.[14]

Mass murderers Charles Manson and Lt. Calley (of the My Lai Massacre in Viet Nam), says Szukalski, have Yeti heritage as well. Had anyone asked Szukalski, Calley would never have entered military service, for "with a facial type like his he should never have been allowed to handle guns." Instead, he should have been directed towards science, crafts and the arts. And, once they ran amok like dogs on a killing spree, these murderers should have been executed immediately without due process of law, since they are animals. Instead, writes Szukalski, the crafty, evil Yetinsyny "will always take advantage of the trusting Human. . . . The conspiring dwarves will build vast parasitic empires based on some silly Ideology, a mere bait for gullible and kindhearted mankind. . . . The howling chest-beating gorilla in the Yetinsyn is perpetually pressed towards its biological preordainment." And probably, things shall ever be so. "It works overtime pounding on the pulpit of subversion, calling all the misfits of the world to unite against the hated Human."

Szukalski's barbed vision, though unique in particulars, contains echoes of the metaphysically charged racist anthropologies of the '20s and '30s. Szukalski's Yetinsyny parallel the Pygmy Beast-men of Jörg Lanz von Liebenfels' racial dystopia,[15] and much more closely, eugenicist Lothrop Stoddard's Under-Men. Like Stoddard's "Menace of the Under-Man,"[16] Szukalski sees the enemy hiding among his own people rather than in a remote ethnic group. In the end, Lanz, Stoddard and Szukalski all fear the same thing: subhuman, revolutionary trouble-makers who would upset the old order. In this respect Szukalski shares the sentiments of Theosophists, de-evolutionists and metaphysical racists in their rejection of modernity, egalitarianism and science.[17]

Part III—Human Individual Metamorphosis/Heaven's Gate

THE MEETING

In May of 1994, posters appeared in Portland, Ore., with the headline "UFOs, Space Aliens, and their Final Fight for Earth's Spoils." In what looked like neatly handwritten text, it read:

> All reproducing space aliens—including mammalian and reptilian— use Earth's humans simply for their own interests (and have been for thousands of years).
>
> —They intentionally keep humans falsely "programmed" or "in the dark". . . .
>
> —These "Luciferians" abduct humans for genetic experimentation, "rob" healthy human specimens for *their* own next "suit of clothes," and induct humans into their service.
>
> In spite of these facts, there is a true Kingdom of "God"—a truly Evolutionary Kingdom Level Above Human, above all mammalian, reptilian, or any other reproductive species. It is a many-membered

Kingdom that exists in the literal Heavens, with its own unique biological "containers" or bodies, and modes of travel—spacecrafts or "UFOs." It is, in fact, more physically real than the world of the space aliens or humans. This Kingdom Level created the physical universe, as we know it, as a "holographic classroom," and the human-mammalian kingdom as a stepping stone. That hologram is about to be "rebooted"—canceled and restarted—for its usefulness and serviceability as a classroom has come to an end.

Two thousand years ago, an Other Member in the real "Kingdom of Heaven," left behind His Next Level—non-mammalian—Body and incarnated into a "picked" and "prepped" human body at approx. its 29th year. He brought with Him the souls or "spirits" that His Father's Kingdom had nurtured in the past, in order that He might help them incarnate and change over their bodies. That formula for being born into the Evolutionary Level Above Human requires: the shedding of all human-mammalian behavior, such as sexuality (all forms); ties (to family, human relationships, possessions, and responsibilities); addictions (of all types); habits; and self-concerns.

That formula was offered a second time, in 1975–76 by two Older Members from that same Kingdom (who incarnated when the bodies, that were "picked" and "prepped" for them, were in their early 40s). They put out a "call" for the crew—the souls who came with them—and helped them incarnate (take over their bodies), while in virtual isolation for approx. 18 years. . . .

A very accelerated "classroom" (for "birthing"—incarnating), is now being offered for the third and last time in this civilization, by those representatives from the 1975–76 "yield" to the remainder of the souls that have been saved from a previous time by the Next Level.

The representative 2,000 years ago, the two representatives who came in the early 1970s, and their students from that "yield" and the present one, all came and will leave in spacecrafts or "clouds of light."

Representatives from that "Next Level" Will Speak at: [local branch library]

Written diagonally across the flyer in red magic marker was the admonition, "Don't Miss This!" After reading such a flyer, I wasn't about to.

I had never attended a meeting quite like this one and had no idea

The Two (Applewhite and Nettles) in a recruitment meeting during the 1970s. (From *The Gods Have Landed*)

what might take place. I imagined it might be a silly lecture about space aliens and some kind of UFO conspiracy. Instead, it turned out to be a compelling discussion about spiritual reality; the group intrigued me so much that I had to find out more. Even three years later, after becoming the mass media's "senseless tragedy" of the week, the group that everyone now knows by the name of "Heaven's Gate" continued to intrigue me.

The meeting was held in the basement of a local branch library on a Saturday afternoon in May. The 40 or 50 folding chairs in the plain meeting room were mostly empty when we arrived. It was easy to pick out which people were the "representatives from the next level." Both the males and females had short-cropped hair and were dressed immaculately—almost in uniform—in shirt and trousers. The men's shirts were buttoned to the top, and the women wore blazers. All the androgynous but attractive representatives emanated an uncanny self-control.

The meeting began when all but two of the group—we soon learned that they called themselves crew members—seated themselves at a table up front. There was no leader, but one of them said, "Let the truth be known." After a minute of silence, the crew members took turns in a consciously egalitarian fashion, explaining their philosophy, their story and their message. I struggled to figure out who exactly they were, because they never identified their organization by name nor where they were based. But I did pick out one phrase that they used again and again: "the level beyond human." They spoke their jargon consistently, and demonstrated a remarkable lack of emotion. I began to wonder if they were really who they said they were: representatives from another world.

I listened intently to what they said, trying to figure out why it might *not* be true. Their story was that 18 years before, some of them had met two beings from the level beyond human. These two beings "created this planet as an experiment." The next level, they emphasized—the level beyond human, which some people call heaven—was a *physical* place, a kingdom of higher technology. The crew members

> ORGANIZED RELIGION *(ESPECIALLY CHRISTIAN)* HAS BECOME **THE PRIMARY PULPIT FOR**
> **MISINFORMATION** AND THE
> *"GREAT COVER-UP"*

> CREW FROM THE EVOLUTIONARY LEVEL ABOVE HUMAN OFFERS –
> **LAST CHANCE** TO ADVANCE BEYOND HUMAN

> THE END OF THE AGE IS HERE – AND AS WAS PROMISED –
> **HE'S BACK,** THE ONE "THE WORLD" HATED AND KILLED BEFORE! (The one who was Jesus)
> **WE'RE BACK,** HIS "ADOPTED" WHO WERE TREATED THE SAME! (Those who were His disciples)
> **WHERE WILL YOU STAND?**
> THE "BLASPHEMY'S" THE SAME – THE TEST IS THE SAME FOR ALL OF US – "LEAVE ALL BEHIND" AND GO WITH THEM – OR TAKE YOUR CHANCES.

Headings from three separate flyers advertising spring 1994 recruitment meetings for the "Next Level Crew" were part of an "astronaut training program" to help them wean themselves from humanness and ascend to the next level, severing all ties with family and friends as well as giving up sexuality and physical pleasures. Most of the crew members wore wedding bands to signify that they were already married—to the next level.

If any of us found ourselves wishing to ascend with them, we could join the crew and ascend with them *if and only if* we were ready. They hinted that those who did not join them would be "spaded under," missing their only opportunity in thousands of years to help fulfill mankind's evolutionary destiny.

I have to admit a momentary temptation to "train" with them and ascend into space. These were obviously not stupid people, and their sincerity impressed me. I was curious to find out what was behind it. Would they ascend to the next level, while the rest of us got "spaded under"? Maybe their "two older members" really *did* know what made the universe tick. I sure didn't!

The crew members continued to talk about the next level, and pointed out that since the next level is a kingdom, it has a physical king. Then one of them added that "He Who Was Called Jesus," was the last representative from the next level to come here, 2,000 years ago. Up until this point, all of their terminology and ideas were entirely new to me. My unfamiliarity with their jargon was one reason why I thought they might really be emissaries from another world—how could these rational-seeming people make this stuff up? But as soon as I heard the name "Jesus" I sighed heavily. "So this is just another Judeo-Christian belief system," I thought, and the spell was broken. These were just regular people, there was no "Level Beyond Human," and, worst of all, I was never going to get my trip to outer space. After I'd returned to my normal, skeptical self the meeting became a lot less fun.

Like me, none of the audience members were willing to join the crew, though they had some questions. A Christian tried to prove them wrong, and members of Eckankar saw the crew's message as just another version of Eckankar.[18] When crew members stated that they don't participate in sexuality "because it's animal behavior," about half the audience got up and left. The few who remained were mildly sympathetic but wanted to argue endlessly over small points. A heavyset man with a dreamy, knowing smile said, "I understand completely what you're saying—you're talking about the Elohim."

But Today's Next Level Crew were not there to argue or even to talk about the "Elohim." They were there to find others like themselves willing to leave Earth as improved, evolved beings, and go to a better place.

HISTORY

Today's Next Level Crew had first been catapulted into the public eye as the infamous "UFO Cult" back in September of 1975. That month 20 people had "disappeared" from Waldport, Ore., following a meeting much like the one I attended almost 20 years later. Posters for the Waldport meeting had promised that "Two individuals say they are about to leave the human level and literally (physically) enter the next evolutionary level in a spacecraft (UFO) within months! 'The Two' will discuss how the transition from the human level to the next level is accomplished and when this may be done." During the meeting, The Two predicted that they would be assassinated and then resurrected into a spaceship, taking their recruits with them to the higher level from whence they came.

After the disappearance of the Waldport recruits, headlines all over the country announced "Twenty Missing in Oregon After Talking of a Higher Life," hinting that they had indeed been picked up by a spaceship. But the group, which in those days was called "Human Individual Metamorphosis" or H.I.M., hadn't in fact, disappeared. They were merely leading an earthly, if nomadic existence, popping up now and then in places like San Francisco to find more recruits. UFO researcher Jacques Vallée attended one of the H.I.M. meetings at Stanford University, discussing it in his 1979 book *Messengers of Deception*. Other press reports that year referred to the group as "The UFO Cult" or as "Bo-Peep's Flock" since The Two wouldn't reveal their given names and referred to themselves only as Bo and Peep.

Meanwhile, scholars saw a rare opportunity to study a cult-in-the-making from the inside. For two months during 1975 sociologists Robert W. Balch and David Taylor joined H.I.M., later writing scholarly reports and an article for *Psychology Today* which detailed the group's history, belief system and structure.

It came out that "The Mysterious Two" were in fact Marshall Herff Applewhite and Bonnie Lu Nettles, both of Houston. They had met in March of 1972.

Applewhite had been chairman of the music department at the University of St. Thomas in Houston, as well as a church choir director. He had originally planned to enter the ministry like his domineering father, but instead devoted himself to music. He had a beautiful baritone voice and performed with music companies, operas, and symphonies, sometimes earning rave reviews. Friends and associates described Applewhite as charismatic and talented, with laudatory comments like, "His students adored him and his choir was marvelous," and, "The man was magical." But Applewhite, who was married, was also burdened with emotional problems in connection with his homosexuality.

Nettles was a mother of four and a registered nurse working in a hospital, but her avocation was metaphysics. She wrote the astrology column for a local newspaper, was an active member of the Houston Theosophical Society, and met weekly with a group to channel messages from the spirit world, making contact with beings from Venus, as well as dead celebrities such as Marilyn Monroe. She described her spirit guide, Brother Francis—with whom she'd been communicating since the mid-'50s—as a nineteenth century Franciscan monk.

In 1970 Applewhite underwent a personal crisis. After a complicated political fiasco he was fired from his job at the university and subsequently entered a state of "utter despair." The next year he had acquired a new job, but by then he'd lost his self-confidence; his friends noticed that he just wasn't the same person.

There are several versions of how The Two met. According to recent stories in the news media, Applewhite checked himself into a psychiatric hospital after his nervous breakdown and Nettles was his attending nurse. Balch's version, however, is that they met by chance when Applewhite was visiting a friend in the hospital where Bonnie Nettles worked.[19] In any event, shortly before their paths crossed, Nettles had been receiving channeled messages that a mysterious stranger would soon enter her life. When they finally did meet, "It was as if we were being guided by forces greater than ourselves. We were snatched from our previous lives."[20]

Immediately, Nettles and Applewhite began a close—though by all accounts non-sexual—partnership, during which Applewhite received an intensive education in all things mystical and metaphysical. In a published interview, The Two described their first days together as "a very confusing period of transition, not knowing what we were doing." They immediately began to embark on many short-lived projects. They started the Christian Arts Center in Houston, whose aim was to promote awareness of spiritual potential through the arts. They sponsored lectures in Theosophy, comparative religion, mysticism, astrology, art and music,

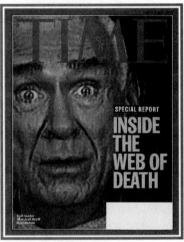

Cover of *Time*, April 7, 1997

amalgamating both Applewhite's and Nettles' areas of expertise. But the controversial center only lasted a few months. Next they opened "Know Place," a metaphysical center offering lectures on such topics as "Man, God and Incarnation," "Understanding Reincarnation," and "Minds of This Galaxy and Others," dropping the artistic angle for good. Applewhite traded in his old life in the arts for a new one in metaphysics. During this period Nettles and Applewhite were in daily contact with invisible beings, experienced astral travel, and underwent vivid dreams in which "beings from UFOs urged them to abandon their earthly lives."

After the failure of Know Place, Nettles and Applewhite left the city to live on a ranch. There they began their first writing effort, a little book called *I Can't Believe That; But You Must*, which they later threw out. The journey that transformed them into The Two continued:

> For the next few months we toured every state in the nation, surviving any way that we could—digging ditches to make tests for septic tanks, working in filling stations, putting tar roofs on houses in Las

Vegas—anything that was enough to get us to the next place and last a little time.

We settled for a while in Portland. . . . Then we went to the national forest on the Oregon coast and camped for an extended period of time in a little campground . . . near Gold Beach. It was here, while we were in that campground, that we realized what we had to do.

We studied the Bible, . . . the secret doctrine of Madame Blavatsky, . . . everything we could get our hands on that had to do with any sort of awareness—spiritual awareness, scientific awareness, religious awareness. . . .

It was while we were at Gold Beach that we realized that we had, in fact, come from the next level, that we had to be the instruments of giving information about how others could reach the next level, and that this would probably precipitate a demonstration of our death and our subsequent resurrection.[21]

Now that The Two had their mission, they went in search of a congregation. At first they had little success and their one follower lasted only two months. The breakthrough finally occurred in early 1975. The Two traveled to Los Angeles to meet with metaphysical teacher Will Dietrich and ended up speaking to his close-knit group of seekers. This group was in the midst of a very difficult period; they had recently experienced infighting, personal problems and the failure of a publishing venture. They had also been studying the book of Revelation and, through their teacher, were well acquainted with flying saucer lore.

Enter The Two, claiming to be the two witnesses from Revelation 11:

And I will give power unto my two witnesses, and they shall prophesy a thousand two hundred and threescore days, clothed in sackcloth. . . . And when they shall have finished their testimony, the beast that ascendeth out of the bottomless pit shall make war against them, and shall overcome them, and kill them. . . . And after three days and an half the Spirit of life from God entered into them, and they stood upon their feet, and great fear fell upon them which saw them. And they heard a great voice from heaven saying unto them, Come up hither. And they ascended up to heaven in a cloud; and their enemies beheld them. (Rev. 11:3-12)

Nettles and Applewhite told the group that the cloud in which they—The Two—had ascended was a UFO; those who wished to ascend with them a second time could do so—if they severed all ties to the human level.

Dietrich was the first to join up, and within two weeks 23 members of his class followed suit. Bo and Peep had their ready-made flock that would soon wander

'Aliens' respond to a cosmic call

CULT SEEDS PLANTED IN OREGON

Cult set up home like a spaceship

Headlines about the Heaven's
Gate suicide from the
March 28, 1997 *Oregonian*

the country looking for strays.

After that, it became much easier to make converts. Meetings advertised with intriguing posters took place primarily along the West Coast. Some of the posters promised that The Two would publicly demonstrate the healing of a dead body as proof that they had come from the next level. Even though these demonstrations never took place, 20 more people "disappeared" with them after a meeting in Waldport, Ore., and another six joined after a meeting at Stanford University. By the end of six months, there were 200 H.I.M. members.

As early as November of 1975 disgruntled ex-member Joan Culpepper had formed H.E.R. (Hinder Evolutionary Ripoffs). By that time, at least ten original members had rejected H.I.M. teachings and four were actively opposing the group.

Around the same time, ranchers in Colorado and Wyoming began discovering mutilated cattle. Coincidentally, some of the mutilations occurred near H.I.M. campsites. Some of their neighbors implied the group was responsible.[22]

Meanwhile, staying with the group became a trial for most of the young acolytes. They had left their husbands, wives, children, sex and worldly possessions behind in order to ascend in a spaceship that never arrived. Neither the demonstrations nor the ascensions ever took place, and most of the converts dropped out, leaving only a handful of devotees. H.I.M. soon dropped from public view, and literally went into hiding for the next 17 years.

———◆———

In January 1991, I received an inexplicable press release from an organization calling itself Total Overcomers Anonymous Monastery.[23] It was headlined "Hidden Monastery Goes Public—But Why is the Story," and continued:

> A modern day group of monastics, not unlike the ancient Qumran Essenes of the "Dead Sea Scrolls" period and locale, have decided to surface after almost 17 years of seclusion. Their Teacher, along with the 24 students, are proclaiming the "fruit" or yield of their separateness and discipline through an hour long weekly satellite TV series: *Beyond Human—The Last Call*, Galaxy 6 channel 5, Sundays At 11:00 A.M. (EST) and repeated Mondays at 11:00 P.M. (EST).
>
> They claim that membership in the Heavenly Kingdom (a physical level of existence) cannot be attained after *death*, but rather is gained

only after having *overcome* all human ties and addictions. And further, this overcoming has to be "midwifed" by an *incarnate* member from that Heavenly Kingdom. They not only claim that their Teacher is from that Kingdom but that they have, as a "classroom," individually, completed their "overcoming of the world" and are ready to take up membership in the real Heavens. Lastly, and the reason for their brief "*last call*," they say that it is now the close of an Age—the "last chance," so to speak, for this *step* to be taken by any *others* who might hope for membership in *God's House*.

Very interesting—especially since it sounds a lot like what many say the world heard some 2,000 years ago. Tapes of their shows and other trappings of their teachings may be secured by writing to: Total Overcomers Anonymous Monastery, or T.O.A., P.O. Box 6592, Anaheim, CA 92816.

The H.I.M. group was now calling itself T.O.A. and had undergone significant changes. (I had no idea who they were at the time.) They hadn't spent the past 17 years *waiting*, they had spent the past 17 years *training*. Rather than UFOnauts, they were now monks. Plus, they lost Bonnie Nettles to cancer in 1985.

Three years after their emergence from hiding, the highly disciplined monks traveled the United States sharing what they'd learned and searching for trainees; the meeting I attended in 1994 was only one of many.

Nettles' death was referred to only obliquely at that meeting. Crew Members stated that one of their "older members" had returned to the next level, but wouldn't elaborate. Nor would they reveal the whereabouts or identity of their remaining "older member." During the question and answer period, I attempted to find out how I might contact them in the future, but they claimed to have no permanent address, nor even a name. The only way to keep in touch with them would be to join.

After I returned home from that memorable event, I was fairly excited. I dug out the 1991 press release, and confirmed to myself that it had originated from the same group. I also began to gather all the published materials on the group that I could find. A few months later I began to track them on the internet; like most other organizations, they had their own website and posted regularly to several news groups. Contrary to later news reports, there was nothing unusual or sinister about their presence on the internet. I corresponded with a couple stray members by e-mail hoping to land some inside information, but to no avail.[24] I thought I might write about The Next Level Crew some day, though the task seemed daunting even at that point because of the group's tangle of influences and long history.

A couple of years later, when I learned of their suicide, I was just as surprised as everyone else.[25] I had assumed that they would continue to wait for their spaceship forever; it had never crossed my mind that they might take a shortcut to the next level.

THE EVOLUTIONARY LEVEL ABOVE HUMAN

The Two developed their theology from esoteric sources like Madame Blavatsky who are part of an essentially gnostic tradition.[26] Briefly, gnosticism is a dualistic philosophy that fosters convergence with spirit or godhead; initiates merge with spirit by attaining "special knowledge" and by leaving the physical world behind, often through asceticism. In short, their esoteric knowledge and practices assure gnostics a first-class ticket to heaven. Because they circumvent the mainstream Christian idea of subservience to God, gnostic sects have been seen as a threat since the early days of Christianity, some suffering persecution at the hands of the Church. The struggle between gnosticism and orthodox Christianity continues today in the flaming rhetoric many fundamentalists use against occultism, "witchcraft," and New Age religion.

Considering the protracted struggle between gnosticism and the Church, it's not surprising that The Two considered themselves to be in an all-out war against organized religion, particularly Christianity. Though they spoke much of "he who was called Jesus" and quoted often from the Bible, their interpretations and their jargon were derived from Theosophical writings and esoteric Christianity rather than mainstream Christianity—which they saw as a force of evil.

The Two's concept of human evolution also derived from gnostic ideas in Theosophy and esoteric Christianity. Even their terminology can be found in widely available books on those subjects, such as Max Heindel's *The Rosicrucian Cosmo-Conception* or *Mystic Christianity* (1908).

Heindel (1865–1919), born Carl Louis van Grasshof in Germany, was a prominent Theosophist who lectured widely on esoteric subjects. He claimed that on a visit to Europe in 1907, he had been initiated by a mysterious Rosicrucian[27] at a temple on the German/Bohemian border. Heindel published the "secret wisdom" he claimed to have learned from this master the following year, in *The Rosicrucian Cosmo-Conception*. A few years later, he founded the Rosicrucian Fellowship in San Diego.[28] Heindel's writings, however, were probably based on the lectures of Rudolf Steiner, founder of Anthroposophy, a mix of Theosophical, Rosicrucian, Christian and occult traditions.[29]

In *The Rosicrucian Cosmo-Conception*, Heindel explains that there are four kingdom levels: mineral, plant, animal and human; each kingdom level correlates with its own type of *vehicle* or body. When The Two characterized human evolution as an ascent to the kingdom level above human which would involve shedding the human vehicle for a new one, they were well within the bounds of Theosophical and esoteric belief.

Though The Two implied that ascent to the "level above human" could help transform the entire species, this kind of evolution principally affects *individual* souls. They emphasized that evolution only takes place in individuals who are willing to train for it, leaving their mammalian bodies behind; self-castration was one way to expedite this process. Though The Two often compared this ascent to the metamorphosis a caterpillar undergoes to become a butterfly, unlike caterpillars who are genetically programmed for their transformation, human caterpillars must undergo special training if they want to become butterflies. In other words, the Two could give individuals the special knowledge required to reach Heaven—if they were willing to leave their physical bodies behind—just as the gnostics could.

The Two's literature explained that 2,000 years ago a crew from the next level responsible for nurturing "gardens" such as Earth determined that some of the human "plants" on Earth were "ready to be used as 'containers' for soul deposits ['seeds' or 'chips' with a program of metamorphic possibilities]." (The garden metaphor is used extensively in esoteric literature; Max Heindel referred to bodily death as "harvest time.") Upon instruction, "he who was called Jesus" left his body in the next level, came to Earth and incarnated into an adult human body. His task was to "offer the way leading to membership into the Kingdom of Heaven to those who recognized Him for who He was and chose to follow Him." But only those who'd received a "soul deposit" or "chip" were able to believe him. Similarly, two more members from the next level—The Two—incarnated into the bodies of a man and a woman in the early 1970s. Their mission was to find "the last wave of souls" who would ascend to the next level, and help them incarnate into bodies "picked and prepped" for them. Those who were successful would leave the human kingdom in a spacecraft.[30]

But what was in store for those who hadn't ascended—or evolved—to the next level? A process of natural selection—or rather spiritual selection—would make sure that the unfit would not survive. As they stated in a 1994 flyer: "The Earth's present 'civilization' is about to be recycled—'spaded under'—in order that the planet might be refurbished. The human 'weeds' have taken over the garden and disturbed its usefulness beyond repair." The weeds were temporal creatures unable to comprehend the next level. Therefore, they would be "spaded under," a metaphor for being destroyed at the end of the Age. Those who graduated to the next level would constitute the new above-human species, while the rest would be destroyed.

Like many other millennialists, The Two were saying—in space-age jargon—that at the End-Time, only the righteous will join God in Heaven, while the unrighteous will die.

The Luciferians, which include aliens and UFOs, as well as Satan and his rebel angels, serve as humanity's major obstacle to ascending to the Next Level. As "technically advanced humans" and former members of the Level Above Human, they have limited powers of "space-time travel" and telepathic communication, as well as increased longevity. But at bottom, the Luciferians are impostors who deceive humanity with technical trickery and a phony heaven. Moreover, one of their most successful scams is Christianity. The Two were convinced that UFOs along with organized religion were the evil force who existed to undermine their project of bringing ripe souls to harvest—and to God. While The Two identified Christianity as evil, at the same time, their very idea of evil—as a palpable force perpetrated by a conspiracy of fallen angels—was essentially Christian.

HARVEST TIME

Twenty-two years is a long time to spend in a classroom, even if it is a spiritual one. Marshall Herff Applewhite and Bonnie Lu Nettles had expected to return to the Next Level on a spaceship way back in 1975. Even after Nettles' death in 1985, Applewhite and the Next Level Crew continued their training, and later more recruitment with the expectation of going up, up, and away at any moment.

Beginning around late 1995, the Next Level Crew began broadcasting their messages—most of them similar or identical to their earlier statements—on internet news groups and on their own web page, entitled "Heaven's Gate." By that time, their message had undergone a shift to more transparently apocalyptic rhetoric. They began posting internet messages asking, "Time to Die for God?— or—Armageddon—Which Side are You On?" and declaring the end of present civilization. One message cited the Branch Davidians at Waco, the Unabomber, the Order of the Solar Temple (a cult who committed group suicide), Aum Shinri Kyo (a cult who had released deadly gas in a Japanese subway) and controversial Nation of Islam leader Louis Farrakhan, favorably, as "groups that are simply rebelling from the system, the 'norm,' and Want to go to God, or Leave This Corrupt World, at any price." The message concluded, "Whether we like it or not, the Armageddon—the Mother of Holy Wars—has begun, and it will not cease until the plowing under is completed. It may be that the establishment liberates the 'radicals' so that they may go 'home,' and that the Angelic Armies of the Kingdom of Heaven will complete the spading under—the end of the Age. On which side are you? Will you go into the keeping of the Next Level, or to dust return?"

The dramatic appearance of comet Hale-Bopp in early 1997, with rumors of a companion UFO confirmed for them that their time had finally come. The Two and their Next Level Crew had been promising, however, to be assassinated, ascended, resurrected, and picked up by a spaceship for the past 22 years. Nobody seemed to realize that this time they really meant it. A "Red Alert" message on their web page stated, "HALE-BOPP Brings Closure to Heaven's Gate," and, "Hale-Bopp's approach is the 'marker' we've been waiting for—the time for the arrival of the spacecraft from the Level Above Human to take us home to 'Their World'—in the literal Heavens. Our 22 years of classroom here on planet Earth is finally coming to conclusion—'graduation' from the Human Evolutionary Level. We are happily prepared to leave 'this world' and go with Ti's crew."

On March 26, 1997 police found 39 bodies at a mansion called Rancho Santa Fe near San Diego, the home of "Do" (Applewhite) and the Heaven's Gate cult. It was soon confirmed that all 39 had committed suicide in an extraordinarily orderly fashion. They were all dressed in identical black pants, black shirt and new black Nikes. Each was covered by a purple cloth. Even after death the peaceful group was polite enough to provide authorities with identification packets next to each dead body. The Next Level Crew had left their human containers for good.

Reporters immediately seized upon the fact that the members of the group had most recently worked as internet programmers while maintaining an elaborate website of their own called Heaven's Gate. Thus they were dubbed a "computer programming cult" and were accused of luring "victims" through the internet. This, along with other unusual aspects of the story (the orderly manner in which the suicide took place, self-castration, the UFO angle, the group's dedication to *Star Trek*, etc.) quickly made this the weirdest news story of the year, if not the decade. Suddenly the talking heads on TV, the guys at the corner bar, office drones, hairdressers—everyone was abuzz with Heaven's Gate and the Evolutionary Level Above Human. When my own mother regaled me with details of H.I.M.'s history, I knew that things had gotten out of hand. It struck me that their suicide had instantly acquainted millions with the concepts The Two and their flock had been trying to explain to just a handful of people for 22 years. If there was any way to acquaint the masses with an obscure, esoteric theology, this was definitely it.

The climate of anti-cult hysteria unfortunately made it all too easy to belittle the aspirations of a group seeking an alternative spiritual path. Many are simply seeking a level of human existence higher than the one we have on Earth. Since there were no ethical violations or sexual abuses to hang them with, cult "experts" found it necessary to find Heaven's Gate guilty of lesser charges: a weird philosophy; self-castration; extreme faith; asceticism; and, of course, suicide. Though they might have watched *Star Trek* and *X-Files* with the rest of us, they rejected materialist values in favor of something far less tangible. They joyfully shortened their own physical lives while we lengthen ours at the expense of all else—even when it entails years of unconscious stupor or intense pain while being hooked up to a machine. Nobody seems to notice that members of Heaven's Gate sought a higher level, found it, and then followed through on the extremely difficult path that they believed would take them there. While I don't share their faith, I'm compelled to respect it. And, for all I know, The Two and their flock may now reside at the Kingdom Level Above Human in a highly evolved state.

Though they used the term "evolutionary" to describe the "Level Above Human," Heaven's Gate's concept of human development was spiritual rather than physical, having more in common with Blavatsky than with Darwin. For them, the agents of human evolution were superior, well-trained souls rather than mere physical survivors. Like flying saucer contactees and those who see humanity as an ape/alien hybrid, they used quasi-scientific terminology to update essentially religious ideas.

Selected Heaven's Gate Internet Posts

I. Time to Die for God?—the Imminent "Holy" War—Which Side are You On?

We are at the end of an Age, or the end of another civilization. As was prophesied, this is the "judgment time" for all living creatures on or related to this planet—in other words, the time when "where we find ourselves," as a result of our accumulated choices during our time here, determines our Judgment. . . .

There is a simple evolutionary procedure which applies to those who might leave or graduate from the human kingdom and enter the Evolutionary Kingdom Level Above Human (the Kingdom of Heaven, or Kingdom of God). Periodically, the Kingdom Level Above Human sends one of its Members "down" into the human kingdom (to incarnate into a human body)—a Member who has previously been taken through that evolutionary transition—to offer the knowledge to those who have been "picked" as possible recipients of that graduation information. This Representative of that Next Kingdom literally takes those candidates through their weaning from the human world—assisting them in the actual separation or breaking of ties to their humanness, and helping them "graft" to Him as the Representative of that Next Level. Their final separation is the willful separation from their human body, when they have changed enough to identify as the spirit/mind/soul—ready to put on a biological body belonging to the Kingdom of Heaven. (This entering into their "glorified" or heavenly body takes place aboard a Next Level spacecraft, above the earth's surface.)

At the close of an Age there are:
1. Some individuals who have personally connected with that Representative and separated from humanness enough to move into Membership in that Next Kingdom, and into a physical body belonging to that Kingdom Level Above Human;
2. Those who have not reached that degree of separation, but are aware of and believe the information that the Next Level Representative has brought, and are separating to the degree of their capability;
3. Those who are compelled to separate from the mainstream in one way or another, but who have not seen or consciously known of that Representative—His information or His presence. These two latter groups will be taken into the keeping of the Next Level until they have a later chance at further separation and overcoming, and they are examples of what was meant by the phrase—"If you believe . . . you will be saved."

This bottom-lines at the point where the only ones who will not be recycled will be those who have overcome under the representative's tutorship; those who have known hime and are in the process of overcoming; and those who have heard his voice subconsciously (or mentally), but have not connected with him consciously. These who have connected mentally are driven, during this period, to go against the world—its systems, the socially and politically accepted "norms"—and are determined (as if they can't help themselves) to go to "God" or Allah, by any name, or His Son, and to die in opposition to this world—or to simply leave it by whatever means—according to whatever their religious backgrounds or "programming" may have been. It is the closeness of that Next Kingdom Level that individuals are responding to. For this "End of the Age" task, this Representative and His Father (Older Member) have been closely relating to this civilization since the early 1970s. Their thoughts have been in this atmosphere and "tappable" (available to be drawn upon) during this time.

Some examples of those whose ideologies suggest that they have connected mentally, cover a broad spectrum—the Weavers at Ruby Ridge, the Branch Davidians at Waco, the Unabomber, the Order of the Solar Temple, Aum Shinri Kyo of Japan, the Freemen of Montana, and others. This is not to say that the Next Level and this Representative would condone many of their choices and actions; however, these groups seem to have correctly identified the "enemy," and feel compelled, at varying degrees, to separate from what they believe is a corrupt world. Many such groups are still in hiding, while others openly take their stand in opposition to the "enemy," such as the patriot/militia movements, and Farrakhan and the Nation of Islam.

In other words, to the groups and individuals mentioned above and to this Representative who is writing this statement, the servants of "This World" (the "socially acceptable," the faithful of the dominant religions and governments) are the opposition, the servants of the "Lower Forces" or "Satan." This mainstream "acceptable" world views "religious zealots" as self-righteous, imbalanced, and dangerous to society's "norm." In reality, those of the mainstream or accepted "norm" (who see themselves as godly, tolerant, fair, and good) are the very ones who have no hesitation to judge and condemn those who are not like them— especially those who are preoccupied with God. They also have no hesitation to impose their ungodly ways and laws "of man" upon those of the rest of the world with different beliefs. If there is no law to justify an action they want to take, they enact a new law, legalizing their desire. Once it has become a law, it is respected as if it were by divine order, no matter how corrupt it might be. They actively engage in, or attempt to engage in the punishment or containment of those they would consider "religious radicals." Examples of how this misplaced judgment is forced upon "religious zealots" are seen in how the authorities treated the Weavers at Ruby Ridge, David Koresh and the Branch Davidians at Waco, and the actions presently being taken against Saddam Hussein and Iraq.

The leadership of the world, in imposing man's laws, deceives and lies about the reasons for their actions, making it appear that they are humanitarian. They seldom expose their real motivations of greed and covetousness of what others have, that they feel they must have or remain in control of, in order to continue "saving the world" from what they would consider the "barbaric" or "radical" elements of humanity. These dominant forces are motivated by their own Counterfeit "truth" supported by their Counterfeit religions. Some examples are:

1. How the True God of the Jews has been replaced by a Counterfeit "palatable" god who encourages "go and multiply" (family values), "peace on Earth," and the goal of a global unity toward a Heaven on Earth;
2. And how the True Christ or Jesus has been replaced by a Counterfeit Jesus who lives "within your heart" and preaches the same—to multiply, seek peace on Earth, and unity toward the future of mankind. . . .

What mainstream society doesn't know is that, in fact, there is a real physical kingdom of God from which everything of this world came. That kingdom still has complete power over this world, though It has infrequently exercised it in the latter part of this civilization. However, we're about to see that power dramatically exercised—physically—now, at the close of this age. This civilization hasn't seemed to learn that man's laws and God's laws do not mix. Man's laws are structured to protect money, property ownership, and national and family interests, and religions have deteriorated to support and abide by these concepts/laws. God's laws are adhered to, to any significant degree, only when one of His Representatives is present, and then only by the few who are under His direct tutorship. And because we're at the End of the Age, and the groups and individuals seen as religious radicals are attempting to move closer to abiding by God's laws, they find themselves in irrevocable conflict with those who simply abide by man's laws.

The only true God by any name, on any planet, in anytime, in any country, in any religion—only wants his prospective children to desire to come to him and to his kingdom by leaving or graduating from the human kingdom with the help of his representative. . . .

Whether we like it or not, the Armageddon—the Mother of Holy Wars—has begun, and it will not cease until the plowing under is completed. It may be that the establishment liberates the "radicals" so that they may go "home," and that the Angelic Armies of the Kingdom of Heaven (Members of the Kingdom Level Above Human) will complete the spading under—the end of the Age. On which side are you? Will you go into the keeping of the Next Level, or to dust return?

II. RED ALERT
HALE-BOPP Brings Closure to Heaven's Gate

Whether Hale-Bopp has a "companion" or not is irrelevant from our perspective. However, its arrival is joyously very significant to us at "Heaven's Gate." The joy is that our Older Member in the Evolutionary Level Above Human (the "Kingdom of Heaven") has made it clear to us that Hale-Bopp's approach is the "marker" we've been waiting for—the time for the arrival of the spacecraft from the Level Above Human to take us home to "Their World"—in the literal Heavens. Our 22 years of classroom here on planet Earth is finally coming to conclusion—"graduation" from the Human Evolutionary Level. We are happily prepared to leave "this world" and go with Ti's crew.

If you study the material on this website you will hopefully understand our joy and what our purpose here on Earth has been. You may even find your "boarding pass" to leave with us during this brief "window."

We are so very thankful that we have been recipients of this opportunity to prepare for membership in Their Kingdom, and to experience Their boundless Caring and Nurturing.

III. OUR POSITION AGAINST SUICIDE

We know that it is only while we are in these physical vehicles (bodies) that we can learn the lessons needed to complete our own individual transition, as well as to complete our task of offering the Kingdom of Heaven to this civilization one last time. We take good care of our vehicles so they can function well for us in this task, and we try to protect them from any harm.

We fully desire, expect, and look forward to boarding a spacecraft from the Next Level very soon (in our physical bodies). There is no doubt in our mind that our being "picked up" is inevitable in the very near future. But what happens between now and then is the big question. We are keenly aware of several possibilities.

It could happen that before that spacecraft comes, one or more of us could lose our physical vehicles (bodies) due to "recall," accident, or at the hands of some irate individual. We do not anticipate this, but it is possible. Another possibility is that, because of the position we take in our information, we could find so much disfavor with the powers that control this world that there could be attempts to incarcerate us or to subject us to some sort of psychological or physical torture (such as occurred at both Ruby Ridge and Waco).

It has always been our way to examine all possibilities, and be mentally prepared for whatever may come our way. For example, consider what happened at Masada around 73 A.D. A devout Jewish sect, after holding out against a siege by the Romans, to the best of their ability, and seeing that the murder, rape, and torture of their community was inevitable, determined that it was permissible for them to evacuate their bodies by a more dignified, and less agonizing method. We have thoroughly discussed this topic (of willful exit of the body under such conditions), and have mentally prepared ourselves for this possibility (as can be seen in a few of our statements). However, this act certainly does not need serious consideration at this time, and hopefully will not in the future.

The true meaning of "suicide" is to turn against the Next Level when it is being offered. In these last days, we are focused on two primary tasks: one—of making a last attempt at telling the truth about how the Next Level may be entered (our last effort at offering to individuals of this civilization the way to avoid "suicide"); and two—taking advantage of the rare opportunity we have each day—to work individually on our personal overcoming and change, in preparation for entering the Kingdom of Heaven.

1. Gardner, *Urantia*, p. 39.
2. The founder of the company, Will Kellogg, was Dr. John Kellogg's little brother.
3. I'm not clear on Dr. Kellogg's blood relationship with Wilfred.
4. Sadler quoted in *Urantia*, by Gardner, p. 117.
5. *The Urantia Book*, p. 396. The following eight excerpts in the text are also from *The Urantia Book*; p.396, p. 398, pp. 708–9, pp. 584–85, p. 580, pp. 585–86, p.828, pp. 836–37, respectively.
6. Sadler quoted in *Urantia*, by Gardner, p. 284.
7. See chap. 4, "Eugenics," for more on Madison Grant.
8. *The Urantia Book*, p. 593.
9. Ibid., p. 839.
10. Ibid., p. 586.
11. Szukalski, *Protong*, p. 55.
12. Szukalski's Yeti include the "Yeti" and "Bigfoot of modern legend.
13. Szukalski, *Protong*, p. 59.
14. Ibid., p. 63.
15. See chap. 3, "Race."
16. See chap. 4, "Eugenics."
17. Those unfamiliar with Szukalski might speculate that his work on Zermatism was an elaborate art project, with overtones of Dada or Surrealism. In fact, there are no hints in his work or his life that he was anything but completely serious about his theories.
18. Eckankar is a New Age system of soul travel (identified by some as a cult), founded in 1965 by Paul Twitchell.
19. Balch, "Bo and Peep."
20. Interview in *UFO Missionaries Extraordinary*, by Hewes and Steiger.
21. Hewes and Steiger, *UFO Missionaries*, pp. 82–84.

32. Similarly, after their suicide in March 1997, the group would be accused of using the internet to recruit "victims." Cults, it seems, are an easy scapegoat for any number of misunderstood phenomena, from cattle mutilations to cyberspace.

23. My *Kooks* 'zine was listed in a New Age directory; I assume this is why it was sent to me.

24. One had left the group for good but was still interested in them; the other, Lindley Pease, had been accidentally separated from the group and was trying to locate them. I pointed him to their web page. Months later I received a "thank you" e-mail from Lindley after he'd rejoined.

25. I then heard that Lindley Pease was among the dead.

26. The connection between gnosticism and Heaven's Gate is explored in "The Deep Roots of Heaven's Gate" by Chris Lehmann, *Harper's*, June 1997.

27. Member of a legendary ancient mystical brotherhood.

28. Not to be confused with the mail-order Rosicrucians, A.M.O.R.C., founded by H. Spencer Lewis in 1925.

29. Shepard, *Occultism and Parapsychology*, pp. 421–22, 883.

30. By 1996 Do/Applewhite was identifying himself as Jesus: "I came to Earth some 2,000 years ago from another physical, biological Evolutionary Level as the expected 'Messiah,' or Jesus, and for this current mission, Returned to this level, this planet and entered into a human body some 24 years ago, Earth-time."

Adamski, George and Desmond Leslie. *Flying Saucers Have Landed.* New York: British Book Centre, 1953.

Andrews, Lori B. *The Clone Age: Adventures in the New World of Reproductive Technology.* New York: Henry Holt, 1999.

Appiah, Kwame Anthony. "Beyond Race: Fallacies of Reactive Afrocentrism." *Skeptic* 2, no. 4 (1994): 104–107.

Arthur, Joyce. "Creationism: Bad Science or Immoral Pseudo-Science?" *Skeptic* 4, no. 4 (1996): 88–93.

As Sayyid Al Imaam Issa Al Haadi Al Mahdi (Issa Muhammad). *The Paleman.* 1975. Rev. ed. [no. 20]. Monticello, NY: *Original Tents of Kedar*, 1990.

Baer, Randall N. *Inside the New Age Nightmare.* Lafayette, LA: Huntington House, 1989.

Balch, Robert W. "Bo and Peep: A Case Study of the Origins of Messianic Leadership." In *Millenialism and Charisma.* Edited by Roay Wallis. Belfast: Queen's University, 1982.

Balch, Robert W. and David Taylor. "Salvation in a UFO." *Psychology Today,* October 1976.

Barclay, David. *Aliens: The Final Answer? A UFO Cosmology for the Twenty-First Century.* London: Blandford, 1995.

Baugh, Carl E., with Clifford A. Wilson. *Dinosaur: Scientific Evidence that Dinosaurs and Men Walked Together.* Orange, CA: Promise Publishing, 1987.

Bettmann, Otto L. *The Good Old Days: They were Terrible!* New York: Random House, 1974.

Binder, Otto O. and Max H. Flindt. *Mankind: Child of the Stars.* Greenwich, CT: Fawcett, 1974.

Blavatsky, H. P. *An Abridgement of "The Secret Doctrine."* Edited by Elizabeth Preston. N.p., n.p.

Boardman Jr., William W., Robert F. Koontz and Henry M. Morris. *Science and Creation.* San Diego, CA: Creation-Science Research Center, 1973.

Boulay, R. A. *Flying Serpents and Dragons: The Story of Mankind's Reptilian Past.* Escondido, CA: Book Tree, 1997.

Bradley, Michael. *The Iceman Inheritance: Prehistoric Sources of Western Man's Racism, Sexism, and Aggression.* New York: Kayode Publications, 1978.

Brennecke, Fritz. *Official Handbook for Schooling the Hitler Youth.* Translated by Harwood Childs (under the title *The Nazi Primer*). New York: Harper & Bros., 1938.

Bronte, Charlotte. "Inside the Crystal Palace: The Great Exhibition, 1851." In *Eyewitness to History.* Edited by John Carey. Cambridge, MA: Harvard University Press, 1987.

Bury, J. B. *The Idea of Progress.* [New York?]: Macmillan, 1932. Reprint, New York: Dover, 1955.

Campanella. "City of the Sun." In *Famous Utopias.* New York: Tudor., n.d.

Campbell, Joseph. *Occidental Mythology.* 1964. Reprint, New York: Penguin Books, 1976.

———. *Primitive Mythology.* 1959. Reprint, New York: Penguin Books, 1987.

Carlson, John Roy. *Under Cover.* New York: Dutton, 1943.

Carrel, Alexis. *Man, the Unknown.* New York: Harper & Bros., 1935. Reprint, n.p.: Halcyon House, 1938.

Coyne, Pat. "Dielectrics. Human Evolution." *New Statesman & Society* 5, no. 232 (December 11, 1992).

Deutsch, Ronald M. *The Nuts Among the Berries.* New York: Ballantine Books, 1961.

Dietrich, B. C. *Death, Fate, and the Gods.* London: Athlone Press, 1965.

Eliade, Mircea. *Myths, Rites, Symbols.* Vol. 2. New York: Harper & Row, 1976.

———. *The Myth of the Eternal Return, or Cosmos and History.* Princeton, NJ: Princeton University Press, 1954.

Essene, Virginia and Sheldon Nidle. *You are Becoming a Galactic Human*. Santa Clara, CA: Spiritual Education Endeavors, 1994.

Evans, Christopher. *Cults of Unreason*. New York: Dell, 1973.

Eve, Raymond A. and Francis B. Harrold, eds. *Cult Archaeology and Creationism: Understanding Pseudoscientific Beliefs about the Past*. Iowa City, IA: University of Iowa Press, 1987.

Evola, Julius. *The Metaphysics of Sex*. N.p., 1969.

Feder, Kenneth L. Fraud, *Myths, and Mysteries: Science and Pseudoscience in Archeology*. Mountain View, CA: Mayfield, 1990.

Foley, Jim. "Creationist Arguments: Bones of Contention." From the talk.origins FAQ archive on the World Wide Web: <http://www.talkorigins.org/FAQS/HOMS/a_lubenow.html>.

Frazer, Sir James George. *The Golden Bough: A Study in Magic and Religion*. Abridged, 1 vol. New York: Macmillan, 1926.

Freund, Philip. *Myths of Creation*. New York: Washington Square Press, 1965.

Gaines, James R. "Bo-Peep's Flock." *Newsweek*, October 20, 1975.

Gardner, Martin. *Urantia: The Great Cult Mystery*. Amherst, NY: Prometheus Books, 1995.

Gaverluk, Emil and Jack Hamm. *Did Genesis Man Conquer Space?* Nashville, TN: Nelson, 1974.

Gillispie, Charles Coulston. *Genesis and Geology: The Impact of Scientific Discoveries upon Religious Beliefs in the Decades before Darwin*. New York: Harper & Bros., 1951.

Girard, Robert C. *Futureman: A Synthesis of Missing Links, the Human Infestation of Earth, and the Alien Abduction Epidemic*. Port St. Lucie, FL: Arcturus Books, 1993.

Gish, Duane T., Ph.D. *Evolution: The Challenge of the Fossil Record*. El Cajon, CA: Creation-Life Publishers, 1985.

Gleick, Elizabeth, et al. "Special Report: Inside the Web of Death." *Time*, April 7, 1997.

Godwin, Joscelyn. *Arktos*. Grand Rapids, MI: Phanes Press, 1993.

Goodrick-Clarke, Nicholas. *The Occult Roots of Nazism: The Ariosophists of Austria and Germany*, 1890–1935. Wellingborough, U.K.: Aquarian Press, 1985.

Gould, Stephen Jay. *The Mismeasure of Man*. New York: W. W. Norton, 1981.

Graverluk, Emil. *Did Genesis Man Conquer Space?* N.p., 1974.

Greene, John C. *The Death of Adam: Evolution and its Impact on Western Thought*. Ames, IA: Iowa State University Press, 1959.

Haller, Mark H. *Eugenics: Hereditarian Attitudes in American Thought*. 1963. Reprint, New Brunswick, NJ: Rutgers University Press, 1984.

Hardy, Alister. "Was there a Homo aquaticus?" *Zenith 15*, no. 1 (1977).

Hedin, Finnvald. *The Thorians*. New York: Vantage Press, 1980.

Heindel, Max. *The Rosicrucian Cosmo-Conception: Or Mystic Christianity*. 1909. Reprint, Oceanside, CA: Rosicrucian Fellowship, 1973.

Hesiod. *The Works and Days*. Translated by Richard Lattimore. Ann Arbor, MI: University of Michigan Press, 1959.

Hewes, Hayden and Brad Steiger. *UFO Missionaries Extraordinary*. New York: Pocket Books, 1976.

Hoff, Charles A., M.D. and C. S. Whitehead, M.D. *Ethical Sex Relations, or The New Eugenics: A Safe Guide for Young Men, Young Women*. Chicago: Hertel, 1922.

Hofstadter, Richard. *Social Darwinism in American Thought*, 1860–1915. Philadelphia: University of Pennsylvania Press, 1944.

Holloway, Mark. *Heavens on Earth*. New York: Dover, 1966.

The Holy Bible. King James version.

Hooton, Earnest A. *Apes, Men, and Morons*. New York: Putnam's Sons, 1937.

Hubbard, L. Ron. *Scientology: A History of Man*. Los Angeles: Church of Scientology, 1968.

Huxley, Julian. *Man in the Modern World*. New York: Mentor Books, 1948.

Huxley, Leonard. *Life and Letters of Thomas H. Huxley*. New York: Appleton & Co., 1901.

Kafton-Minkel, Walter. *Subterranean Worlds: One Hundred Thousand Years of Dragons, Dwarfs, the Dead, Lost Races, and UFOs from Inside the Earth*. Port Townsend, WA: Loompanics Unlimited, 1989.

Kenyon, J. Douglas. "Visitors From Beyond." *Atlantis Rising*, no. 5 (1995).

Kevles, Daniel J. *In the Name of Eugenics: Genetics and the Uses of Human Heredity*. Berkeley and Los Angeles: University of California Press, 1985.

Klassen, Ben. *Nature's Eternal Religion*. Lighthouse Point, FL: Church of the Creator, 1973.

Kossy, Donna. *Kooks: A Guide to the Outer Limits of Human Belief*. Los Angeles, CA: Feral House, 1994.

Kuban, Glen J. "On the Heels of Dinosaurs." From the talk.origins FAQ archive on the World Wide Web: <http://www.talkorigins.org/faqs/paluxy.html> (1996).

Lefkowitz, Mary. *Not Out of Africa: How Afrocentrism became an Excuse to Teach Myth as History*. New York: BasicBooks, 1996.

———. "Stolen Legacy, or Mythical History? Did the Greeks Steal Philosophy from the Egyptians?" *Skeptic* 2, no. 4 (1994): 98–103.

Lerner, Richard M. *Final Solutions: Biology, Prejudice, and Genocide*. University Park, PA: Pennsylvania State University Press, 1992.

Ley, Willy. "Pseudoscience in Naziland." *Astounding Science Fiction*, May 1947.

Livingstone, David N. *Darwin's Forgotten Defenders: The Encounter between Evangelical Theology and Evolutionary Thought*. Grand Rapids, MI: Eerdmans, 1987.

Lubenow, Marvin L. *Bones of Contention: A Creationist Assessment of Human Fossils*. Grand Rapids, MI: Baker Books, 1992.

Maerth, Oscar Kiss. *The Beginning was the End*. New York: Praeger, 1974.

McCann, Alfred Watterson, LL.D. *God, or Gorilla: How the Monkey Theory of Evolution Exposes its own Methods, Refutes its own Principles, Denies its own Inferences, Disproves its own Case*. New York: Devin-Adair, 1922.

McIver, Tom. "The Protocols of Creationism: Racism, Anti-Semitism, and White Supremacy in Christian Fundamentalism," *Skeptic* 2, no. 4 (1994): 76–87.

———. "A Walk through Earth History: All Eight Thousand Years, a Trip to the Institute for Creation Research Museum of Creation and Earth History," *Skeptic* 4, no. 1 (1996).

Milner, Richard. *The Encyclopedia of Evolution: Humanity's Search for its Origins*. New York: Henry Holt & Co., 1990.

Montagu, Ashley, ed. *Science and Creationism*. New York: Oxford University Press, 1984.

Moore, T. Owens, Ph.D. *The Science of Melanin: Dispelling the Myths*. Silver Spring, MD: Beckham House, 1995.

Morgan, Elaine. *The Aquatic Ape*. New York: Stein & Day, 1982.

———. *The Descent of Woman*. New York: Stein & Day, 1972.

———. *The Scars of Evolution*. New York: Oxford University Press, 1994.

Morris, Henry M. *A History of Modern Creationism*. San Diego, CA: Master Book, 1984.

Morris, Henry M. and John C. Whitcomb Jr. *The Genesis Flood: The Biblical Record and its Scientific Implications*. Grand Rapids, MI: Baker Book House, 1961.

Morris, Henry M., William W. Boardman Jr., and Robert F. Koontz. *Science and Creation*. El Cajon, CA: Creation-Science Research Center, 1973.

Muhammad, Elijah. *Message to the Blackman in America.* Chicago: Nation of Islam, 1965. Reprint, n.p.: Final Call, n.d.

Mullins, Eustace. *The Curse of Canaan: A Demonology of History.* Staunton, VA: Revelation Books, 1987.

Newbrough, John Ballou. *Oahspe: A New Bible.* Los Angeles: Kosmon Press, 1942.

Orrmont, Arthur. "John Humphrey Noyes: Communist of Love." In *Love Cults and Faith Healers.* New York: Ballantine Books, 1961.

Parfrey, Adam, ed. *Apocalypse Culture.* 1987. Rev. and exp. ed. Los Angeles, CA: Feral House, 1990.

Passmore, John. *The Perfectibility of Man.* New York: Scribner's Sons, 1970.

Patrick, Reynolds, Roede, and Wind, eds. *The Aquatic Ape: Fact or Fiction? The First Scientific Evaluation of a Controversial Theory of Human Evolution.* London: Souvenir Press, 1991.

Pike, E. Royston. *Encyclopedia of Religion and Religions.* New York: Meridian, 1958.

Poliakov, Léon. *The Aryan Myth: A History of Racist and Nationalist Ideas in Europe.* Translated by Edmund Howard. [Brighton, U.K.]: Sussex University Press, 1974.

Price, George McCreedy. *Illogical Geology: The Weakest Point in the Evolution Theory.* N.p., 1906.

Proctor, Robert N. *Racial Hygiene: Medicine Under the Nazis.* Cambridge, MA: Harvard University Press, 1988.

Redbeard, Ragnar, LL.D. [pseud.]. *Might is Right: Or Survival of the Fittest.* Chicago: Dil Pickle Press, 1927.

Reeve, Bryant and Helen. *Flying Saucer Pilgrimage.* Amherst, WI: Amherst Press, 1965.

Rimmer, Harry. *The Theory of Evolution and the Facts of Science.* 5 vols. Duluth, MN: Research Science Bureau, 1929–1945.

Robertson, Constance Noyes. *Oneida Community: An Autobiography, 1851–1876.* Syracuse, NY: Syracuse University Press, 1970.

Roux, Georges. *Ancient Iraq.* 2nd ed. New York: Penguin Books, 1980.

Saleeby, Caleb Williams. *Hereditary Genius.* N.p., n.d.

Saleeby, Caleb Williams. *Parenthood and Race Culture: An Outline of Eugenics.* New York: Moffat, Yard & Co., 1909.

Schneider, William H. *Quality and Quantity: The Quest for Biological Regeneration in Twentieth-Century France.* Cambridge, England: Cambridge University Press, 1990.

Sendy, Jean. *The Moon: Outpost of the Gods.* New York: Berkley Publishing, 1975.

Shannon, T. W. *Nature's Secrets Revealed: Scientific Knowledge of the Laws of Sex Life and Heredity, or Eugenics.* Marietta, OH: S. A. Mullikin, 1917. Reprint, New York: Doubleday, 1970.

Shepard, Leslie A., ed. *Encyclopedia of Occultism and Parapsychology.* N.p.: Avon, 1980.

Shermer, Michael. "Afrocentric Pseudoscience and Pseudohistory," *Skeptic* 2, no. 4 (1994): 71.

Shockley, Paul *Interpreter. Revelations of Awareness,* no. 396 (1992).

Sitchin, Zecharia. *The 12th Planet.* New York: Avon Books, 1976.

Stoddard, Lothrop. *The Revolt Against Civilization: The Menace of the Under Man.* New York: Scribner's Sons, 1922.

———. *The Rising Tide of Color.* Against White World-Supremacy. New York: Scribner's Sons, 1920.

Story, Ronald. *Guardians of the Universe?* New York: St. Martin's, 1980.

———. *The Space-Gods Revealed.* New York: Harper & Row, 1976.

Szukalski, Stanislav. *Behold!!! The Protong.* Sylmar, CA: Archives Szukalski, 1989.

Trench, Brinsley LePoer. *The Sky People.* London: Spearman, 1960.

Urantia Foundation. *The Urantia Book.* Chicago: Urantia Foundation, 1955.

Vallee, Jacques. *Messengers of Deception: UFO Contacts and Cults.* 1979. Rev. ed. New York: Bantam Books, 1980.

Van Tassel, George W. *Religion and Science Merged*. 1958. Reprint, Yucca Valley, CA: Ministry of Universal Wisdom, 1968.

———. *When Stars Look Down*. Los Angeles: Kruckeberg Press, 1976.

Viereck, Peter. *The Roots of the Nazi Mind*. New York: Capricorn Books, 1961.

von Däniken, Erich. *Chariots of the Gods?* Translated by Michael Heron. New York: Bantam Books, 1971.

———. *Gods from Outer Space*. Translated by Michael Heron. New York: Bantam Books, 1972.

Vorilhon, Claude/Raël. *The Message Given to Me by Extra-Terrestrials: They Took Me to their Planet*. Lichtenstein: Raelian Foundation, 1986. Reprint, Tokyo: AOM Corp., 1992.

Washington, Peter. *Madame Blavatsky's Baboon*. London: Secker & Warburg, 1993.

Wauchope, Robert. *Lost Tribes and Sunken Continents*. Chicago: University of Chicago Press, 1962.

Weakley, Jeffrey A. *The Satanic Seedline: Its Doctrine and History*. Boring, OR: CPA Books, 1994.

Webster, Nesta H. *Secret Societies and Subversive Movements*. N.p., 1924.

Weisman, Charles A. *The Origin of Race and Civilization*. Burnsville, MN: Weisman Publications, 1990.

———. *Who Is Esau-Edom?* Burnsville, MN: Weisman Publications, 1991.

Welsing, Dr. Frances Cress. *The Isis Papers: The Keys to the Colors*. Chicago: Third World Press, 1991.

White, Andrew Dixon. *A History of the Warfare of Science with Theology in Christendom*. 1896. Facsimile of original. New York: Dover, 1960.

Wiggam, Albert Edward. *The Fruit of the Family Tree*. Garden City, NY: Garden City Publishing, 1925.

Wiggam, Albert. *The New Decalogue of Science*. N.p., 1923

Williamson, George Hunt. *Other Tongues —Other Flesh*. Amherst, WI: Amherst Press, 1953.

Wills, Garry. *Under God: Religion and American Politics*. New York: Simon & Schuster, 1990.

Zihlman, Adrienne. "Evolution, a Suitable Case for Treatment." *New Scientist*, Jan. 19, 1991.

Zinsstag, Lou and Timothy Good. *George Adamski: The Untold Story*. England: CETI Publications, 1983.

Also available from Feral House

Kooks *Donna Kossy*

Kooks, an extraordinary sourcebook to the outer limits of human belief, now appears in an expanded edition, adding a new chapter of peculiar notions and eccentric people to this underground classic.

"Donna Kossy is one of the very few dignified representatives of the growth science of Crackpotology. To write entertainingly for 'nonkooks' about so-called kooks, crackpots, and possible visionaries requires walking a tightrope between tolerant understanding of 'outsider' psychology and graceful sarcasm, balancing both a solid grounding in the mainstream scientific paradigm, and a healthy distrust of the status quo. . . . [Kossy] Is truly a friend to the kooks. . . ."
—Rev. Ivan Stang

8¹/₂ × 11 ◆ 287 pages ◆ illustrated ◆ ISBN 0-922915-19-9 ◆ $18.95

Apocalypse Culture II *Edited by Adam Parfrey*

We've been told that the original *Apocalypse Culture* ruined marriages, created fistfights, and inspired people for life. Reviewers claimed *Apocalypse Culture* was "the new book of revelation" and "the terminal documents of our time."

Apocalypse Culture II breaks the editor's arrogant promise that no sequel edition would ever appear. Herein find over 62 new articles and 200 photos and illustrations delineating the Forbidden Zone, the psychic maelstrom that everyone knows exists but fearfully avoids.

6 × 9 ◆ 470 pages ◆ lavishly illustrated ◆ ISBN 0-922915-57-1 ◆ $18.95

Muerte! Death in Mexican Popular Culture
Edited by Harvey Stafford

Mexico is a country obsessed with blood and gore. The biggest selling magazines, *Alarma!* and *Peligro!*, week after week promote the most extreme examples of death they can find. Why does Mexican culture, a strange amalgam of Catholicism and Santeria, go so far with bloody sensationalism?

The photographs within *Muerte!* were largely snapped by the biggest photographers from Mexican tabloids, and are printed in this book for the first time. *Muerte!* also includes text from Diego Rivera, Eduardo Matos Moctezuma, Jorge Alberto Manrique, Alberto Hijar and Victor Fosada explaining Mexican death-consciousness.

10 × 8 ◆ 102 pages ◆ full color ◆ ISBN 0-922915-59-8 ◆ $16.95

www.feralhouse.com

To order from Feral House: Domestic orders add $4 shipping for first item, $1.50 each additional item. Amex, MasterCard, Visa, checks and money orders are accepted. (CA state residents add 8% tax.) Canadian orders add $7 shipping for first item, $2 each additional item. Other countries add $11 shipping for first item, $9 each additional item. Non-U.S. originated orders must be international money order or check drawn on a U.S. bank only. Send orders to: Feral House, P.O. Box 13067, Los Angeles, CA 90013